DEATH AND THE EMPEROR

30/11/17

PENELOPE J. E. DAVIES

DEATH AND THE EMPEROR

ROMAN IMPERIAL FUNERARY
MONUMENTS FROM AUGUSTUS
TO MARCUS AURELIUS

UNIVERSITY OF TEXAS PRESS

AUSTIN

The publication of this book was assisted by a University Cooperative Society Subvention Grant awarded by the University of Texas at Austin.

First University of Texas Press edition, 2004

Figures 41, 63, 66, 67, and 71 are reprinted with the kind permission of Yale University Press.

∞
The paper used in this book meets the nimimum requirements of ANSI/NISO Z39.48-1992 (R1997) (Permanence of Paper).

Library of Congress Cataloging-in-Publication Data

Davies, Penelope J. E., 1964–
Death and the emperor : Roman imperial funerary monuments, from Augustus to Marcus Aurelius / Penelope J. E. Davies.— 1st University of Texas Press ed.
p.   cm.
Originally published: Cambridge, U.K. ; New York, NY, USA: Cambridge University Press, 2000.
Includes bibliographical references and index.
ISBN 0-292-70275-2 (alk. paper)
1. Sculpture, Roman—Italy—Rome.   2. Relief (Sculpture), Roman—Italy—Rome.
3. Emperors—Monuments—Italy—Rome.   4. Sepulchral monuments—Political aspects—Italy—Rome.
5. Rome (Italy)—Buildings, structures, etc.   1. Title.
NB1875.D38   2004
733'.5—dc22
2003056529

For Maureen, Michael, and Sarah,
and in Memory of Justin

CONTENTS

ILLUSTRATIONS

ACKNOWLEDGMENTS

My fascination with imperial funerary monuments began while I was a graduate student at Yale University and developed into a doctoral dissertation submitted in 1994. I am greatly indebted to my advisor, Diana E. E. Kleiner, for the guidance she offered, and for her unwaning enthusiasm for the topic. I am also grateful to Jerome J. Pollitt and Maria Georgopoulos for their suggestions for revisions.

Yale University provided generous support for travel and research from various funds, including the John F. Enders Grant, the Berkeley and Biddle Grants, the Augusta Hazard Grant, and the Tarbell Fund administered through the Classics Department. My initial research in Rome was supported by a Samuel H. Kress Foundation travel grant; and a Summer Grant from the University Research Institute and a John D. Murchison Fellowship in Fine Arts at the University of Texas at Austin allowed me to continue my research. A Getty Postdoctoral Fellowship permitted me the luxury of dedicating 1997–1998 to completing the manuscript. A special note of thanks is also due to Sherry and Tommy Jacks for their extraordinary generosity in helping to fund return trips to Rome.

I am grateful to the Soprintendenza Archeologica di Roma for permission to visit those monuments that are closed to the public, and especially to Giangiacomo Martines and Eugenio Gatti for their warm welcome; thanks also to Paolo Liverani of the Vatican Museums. My visits to the mosaics beneath the Caserma dei Corazzieri with Paola Ciuferri and to Hadrian's "Underworld" with Adriano D'Offizi are still magical memories.

While writing this book I have sought the expertise of many friends and colleagues, whose insights have enriched my work in countless ways. Foremost among them I name John R. Clarke, who has helped immeasurably with this project and many others; I thank him for his friendship and unhesitating encouragement. Ann L. Kuttner and William L. MacDonald read the manuscript with a critical eye and made many an astute suggestion, as did the anonymous reviewers for Cambridge University Press; Judith M. Barringer did the same at an earlier stage. Others have read individual chapters and improved them: Pieter B. F. J. Broucke, Eve D'Ambra, Richard

Etlin, Fred S. Kleiner, Tanya M. Luhrmann, Ramsay MacMullen, Sarah P. Morris, James E. Packer, Andrew M. Riggsby, and Salvatore Settis. They have helped me more than these meagre words express, and I thank them all. I have also learned much and benefited in myriad ways from wide-ranging conversations with Janice Leoshko. To the graduate students in the Department of Art and Art History at the University of Texas at Austin who pondered these monuments in seminars I also offer my thanks, and to Debbie Esquenazi for her invaluable assistance.

Many individuals and institutions have generously assisted in providing illustrations. I thank Edmund Buchner, Amanda Claridge, Sir Howard Colvin, Michael Eisner, Rudolf Fellmann, Ron Jameson, Martina Jordan-Ruwe, Eugenio La Rocca, James E. Packer, Rita Paris, Stephen Petersen, Mario Torelli, and Henner von Hesberg, as well as William E. Metcalf of the American Numismatic Society, Michael Slade at Art Resource, Janet Larkin at the Photographic Service of the British Museum, Marion Schröder of the Deutsches Archäologisches Institut in Rome, Robin Meador-Woodruff at the Kelsey Museum of Archaeology at the University of Michigan, Rosanna Friggeri at the Museo Nazionale Romano, Francesco Riccardi at the Vatican Museums, the Photographic Archives and Fototeca Unione at the American Academy in Rome, and Hirmer Verlag in Munich. Special thanks to Michael Larvey and Constanze Witt for their help. A subvention from the Samuel H. Kress Foundation helped to cover the cost of illustrations, along with a British Studies Fellowship and a Special Research Grant from the University of Texas at Austin.

Working with Cambridge University Press on this book has been a great pleasure. A thousand thanks to Beatrice Rehl for her expertise and encouragement and to Andy Beck, Humanities Development Editor; thanks also to Ernie Haim and Alan Gold for overseeing production, and to Barbara Folsom for her meticulous care in copyediting.

My greatest debt is to my family, and especially my parents, Maureen and Michael Ellis Davies, who introduced me to Rome, who taught me to listen for the haunting voices of history, and who know the irrefutable lure of old stones. Their unqualified support and loyal friendship have sustained me in this as in all things. I dedicate this book to them with gratitude and respect.

"Truth is independent of fact. It does not mind being disproved. It is already dispossessed in utterance."

– Lawrence Durrell, *Balthazar, The Alexandria Quartet* (1958)

INTRODUCTION

B ETWEEN THE YEARS 28 B.C. and A.D. 193, eighteen rulers acceded
to the Roman imperial throne. Of these, seven left behind magnificent
monumental memorials in Rome; others were buried in existing dynastic
sepulchers, while others still were cast into official oblivion by senatorial decree,
their bodies mutilated, thrown into the Tiber, and washed out to sea. The body's
final resting place was as important in antiquity as it is today, if not more so: the
souls of the unburied were believed to wander interminably in a cruel limbo of
mythology's making. For the ruling family, however, even more was at stake: the
future of the living was dependent, to a large degree, upon the honors (or lack
thereof) bestowed upon the dead. This dependency is visible in the design of
imperial memorials. This book analyzes the funerary monuments of the Roman
emperors as a genre for the first time, beginning with the Mausoleum of Augustus and concluding with the Column of Marcus Aurelius.[1] Its aim is to uncover
political or ritual motivation behind their design, decoration, and location. In
doing so, this study brings together two different kinds of funerary monument:
the tomb proper and the commemorative monument erected after an emperor's
death. The latter has proven hard to define; for some, it is a cenotaph;[2] for others,
a public memorial.[3] The monuments I discuss in these pages were erected in
the city of Rome to commemorate a deceased emperor, and they refer in their
decoration, either explicitly or implicitly, to his change of state from mortal to
immortal. They are therefore occasioned by the emperor's death, even if he was
buried in an existing imperial tomb to stress his dynastic affiliation. In this work,
I term them both commemorative monuments and funerary monuments.[4]

None of the imperial funerary monuments is unfamiliar to scholars of
Roman art; few, indeed, are unknown to tourists in Rome. The Mausoleum of
Augustus still stands, derelict, the haunting focus of Mussolini's Piazza Augusto
Imperatore in the heart of historic Rome; Hadrian's tomb, of similar form, was a
jealously guarded fortress in medieval times and, renamed Castel Sant'Angelo, be-
came the seat of Renaissance popes and the stronghold of Vatican City. The Arch
of Titus, for its part, rightly admired for its harmonious proportions, crowns the
Velian ridge now as it did in antiquity, visually defining the eastern side of the
Roman Forum. The Columns of Trajan and Marcus Aurelius have weathered land

shifts and world wars, and survive to be lauded as landmarks of the modern city and Western art alike. And newly restored and relocated in the Cortile del Belvedere, the Column base of Antoninus Pius is one of the first sights to welcome a visitor to the Vatican Museums. Only the Temple of the Flavian Dynasty is mostly lost to us, destroyed and buried beneath the streets of modern Rome.

Not only well known, these monuments have been extensively excavated, and their architectural forms and sculptural decoration comprehensively documented. Yet for the most part scholars have examined them in isolation from one another and often from a limited number of perspectives; generally speaking, dominant concerns have been to establish a monument's original appearance and to identify its prototype. Another approach has been to discuss the funerary monuments individually or in small groups in studies on specific monument types, or to view the monuments within the wider context of the artistic production of their day. The Columns' sculptural friezes lie at the heart of any discussion of the development of pictorial narrative, and the sepulchers naturally find their way into works on Roman tombs or tomb architecture throughout history and general works on Roman art and architecture.[5] While each of these approaches is valid in its own right, they have the collective effect of blurring links between monuments of different types. This study, in contrast, analyzes the monuments as a group, despite their diverse forms and decoration. I treat architectural and sculptural form in a single sweep, dissolving the conventional barrier between the two media; I justify this unusual approach for this body of material on the assumption that the tomb, as a monument, belongs properly in neither category and might usefully be considered monumental sculpture even at its most architectural. This characterization finds ancient corroboration in the writings of Petronius, who describes a tomb designer and builder not as an architect but as a *lapidarius,* or monumental mason.[6]

I have taken several different approaches to the monuments, and always with the firm conviction that each one can bear numerous meanings. Roman art is by nature polysemous, but in few areas are there greater possibilities for mixed significances than in the funerary, where beliefs are often confused and illogical; in few areas is there greater possibility for accrual of meaning than in ritual practice, funerary or otherwise, since a pervasive conservatism allows rituals to persist long after their original meanings have been lost, necessitating the post facto creation of new meaning. Different levels of meaning for a symbol or practice, then, might appear contradictory, but we should not for that reason alone consider them mutually exclusive. This conservatism, in turn, renders less hazardous an attempt to draw comparisons between monuments at the beginning and end of the two centuries under scrutiny.[7]

Alongside the funerary monuments that are my primary focus, I discuss a select group of other works when their association with a funerary monument, topographical or otherwise, implicates them either as part of a program or as necessary *comparanda* to tease out meaning. I have not, however, set out to do this exhaustively here; thus I discuss the Ara Pacis and the Solarium in some depth as part of Augustus's Campus Martius complex, but I have not attempted a thorough reading of the Basilica Ulpia (for instance) in the light of Trajan's Column as a tomb. Similarly, I discuss the Apotheosis of Sabina panel in some detail alongside the apotheosis relief on the Column base of Antoninus Pius, but I do not include an analysis of the full range of commemorative coins struck or altars erected in honor of deceased empresses. I stress that this book does not aim to be an exhaustive overview, and most emphatically I do not claim to offer the definitive reading of these monuments; on the contrary, many of the ideas I present here are highly speculative. I hope only to suggest ways in which we might reach beyond the archaeological data, primarily by moving within the monuments themselves, and inevitably my suggestions are tempered if not entirely formulated by my own experience of space. As William MacDonald so aptly puts it: "architecture, through its unavoidable imagery, is like the other arts an affective one: the sense and memory are strongly engaged. Awareness of historical continuities and sensory factors is essential to the understanding of Roman architecture and the construction of an approximate definition of it; the scholarly tradition of authorial non-involvement, in matters of judgement, should be reconsidered."[8]

I direct my inquiry toward uncovering ideological or ritual motivation behind imperial funerary monument design. I have not focused on assessing them as expressions of individual eschatological views, not because they are devoid of such intent but because it is notoriously difficult to penetrate Roman belief systems and to separate temple from state, let alone to assess the emperor's personally held creed when so many options were open to him. Pontifex Maximus, head of the state religion (after 12 B.C.), he could also elect to be initiated into mystery cults promising salvation; Augustus, for instance, like Hadrian, took the Eleusinian vows of silence and perhaps the Samothracian ones too.[9] Yet how deeply he or any initiate believed he or she would inherit eternal life is open to debate, and in Augustus's case participation may have been a spiritual or a political act or both.[10] Adherents to philosophical doctrines contemplated a different form of afterlife in the soul's separation from the body and existence elsewhere. Augustus rubbed shoulders with one Stoic of note, his tutor Athenodorus of Tarsus, and a work probably advocating Stoicism, the *Hortationes ad Philosophiam,* is even attributed to the future emperor.[11] Hadrian, for his part, fraternized with philosophers such as Epictetus and Heliodorus, and claimed to see a new star when Antinous died, which may indicate familiarity with the concept of astral immortality;[12] all the same, no single doctrine appears to have claimed his exclusive attention. Not so Marcus Aurelius, whose musings on Stoicism survive as his *Meditations;*[13] yet even in the face of his personal testimony there is no guarantee that Commodus respected his father's beliefs when designing his column. Despite the range of possibilities, Romans on the whole appear to have held out no great hope for an afterlife. Indeed, few early imperial epitaphs express more than an open question: "If there is something else. . . ."[14]

Even if his beliefs were known, evidence for the emperor's level of engagement, as patron, in the design of a funerary monument is exceedingly sparse.

All the same, I argue that an imperial funerary monument was not just a burial marker but an accession monument as well, and it is hard to imagine that the emperor, the incumbent, or other members of the imperial family did not take an active role in the design of such a critical work. Since several of the monuments were private commissions funded by the emperor and sometimes built on imperial land, the Senate as a body presumably did not have the final say over blueprints. Evidence concerning other posthumous honors, though admittedly tangential, seems to support such a notion. It was commonplace, for instance, for a Roman of any rank to specify the format of his funeral in his will. Drusus read Augustus's *mandata de funere* to the Senate after his death; Nero instructed that his body should be cremated and saved from mutilation; Otho that he should not be decapitated.[15] Moreover, the *Tabula Siarensis,* bronze inscriptions preserving parts of the *senatus consulta* for Germanicus, indicate that, though the Senate was in charge of his honors after his death in Syria in 19, they made sure to include Tiberius, Livia, Drusus, and Antonia in their deliberations.[16] In the *Satyricon,* Trimalchio's dinner conversation with Habinnas presupposes an ongoing discussion between the two concerning the appearance of Trimalchio's tomb, and Trimalchio states his desires with the apparent expectation that they will be fulfilled.[17] All the same, such instructions were not necessarily followed verbatim. Sometimes they might be embellished; as senators such as Asinius Galo and Lucius Arruntius vied to heap honors upon Augustus, the Senate added its own flourishes to his funeral, such as parading his body beneath the Porta Triumphalis and including at the head of the procession *tituli* with the laws he had passed and the names of nations he had conquered.[18] At other times, they were simply disregarded: in the interest of public safety the Senate had prevailed over Sulla's expressed wishes to be inhumed and arranged instead for his cremation.[19] At the least one might posit a design committee for an imperial funerary monument, such as the board Frank Lepper and Sheppard Frere suggest for Trajan's Column, possibly headed by the emperor but certainly partisan to the monarchy's cause;[20] the committee for Augustus's Mausoleum, for instance, probably included Agrippa as well as an architect.

Logic suggests that each case was quite individual. Scholars usually conclude that Augustus played a relatively active role in determining the design of monuments that he commissioned, and likewise those dedicated to him by the Senate and People of Rome;[21] if, as I argue in Chapter 2, the Mausoleum relied on Egyptian construction techniques and models, then the emperor's (or Agrippa's) firsthand knowledge of Egypt must have been a forceful factor in its design. The same is true of Hadrian, whose renowned interest in all the arts and sciences was amply matched, by all accounts, by his determination to engage with the experts; ancient sources speak repeatedly of his aggressive demand to be heard in discussion with professionals of all sorts.[22] He harbored personal ambitions as an architect, and although scholars generally discredit Cassius Dio's report that the demise of Trajan's architect Apollodorus was a direct consequence of his criticism of Hadrian's blueprints for the Temple of Venus and Roma, the anecdote, and Apollodorus's snide comment that Hadrian should go back to drawing his pumpkins, reveal that the emperor at least dabbled in architectural design.[23] Many buildings in Rome and elsewhere are firmly linked with his name, and it is fair to suppose that he was closely involved in the monument that would hold his mortal remains in perpetuity and would inaugurate his dynasty; indeed, the *Scriptores* state as much unequivocally: *fecit et sui nominis pontem et sepulchrum iuxta Tiberim* ("he also built the bridge bearing his name and a tomb next to the Tiber").[24] Perhaps he also chose the site for his tomb, for Hadrian was no novice when it came to topographical reasoning: he may have commissioned or even written a topographical study of Rome, "On the Places in Rome, and the Names by Which They Are Called," attributed to his freedman P. Aelius Phlegon.[25]

The role of other emperors is harder to gauge. A ferocious patron of building activity in Rome, Domitian raised so many arches that "somebody scrawled on one of them 'arci,' meaning 'arches,' spelling out the Greek word for 'enough!' in Greek letters."[26] Could he conceivably have overseen the design of all of them personally, even one – ostensibly at least – dedicated by the Senate and People of Rome? On the other hand, the Temple of the Flavian Dynasty was so intimately bound up in its very conception with the emperor's person that Domitian probably had a hand in its design, perhaps hiring Rabirius as architect, as he did for his Palatine residence and many other buildings in Rome.[27] Trajan may have relied heavily upon his architect. His Column is the work of an unknown artist whom Ranuccio Bianchi-Bandinelli nicknamed "The Maestro," yet there is good reason to believe that he may have been Apollodorus, architect, engineer, and *praefectus fabrum* (minister of works) who accompanied Trajan across the Danube and indeed made his crossing possible by constructing the pontoon bridge pictured prominently on the Column's frieze. His talents were famous in antiquity and his name has long been associated with Trajan's Forum and adjacent markets; the subtle engineering of the Column stands on a level footing with these. He may have designed the frieze too.[28] On the whole, however, architects are difficult to identify, and no names of master architects after Apollodorus are known to us. For the Columns of Antoninus Pius and Marcus Aurelius one must proceed on guesswork alone.[29]

Despite its obviously innovative quality as the first imperial tomb, the Mausoleum of Augustus emerged against the backdrop of an established Republican tradition of tomb building in Rome and beyond. It began as early as the sixth century B.C., when loosely scattered cemeteries started to spring up outside the city gates, and the practice remained more or less consistent until the third century.[30] Mainly earthen mounds or subterranean chambers carved out of the living tufa, these early burials lacked extravagant external markers, perhaps because of archaic sumptuary laws restricting lavish expense for funerary arrangements.[31] The Tomb of the Scipios on the Via Appia is the best-known example, a hypogeum with four subterranean galleries arranged in a quadrangular plan with two intersecting corridors in the center, whose first phase of construction, attributed to L. Cornelius Scipio Barbatus (cos. 298) or his son, dates to the first decades of the third century.[32] In the fourth and third centuries, members of the elite developed another type of monument, exemplified by the Esquiline Tomb associated with Q. Fabius, which consists of a masonry tomb sunk into the earth and painted on the walls. Interspersed with these grander tombs were the humbler burials of the nonelite, and the poor found burial in mass graves.[33]

It was in the second century that a first step toward the conspicuous monumentality that characterizes the imperial funerary monuments occurred, when newfound prosperity from foreign campaigns led increasing numbers of elite families, as well as nonelite men with military careers, to build tombs, and the external appearance of the tomb became increasingly important. A second construction phase at the Tomb of the Scipios illustrates this well. In circa 150–35, Scipio Aemilianus built subsidiary galleries for additional burials in the tomb of his forebears; more notably, he expressed his status, wealth, and philhellenic leanings by adding to it a monumental tufa facade with engaged Corinthian columns. Paintings on the base represented scenes of warfare, and in niches, statues of Scipio Africanus, Scipio Asiaticus, and Ennius placed new emphasis on the individuals interred within and their learned associates. This incipient trend toward conspicuous display and self-representation went hand in hand with the expansion of the Roman Empire and a developing rivalry for positions of political prominence in its capital.[34]

By the end of the second century, the art of ostentatious tomb construction was flourishing. With escalating social unrest in Italy, a tomb became a means to express status publicly yet through private means, to establish one's position, not merely in relation to one's peers, but also in relation to members of other social ranks. More and more families erected tombs in ever more varied form. The familiar earthen tumulus took on architectonic articulation, as seen in Casal Rotondo on the Via Appia (third quarter of the first century), where a high stone socle serves as a monumental base, and the earthen tumulus is reduced almost to a crowning element (fig. 1). Circular tombs of this sort jostled for attention with altar tombs, such as the Tomb of consul C. Sulpicius Galba by the Horrea Galbana and aedicular tombs such as that on Via Salaria; other patrons selected exedra tombs on the Via Appia. More playful were the variations on themes, such as the so-called Tomb of the Curatii and the Horatii on the Via Appia outside Albano. With four conical pyramids on a high base, the tomb is reminiscent of descriptions of the Tomb of Porsenna in Chiusi. Types intermingled to produce hybrids and dimensions escalated dramatically: routinely 10 meters in diameter, tumuli built by prominent families reached 34 meters (in Magliana, west of Rome), and all types of tomb stood on tall bases to increase monumentality. Subsidiary architectural elements, such as columns, and contrasting materials and lavish sculpture, were increasingly coopted to draw a passerby's attention. In contrast to the third and second centuries, when tombs were oriented vaguely toward roads, now the tomb's facade was aligned with the edge of the road for maximum impact on a passerby, and families vied for prominent locations at

Figure 1. "Casal Rotondo," Via Appia, Rome, first century B.C. Photo: Penelope J. E. Davies

gateways or major junctions. A single motive appears to have driven all of these changes: to promote a *gens,* helping to establish or maintain its position in the social and political order. Although privately funded, then, late Republican tombs took on an increasingly public role, and inscriptions and statuary emphasized, not intimate tidings of farewell, but biographical and genealogical details.[35]

The public role of these privately funded monuments became all the more intense with Augustus. Constitutionally speaking, to be sure, he was a private citizen at the time of his mausoleum's construction. Yet the reality was that with Mark Antony dead and Lepidus ineffectual, he was the de facto ruler of Rome and his person was anything but private. The ambiguous if not outright paradoxical nature of his position plays itself out even in the location of his tomb on public land, along with monuments for public use; its construction also marked the end of a public disaster, civil war. At some level, it must have called to mind the public burials on the Campus Martius that the Senate and People of Rome granted to Rome's *summi viri,* including Sulla, the consuls A. Hirtius and C. Vibius Pansa, and Julius Caesar.[36] More than that, though, like the Late Republican tombs it belongs in the context of a general tradition of commemorative monuments dedicated by the Senate and People of Rome or by private individuals to acknowledge civic benefaction, especially military virtue on behalf of the state. While many of these took the form of statues (so many, indeed, that a law was passed to restrict their numbers), grander monuments included statue groups dedicated on elaborate bases, such as the Base of Marcus Antonius on the Circus Flaminius,[37] columns (such as the *columna rostrata* erected in the Forum by the state to honor C. Duilius in ca. 260 for his victory over the Carthaginians),[38] or arches (such as those in the Circus Maximus and the Forum Boarium celebrating L. Stertinius's success in Spanish campaigns).[39] These monuments were unabashedly propagandistic; for the most part, their raison d'être was to promote an individual and his family, proclaiming their message through inscriptions, sculpture, and sheer physical presence.[40] Even when a monument took the form of a votive offering to a patron god, political intention rang through; when Marcus Antonius, for instance, dedicated his statue group to Mars and Neptune for their part in his victories over Cilician pirates and erected it between their temples, he must have recognized that the tutelage of a god implied divine favor, which was politically expedient. Moreover, the incorporation of a Hellenistic marine *thiasos* relief emphasized through physical spoliation the highpoint of his military career, the triumph he celebrated late in 100.[41] In their grandest incarnations these commemorative monuments became entire architectural complexes, and this was the intention behind Pompey's triumphal complex on the Campus Martius, dedicated in 55 B.C., where a monumental trophy stood side by side with a stone theater, a huge portico, a Curia, and a Temple to Pompey's guiding goddess, Venus Victrix.[42] The vast scale of this complex, and of Julius Caesar's Forum after it, tellingly reflects the faltering hold of the Republic's ideals and the concurrent rise of prominent individuals to positions of sole leadership. Standing proud on the northern Campus Martius, the Mausoleum of Augustus relates as closely to these overwhelming monuments to victory as it does to the tradition of Late Republican tombs that it brings to a close.

As we have seen, it was customary for an emperor (and indeed for any Roman, regardless of social standing) to prescribe in his will the manner in which he wished his funeral to be conducted, and the Senate might choose, as it did with Augustus, to add its own honors to his instructions.[43] Literary sources on imperial funerals are relatively detailed; Cassius Dio, Suetonius, and Tacitus report on Augustus's funeral, while Cassius Dio recalls that of Pertinax, and Herodian describes that of Septimius Severus. Their accounts indicate that an imperial funeral followed the broad lines of the public funeral, *funus publicum,* initially a burial at public expense for foreign dignitaries or for those, like Valerius Poplicola, Agrippa Menenius, and Siccius Dentatus, who had earned spectacular funerary ceremonies but had left insufficient funds. Sulla was the first to receive a public burial as an extravagant state honor after his death in Campania in 78 B.C., by his own testamentary instruction and by request of the consul, Q. Lutatius.[44] Appian describes how a magnificent procession accompanied his embalmed body to Rome, resting on a gilded couch or *kline,* and presumably on a chariot. Standard-bearers and lictors led the procession, and after the body came trumpeters, dancers, mimes, and armed soldiers interspersed with veterans; crowds of people brought up the rear. Once the cortège passed beneath the city gates, the trumpeters moved to the front, intoning dirgeful music to herald their arrival. Behind the corpse were gifts, including two thousand crowns of gold from cities, friends, and soldiers, as well as six thousand beds (perhaps for celebrants of the funerary banquet); from married women there were enough aromatic offerings, according to Plutarch, to fill two hundred and sixty *fercula* (trays for spoils) and to allow for a sculpture of the dictator with a lictor to be carved from the wood of frankincense and cinnamon trees. Priests and Vestal Virgins came next in the procession, followed by senators, magistrates, the *equites,* and the legions. The parade proceeded to the Curia, where a cry or ordered greeting, a *conclamatio,* took place.[45]

Plutarch's account suggests that a passage of time may have elapsed between this *translatio* and the day of cremation, when Sulla's body was transported from the Curia to the Rostra in the Forum, and there, since his son was too young, the most talented orator of the day pronounced the eulogy, or *laudatio,* over the body. At about the ninth hour (approximately 3 P.M.), the strongest of the senators carried it to the Campus Martius where, in a strong wind and driving rain, body and statue were consumed by flames, amid a procession of cavalry and infantry. The ashes were taken to a tumulus on the Campus Martius that the Senate had provided.[46] After his death, as a response to the state of emergency and to prevent an outbreak of civil strife during the power transition, there followed a period of *iustitium,* during which normal duties were suspended; baths and taverns were closed, spectacles and banquets ceased; and women grieved for a year. This practice eventually became an expression of homage.[47]

Although the funerals of the elite formed the broad basis of this *funus publicum,* the extravagance of the trappings, along with certain notable differences in procedure, signal an incipient inclination to treat the deceased as a divinity, an inclination that finds fuller development in Julius Caesar's funeral. Indeed, the magistrates and ex-magistrates (not family members, as was customary) conveyed Caesar's body concealed within a couch of ivory with coverlets of gold and purple. A wax image represented the dictator. The procession progressed from the *domus publica* at the Regia to a shrine on the Rostra modeled after the Temple of Venus Genetrix, to suggest that Caesar had joined his progenitress in immortality. Gladiatorial contests were held, and Mark Antony, rather than a member of the family, delivered an oration.[48] Moreover, though a pyre had been assembled on the Campus Martius next to the tomb of his daughter Julia, frenzied crowds of mourners seized Caesar's body on their shoulders and carried it to the Capitol, where they intended to cremate and bury it in the cella of the Temple of Jupiter Capitolinus, where he would take his place among the gods. Upon the priests' refusal, they cremated him instead on an improvised pyre in the Roman Forum before sealing his ashes in Julia's tumulus on the Campus Martius.[49]

Imperial funerals followed a similar outline, with additional participants and representations, such as personifications of subject nations.[50] The *translatio* normally processed from the emperor's Palatine residence to the Rostra, by way of the Sacra Via, with the successor behind the bier. There, like Caesar's, the body was placed in a shrine, a baldachino composed of columns and a roof, as was the custom in the East for shrines of gods and kings and as described as having been on Alexander the Great's funeral carriage.[51] Cassius Dio reports that, like Caesar's, Augustus's body, and Pertinax's too, were represented by waxen images; this may have been true for other emperors as well.[52] After the oration the body was conveyed to the imperial *ustrinum* or pyre on the Campus Martius for cremation which, real or simulated, was essential for divinization and persisted for emperors long after other Romans had begun to favor inhumation.[53] The pyre itself, apparently modeled on Hellenistic examples, and especially that erected in Babylon for Alexander the Great's friend Hephaistion in 325, appears to have become more elaborate with passing time.[54] Coin depictions survive from the time of Faustina the Elder's death and after, and mesh well with literary descriptions. An eyewitness, Cassius Dio, recalled Pertinax's pyre as a towerlike structure in three levels, adorned with marble and gold and a series of statues. On top was a figure of Pertinax driving a gilded chariot. Herodian, though not present at Septimius Severus's funeral, describes a building of many levels, decreasing in size toward the top like a lighthouse. The body was lodged on the second storey, and the inside, he states, was filled with wood. The exterior was hung with tapestries woven in gold, and adorned with marble statues and paintings of various sorts; the upper levels had doors and windows. Bystanders, he records, scattered incense of all sorts and piles of fruit and herbs, and poured on aromatic liquids.

Cremation often led to apotheosis, on the models of heroes such as Romulus and Hercules.[55] Many believed Caesar's soul to have departed his body immediately after his assassination in the Curia Pompeiana,[56] and during the games after his death a comet shone in the sky for seven days; the people interpreted this omen to mean he was divine.[57] Seizing advantage of this response years later, Livia paid one Numerius Aticus to claim to have seen Augustus's spirit rise to the heavens.[58] By Cassius Dio's account written some two centuries later, when soldiers set fire to Augustus's pyre, an eagle soared up from it into the sky; recording a similar phenomenon at the funeral of Pertinax, Dio interjects, "and thus Pertinax became immortal." Though featured in visual representations of or allusions to the emperor's apotheosis from the early empire, the event is absent from other earlier accounts of Augustus's funeral by Suetonius and Tacitus. It appears only to have entered official ceremony in the second century, perhaps from the East, as an abstract means of expressing the soul's liberation from the burning body.[59]

The Senate's official declaration of apotheosis, or *consecratio,* occurred after the funeral, generally at the successor's instigation. Tiberius, for instance, addressed the Senate to plead for a public funeral for Augustus, at which point the late emperor's *Res Gestae* and other writings were recited; after the funeral the Senate met again and conferred the decree of apotheosis. The decree may have had little to do with religion and most to do with politics and the Senate's approval of the emperor's policies;[60] in any event, the emperor's consecration rapidly became an expected consequence of his lifetime achievements or virtue on behalf of the state; an alternative was his *damnatio memoriae,* or condemnation of memory for bad government, as was the posthumous fate of Nero, among others.[61] By the second century, apotheosis was becoming more and more of a formality (Simon Price calculates that thirty-six of the sixty emperors from Augustus to Constantine received the honor, along with twenty-seven members of their families), and the official decree came in some cases to precede the funeral; the funeral, in turn, focused increasingly upon the moment of cremation and the magnificence of the pyre, as the pyre and its lighting became the spectacular enactment of apotheosis.[62]

Upon apotheosis, the new *divus* was entitled to the trappings of a cult, such as a temple (sometimes shared with already deified members of the imperial family), a *flamen,* and a *pulvinar,* or cushion used in rituals and festivals.[63] After Julius Caesar's funeral, the people established a cult where his pyre had stood in the Roman Forum, probably administered by Mark Antony; the Senate and people decreed his official consecration in January of 42, and Augustus began construction of a temple to him on the site in circa 36 B.C., dedicating it after his Actian triumph on August 18 of 29.[64] Caligula completed a temple to the Divine Augustus on the edge of the Roman Forum, and Agrippina began a temple to the Divine Claudius on the Caelian Hill, which Nero promptly expropriated as a monumental nymphaeum within his Domus Aurea and which Vespasian later completed.[65] Domitian built a temple to his divine father, Vespasian, and brother Titus at the west end of the Roman Forum, and additional shrines in their names were attached to the Porticus Divorum on the Campus Martius;[66] the cult of Divine Trajan and Plotina was centered in the temple in his forum.[67] Antoninus Pius dedicated the Hadrianeum on the Campus Martius for Hadrian in 145, after he had managed to secure his apotheosis from a reluctant Senate;[68] still partially preserved within the Borsa in Piazza di Pietra, it stood alongside Hadrian's temple to his mother-in-law, Diva Matidia, with its basilicas to Matidia and her mother, Trajan's sister, Diva Marciana.[69] At Antoninus Pius's own death, his cult joined that of his wife Faustina in a temple built in 141 in the Roman Forum.[70] Marcus Aurelius's temple is known from literary sources and the *Regionary Catalogues,* and probably stood within a spacious courtyard surrounding his column on the Campus Martius.[71]

The name of the new *divus* was evoked in prayers and formulae, and on the anniversary of his *natalis* or birthday, games were held and prayers recited to the emperor as god.[72] On days when games were not specifically in honor of the *divus,* his statue took its place among those of other gods. Augustus's statue, for instance, was paraded around the circus in a chariot drawn by elephants.[73] The image and memory of a *divus* were correspondingly removed from the context of mortal ancestors, as exemplified by the exclusion of Julius Caesar's image from the crowd of illustrious predecessors imitated by actors at Augustus's funeral.[74]

THE MONUMENTS

THE MAUSOLEUM OF AUGUSTUS

I N 29 B.C., TWO years after conquering Mark Antony and Cleopatra, Augustus (then Octavian) returned to Rome to celebrate a triple triumph for his victory at Actium, the annexation of Egypt, and his conquest of Illyricum. Determined to establish himself in supreme power, he undertook the task of rebuilding the shaken city. Though neither he nor his minister of works, Agrippa, was new to the art of building in Rome, this initiative on his return tackled the city's infrastructure and urban image with unprecedented vigor. Completing Julius Caesar's Curia and a Temple to the Divine Julius in the Roman Forum in 29, in 28 Augustus turned his attention to a Temple of Apollo, his epiphanous patron at Actium, as one of eighty-two temples he later claimed to have built or restored. Work on the Campus Martius began in earnest with the restoration of Pompey's vast triumphal complex and the provision, in 25, of public amenities such as the Thermae Agrippae and the Basilica Neptuni. Also in 28, Agrippa began the first Pantheon and dedicated it in 25 as a cult center for all the gods, including Augustus's mortal predecessor, Julius Caesar.[1] To the north of this, as one of the first buildings of this extensive program, Augustus constructed a magnificent Mausoleum for himself and his family (figs. 2, 3). Its doors opened in 23 B.C. when Marcellus, Augustus's nephew, died prematurely, and it found constant use over the next two decades as, one by one, Augustus's descendants predeceased him; finally, in A.D. 14, he was laid to rest there himself.[2] The long years since its construction have not been kind, and, despoiled of its revetment in the Middle Ages when it was a marble workshop (the Calcare dell'Agosta), it has been used as a fortress for the Colonna family, a hanging garden, a bullring, amphitheater, and concert hall. Excavated in 1907–8 and 1926–30, it was finally "liberated" by Mussolini in 1939.[3]

Soon after its construction, Strabo wrote:

> Most worth seeing is the so-called Mausoleion, a large mound set upon a tall socle by the river, planted with evergreen trees up to the top. Above stands the bronze statue of the Emperor Augustus. Within the mound are the graves intended for him, his relatives, and friends. Behind there is a large grove with

Figure 2. Mausoleum of Augustus, Rome, ca 28 B.C., actual state. Photo: Penelope J. E. Davies

splendid walks, in the midst of which is an elevated place (the ustrinum), where Augustus's corpse was burnt.[4]

Reconstructions of the tomb have traditionally fallen into two main camps.[5] One sees the tomb as a simple earthen tumulus planted with grass and black cypress trees, surmounting a two-tiered circular base wall with a decorative entablature.[6] More convincing are reconstructions with greater architectonic articulation, most recently Henner von Hesberg's (fig. 4). This posits a masonry drum reveted with travertine and with Carrara marble to either side of the entrance, where inscriptions named those interred inside. Above the drum rose the grass tumulus, broken by a ring of masonry above walls 4 and 3. Above wall 2 was a tholos with a Doric entablature and crenellations. The tumulus continued above the tholos, and at the apex were steps and a statue of Augustus on a podium, melted down in the Middle Ages. Sparse fragments of surviving sculptural decoration are comprehensively catalogued by Panciera.[7]

In plan, five concentric walls (the outermost 300 Roman feet in diameter) surrounded a 150-foot-high rectangular travertine pillar, coated with concrete to appear cylindrical above ground level (fig. 5).[8] From the entrance on the south, a vaulted vestibule led to an annular corridor between walls 2 and 1. From this passageway one entered the burial chamber proper, which contained niches for urns or statuary at the cardinal points. Inside the travertine pillar in the center of the cella was a smaller chamber, presumably for Augustus's cinerary urn.[9] Between walls 5 and 4 were semicircular chambers divided by radial walls to make quarter circles, and radial walls also linked walls 4 and 3 to form 12 rectangular chambers. There was no access to either set of chambers.

Just outside the entrance to the Mausoleum was a pair of pillars on which a copy of Augustus's *Res Gestae,* or Things Achieved, was inscribed after his death as specified in his will. This document, which Augustus updated gradually throughout his reign, detailed honors and offices he received, his personal expenditure for public good, and his military accomplishments.[10] Flanking the pillars, and standing some 22 meters from either side of the entrance, was a pair of small, uninscribed red granite obelisks (figs. 6, 7).[11]

The Mausoleum did not stand in isolation on the northern Campus Martius; rather, as Edmund Buchner and other scholars have suggested, it was but

Figure 3. Mausoleum of Augustus, Rome, ca 28 B.C., actual state. Photo: Penelope J. E. Davies

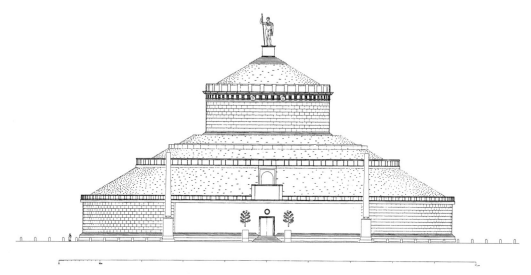

Figure 4. Reconstruction of the Mausoleum of Augustus by H. von Hesberg. Courtesy of Henner von Hesberg

Figure 5. Plan of the Mausoleum of Augustus, Rome, ca. 28 B.C., actual state. Photo: Deutsches Archäologisches Institut, Rom–InstNegNr 61.1181

Figure 6. Obelisk from the Mausoleum of Augustus in Piazza dell'Esquilino, Rome. Photo: Penelope J. E. Davies

Figure 7. Obelisk from the Mausoleum of Augustus in Piazza del Quirinale, Rome. Photo: Penelope J. E. Davies

one component of a tripartite complex, consisting also of the Ara Pacis Augustae and Solarium or Horologium Augusti. The Ara Pacis or Altar of Augustan Peace (13–9 B.C.), a small marble altar within a hypaethral rectangular enclosure, celebrated Augustus's safe return from Spain and Gaul (fig. 8). Lavish relief sculpture ornaments the entire monument. On the lower half of the exterior of the enclosure wall is a rich carpet of acanthus. In the upper register, four panels flank the doors on east and west sides: on the west, Aeneas sacrifices on his arrival in Latium, and the she-wolf suckles Romulus and Remus; on the east, two seated figures represent the goddess Roma and a female of disputed identity, nursing two infants and surrounded by animals, vegetation, and two female personifications of winds or seasons (fig. 82). Friezes on north and south sides depict a procession of priests, senators, and imperial personages (fig. 78). The interior of the enclosure is carved to imitate wooden laths and pilasters, decorated with bucrania, garlands, and paterae (fig. 73), and a procession in honor of peace winds around the altar itself.[12] The Solarium or Sundial (10–9 B.C.), for its part, consisted of a huge bronze grid laid into the pavement around an Egyptian obelisk, with mosaics of the winds and various celestial symbols (figs. 9, 60–61).[13] Though constructed over a period of approximately twenty years, the monu-

Figure 8. Ara Pacis Augustae, Rome, 13–9 B.C., view of the west side. Photo: Michael Larvey

Figure 9. Reconstruction of the Solarium Augusti with the Mausoleum of Augustus and the Ara Pacis Augustae, Campus Martius, Rome, ca. 28–9 B.C., by E. Buchner. Courtesy of Edmund Buchner

ments were visibly united by their topographical proximity to one another and their isolation from other buildings (since the area around them was desolate), even if they were not joined by the movement of the needle's shadow, as Buchner supposed. They also shared commonalities in symbolic themes, such as references to the Actian victory. All, we might suppose, were part of Augustus's commemorative scheme.[14]

Tiberius's ashes, and probably those of Claudius as well, joined Augustus's in the Mausoleum, a testimony to the dynastic basis of Julio-Claudian authority.[15] Following Caligula's assassination in 41, his body was "carried away secretly to the Lamian Gardens and, half-cremated on a hastily-built pyre, it was buried under shallow turf. Later, it was exhumed, cremated, and entombed by his sisters on their return from exile. It is well known that until then the custodians of the Gardens were haunted by ghosts; in the building where he died not a night passed without some kind of terror, until at last the house itself was consumed by fire."[16] After Nero's ignominious death in 68, his ashes found burial in a prophyry urn beneath a marble altar in the family tomb of the Domitii on the Pincio; the memory of his burial there was so powerful that in 1099 Pascal II built the church of Santa Maria del Popolo at the location of his tomb to dispel his evil spirit.[17] The brevity of their reigns and the violent circumstances of their deaths prevented the construction of impressive memorials for Galba, Otho, and Vitellius, but with the demise of the first Flavian emperor, Vespasian, in 79, the doors of Augustus's Mausoleum appear to have opened once more for his burial.[18]

THE ARCH OF TITUS

On 1 September A.D. 81, after a reign of only two years, two months, and twenty days, the second Flavian emperor, Titus, died in the country house where his father, Vespasian, had passed away. His younger brother, Domitian, assumed the throne and, despite Suetonius's assertion that the new emperor "granted [Titus] no honour at all, except for his deification," he appears to have embarked upon a systematic architectural program in the names of his late father and brother, building temples in their honor in the Roman Forum and in the Porticus Divorum on the Campus Martius, and completing their projects.[19] As part of this policy, the Senate and People of Rome dedicated an arch to his newly deified brother at the eastern end of the Roman Forum on the brow of the Velian Hill (figs. 10, 97).

The history of the Arch is complex but well documented. It was still visible in the sixth or seventh century, when an apprentice scribe recorded its inscription. By the thirteenth century the Frangipani had incorporated it into their fortress, and it was subsequently enveloped in the Santa Maria Nuova building complex along with an olive tannery and a silo; by 1715, monks were using its attic chamber as a retreat. In 1817/18, Raffaele Stern, architect to the Apostolic See, was

Figure 10. Arch of Titus, Rome, 81, view from the east. Photo: Michael Larvey

appointed to restore it, and after his accidental death in 1820 Giuseppe Valadier resumed his work. Between 1822 and 1824 dismantling the Arch almost entirely, he reconstructed it, basing his restorations on surviving fragments and comparisons with the Arch of Trajan at Benevento, distinguishing modern from ancient work by leaving moldings unsculpted and using travertine instead of marble.[20]

The design of this single-bayed Arch is exquisitely simple. Eight engaged composite columns framing the bay divide the three horizontal sections – socle, central area, and attic – into a matching tripartite vertical configuration. The Arch's core is travertine, and its outer skin marble; lower, more visible sections are worked in Pentelic marble, upper parts in less costly marble from Carrara.[21] The exterior surfaces are undecorated except for three areas.[22] Winged victories grace the spandrels, each with her left foot on a globe and each with a different attribute referring to the Jewish war; and on the keystones are personifications of Virtus and Honos. A small figural frieze running around the Arch at cornice level, of which only thirty-eight figures survive, depicts the triumphal procession of June 71.[23] More elaborate decoration is reserved for the interior of the bay, where two relief panels depict moments from the triumph. On the north side, Titus rides in his triumphal chariot, pulled by four spirited horses and accompanied by a crowd of lictors and other unidentified figures (fig. 11). The relief on the south side illustrates the display of booty in the triumphal procession (fig. 12). Two groups of ministrants bearing *fercula* on their shoulders move toward a triumphal archway at the right, preceded by ministrants with placards, probably describing the

Figure 11. Arch of Titus, triumphator relief, Rome, 81. Photo: Alinari/Art Resource, New York, AL5839

Figure 12. Arch of Titus, spoils relief, Rome, 81. Photo: Alinari/Art Resource, New York, AL5840

booty.[24] In the vaulting of the bay are coffers sculpted with rosettes, and at the summit a small relief panel, framed by laurel garlands clasped by putti, depicts Titus soaring heavenward on the back of an eagle (fig. 13).[25] The Arch's crowning statuary does not survive, but literary evidence suggests that it may have represented Titus in a quadriga drawn by elephants: in 535/6 Theodahad, the Ostrogoth king, ordered the restoration of bronze elephants that were about to fall from place onto the Sacra Via.[26]

A dedicatory inscription in bronze letters on the east side of the attic (and probably originally on the west as well) provides a terminus post quem for the Arch:

SENATUS POPULUSQUE ROMANUS DIVO TITO DIVI VESPASIANI F. VESPASIANO AUGUSTO

[The Senate and People of Rome to the deified Titus Vespasian Augustus, son of the deified Vespasian].[27]

Titus's divine status indicates that the Arch was not begun during his reign, as some suppose,[28] but must postdate his apotheosis, which the Senate probably decreed by the end of 81.[29] F. S. Kleiner's identification of Domitian on horse-

Figure 13. Arch of Titus, apotheosis relief, Rome, 81. Photo: Penelope J. E. Davies

back between two chariots on top of the arch in the spoils relief argues for a date before Domitian's *damnatio memoriae* in 96 (fig. 14).[30]

In 1934, Karl Lehmann-Hartleben suggested that Domitian built the Arch as a sepulcher rather than a triumphal monument.[31] His reasoning was, first, that the inscription is more consistent with sepulchral inscriptions than with those on triumphal arches, since it omits Titus's military titles and provides no more than his name and patronymic and the identity of the dedicator. The Arch of Titus near the Circus Maximus, in contrast, details the motive for the arch's construction as well as the honoree's titles.[32] Since the latter monument was erected in 80 to celebrate the capture of Jerusalem, Lehmann-Hartleben argued that the Arch of Titus on the Velian could hardly have been built for the same motive. Instead, he concludes that it stood as a tomb for Domitian's late brother, whose ashes he deposited in its hollow attic. This chamber, reached by a travertine staircase on the Colosseum side of the north pylon, was appropriately located above the apotheosis scene and behind the inscription that described Titus's new divine status.[33] Lacking more conclusive evidence, Lehmann-Hartleben's argument has not found widespread acceptance. However, it has forced scholars to recognize that, although the Arch cannot be termed a tomb, it cannot be regarded as a simple triumphal monument either. Rather, with its apotheosis scene and its celebration of Titus as a *divus,* it functioned as a commemorative monument occasioned by his death.[34]

Figure 14. Detail of the arch in the spoils relief on the Arch of Titus, Rome, 81. Photo: Penelope J. E. Davies

THE TEMPLE OF THE FLAVIAN DYNASTY

"Domitian was born on the ninth day before the Kalends of November [24 October], when his father was consul designate [51], . . . in Pomegranate Street in the sixth district of the city, in a house that he later converted into the Temple of the Flavian Gens."[35] So writes Suetonius. When Julia, daughter of Titus, died and was deified in 91, her ashes were brought to this temple, and so, scholars believe, were those of Domitian's father, Vespasian (from the Mausoleum of Augustus), and brother, Titus.[36] When a conspiracy against Domitian's life came to fruition on 18 September 96, public undertakers carried his body away on a common bier. His nurse, Phyllis, cremated him in her garden on the Via Latina, then took his ashes secretly to the Flavian temple, where she mixed them with Julia's.[37] The Temple of the Flavian Dynasty was therefore its Mausoleum, and it is also one of the great enigmas of Roman architecture. Frequent allusions to the temple by Martial and Statius amount to little of substance, and besides the statement quoted above, Suetonius records only that lightning struck it in 96. Claudius Gothicus may have undertaken its enlargement, and presumably it was still visible when the Chronographer of A.D. 354 took note of it;[38] sometime thereafter it perished, leaving behind a legacy of uncertainty on almost every count: the date of its construction, its location, and its very appearance.

When he came to power, Domitian was confronted by a city in desperate need of repair. Devastating fires had devoured major portions of the capital, and a year of civil war had bequeathed it a haunting legacy of neglect, despite Nero's far-reaching rebuilding program. The only substantial Domitianic buildings to survive the centuries are the Domus Flavia on the Palatine and the Forum Transitorium, completed by Nerva; yet Brian Jones calculates that Domitian erected, restored, or completed some fifty structures. As well as the Temple of the Flavian Dynasty, his projects included a spectacular Temple to Jupiter Capitolinus and a new Pantheon; he even began to develop the area of Trajan's Forum, the most magnificent of all the imperial fora, removing the saddle between the Capitoline and the Quirinal in a massive excavation initiative.[39]

Construction on the Templum Gentis Flaviae began some time after Domitian assumed the throne in 81. The date of its completion is unknown; estimates range from 89 to 96.[40] The *Curiosum urbis Romae Regionum XIIII* and the *Notitia urbis Romae Regionum XIIII* place it in Regio VI, the Alta Semita (which stretches from the present Piazza del Quirinale toward the Porta Colina), listing it after the Temple of Quirinus and the Horti Sallustiani and before the Baths of Diocletian. Suetonius's testimony indicates that it stood somewhere on the vicus ad Malum Punicum, south of the Alta Semita on the Quirinal Hill, a favorite and densely packed region for patrician residents.[41] Early conjectures located it near the church of San Carlo alle Quattro Fontane or Sant'Andrea al Quirinale, but in the 1980s, excavations beneath the Caserma dei Corazzieri at Via XX Settembre 12, near Santa Susanna, uncovered a concrete core for a huge podium, possibly facing south onto the Alta Semita. In the vicinity are parts of Republican walls in *opus reticulatum,* some of which were decorated in a later restoration with glass paste polychrome mosaics of fantastic architecture and human figures, analogous to fourth-style paintings and probably dating to the Neronian or Flavian period (figs. 15, 16). A lead water pipe leading to the mosaics suggests that the structure they decorated was a nymphaeum, and the level of workmanship intimates an aristocratic residence.[42]

Two inscriptions suggest that the owner of the house was Flavius Sabinus, brother of Vespasian, prefect of the city in 69. One, a cippus inscribed *Inter duos / parietes / ambitus privat(us) / Flavi Sabini* ("between these two walls, private passage, belonging to Flavius Sabinus"), was discovered in the sixteenth century in the Vigna Sadoleto on the Quirinal, probably in the vicinity of the church of Santa Susanna; the other, a lead water pipe, found near the Methodist church on Via Firenze opposite the Caserma dei Corazzieri, is inscribed: *T. Flavi Sabini* ("[property of] Titus Flavius Sabinus"). Domitian was probably born in a neighboring residence belonging to Vespasian, or even in this very house, home of his wealthiest and most influential relative, to whom the impoverished Vespasian mortgaged all his property in 60. If so, the concrete podium may mark the site of the Temple of the Flavian Dynasty, built on Domitian's birthplace.[43]

There is little evidence for the temple's form, except that it was monumental in proportion and lavishly decorated. In *Epigram* 9.1.8 Martial describes it as an *altum decus,* a lofty glory; in 9.20.1–2, he adds, "This piece of land, which now stands wholly exposed, and is being covered with marble and gold, was privy to our lord's infant years." Indeed, such was its splendor that "Zeus ridicules the falsehoods of his tomb on Crete when he espied the Flavian temple of the Augustan heaven. . . .

Figure 15. Mosaic from a house on the Quirinal beneath the Caserma dei Corazzieri, Rome, Neronian or Flavian period. Photo: Penelope J. E. Davies

Figure 16. Mosaic from a house on the Quirinal beneath the Caserma dei Corazzieri, Rome, Neronian or Flavian period. Photo: Penelope J. E. Davies

Figure 17. Sestertius of 95/96 possibly showing the Temple of the Flavian Dynasty. Photo: Fototeca Unione, American Academy in Rome

'You have given me a monument at Gnossos,' he said, 'see how much better it is to be Caesar's father.' "[44] Statius terms it a *Flavium caelum,* a Flavian heaven,[45] and many scholars have taken this to mean that the temple was round or oval, perhaps topped by a dome to complete the impression of the skies. However, Torelli insists that the notion of a circular building still relies largely on sixteenth-century sketches no longer associated with the Flavian Temple,[46] and prefers to recognize it on a rare Domitianic sestertius showing a decastyle gabled porch within a double precinct, complete with porticoes and a facade marked by an arch and two lateral entrances; the coin was minted in Rome in 95/96, arguably the year of the temple's description by Martial and Statius (fig. 17).[47] He envisages a rectangular peripteral building with cryptoporticoes and nymphea, along the lines of the Claudianum on the Caelian Hill, and remarks that a fragmentary relief in the Museo Gregoriano Profano and the Museo Nazionale delle Terme shows the emperor (restored as Trajan) and lictors before an appropriate decastyle temple (fig. 107).[48] Sculptural fragments assigned to the complex's decorative program are described in Chapter 6.

Use of the temple as the imperial mausoleum ceased with the end of the Flavian dynasty. Domitian's successor, Nerva, aged approximately sixty-eight, died of natural causes in 98, after appointing Trajan his successor. His ashes were placed in the Mausoleum of Augustus.[49]

TRAJAN'S COLUMN

In 117, partly paralyzed by a stroke and plagued by dropsy, Trajan determined to leave his army in Syria and sail for Italy. Overcome by illness, he broke his journey at Selinus in Cilicia, where he died, probably on 8 August. His body was cremated and his ashes conveyed to Rome by the returning army. Sealed in a golden urn, they were deposited in the base of his sculpted Column in his Forum, where they remained until their theft in the Middle Ages (fig. 18).

Figure 18. Trajan's Column, Rome, 113, actual state. Photo: Alinari/Art Resource, New York, AL7008

As its inscription indicates, Trajan's Column was dedicated in 113 by the Senate and People of Rome; it must therefore have been under construction contemporaneously with Trajan's new Baths (dedicated in 109), the adjacent Markets (100–12), and the Forum within which it stands (113), in a small court defined by the Basilica Ulpia on the southeast side, and flanking Greek and

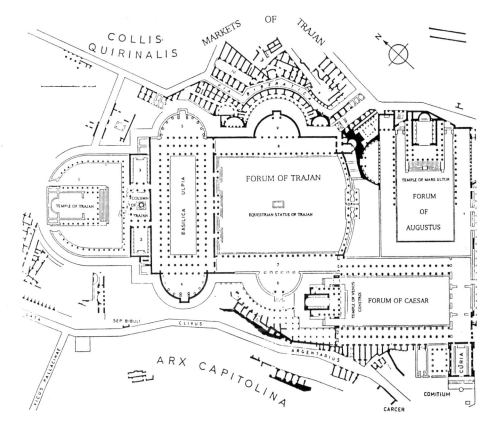

Figure 19. Plan of Trajan's Forum, Rome, ca. 100–112

Figure 20. Restored north–south section of Trajan's Forum, Rome. From J. E. Packer, *The Forum of Trajan in Rome: A Study of the Monuments* (Berkeley, 1997). Courtesy of James E. Packer

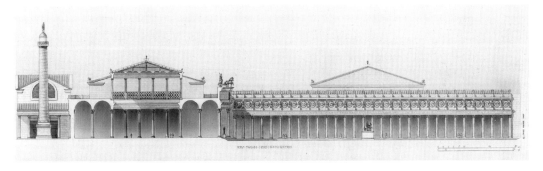

Latin libraries collectively termed the Bibliotheca Ulpia. Traditionally, scholars place the Temple of Divine Trajan on the northwest (figs. 19, 20, 91), although a recent hypothesis would locate it on the southeast end of the Forum, replacing it at the northwest with a massive propylon.[50]

Soaring 150 Roman feet (44.07 m) high, the Column is sculpted on the base with weapons and trophies and on the shaft with a spiraling narrative frieze. The

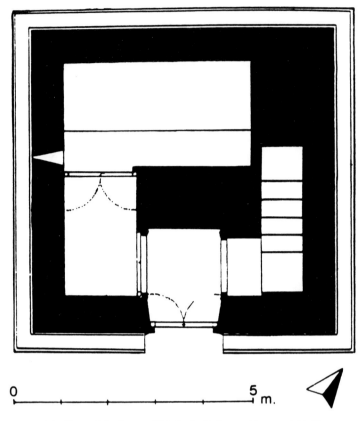

Figure 21. Plan of the base of Trajan's Column, Rome, 113. By permission of Amanda Claridge

Tuscan capital supports a platform, on which there was a colossal gilded statue of Trajan standing on a low dome.[51] Inside the base is a vestibule. A short corridor to the left leads to a small rectangular room, presumably Trajan's burial chamber (fig. 21), and to the right begins a staircase to the upper platform, carved out of the marble drums before the Column was assembled. Rectilinear in the base and spiral in the shaft, the staircase rises in a hundred and eighty-five steps lit by forty-three small slit windows (fig. 22).

There is, admittedly, no incontrovertible evidence that Trajan's Column was designed from the outset as his sepulcher. Literary sources state clearly that his ashes were buried *sub columna* (under the column), yet they are equally unclear about when the decision to place them there was taken and by whom.[52] There is nothing inherent in the Column itself that unambiguously certifies a primary, or even a secondary, funerary function. Furthermore, protocol denied an emperor public burial until the Senate decreed it, and this could not happen until after his death. Burial within the *pomerium* was an extraordinary honor, which Trajan could not have presumed himself to merit with impunity.[53] Three scenarios are possible: (1) that the Column was built purely as an honorary monument, exalting Trajan for his spectacular victories across the Danube and only conceived of,

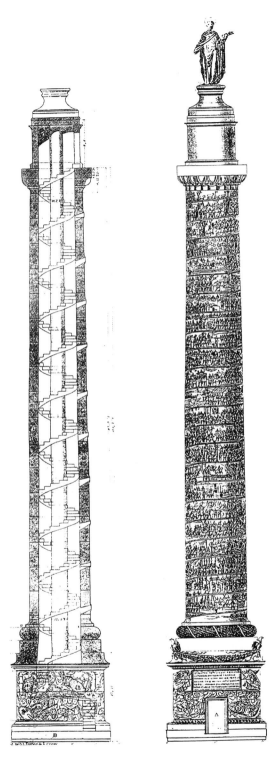

Figure 22. Section of Trajan's Column, Rome, 113. From E. Cresy and G. L. Taylor, *The Architectural Antiquities of Rome,* vol. 2 (London, 1922), pl. CIII

unaltered, as a tomb after his death; (2) that it was initially conceived as an honorary monument and redesigned in a separate construction/decoration phase as a tomb; and (3) that it was designed for Trajan's burial.

Amanda Claridge argues that the present Column as an entirety, with sculpted base and shaft, is troublingly busy; in Trajan's time, she proposes, only the base was sculpted, and the shaft was left plain. The spiral frieze was added in Hadrian's reign, when the Column became Trajan's tomb.[54] However, one might expect Hadrian to feature more prominently in a frieze that he commissioned, and, in general, arguments against an initial funerary intention for the Column fail to account for some disquieting problems. First, be it ever so small, there *is* a chamber in the Column's base, which must have added further complications to an already challenging engineering problem.[55] Moreover, in the back wall of that chamber are traces of a bench or altar that was subsequently hacked away, and marks above it indicate that there was once a bracket, which probably held Trajan's golden urn in place. A rectangular window with an internal splay guided rays of light onto the altar and pavement.[56] The chamber may have been a location for propitiatory sacrifices or a depository for votive objects (such as the spoils depicted on the exterior) before becoming a burial chamber in 117; it may even have housed military standards or the scrolls of Trajan's *Dacica,* as an extension of the Bibliotheca Ulpia.[57] Yet its use for any one of these functions between 113 and 117 does not preclude an ulterior motive for its construction. One might compare it with Marcus Aurelius's Column, designed as a commemorative monument and not a tomb, which has no such chamber.[58] Second, there is a formal similarity between the Column base and a widely used type of Roman funerary altar, often having a double door on the front surmounted by an inscription, and iconographical features including eagles, victories, and weaponry (fig. 23).[59] Columns had been used to mark burials in Greek lands since archaic times, as Elizabeth McGowan documents, as well as in Italy; a column outside the Porta del Vesuvio in Pompeii, for instance, records the burial of a woman named Septumia, and Numerius Erennius Celso erected a column for his wife, Esquilla Polla, near the Porta di Nola.[60] Trajan's Column in its entirety therefore represents the superimposition of two traditional funerary elements, the altar and the column.[61]

The prevalent view on the Column's function is one championed by Zanker in 1970, namely, that Trajan intended his Column to be his final resting place from the outset.[62] According to Greek tradition, as a scholiast on Pindar records, a local hero, especially a founding hero, might be buried within the walls of the city, often in the marketplace;[63] Alexander the Great, for instance, was buried inside Alexandria.[64] The place of burial then became a form of *heroön,* which may explain the isolation of the northern part of Trajan's Forum, with tomb and temple.[65] In Republican times, burial within the *pomerium* was an honor reserved for the *summi viri,* great men whose virtues Trajan was intent upon reviving.[66] Perhaps this explains why he set himself apart from the Flavians and opted to be buried in a style reminiscent of the honors paid to the great soldier leader of the Late Republic, Julius Caesar. Suetonius describes a monument erected in Caesar's

Figure 23. Funerary altar of P. Ciartius Actus, Musei Capitolini. Photo: Archivio Fotografico dei Musei Capitolini, Inv. 2112/S

honor: "[After the funeral the Roman people] raised a solid, nearly twenty-foot-high column of Numidian marble (*solidam columnam prope viginti pedum lapidis Numidici*) in the Forum, and inscribed on it: To the father of his country. For a long time thereafter they continued to make sacrifices there, and to take vows and decide certain disputes by swearing an oath in Caesar's name."[67] What-ever the precedents, the choice of a site within the *pomerium* was an act of enormous presumption, not dissimilar to one that had contributed to Julius Caesar's assassination.[68] Admittedly, Domitian had redefined the boundaries for self-aggrandizement since the relatively austere times of the Republic, and even though Trajan reaffirmed the emperor's status as *princeps* rather than *deus,* he was judged by different rules from those which had governed Caesar.[69] Nevertheless, Zanker argues that Trajan masked his future tomb as a victory monument whose full glory as a sepulcher would be revealed upon his burial there,[70] and sculptural reliefs with distinctly funereal associations located throughout the Forum support his argument. A frieze of winged tauroctonous victories decorating candelabra in the Basilica Ulpia refers both to the emperor's victorious power and to his eventual victory over death in apotheosis.[71] A lion-griffin, putto, and kantharos frieze was sculpted on the temple temenos portico (fig. 24),[72] and a griffin and candelabra frieze decorated the exterior of the portico around the column.[73] As companion of Nemesis, the griffin was symbolic of military might and the

Figure 24. Griffin and putto frieze from Trajan's Forum, Rome, ca. 100–112. Musei Vaticani. Photo: Penelope J. E. Davies

unavoidable necessity for vengeance, *ineffugibilis necessitas ultionis.*[74] Yet a long tradition also associated it with both Apollo and Dionysos, in the role of watchful guardian (over god, ruler, or the dead) and vehicle of apotheosis or Dionysiac regeneration; as such, the griffin was often carved on the side panels of sarcophagi.[75] Putti, moreover, have a well-documented place in funerary iconography.[76] These sculptural themes appear to have been chosen for the Forum according to a program of purposeful ambiguity. In another frieze, representing candelabra and sphinxes and probably to be located inside the colonnades of the column courtyard, the ambiguity vanishes; the sphinx, as Marina Millela puts it, has no other significance than decorative and apotropaic, "the latter connected with its function as guardian of the tomb."[77]

HADRIAN'S MAUSOLEUM

Forced in 130 to confront the loss of his beloved Antinous, Hadrian appears to have anticipated his own demise philosophically. As his popularity waned and his health failed, he attempted suicide in the last year of his life, hoping as his time drew near to find relief in death: "I am being released from my life neither before my time," the dying emperor wrote to his successor, "nor unreasonably, nor piteously, nor unexpectedly, nor with faculties impaired."[78] On his deathbed, so the story goes, he composed a verse for his soul,

Little charmer, wanderer, little sprite
Body's companion and guest
To what places now will you take flight
Forbidding and empty and dim as night?
And you won't make your wonted jest,[79]

in which his apparent levity is tinged with a note of pessimism. He even fashioned his own Underworld on his extensive property at Tivoli, identified with a cavernous grotto and a series of gloomy subterranean corridors.[80] Not merely introspective, Hadrian was also a great lover of the arts: "He was intensely interested in poetry and letters. Highly skilled in arithmetic, geometry, and painting, he made no secret of his knowledge of lyre-playing and singing." Instigator of a comprehensive building program in Rome, he practised architecture in his own right, vying in creativity with the unfortunate Apollodorus.[81] It comes as no surprise that at some point before 123, while building was under way on the Pantheon and his villa at Tivoli, Hadrian began construction of a new mausoleum.[82] When he died of haemorrhaging and dropsy in Baiae on 10 July 138, "hated by all," the tomb was unfinished, and his ashes found private burial in the gardens of Cicero's old villa at Puteoli.[83] In 140, his successor, Antoninus Pius, arranged for their disinterment and burial in the Mausoleum, which he duly completed. In ensuing years, the Antinoeion, as it was known to many, became the last resting place for Antonines and Severans alike (fig. 25).

Figure 25. Mausoleum of Hadrian, Rome, ca. 125–39, actual state. Photo: Penelope J. E. Davies

The Mausoleum has often been the focal point of Rome's tumultuous history, and scholars' difficulties in understanding it stem less from destruction than from medieval and Renaissance accretions. By the sixth century, it had been incorporated into the city's fortifications as a fortress guarding the Pons Aelius, and in 590 a small church of Sant'Angelo di Castro Sant'Angelo was constructed on the summit, which the Crescenzi family replaced with a fortification tower in about the tenth century. In 1277, a covered walkway was built to link the fortress to the Vatican palace, and Hadrian's tomb became a papal stronghold. A long succession of popes built apartments there, decorated with a splendor still visible today.[84]

The Mausoleum stands on the Ager Vaticanus on the Tiber's west bank. To grant access from the Campus Martius, Hadrian built a bridge across the Tiber, the Pons Aelius, and dedicated it in 134 (figs. 109–10).[85] Oriented to the cardinal points, the Mausoleum was set off from surrounding land by a rectangular fence, with a triple-arched entrance between the bridge and the tomb.[86] The tomb consisted of three elements.[87] The first was a square base, measuring 300 Roman feet on a side, composed of a double wall of brick and marble-faced travertine on a low socle. Around its entablature ran a frieze of bucrania, paterae, and garlands of poppies and oak leaves, surmounted by a cornice decorated with palmettes and lion's head protomes. On the south side was an upper register of pilasters and marble revetment simulating rusticated ashlar. Inscriptions affixed to the podium provided epitaphs of those interred within. At the corners were Corinthian pilasters, supporting statue groups of horses and men; these sculptures may have served as weapons against the Goths in 537.[88]

Behind the podium's marble-revetted wall was a brick-faced concrete wall, tied by sixty-eight radial walls to the tomb's second component, a circular concrete drum faced with tufa and travertine. The radial walls defined chambers with interconnecting doors and probably formed a sort of raft to stabilize the tomb on the unfirm, marshy ground. Standing 31 meters high, the drum measured approximately 74 meters in diameter up to the height of the podium (10–12 meters) and 68 meters above. A second drum rose within the first and supported the crowning element, perhaps a tempietto or a portrait of Hadrian in a quadriga (fig. 26).[89]

Tradition ascribes a number of sculptures to the Mausoleum, including a bronze bull on the ramparts, *mugituro et moturo similis, in specie illius quo Iupiter Europam iuxta fabulam decepit,* sometimes associated with the rear half of a bronze bull in the Capitoline Museums.[90] Archaeological finds present problems: numerous sculptural fragments have come to light in the area of the tomb, but probably belong to the imperial gardens surrounding it rather than to the Mausoleum itself. Such is probably the case with the Barberini Faun, found in fortification ditches for Castel Sant'Angelo in 1624–28, as well as a dancing satyr now in the Uffizi, a river personification, and fragments of a discobolos. Maria Antonietta Tomei suggests that the Mausoleum featured a row of colossal statues as part of its crowning element, on the model of Hellenistic tombs such as the

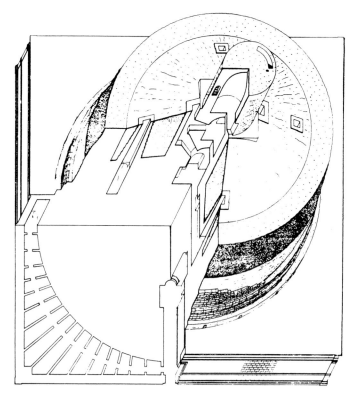

Figure 26. Isonometric reconstruction of the Mausoleum of Hadrian, Rome, ca. 125–39, by M. Eisner. By permission of Michael Eisner

Mausoleum at Halicarnassos. Fragments of suitable sculptures survive, among which are four colossal male heads now displayed in the Ambulatory of Bonifacio IX. Of these, one bears the characteristic features of Antinous, with his hair grasped by a fragmentary hand belonging to a lost figure; another is probably a divinity, judging by the *taenia* in his hair.[91]

A large bronze door in the Mausoleum's south facade opened into a barrel-vaulted vestibule, leading to a square atrium (fig. 27). Both vestibule and atrium were lined with travertine then revetted with colored marble. On the atrium's north side, a large apse framed a colossal statue of Hadrian (fig. 28).[92] A second, smaller rectangular niche on the west side is balanced on the east by the entrance to an annular corridor, rising in an anticlockwise direction and turning a full 360 degrees to culminate above the vestibule.[93] There a second, radial corridor led to the main burial chamber, corresponding in level to the change in diameter in the first cylindrical drum. The chamber is a vaulted square cella, with large niches on the north, east, and west sides that probably held cinerary urns for Hadrian, Sabina, and Lucius Aelius (fig. 29); a vast porphyry sarcophagus is rumored to have been found on the ramp and may belong in this room.[94] The ramp's spiraling movement (fig. 30) continued through a series of wedge-shaped

Figure 27. Entrance vestibule of the Mausoleum of Hadrian, Rome, ca. 125–39. Photo: Penelope J. E. Davies

Figure 28. Portrait of Hadrian from the Mausoleum, ca. 125–39, Musei Vaticani. Photo: Penelope J. E. Davies

Figure 29. Niche in the burial chamber of the Mausoleum of Hadrian, Rome, ca. 125–39. Photo: Penelope J. E. Davies

chambers radiating out from the cella; the interior face of the drum was therefore polygonal at this level, a device perhaps designed to reduce weight. A staircase curled around the cella, leading to two or three additional rooms of uncertain purpose above the main chamber, and on to the tomb's summit.[95] Thus, as Angeletti puts it,

> If at the first level we have a peripheral circular corridor, echoing the exterior, joined to the burial chamber by an orthogonal axis, on the second level the central chamber is the newel of a series of rooms which, in star-like fashion, unite the center and the periphery volumetrically, at the same time fulfilling the necessary function of passageway to the upper level, which in plan repeats the first.[96]

Finds suggest that sculptures embellished the interior of the Mausoleum as well as the exterior. Surviving pieces include two female statues draped in peploi,

Figure 30. Staircase in the Mausoleum of Hadrian leading to the upper room, Rome, ca. 125–39. Photo: Penelope J. E. Davies

perhaps positioned as guardians of the cella, and portraits representing Hadrian, Antoninus Pius, and possibly Julius Caesar.

THE COLUMN OF ANTONINUS PIUS

In March of 161, twenty years after losing his wife Faustina, Antoninus Pius fell ill at his villa in Lorium "after eating Alpine cheese at dinner rather greedily."[97] Commending the Republic to his adoptive son, Marcus Aurelius, and uttering the final word "Equanimity," he died in his sleep. His body was cremated and his ashes delivered to Hadrian's Mausoleum.[98] Marcus Aurelius promptly coopted his adoptive brother, Lucius Verus, as joint emperor, and together they erected a column on the Campus Martius, their first recorded artistic venture, to celebrate their father's memory.

Only the column's base survives. Bronze coins minted by the new co-emperors at the time of its construction show that it was surrounded by an openwork balustrade and topped by a Corinthian capital supporting a male statue, presumably Antoninus Pius, holding a spear and an orb (fig. 31).[99] The shaft, a 50-foot red granite monolith, was not sculpted but polished smooth, and stood in situ, protruding six meters from the Mons Citatorius, until 1703, when Francesco Fontana directed the excavation of shaft and pedestal, and their subsequent removal to Piazza di Montecitorio.[100] Despite numerous projects to reerect the shaft, it was finally dragged behind the Curia Innocenziana where, in 1759, it sustained heavy damages in a fire; in 1789–90, Giovanni Antinori used surviving fragments to restore the obelisk of Augustus's sundial.[101] A small piece of the shaft, however, preserves an antique mason's inscription in Greek, indicating that it was not quarried for the special purpose of commemorating Antoninus Pius but during Trajan's reign in 105–6 as one of a pair of 50-foot columns;[102] this may indicate haste in erecting the monument.

After its excavation, Vincenzo Felici and Francesco Giuseppe Napoleoni restored the Column's monolithic white marble pedestal. It was then transferred to the Vatican's Giardino della Pigna in 1789, and a second restoration, by Giuseppe de Fabris, was concluded in 1846. In 1855 it was moved to the Cortile della Pigna; it is presently located in the Belvedere Courtyard.[103]

On the north face of the Column base an inscription in bronze letters names Antoninus Pius as the honoree, and Marcus Aurelius and Lucius Verus as dedicants:

DIVO ANTONINO AUG. PIO
ANTONINUS AUGUSTUS ET
VERUS AUGUSTUS FILII

[Antoninus Augustus and Verus Augustus, his sons, to the Divine Antoninus Pius Augustus] (fig. 32).[104]

A relief panel on the south side shows bustlike figures of Antoninus Pius and Faustina ascending heavenward on the back of a winged male figure (fig. 33). On either side of the imperial couple, in the upper corners, are two eagles, flying from left to right. Two personifications fill the lower half of the relief: on the left, the seminude figure of Campus Martius, reclining against a pile of rocks and

Figure 31. Bronze coin showing the Column of Antoninus Pius, ca. 161. Photo: Courtesy of the American Numismatic Society, New York

Figure 32. Column of Antoninus Pius, inscription, Rome, 161. Photo: Penelope J. E. Davies

supporting an obelisk with his left hand; on the right, the goddess Roma in Amazon attire, a pile of weapons at her feet. On east and west sides of the pedestal are two near-identical reliefs, showing seventeen mounted Roman soldiers encircling a group of ten infantrymen carrying Roman standards (figs. 34, 89). In 1703, Bianchini suggested that the reliefs represent a *decursio,* the army's ritual encirclement of an emperor's pyre, and despite the absence of a pyre, this identification is widely accepted.[105]

THE COLUMN OF MARCUS AURELIUS

In 169, on his return to Rome from the German war, Lucius Verus died of apoplexy, leaving Marcus Aurelius in sole command of the empire. His body was

Figure 33. (*facing page top*) Column of Antoninus Pius, apotheosis relief, Rome, 161. Photo: Penelope J. E. Davies

Figure 34. (*facing page bottom*) Column of Antoninus Pius, decursio relief, Rome, 161. Photo: Penelope J. E. Davies

Figure 35. Column of Marcus Aurelius, actual state, Rome, ca. 180–93. Photo: Alinari/Art Resource, New York, AL6697

laid to rest in Hadrian's Mausoleum.[106] In 180, Marcus Aurelius, the philosopher-emperor, in his turn became ill at his military camp near Vienna, and seven days later he died. The cause of his illness is unknown: perhaps he fell victim to the plague, brought by the army from Mesopotamia; perhaps he developed cancer. There was even a rumor that his doctors precipitated his demise in their anxiety to curry favor with Commodus, his son and heir. His ashes were conveyed to Hadrian's Mausoleum, and "temples, columns, and priests" celebrated his memory.[107] Among these honors was the Column of Marcus Aurelius, in today's Piazza Colonna, one of Commodus's few building projects (fig. 35).

The Column's base as it now appears belies its original appearance, for as part of an extensive "restoration" project in 1589, at Sixtus V's initiative, Domenico Fontana entirely rebuilt it with marble from the recently dismantled Septizodium. Excavations reveal that the ancient pedestal was approximately twice the height of the base of Trajan's Column and differed from its modern replacement in ground level, proportions, decoration, and even orientation (the door, now on the south side, originally faced east).[108] Since no numismatic images of the column exist, scholars base their reconstructions of the pedestal on sketches executed shortly before the restoration, especially those made by Enea Vico in 1540 and Francisco d'Hollanda in 1539–40 and reflected in G. B. Piranesi's fantasy reconstruction (fig. 36). They show a heavily damaged socle,

Figure 36. Drawing of the Column of Marcus Aurelius by G. B. Piranesi. Photo: Deutsches Archäologisches Institut, Rom-InstNegNr 37.1356

45

buried up to circa 3 meters, and four to five layers of masonry above ground level. Rectangular dowel holes indicate that all layers were revetted, although sculpture survives only on the fourth: on the east was a horizontal rectangular relief representing a barbarian submission, and on the north (and presumably also on the south and west) were four winged victories with wreaths and garlands.[109] No inscription survives. In a new reconstruction based on Trajan's Column and Arcadius's Column in Constantinople as well as the above-mentioned sketches, Martina Jordan-Ruwe proposes a single, tall base element rising from a molding and crowned by a cornice (fig. 37). Marble eagles grace the corners of the plinth above cornice level, and hanging garlands ornament the sides. She restores a weapon frieze below the figural relief on the fourth layer, and above it, on the east side, winged victories supporting an inscription.[110]

The Column shaft rests upon an oak-leaf torus and is formed of twenty-six drums of Luna marble.[111] Concealed inside it is a two hundred-step spiral staircase, lit by fifty-six small rectangular windows, leading to a platform on the Doric capital (fig. 114). On the summit stood a bronze statue of Marcus Aurelius, destroyed by barbarian raiders and replaced in the sixteenth century with a statue of Saint Paul, to whom the column was rededicated.[112] A continuous narrative frieze adorns the shaft in twenty-one turns, describing Marcus Aurelius's repeated campaigns against German and Sarmatian tribes in the Danube area.[113]

Determining the date of the Column's construction is difficult but vital, for an early date in Marcus Aurelius's reign would imply that it was commissioned not by Commodus but by Marcus Aurelius himself; this in turn might suggest that it was not intended as a commemorative monument. The only secure information comes from an inscription recording the construction of a house for

Figure 37. Reconstruction of the base of the Column of Marcus Aurelius by M. Jordan-Ruwe. By permission of Martina Jordan-Ruwe

the Column's custodian, Adrastus, in 193, providing a terminus ante quem for its completion.[114] Any further data must be gleaned from the frieze.

The dating of events narrated by the frieze depends upon three crucial scenes: the crossing of the Danube (Scene III), the "Rain Miracle" (Scene XVI) (fig. 38), and the personification of Victory (Scene LV). Interpretations of these episodes have led to widely differing chronologies for the events depicted on the frieze as a whole and differing dates for the Column's construction. The frieze probably opens after the inception of war in 171, either in 172–73 (when coin issues may depict the bridge over the Danube, and when Marcus Aurelius's offensive in enemy territory began, as opposed to his regaining of Roman land), or even as late as 174, shortly before the rain miracle.[115] Scholars concur that the rain miracle scene represents an episode known from literary sources, which together with numismatic evidence suggests that the event took place in 174.[116] The Victory marks a division of the war between 175 and 177, recorded in literary, epigraphic, and numismatic sources (not between two distinct campaigns, against Germans in 171–73, and Sarmatians in 174–75, as von Domaszewski contends).[117] The second half of the frieze depicts events from continued campaigns, extending to at least 179.[118]

The most convincing reading of the datable scenes on the Column strongly suggests that it was erected after Marcus Aurelius's death in 180 as a commemora-

Figure 38. Column of Marcus Aurelius, "Rain Miracle" scene, Rome, ca. 180–93. Photo: Alinari/Art Resource, New York, AN1904

tive monument, presumably by the Senate and People of Rome with Commodus's encouragement; it was not, as von Domaszewski would have it, a triumphal monument to the early campaigns, which the Senate appears to have celebrated in 176 with an arch over the Clivus Argentarius.[119] The obvious precedents, Trajan's and Antoninus Pius's Columns, argue for a funerary function, as does the Column's location on the Campus Martius, between the Temple of Hadrian and Antoninus Pius's Column.[120]

AN IMAGE OF THINGS
ACHIEVED

Tʜᴇ ᴋɪɴɢ's (ᴏʀ ǫᴜᴇᴇɴ's) mortality presents a precarious challenge to
a monarchy. At the monarch's death, such stability as he or she offered
crumbles; power is momentarily unthroned and waits uncomfortably in
the wings; an heir warily steps in to assume it. For that heir, there is no guarantee of a swift or trouble-free succession; for the society he governs, no certainty
of renewed stability. In this chapter, I propose that the funerary monuments of
the Roman emperors arose in response to this challenge. Although purportedly
memorials to the dead, they spoke to the living about the living; and just as they
commemorated one emperor's death, so they promoted another emperor's rise. I
suggest that, starting with Augustus, the emperors often designed tombs with a
marked dual valency that highlighted critical aspects of the emperor's life, most
notably the triumph upon which his authority was at least partially predicated. I
explore the purpose behind this practice and suggest that one of the functions of
an imperial tomb was to justify the deceased emperor's apotheosis so as to promote dynastic succession.

AUGUSTUS'S MAUSOLEUM: SETTING A STANDARD

A set of recurrent questions confronts the scholar who endeavors to understand
the Mausoleum of Augustus. How, for instance, did Augustus justify building his
tomb on public land? Why did he build it so early in his life, as one of his first
major commissions after Actium? And what exactly is its place in architectural
history? These questions are crucial, for in many ways Augustus's Mausoleum set
the standard for imperial tombs to come. In the following pages, I propose that a
solution to these questions and a richer reading of the tomb as a dynastic statement reside in a deliberate multivalency in its design.

A Time and a Place

Augustus chose the northern Campus Martius as the site for his Mausoleum.
Tradition held this to be one of the oldest, most sacred regions of the city.

Apparently no law prohibited private buildings there, for they existed from a Republican date; numerous buildings stood in the area of the Saepta, for instance, and Pompey owned a house and gardens close to his theater. As a site for a private tomb, however, it posed a distinct problem: although it was outside the *pomerium,* as the laws of the Twelve Tables dictated for a burial site, it was a public, honorary place, and burial there was a privilege reserved for Rome's favorites, chosen posthumously by senatorial decree.[1] When Augustus elected to build a huge mausoleum within his lifetime on the sacred Field of Mars, fewer than two decades had elapsed since Julius Caesar's assassination, prompted by his kingly aspirations and partially, if Cassius Dio is to be believed, by the Senate's second thoughts concerning its own conferral on him of the right to burial within the city.[2] How could Augustus claim a similar honor with impunity? In solution to this question some scholars have concluded, in the face of Strabo's eyewitness testimony to the contrary, that the Mausoleum was not on the Campus Martius at all, but just over its northern boundary in part of a cemetery located there.[3]

The early date of the Mausoleum's construction presents a second complication. Most scholars concur that building began no later than 28 B.C., the date to which Suetonius assigns it. It may have been complete by the time of Marcellus's death in 23, when Virgil termed it the recent tumulus, *tumulus recens.*[4] This being so, the tomb must have been one of the first, if not *the* first building of Augustus's new regime, begun immediately upon his delayed return to Rome after Actium. It was also in all likelihood the largest building he executed throughout his reign.[5] Both of these facts, coupled with Augustus's use of Carrara marble, a relatively new and ostentatiously luxurious building material, must have made the monument an impressive sight as it rose in the urban landscape. What was the message he wanted it to broadcast?

To account for its early date, some scholars have concluded that, alarmed at his own ill health, Augustus feared that he was not destined for longevity, an unlikely explanation, as advertisement of his illness (which was not severe in the early twenties) would have cost him valuable support at a critical time.[6] Other explanations have been to regard his speedy construction of a mausoleum as a simple reflection of his anxiety to establish a dynasty, or as the most eloquent manifestation of an early absolutist "Romulan epoch."[7] Konrad Kraft would set the date of the tomb's conception to 32, a year before the victory at Actium, in response to an episode known from Plutarch and Suetonius, in which Augustus daringly, and quite illegally, procured Mark Antony's will from the Vestal Virgins and publicized its contents to a scandalized Senate. Among its stipulations were Mark Antony's recognition of Cleopatra's eldest son, Caesarion, as Caesar's true heir (an open challenge to Augustus) and his bestowal of substantial inheritances upon Cleopatra's children. These provisions were not popular but were already public knowledge. News to Rome, however, was Mark Antony's expressed desire to be buried in Alexandria even if he should die in Rome, a clause that, according to Plutarch, Augustus emphasized "most strongly."[8] Incensed by this revelation, Romans took it to be a breach of loyalty, a desire to shift the center of power from Italy to the land of his Egyptian queen.[9] The projected shift in turn marked his subservience to Cleopatra. Her foreignness, her gender, and Mark Antony's infatuation with her became literary tropes in the early Augustan Age, and Augustus had every reason to encourage their repetition: his former colleague's collusion with a foreign woman made Augustus the victor in a foreign war, while a war against Mark Antony alone, a fellow Roman, bore the undesirable mark of a civil war. By building a prominent tomb in Rome, Kraft concludes, Augustus furnished a perfect antithesis to Antony's plans and publicly declared his own commitment to the city.[10] Kraft's analysis has received relatively widespread support, but does it go far enough? We shall return to this question later in the chapter.

Echoes of Egypt

A third and major problem resides in the Mausoleum's design. Inspiration for its appearance seems to have come from a number of sources. For its essential form Augustus may have looked to Etruria, where necropoleis such as the Banditaccia Cemetery at Caere hosted crowds of grass-covered earthen tumuli (fig. 39), whose archaic simplicity and monumentality may have signaled the *mos maiorum*

Figure 39. Tumulus in the Banditaccia cemetery, Cerveteri (Caere). Photo: Alinari/Art Resource, New York, AL35852

of the Republic that Augustus claimed to restore.[11] Perhaps he also thought of Troy, lost homeland of Rome's ancestors, where huge mounds covering prehistoric villages appeared to Roman eyes to be royal graves of magnificent proportions. As Virgil penned the glorious epic of Aeneas's flight from his burning home, Romans of the Augustan Age deliberately glorified Troy as their true motherland.[12] However, the masonry articulation dividing the slopes, as well as the prominent base wall, gave the Mausoleum a more architectonic presence than these alone, which may have found its inspiration in the Republican tombs of modest size lining the roads into Rome (figs. 1, 40).[13] Its architectural quality, as well as its sheer size, recalled dynastic tombs of Asia Minor, such as the Mausoleum at Halicarnassos (fig. 41), a vast sepulcher built in circa 350 for Mausollus, satrap of Caria, to a design by architects Satyros and Pytheos. Rectangular in plan, the tomb featured a colonnade on a high base; above, a stepped pyramid supported a four-horse chariot. Freestanding and relief sculptures ornamented every stage of the building, by the hands of great sculptors of the day, Scopas, Bryaxis, Timotheos, and Leochares.[14] A perceived similarity between this wonder of the ancient world and the Mausoleum of Augustus presumably led to the naming of the latter, although the perception may have been belated, for the term was not applied to it until after A.D. 4 and Gaius's death in south Lycia. In the following pages, I shall focus upon a further proposal: that Augustus was deeply influenced by the Mausoleum of Alexander (the Sema or Soma). I shall

Figure 40. Tomb of Caecilia Metella, Via Appia, Rome, first century B.C. Photo: Penelope J. E. Davies

Metres 5   0   10   Feet 15   0   30

Figure 41. Reconstruction of the Mausoleum of Halicarnassos, ca. 350 B.C. From Howard Colvin, *Architecture and the Afterlife* (New Haven-London, 1991), fig. 31. Copyright Yale University Press

attempt to bolster the existing argument in favor of Egyptian prototypes by tracing models for two aspects of the Mausoleum's internal structure: its concrete core and its ground plan. These hypotheses are by no means intended to supplant other proposals; on the contrary, I hope to show that, for all the attempts to isolate a single model for the Mausoleum, the tomb is an extraordinarily complex building, drawing on numerous sources of inspiration.

Figure 42. Medracen, Algeria, end of the third century B.C. or first half of the second, actual state. Photo: Deutsches Archäologisches Institut, Rom-InstNegNr 1971.2353

Scholars have long conjectured that Augustus's Mausoleum finds its prototype in the Mausoleum of Alexander in Alexandria, built in 215–14 by Ptolemy IV Philopator, where by Cassius Dio's account Augustus paid homage to the king: "He viewed Alexander's body, and even touched it, with the result that the nose shattered, so they say. But he declined an invitation to look at the Ptolemies' bodies, although the Alexandrians were very eager to show them to him; he said, 'I longed to see a king, but not corpses.' "[15] The dramatic obstacle to this thesis is the dearth of evidence for the tomb's appearance. Strabo records that it stood within the royal palaces; Lucan adds that there was a consecrated vault (*sacrato antro*) to which the visitor descended, capped by an earthen tumulus, *effossum tumulis cupide descendit in antrum.* Around it were tombs for members of Ptolemy's line.[16]

Filippo Coarelli and Yvon Thébert contend that the Sema belonged to a geographically widespread Mediterranean *koine* of monumental and finely crafted dynastic tombs that stood distinctly apart from humbler burial markers in their own locales. Cyrus's tomb at Pasargadae is an early example (sixth century), followed by well-known sepulchers such as the Nereid Monument at Xanthos (ca. 390) and the Mausoleum at Halicarnassos.[17] They focus on two members of the *koine* in modern Algeria as reflections of Alexander's tomb: Medracen (end

Figure 43. "Tomb of the Christian," Kbour-er-Roumia, Algeria, end of the second century or first half of the first, actual state. Photo: Deutsches Archäologisches Institut, Rom-InstNegNr 1971.2181

of the third century B.C. or first half of the second) and the "Tomb of the Christian," Kbour-er-Roumia (end of the second century or first half of the first) (figs. 42, 43). Both consist of a cylindrical drum ornamented with sixty engaged columns and false doors. Above the cylinder is a stepped cone reminiscent of man-made burial tumuli in Alexander's native Macedonia, crowned by a platform with a pyramid or a sculptural group.[18] Telltale Egyptian characteristics (such as Medracen's Egyptian molding surmounting the Doric order and Eypgtian architraves framing its false doors) led Coarelli and Thébert to suppose that the architects of these tombs found their model in the Sema; closer than the regal examples of Asia Minor, it was also a relatively recent building whose fame must have rapidly traveled the trade routes of the north African shore. The Sema's role as prototype for both the Algerian tombs and the Mausoleum of Augustus would explain similarities in general appearance among these tombs.

Whatever the Sema's role, the construction technique of the Mausoleum of Augustus supports an argument for an Egyptian influence. One of the architect's primary ambitions was to achieve height for visibility, and standing some 150 feet tall it was probably the tallest building in Augustan Rome.[19] The tomb also had to support the weight of a bronze statue of the emperor at its towering height. To achieve load-bearing height on the marshy Campus Martius, the tomb's internal structure had to be both solid and light, and since no Roman before Augustus had raised a tumulus of such momentous proportions, there were no local prototypes to follow. Smaller tumuli (ca. 34 meters at the largest, as opposed to 100) were solid concrete throughout (faced with stone) or packed with earth inside a hollow drum, as seen in the "Tomb of the Horatii" at the Via Appia's sixth milestone. In other cases a series of walls contained the earth filling, diminishing in height as they radiated like cartwheel spokes from the center to the drum wall (as in the tomb at Via Lucio Fabio Cilone 19 [fig. 44]).[20] Construction on the Mausoleum, in contrast, centered around the massive travertine pillar; as it rose, the architect encircled it with concrete rings of ever-diminishing size as buttresses.[21] A new technique in Italy, this was not one suggested by tomb construction in Greece or Asia Minor, or, as Jane Reeder suggests, by the Samothracian Arsinoeion, where the primary concern was to create a large, usable internal space, not to support heavy crowning statuary.[22] However, it *is* a well-attested technique in Egypt.

As far as it is understood, the early method of pyramid construction, developed in the second to third dynasties and exemplified by the Pyramids of Djeser at Saqqara, Sneferu at Meydûm, and Cheops at Gizeh, involved a "layering" technique, in which a central core was encased with inclined accretion layers, diminishing in height from the inside out to resemble steps (fig. 45).[23] In modified form, the same technique was used for the renowned lighthouse or Pharos at Alexandria on the northwest coast of the Egyptian delta, begun in the reign of Ptolemy I Soter (305–282 B.C.) and sometimes attributed to one Sostratus as architect (fig. 46). To judge by its appearance in mosaics and medieval descriptions, this building was composed of a square, slightly tapering base, an octagonal central drum, and a crowning *tholos*-like element. The outer layers (square and

Figure 44. Plan of the round tomb at Via Lucio Fabio Cilone 19, Rome, first century B.C., by M. Eisner. By permission of Michael Eisner

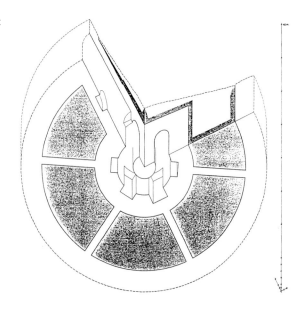

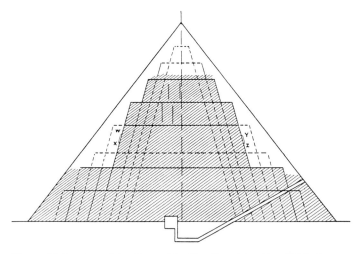

Figure 45. Section of the Pyramid of Sneferu, Meydûm, IVth dynasty. After W. M. F. Petrie, *Medum* (London, 1892), pl. II

octagon) buttressed the hollow central tower, which housed the lighthouse's machinery. Through this vertical layering technique, the lighthouse supported a huge bronze statue at the towering height of approximately 117 meters.[24] The similarity extends to the Mausoleum of Hadrian, approached by a bridge reminiscent of the famous Heptastadion leading across the water to the Alexandrian

Figure 46. Sections of the Pharos at Alexandria and the Mausoleum of Augustus. Drawing: Penelope J. E. Davies

lighthouse; its superimposed elements correspond more closely in shape (square, cylinder-octagon, cylinder), and a spiraling ramp leads up through the interior, transformed into a staircase at higher levels.[25]

These similarities in construction technique suggest that Augustus's architect turned to Egypt for a solution to structural requirements that he recognized to be close to those of the Pharos or other Egyptian buildings; he then adapted the technique to complement Roman construction materials (cement for all but the central pillar, for ease of construction, economy, and lightness), to combine with known Roman building procedures (radial walls and recumbent arches between the outer three walls), and to suit the chosen location.[26]

I propose that this borrowing played itself out in the appearance of the tomb as well. As a result of this building technique, the Mausoleum had ring walls, between which the architect incorporated annular corridors, just as the Egyptian architect did (fig. 5). In other Roman circular tombs with annular corridors, a visitor reached the central burial chamber by a linear corridor from the entrance (for instance, the tomb on Via Lucio Fabio Cilone [fig. 44]).[27] In some cases (such as the tomb of L. Munatius Plancus at Gaeta [fig. 47]), a straight corridor leads to the chamber, and a second, annular corridor surrounds the cella.[28] In the later Mausoleum of Hadrian, as in the Tomb of the Christian, a circular corridor actually hinders the visitor's progress to the chamber by forcing him to circumambulate it before entering; there is no rectilinear path from exterior

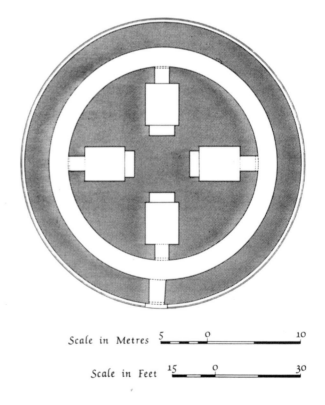

Figure 47. Plan of the Tomb of Lucius Munatius Plancus, Gaëta, first century B.C., by Prof. Dr. Rudolf Fellmann. From *Das Grabmal des Lucius Munatius Plancus bei Gaëta* (Basel, 1957). By permission of Prof. Dr. Rudolf Fellmann

Scale in Metres 5 0 10

Scale in Feet 15 0 30

to interior (figs. 48, 67). Augustus's Mausoleum is more closely related to these tombs than to the smaller Roman examples, yet it does not conform to either type (fig. 5): its entrance corridor ends in a T-junction, forcing a visitor to left or right into an annular corridor, from which she could enter a second annular corridor through one of two openings, offset from the entrance corridor. From the second corridor, a doorway on the south led to the burial chamber.[29] The deliberately indirect access to the burial chamber does not compel a visitor to encircle it (although it does accommodate circumambulation); rather than coercing a visitor in any one direction, it offers a choice of path so that she is uncertain which way to progress. As Reeder also noted, the interior of the Mausoleum resembles nothing so much as a stylized labyrinth.[30]

Just as the tomb's construction technique belonged in Egypt, so too did the earliest and most renowned labyrinths, such as that near the Lake of Moeris on the west side of the Nile, known from Herodotus and Strabo but as yet unidentified; from these, later labyrinths such as Daedalus's mythical maze took their essential characteristics.[31] Ancient descriptions are often incomprehensible, yet they attest unanimously to the Eypgtian labyrinth's magnificence and to an intense awe that it inspired in visitors: "Greater than words could express, for,

Figure 48. Plan of the "Tomb of the Christian," Kbour-er-Roumia, Algeria, end of the second century or first half of the first, by Gsell. From M. Christofle, *Le tombeau de la Chrétienne* (Paris, 1951)

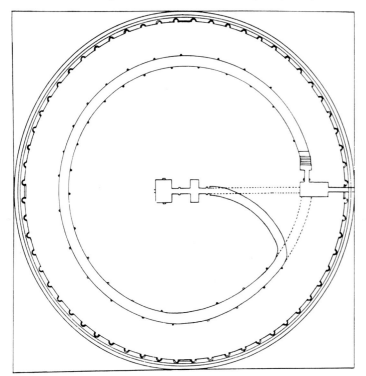

if one were to collect together all the buildings of the Greeks and all their works on display, they would be seen to be inferior to labyrinths in terms of both labour and expense, even though the temples at Ephesus and Samos are noteworthy buildings."[32] Indeed, for Pliny labyrinths as an architectural genre were "the most extraordinary works of human expenditure."[33]

Both of these characteristics, building technique and labyrinthine plan, can be explained if Augustus was consciously quoting from the Pharos and the famous Egyptian labyrinths. The scenario may, however, be simpler; for both features may also have been present in Alexander's Sema: the building technique as a standard form of Egyptian construction, and the labyrinth following a long-standing Egyptian tradition for protecting a dead king.[34] Ancient sources insist that Augustus visited Alexander's tomb, and, interestingly, Suetonius states that he had the sarcophagus containing Alexander's body removed from its shrine (*prolatum e penetrali*) in order to view it.[35] Perhaps he was spared the passage to the inner shrine because it was treacherous and confusing; in other words, perhaps the path to Alexander's burial chamber took the form of a labyrinth. A specific reference to Alexander's Sema would be in keeping with Augustus's evident admiration for the Macedonian king, for his act of homage there was not an isolated incident: as scholars have long noted, like other Late Republican generals, Augustus liked to conceive of himself as a second Alexander, and such was his feeling of special accord with him that while still in Egypt after the Actian war he granted a pardon to all Egyptians, especially Alexandrians, and claimed the province of Egypt as his private domain. Coarelli and Thébert note that circumstances conspired to present Augustus as Alexander's literal successor when he appeared in Egypt at about the age at which Alexander had died, and on his return to Rome, "the first seal Augustus used for safe-conducts, dispatches, and private letters was a sphinx; next came a head of Alexander the Great; lastly his own head, cut by Dioscurides, the seal which his successors continued to employ."[36] This *imitatio Alexandri* found a suitable context in Rome after the Mausoleum's construction (or contemporaneous with it), when Egyptianizing motifs were introduced into art and architecture in a steady stream, best exemplified by the pyramid tomb of Gaius Cestius (fig. 49) and the similar Meta Romuli on the Vatican plain.[37] Augustus promoted the fashion himself, in, for instance, the Egyptianizing themes that decorated his Palatine home, and in the Egyptianizing buildings he constructed with Agrippa's help south of the Mausoleum on the Campus Martius, such as the Iseum and the Canopus.[38] A coffer on one of these buildings was even decorated with a *corona atef,* a pharaonic ruler-cult emblem.[39] Egyptian elements feature blatantly in the Mausoleum's decoration. The obelisks flanking the entrance, fashioned of exotic red granite quarried in Syene (Assuan) in Egypt, may have reminded Romans of pharaonic mortuary practice; the Sundial, which with its Greek lettering and Egyptian seasonal changes probably followed an Alexandrian model,[40] and sculptural details on the Ara Pacis (the meander pattern and a lotus frieze) reinforced the Egyptianizing mood in the complex as a whole (fig. 8).

Figure 49. Pyramid tomb of Gaius Cestius, Rome, ca. 15 B.C. Photo: Michael Larvey

MAUSOLEUM-TROPAEUM

Archaeological and literary evidence supports a hypothesis that Augustus looked to Egypt among other places for models for his Mausoleum. However, the imprecise nature of the evidence makes it difficult to determine exactly which models inspired him: Pharos and pyramids; Pharos, pyramids, and Sema; or just the Sema, which incorporated elements found in the Pharos and pyramids. Together, the archaeological evidence for Egyptianizing motifs on the Campus

Martius and the literary evidence for Augustus's *imitatio Alexandri* strongly suggest that the Sema loomed large in Augustus's mind, and that the influence of construction betrays a similarity in appearance as well. Is there any reason, besides his admiration for Alexander, that he turned to Egypt for inspiration?

Perhaps the powerful and well-documented funereal associations of these Egyptian buildings made them logical selections for a prototype. Lighthouses were a metaphor for death as a final haven from life's adversities,[41] while labyrinths originated in royal tombs and mortuary temples, defending deceased rulers from robbers and the powers of hostile spirits.[42] Yet a propagandistic motive may have dominated Augustus's reasoning. As Strabo and Pliny bear witness, Romans visualized Egypt through its famous buildings; any one of them, alone, could represent the land of the Nile. The Sema and the Pharos were the great showpieces of Alexandria with which a Roman visitor's tour of Egypt invariably began.[43] As burial place of Alexandria's founder, the Sema was in essence the city's foundation stone, *heroön* for its eponymous hero; the towering Pharos, for its part, was Alexandria's most visible building, the first sign of civilization on shore for an approaching seafarer; and on lamps, coins, and mosaics it became an easily recognized locating device.[44] Thus both structures were symbolic of the land that Augustus was anxious to cast as the defeated enemy of Actium in lieu of Mark Antony, if not the very city where the Actian victory was sealed through his ignoble death.

A richer reading of the Mausoleum emerges, along with solutions to the problems of its location, date, and place in architectural history, if we consider it as a monument with a dual role. In all likelihood, upon his return to Rome after the battle of Actium at the age of about thirty-five, Augustus was more preoccupied with his recent triumph than with his mortality. Like other generals before him, he was probably eager to erect a monument to celebrate his military prowess, in part to dispel the unglamorous truth about the battle and recast it in the mold of the Antigonids' renowned naval victories at Cos and Salamis.[45] Since the victory was to double as cause and justification of his family's subsequent prominence, he also determined, in Republican tradition, to fashion a magnificent tomb to mark his name. These two monuments, trophy and tomb, were one and the same building.[46] In its appearance, whether resembling Sema or Pharos, it reflected the character of the enemy, a foreign enemy, whose defeat it commemorated. If a Roman recognized the lighthouse in its design, then the trophy not only described the nationality of the enemy but also the nature of the battle: that is, the lighthouse signified a naval battle, just as the trophy erected at the new city of Nikopolis, near the location of the battle, incorporated ships' prows captured from the enemy.[47]

In using Egyptian models for the design of his mausoleum-trophy, Augustus followed a well-established tradition of denoting the victory won in the trophy's form, which can be seen in numerous examples including the group of battling horsemen of Lysippos's Granikos Monument at Dion, Macedonia (ca. 330 B.C.) memorializing the heroic dead of Alexander's Persian campaign (fig. 50).[48] By bringing Egyptian forms to Rome, Augustus was following a second tradition,

Figure 50. Bronze equestrian statuette of Alexander the Great, Naples Archaeological Museum, first century B.C. or A.C., based on an original of ca. 330 B.C. Photo: Alinari/Art Resource, New York, AL11192

too, that of "capturing" a work of art as spoils or emblems of triumph. This tradition cast the expropriator as cultural heir – and superior – to the vanquished, as well as military victor. Examples might include, again, the Granikos Monument, which Metellus brought to Rome in 148 B.C., or the Aemilius Paullus Monument, which Perseus originally installed at Delphi as a statue base for himself and which Aemilius Paullus expropriated for his own image after his Macedonian conquest, stating that "it was only proper that the conquered should give way to the victors."[49] If the captured work of art was a victory monument, it presumably also signified the expropriation of triumphant forces. The Egyptian forms of Augustus's Mausoleum complex, then, were part of his declaration of victory, as he "captured" the Egyptian architectural heritage and even expropriated Egyptian triumphal symbols in his display of obelisks, traditionally produced by Egyptian kings "when they had subdued nations in war or prided themselves on the prosperity of their kingdoms."[50] The tomb, then, was more than just a demonstration of wealth and power: as a monumental trophy characterizing the battle that had brought him fame, it was designed as a visual *res gestae,* an image of things achieved, defined by symbols of Egypt, perhaps specifically of Alexandria; complete with "spoils" as proof of its authenticity, it complemented the more extensive written *res gestae* mounted on pillars by its doors.[51]

Kraft's argument linking the Mausoleum to Mark Antony's will, when applied to a mausoleum conceived not in 32 but after Antony's death, shows how powerful an affiliation between tomb and triumph would be, promoting Augustus's commitment to Rome in opposition to the late Mark Antony's disloyalty. Moreover, for those who knew the details of the capture of Alexandria, a trophy in the form of a tomb also bore a delicious irony, for, as Cassius Dio relates, it was inside the walls of Cleopatra's unfinished tomb that Mark Antony met his death. While he was preparing to set sail after a last battle against Augustus at Alexandria, Cleopatra fled to a mausoleum that was under construction for her near a temple of Isis by the sea, and from there she sent him word that she was dead. Succumbing to her deceit, he tried to end his life by the sword. When he discovered that she was alive and secured within her tomb: "He struggled to his feet as though still strong enough to survive. But since he had lost much blood, he knew that his end was near, and entreated bystanders to carry him to the monument and pull him up by the ropes which had been left hanging there to raise the stone blocks. Thus Antony died there in Cleopatra's bosom."[52] When Cleopatra had taken her life too, Augustus arranged that they should be "embalmed in the same way and buried in the same tomb," as if purposely to emphasize Mark Antony's foreign loyalty and ignominious end.[53]

A hypothesis of a dual role as tomb and trophy harmonizes well with the Mausoleum's place in subsequent architectural history. If its prototypes are difficult to pinpoint, its successors, in contrast, are not. Yet with the exception of the Mausoleum of Hadrian, which was clearly inspired by Augustus's tomb, they are found less consistently in funerary architecture than in the architecture of triumph. The closest parallels are two huge victory monuments at La Turbie near Monte Carlo and Adamklissi in Rumania. The trophy at La Turbie celebrated the subjugation of Alpine tribes in 7–6 B.C. (fig. 51). Its cylindrical drum and Tuscan colonnade supported a cone-like element, probably crowned by a statue of the *Genius Augusti in formam deorum.*[54] Adamklissi, dedicated by Trajan to Mars the Avenger in 107/8 after his Dacian campaigns, consisted of a stepped platform, a crenelated drum with a Doric entablature, a truncated cone, and a pedestal for a trophy (fig. 52).[55] Similarities between these monuments and the Mausoleum are remarkable: at La Turbie they exist even in minor details such as letter fragments from the inscription and the dependence of both monuments on a module of twelve, while formal similarities with Adamklissi are pronounced enough to make an independent development unlikely.[56] The sudden appearance of these monumental trophies is something of an embarrassment to those who would trace the history of Roman trophy development, for tumulus trophies did not appear until Drusus and Tiberius built one on the banks of the Elbe to mark their victories over the Cherusci and the Marcomanni after the Mausoleum's construction in 9 B.C.[57] Instead, during the early Re-

Figure 51. Model of the trophy at La Turbie, France, 7–6 B.C., Museo della Civiltà Romana. Photo: Deutsches Archäologisches Institut, Rom-InstNegNr 73.1179

public, upon returning to Rome victorious generals would consecrate to Jupiter, Mars, or Quirinus a portable, processional version of the Greek cruciform mannequin-type trophy, dressed with weapons and armor. As time passed, they began to transport statuary groups to Rome as part of their trophies, initiating a tradition of Roman triumphal art. Pompey's victory complex on the Campus Martius monumentalized this development, and its dedication to his patron goddess, Venus,

Figure 52. Model of the trophy at Adamklissi, Rumania, 107–8, Museo della Civiltà Romana. Photo: Deutsches Archäologisches Institut, Rom-InstNegNr 37.377

underlines a gradual transformation in the trophy's character, from an object conceived to be impregnated with war's destructive forces (*Theos Tropaios*) to a permanent marker of the *imperator's Felicitas.* By way of explanation for the tumulus's conspicuous absence, Picard concludes, "The monument built by Drusus takes its inspiration from La Turbie, which was under construction at that time, but since it had to be improvised in haste in barbarian territory, one can conjecture that it consisted above all of a mound of earth, analogous in form to the Mausoleum of Augustus, or perhaps Trajan's trophy at Adamklissi." As for La Turbie, "The monument belongs to a very well known architectural family . . . of Hellenistic tombs dating back to the fourth century. . . . The most famous example is the Mausoleum of Halicarnassos, whose proportions, as Formigé emphasized, suggested a geometric scheme to the architect of the Mausoleum of Augustus."[58]

This hypothesis also meshes well with the funerary ceremonies following Augustus's death, apparently scripted at least in part by the emperor. The emphasis was distinctly triumphal: "His body was hidden in a coffin; a wax effigy was displayed above it in triumphal dress. This image was borne from the palace by the officials who had been appointed for the following year; another one of gold was carried from the Senate House, and yet another was conveyed on a triumphal chariot." Behind the parade of ancestral and historical images "were all the peoples that he had added to the empire, each represented by an image possessing some indigenous characteristics." Moreover, during a discussion of the funeral senators proposed that "the procession should pass through the Triumphal Gate preceded by the image of Victory from the Senate House."[59] In short, H. S. Versnel notes that a significant affiliation between triumphs and funerals was established precisely at Augustus's death, even though the emperor had not celebrated a triumph since 29 B.C.[60]

Both Dietrich Boschung and Henner von Hesberg have pondered a dual role for the Mausoleum as trophy and tomb in passing, but without appraising its full implications.[61] Consider the impact of such a bivalency upon the unresolved complications of location and date described at the beginning of this chapter. Augustus chooses the Campus Martius for his trophy-tomb in the knowledge that, even though he does not have senatorial permission to build a tomb there, as a victory monument this is where it belongs, near the ancient altar of Mars, god of war. From earliest times Romans had considered the Campus sacred to Mars and used it for military exercises.[62] On the whole, dedications and monuments on the Campus Martius were closely linked with the army or navy, and most of the temples built there between the Punic Wars and the battle of Actium were tied to victories.[63] It was the starting point for triumphal processions, and burial there following senatorial decree was typically for generals who had celebrated a triumph.[64] It was also, perhaps most significantly, the site of Pompey's huge triumphal complex, with its vast stone theater, massive portico, Curia, and Temple to Venus Victrix. Sculpted figures on the theater representing the nations he had subdued underlined the triumphal nature of the complex, and adjoining it was a monumental trophy.[65] Augustus's choice of the Campus for monumentalization in the name of triumph followed directly on Pompey's lead; so too did the concept of ambiguous architecture, for Pompey was able to dedicate his theater only (a type of building about which many Romans were still at best ambivalent) by declaring it a staircase for shows subjoined to the temple.[66] In a similar way, Augustus's tomb in the guise of a trophy circumvented the need for a senatorial decree to build a private burial monument on public land.

An Image of Things Achieved

Augustus was not the first to describe selected lifetime achievements in his tomb's design. Mural paintings from the above-mentioned third- or second-century tomb on the Esquiline, for instance, represent memorable moments in the Samnite War, with scenes of parley, siege, and battle, and labels identifying two soldiers as M. Fannius and Q. Fabius (with whom the tomb is associated) (fig. 53). Likewise, fragmentary paintings on the podium facade of the Tomb of the Scipios apparently depicted wartime achievements of those interred within.[67] After Augustus, and presumably at least partially because of the precedent he set, many of

Figure 53. Paintings from the Tomb of Q. Fabius on the Esquiline, Rome, third or second century B.C., Museo dei Conservatori. Photo: Deutsches Archäologisches Institut, Rom-InstNegNr 34.1929

the emperors who designed funerary monuments emphatically included a visual representation of highpoints from their respective *res gestae;* moreover, like Augustus, they selected for their tombs bivalent architectural types, referring both to death and to triumph. An examination of these later monuments yields a possible explanation for this practice.

Titus reached his military apogee before he acceded to the throne, when he and Vespasian forced a rebellious Jerusalem into submission in 70. Together, they celebrated a triumph on their return to Rome in 71. It is this triumph that is illustrated in the relief panels inside the bay of the Arch of Titus (as well as in the small frieze at cornice level). A comparison of the Arch's representation of the triumph with a firsthand account by Josephus foregrounds the design committee's concerns when conceiving the Arch. According to Josephus, behind the spoils "drove Vespasian first with Titus behind him; Domitian rode alongside them, gloriously adorned, a magnificent sight with his horse."[68] In the *Triumphator* panel on the north side of the bay, only Titus appears in his chariot (fig. 11); omissions in the visual narrative recharacterize the event to glorify Titus alone. The presence of personifications further compromises the relief's historical accuracy: Virtus, holding the horses' reins, represents the emperor's military virtue; and Honos, in front of the chariot, personifies the glory his virtue earned him. Behind the emperor a personification of *Victoria Augusti* stands in the place reserved for the triumphator's slave and holds a *corona civica* of oak and acorn above his head, a sign of divine force bestowed upon a victor. Evidently the aim of this panel was not so much to illustrate the overthrow of the Jews as to extol Titus through depicting the most important event of his career.[69] Furthermore, just as the obelisks outside Augustus's Mausoleum validated the Actian triumph, so in the south relief spoils symbolically validate Titus's triumph. The items on the *fercula* – the shewbread table topped with two cups and with trumpets between the legs, and a menorah – came from the innermost shrine of Jerusalem's Temple (figs. 54, 55); until their "capture" and subsequent display in the nearby

Figure 54. Arch of Titus, detail of the spoils relief showing the menorah, Rome, 81. Photo: Penelope J. E. Davies

Figure 55. Arch of Titus, detail of the spoils relief showing the shewbread table, Rome, 81. Photo: Penelope J. E. Davies

Forum Pacis, only high priests had seen these ultimate tokens of Judaism, the enemy conquered.[70]

The third panel in the Arch, suspended in the summit of the bay and sur-rounded by starlike rosettes, shows Titus borne aloft on an eagle's back, denoting his apotheosis (fig. 13). Herein lies a crucial clue to the role of the *res gestae* in this arch and in the Mausoleum of Augustus. The triangular arrangement of the three bay reliefs establishes a causal relationship between deeds and apotheosis, speaking a simple message: through his military accomplishments (side panels), Titus earns

Figure 56. Arch of Titus, detail of the triumphator relief showing the frieze on Titus's chariot, Rome, 81. Photo: Penelope J. E. Davies

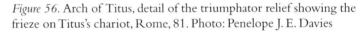

apotheosis (apex).[71] This was the explicit message of the Arch, and this was the implicit message of Augustus's visual *res gestae,* crowned by his gleaming godlike statue. The ambivalence of the Arch's form confirms what is spelt out so eloquently in its panel decorations. To be sure, arches played an increasingly present role in commemorating the dead, as is seen in the cenotaph of the Sergii at Pola, where the only precursor for the apotheosis relief is found; and, indeed, they seem to have been the monument of choice for Julio-Claudian princes, as exemplified by the Arch of Gaius in Pisa and those erected in Rome in honor of Drusus the Elder and Younger and Germanicus.[72] This tradition may have partially guided Domitian's choice for his brother's memorial. Yet just as often arches marked triumphs, as was the case with two nearby monuments, the Parthian Arch of Augustus and the Fornix Fabiorum.[73] Muted innuendoes in the Arch's panels further emphasize the ambiguity: the bilevel composition of the Triumphator panel, isolating Titus above horses and soldiers in the company of a winged female figure, recalls the developing iconography of imperial deification, which employed an ascending horse-drawn chariot and celestial or winged figures as vehicles of apotheosis, as seen on the Belvedere Altar of 12–2 B.C.; the sculptural details on Titus's chariot – a frieze of baetyls, sacred to Apollo, and two heraldically poised eagles on thunderbolts (figs. 56, 57 – belong in both a triumphal and an apotheosic context.[74]

A similar visual causality is established on the Columns of Trajan and Marcus Aurelius. There, the dead ruler's accomplishments wind in a sculpted narrative around the shaft, with a winged Victoria inscribing a shield as a title page.[75]

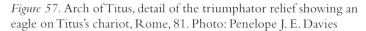

Figure 57. Arch of Titus, detail of the triumphator relief showing an eagle on Titus's chariot, Rome, 81. Photo: Penelope J. E. Davies

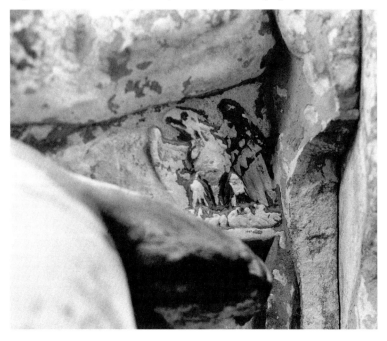

Scholars believe that the narrative format of the Column's sculptural frieze on Trajan's Column was based either upon the continuous illustrated *rotulus* (even though no example of such a scroll is documented) or upon a painted length of fabric of the kind that was wound around columns of temples on feast days.[76] Most agree that its content relied to some extent upon Trajan's own account of the Dacian campaigns known as his *Dacica,* of which a mere four words survive.[77] Yet the events depicted in both friezes appear to have been edited in a similar way to the triumph panel on the Arch of Titus; both are made up of programmatically placed formulaic motifs (such as *adlocutiones,* sacrifices, marches, and *clementia* scenes), which succinctly epitomize the emperor's cardinal virtues. The frieze on the later column also uses unnaturalistic devices such as hieratic frontality and size differentiation to isolate the emperor's figure amid crowds of soldiers.[78] The friezes are not, then, historically "accurate," but extol the emperor's character (at the expense of other generals active in the campaigns) in a selective visual *res gestae.*[79] With its slow spiraling, the narrative of virtue draws the eye up to the column's crowning climax, the emperor in his gleaming divinity. Again, the emphasis on the emperor's military valor is underlined by the monument's ambivalent quality: like the tumulus and the arch, the column had a long-standing dual role as triumphal monument (seen, for instance, in the third-century rostral column of C. Duilius in the Roman Forum) and funerary monument (the Column of Septumia outside the Porta del Vesuvio in Pompeii, for instance).[80] This ambiguity must have been instrumental in Trajan's selection of a column and extends throughout his whole forum, which was decorated according to what might be termed a program of ambiguity to disguise his choice of location for his tomb, just as the trophy form had obscured that of Augustus.[81]

Inevitably, as a Roman anticipated his own demise he hoped to be remembered at his best, for beneficent works and good character. Yet admirable deeds could also offer a path to immortality through remembrance, since they transformed the deceased into an exemplum for the living.[82] An excerpt from Polybius's description of Roman customs lends insight into the process. The passage records a practice of creating wax masks of the dead and placing them in wooden cupboards in the atrium, the most conspicuous part of a Roman house. At family funerals, he explains, living substitutes wore the masks in procession, dressed according to the rank of the deceased, riding in chariots and bearing the appropriate insignia of office; they would then sit, in ivory chairs, upon the Rostra. "There could not be a more impressive sight for a young man who aspires to fame and virtue," he interjects. "For who could remain unmoved at the sight of the images of these men who have won renown for their virtue, all gathered together as if they were alive and breathing? What spectacle could be more glorious than this?" A speaker delivers an oration over the body and "proceeds to relate the successes and accomplishments of the others whose images are displayed, beginning with the oldest. By this constant renewal of the good report of heroic men, the fame of those who have performed any noble deed is made immortal, and the renown of those who have served their country well becomes a matter of common knowledge and a heritage for generations to come. But the most important consequence is that young men are inspired to stand firm through extremes of suffering for the common good in the hope of attaining the glory that attends upon the great."[83] In the role of exemplum, then, lay perpetuation in the respectful and emulative minds of the living. For the living, in turn, the achievements of ancestors, recounted or represented in public places and as part of public ceremonies, offered prominent families recurrent validation, and a pedigree of civic "heroes," as Harriet Flower notes, offered critical support to a man seeking office. In effect, exalted histories maintained the fabric of republican society.[84]

Yet more was at stake for the imperial family. As we have seen, the emperor emphasized his triumph, an achievement that had long held an exalted, near-divine, place among human endeavors, in such a way as to suggest that his deeds justified his apotheosis, returning him perhaps to the godlike status from which he had come.[85] A bountiful source of flattery and panegyric for poets,[86] perhaps even a deep-seated belief, this apotheosis played a crucial role in counteracting the immediate and inevitable instability that resulted from the emperor's death. By allowing his successor to be "reborn" as the son of a god, it could facilitate smooth dynastic succession, and was all the more important in the absence of a formal investiture ceremony.

Caesar's words at his aunt's funeral indicate an early consciousness of the legitimizing power of divine ancestry: "My aunt Julia's maternal family descends from kings, and her father's side is related to immortal gods. For the Marcii Reges claim descent from Ancus Marcius, hence her mother's name. The Julii, to whom our family belongs, are descendants of Venus. Therefore, our family has both the sanctity of kings, the mightiest of men, and the ceremony due to gods, who rule the kings themselves."[87] The young Augustus recognized it, too: "At the first Games provided by [Caesar's] successor Augustus in honor of his apotheosis, a comet shone for seven days on end, rising in about the eleventh hour. This was thought to be Caesar's soul, received in heaven; and for this reason a star was added to the forehead of his divine image."[88] By sacred law, Caesar became a god in 42, and in subsequent years, as Augustus struggled for a subtle supremacy, he minted coins that traded on this apotheosis: in 36, denarii juxtaposed his portrait as *divi filius* with an image of the Temple of Divine Julius (fig. 58);[89] on the obverse of a second issue, the comet, inscribed *Divus Iulius,* accompanied Augustus's portrait on the reverse, inscribed *Caesar Augustus.* Another type was even more explicit: an inscribed bust of Divus Julius on the obverse was paired with Augustus's portrait on the reverse, with the legend *Divi Filius* (fig. 59).[90] By stressing Augustus's descent from a god, the coins set him above

Figure 58. Denarius of Octavian showing the Temple of Divus Julius, 36 B.C. Photo: Courtesy of the American Numismatic Society, New York

Figure 59. Sestertius of Octavian as *divi filius,* 37 B.C. Photo: Courtesy of the American Numismatic Society, New York

Mark Antony through the nuance of Caesar's divine charisma, to win him support from veterans and the populace at large.

In this way, Augustus benefited directly from Caesar's alleged divinity. Since he risked leaving Rome with an even more fragile constitution than the tottering republic he had abolished, and since he had reason to be particularly concerned about succession, Augustus endeavored to secure the throne for his chosen successor by bequeathing him divine parentage. Thus he advertised his achievements in the monument in which he would lie buried, in both written and visual form, in the hope that his deeds would win him deification. Then, as descendant of a god, his successor (who features prominently in the final version of the written *res gestae*) would be imbued with a special charisma emanating from Augustus, his divine ancestor; this charisma should, Augustus hoped, elevate him above the vacillations of popular opinion to facilitate his accession.[91]

On subsequent monuments, whether commissioned by the emperor who would lie buried there or by a successor, the process was similar: apotheosis promoted or justified dynastic succession. On the Arch of Titus, Titus, now divinized, provides Domitian with a divine sibling, making him, as the inscription spells out, son and brother of a god. In Trajan's case, the *res gestae* were particularly important because he came from a relatively obscure background and could not rest upon Nerva's meagre laurels in his hope for deification.

The decision of apotheosis for a dead emperor rested with the Senate, who would judge the deceased on the basis of his virtues (or popularity).[92] As L. Cerfaux and J. Tondriau aptly put it: "The Roman emperor is simply a candidate for apotheosis, and his reign constitutes an examination of his abilities."[93] However, the illustrated *res gestae* seen on imperial tombs were an attempt to justify his deification, and, when apotheosis became the norm in the second century, they served to emphasize it. Apotheosis was in part a means of securing a personal afterlife, either with the gods or in men's memory and worship, but just as important, it was also a political move to further the dynasty, to ensure that kingship did not die with the passing of the king.[94] Having identified this motive for the funerary monument's design, one perceives that the tomb was not simply a monument to a dead ruler, but, perhaps more significantly, an accession monument as well, erected either by an emperor for himself out of concern for his descendants or by an heir to validate his claim to the throne. This role as accession monument will be central to the themes developed in the following chapters.

AN IMPERIAL COSMOS:
THE CREATION
OF ETERNITY

The King has two capacities, for he has two bodies, the one whereof is a
Body natural, consisting of natural Members as every other Man has, and in
this he is subject to Passions and Death as other Men are; the other is a Body
politic, and the Members thereof are his Subjects, and he and his Subjects
together compose the Corporation. . . . And this Body is not subject to Passions as the other is, nor to Death, for as to this Body the King never dies,
and his natural Death is not called in our Law, the Death of the King, but
the Demise of the King, not signifying by the Word (*Demise*) that the Body
politic of the King is dead, but that there is a Separation of two Bodies, and
that the Body politic is transferred and conveyed over from the Body natural
now dead, or now removed from the Dignity royal, to another Body natural.
So that it signifies a Removal of the Body politic of the King of this Realm
from one Body natural to another.[1]

IN THE PREVIOUS chapter, I suggested that references to *res gestae* in imperial funerary monument design justified the deceased emperor's apotheosis in
order to bequeath to his successor a divine parentage, which in turn would
ease dynastic accession. This chapter follows on from these conclusions, tracing a
pattern of cosmic references and metaphors that emerges when one analyzes the
monuments as a group. In two cases, the funerary complex of Augustus and the
Antonine Column base, the cosmic allusion is explicit. In the cases of the Templum Gentis Flaviae and the Mausoleum of Hadrian, I attempt to understand
architectural form as a metaphor through a combination of literary, experiential,
and circumstantial evidence. I argue that cosmic allusions imply an association
between the emperor and the cosmocrator, a link that is consistent with references in literature and other media, where it might find an explanation in terms
of panegyrical adulation or absolutism. In the last section of the chapter, however, it becomes apparent that the association plays an additional role in an imperial funerary context, where it implies dynastic continuity by suggesting the
emperor's regeneration in his successors.

COSMIC ALLUSIONS: THE FUNERARY COMPLEX OF AUGUSTUS AND THE ANTONINE COLUMN BASE

Between 27 June 10 and 27 June 9 B.C., Augustus arranged for the transportation of Psammetichus II's red granite obelisk to Rome from Heliopolis, Egyptian City of the Sun. He hired mathematician and astrologer Facundus Novius to install it in the northern Campus Martius, near his Mausoleum. The obelisk, now relocated in Piazza di Montecitorio, stood on five steps atop travertine and peperino slabs (fig. 60). On its base, an inscription recalled the Actian triumph:

IMP. CAESAR. DIVI F.
AUGUSTUS
PONTIFEX MAXIMUS
IMP. XII COS. XI TRIB. POT. XIV
AEGYPTO IN POTESTATEM
POPULI ROMANI REDACTA
SOLI DONUM DEDIT

(The Emperor Caesar, son of a God, Augustus, Pontifex Maximus, Imperator for the twelfth time, in his eleventh consulship, with tribunician power for the fourteenth time, gave [this] as a gift to the sun when Egypt had been made subject to the Roman people)

At the top of the shaft were a pyramidion and a sphere.[2]

Figure 60. Obelisk from the Solarium Augusti, in Piazza di Montecitorio, Rome, 10–9 B.C. Photo: Penelope J. E. Davies

The obelisk was the gnomon for a huge meridian or sundial, the purpose of which was to signal midday or all the hours of the day and to divulge the sun's position in relation to the zodiac circle. For this task an obelisk was eminently appropriate, for Romans associated obelisks with the sun: as Ammianus Marcellinus put it, "An obelisk is a very pointed stone, rising gradually somewhat in the shape of a turning post to a lofty height; gradually it grows slenderer, to resemble a sunbeam. . . ."[3] Excavations begun in 1980 beneath Via di Campo Marzio uncovered the pavement into which it was set as it survived from a Domitianic restoration, with a bronze line against which the progress of the needle's shadow could be read. Greek letters adjacent to the line spelt out *Parthenos, Leon, Taurus* and probably *Krios,* as well as seasonal changes: *Etesiai pauontai* (Etesian winds calm) and *therous arche* (summer begins) (fig. 61).

Figure 61. Solarium Augusti, excavated section beneath Via di Campo Marzio, Rome, 10–9 B.C. Photo: Deutsches Archäologisches Institut, Rom-InstNegNr 82.3636

Reports of Renaissance construction works record mosaics of wind personifications at the corners of the obelisk with inscriptions such as "Boreas [the North Wind] blows," as well as bronze "steps" (divisions of the zodiac) and various celestial signs, *varia signa caelestia*.[4] Revolving eternally around and ordered by the obelisk, symbol of the sun, the whole instrument formed a magnificent symbol of the cosmos.

The Antonine Column base incorporates another explicit cosmic reference. In the apotheosis relief, a nude winged figure, spread diagonally across the panel, carries the imperial couple heavenward. About his shoulders flutters a stretch of cloth, and his huge wings span almost the entire width of the relief. A crown of baroque, flamelike curls frames his youthful, idealized head, and he gazes away into the distance. In his left hand he holds a globe, on which are sculpted five stars, a crescent moon, and a zodiac band (fig. 62). The band, in turn, is carved with three signs, Pisces, Aries, and Taurus, and coiled around the globe is a serpent.

Figure 62. Column of Antoninus Pius, detail of apotheosis relief showing Aion holding a globe, Rome, 161. Photo: Penelope J. E. Davies

ARCHITECTURAL METAPHOR: THE TEMPLUM GENTIS FLAVIAE AND HADRIAN'S MAUSOLEUM

> [The architect's task is] to vitalize building materials, to animate them collectively with a thought, a state of feeling, to charge them with a subjective significance (Louis Sullivan).[5]

Difficult as it is to reconstruct the essential forms of many ancient buildings, there have been only limited attempts to penetrate their metaphorical role. Indeed, in the absence of the architect's or patron's direct testimony, attempting to prove an intended symbolic value in a building is an uphill task. All the same, ancient authors make it abundantly clear that Romans were inclined to assign meaning to buildings with or without the architect's or patron's encouragement, and the Templum Gentis Flaviae was one such building, as Statius and Martial bear witness. In 95, Statius addressed *Silvae* 4 to Domitian on the opening of a new coastal road from Sinuessa to Naples. In a quasi catalogue of imperial improvements made to Rome, he refers to a "Flavian heaven," apparently the Flavian Temple, which, he indicates, would ensure the eternity of Vespasian's dynasty: *Qui genti patriae futura semper / sancit limina Flaviumque caelum* ("He who sanctifies in the name of his father's family thresholds that will last forever, a Flavian heaven").[6] The image recurs in 5.1.236–41: *Est hic . . . minister / illius, aeternae modo qui sacraria genti / condidit inque alio posuit sua sidera caelo* ("Here is the minister of the man who recently founded a sacred shrine for his eternal race, and set his stars in another heaven"). The Temple evokes a similar response in Martial-9.1.8–10): *Manebit altum Flaviae decus gentis / cum sole et astris cumque luce Romana. / Invicta quidquid condidit manus, caeli est* ("The exalted glory of the Flavian race will endure with sun and stars, and with the light of Rome. Whatever an unconquered hand has founded, it is of heaven!")

Illuminating as it might be, this method of gaining a glimpse into the metaphorical role of architecture stands the risk of privileging a text over the building itself, and some Roman buildings speak louder through their very forms than a textual commentary might. The scholar's task is to find a way to read the built form in the context of ancient thought, recognizing all the while that any hypotheses will remain tenuous and hard to prove. Few would disagree that Hadrian's Pantheon, begun in 118, has a symbolic presence, even though its extent and precise message may be hard to pin down. The temple's spectacular dome, pierced by a twenty-seven foot oculus, is a perfect hemisphere, sitting on a vertical cylinder whose height and radius are equal to its own (fig. 63); as a result, within the temple is contained a perfect sphere or globe, variously interpreted as a symbol of empire, harmony and eternity, and the cosmos. The building speaks for itself: regardless of which gods were worshipped there and how, it functions as a massive celebration of light (figs. 64, 65). William Loerke writes: "The major visual experience in the Rotunda, apparent to anyone immediately upon entry, whether or not he knows anything about Roman temples, Roman religion, or

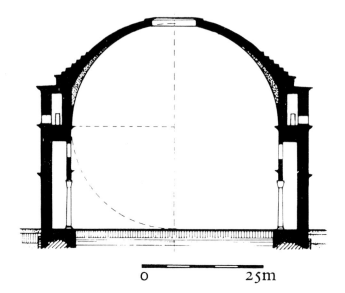

Figure 63. Section of the Pantheon showing inscribed circle, Rome, ca. 117–28. From J. B. Ward-Perkins, *Roman Imperial Architecture* (Harmondsworth, 1981), fig. 54. Copyright Yale University Press

0   25m

Figure 64. View of the interior of the Pantheon's dome, Rome, ca. 117–28. Photo: Penelope J. E. Davies

Figure 65. Disc of light from the Pantheon's oculus, Rome, ca. 117–28. Photo: Penelope J. E. Davies

Roman history, is the single shaft of sunlight slowly moving through space. The Rotunda isolates the sun's motion. It has always offered its visitors a palpable experience of celestial motion."[7] The oculus hovered, sunlike, above worshippers, allowing the sun's powerful beam to cut through the temple, just as Vitruvius prescribed for temples to Sol.[8] More systemic symbolism may or may not be present: for instance, six large exedrae and an apse may have housed statues of the cosmic deities: the sun and moon, and five planets (fig. 66).[9] For Loerke, the fact

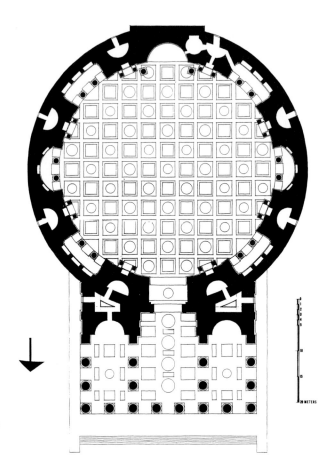

Figure 66. Plan of the Pantheon, Rome, ca. 117–28. From W. L. MacDonald, *The Architecture of the Roman Empire* (New Haven, 1982), vol. 1, fig. 98. Copyright Yale University Press

that the twenty-eight vertical rows of dome coffers do not derive from the ground plan demonstrates that their number was contrived to represent the twenty-eight days (four seven-day weeks) it takes the moon to orbit the earth, and the five horizontal rows may correspond to the five circles on ancient globes: two arctic circles, two tropics, and the equator.[10] If the center of each coffer held a starlike rosette, the entire ceiling must have conjured up a glittering image of the heavens. This at least was Cassius Dio's impression: "It is called [the Pantheon], perhaps because amongst the images that decorate it are the statues of many gods, including Mars and Venus; but my opinion of the name is that, because of its vaulted roof, it resembles the heavens." Animating this cosmic image, and using it as an Aula Regia, sat Hadrian, the sun's implicit associate, co-cosmocrator.[11]

Hadrian's predilection for architectural metaphor suggests the possibility of symbolism in the form of his Mausoleum. On the whole its damaged state has rendered attempts to understand its symbolism relatively rare. One proposal would align each of its three elements with the three stages of the soul's progression from mortal to immortal (human status, ascent of the soul, and apotheosis).[12] In another attempt, Tina Squadrilli hypothetically reconstructed the tomb with two doors on east and west sides of the base, suggesting that they symbolized the sun's rising and setting, a metaphor for the cycle of Hadrian's life. This reconstruction, and a posited statue of Hadrian "in the guise of the sun" on the tomb's summit, led her to describe the building "not only as an imperial tomb but almost as a temple dedicated to a solar god."[13] Scholars can now be certain that a single door on the south side led into the Mausoleum, and opinions differ over whether the tomb supported a tempietto or a statue. Still, Hadrian fostered a special relationship with the sun; he expressed that relationship through art, and his tomb's basic structure, coupled with circumstantial evidence and an experiential analysis of its form, constitute a plausible argument for a metaphorical interpretation of the tomb as an image of the cosmos.

Son of Publius Aelius Hadrianus Afer and Domitia Paulina, Hadrian's given name was Publius Aelius Hadrianus, to which he added Traianus after his adoption. As scholars have noted, his *nomen,* Aelius, was a "Latinization" of the Greek ἥλιος, "sun." It was this name, and not Hadrianus, that he intended to pass on, for when he adopted the short-lived Lucius Ceionius Commodus as his heir in 136, he renamed him, not Hadrianus, but Lucius Aelius Caesar, and the *Historia Augusta* consistently refers to him as "Helius." On coins, his actual successor Antoninus Pius took the name Aelius as well, dropping Aurelius.[14] Hadrian's newly established dynasty, it seems, was to be the dynasty of the sun, and it was this name that was given to the bridge connected to his tomb.[15] Circumstantial evidence to support this observation accumulates rapidly: peacocks, thought to have the eye of the sun in their tails, in gilded bronze outside Hadrian's Mausoleum (fig. 81); a peacock dedicated by Hadrian at the Argive Temple of Hera, perhaps to acknowledge their common symbol; a painting of a peacock on the wall of the tomb of the Aelii (E), freedmen of Hadrian's family, in the Vatican necropolis; Hadrian's predilection for sunrises, either real or reported; a special request to be Archon of Delphi in 120 and reelection to the post in 125; and so on.[16]

The annular corridor by which one reached the burial chamber in Hadrian's Mausoleum was unusual (though not unique).[17] The corridor, and the chamber's location at an upper level in the Mausoleum (together a unique combination) placed Hadrian's ashes in the center of the tomb, both horizontally and vertically (fig. 67).[18] Visitors who hoped to enter the burial chamber were compelled first to encircle the emperor's body in an anti-clockwise direction, a form of circumambulation that is consistent with ancient funerary rituals as they are described in Chapter 5. Yet ancient sources also indicate that in at least one other form of architecture, the circus, Romans construed this kind of anti-clockwise circular movement, when enacted around a solar symbol, as a metaphor for the cosmos (even though they viewed the universe as geocentric).

In ca. 193–220, Tertullian described the symbolism of the circus games in this way:

> They consecrated the four-horse chariot to the sun, the two-horse to the moon. . . . At first there were only two colors [for drivers], white and red.

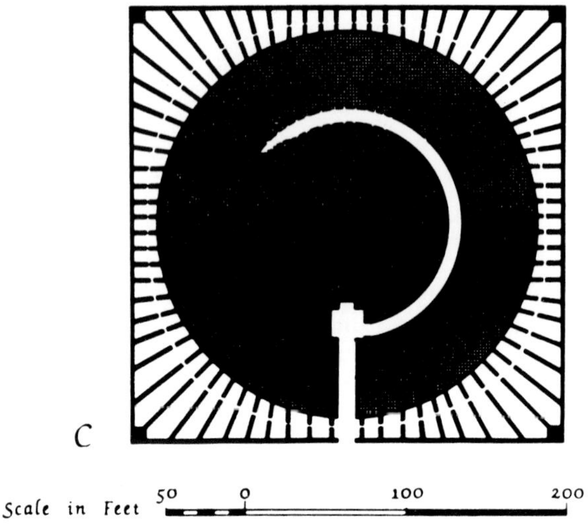

Figure 67. Plan of Hadrian's Mausoleum at ground level, Rome, ca. 125–39. From H. Colvin, *Architecture and the Afterlife* (New Haven-London, 1991), fig. 41C. Copyright Yale University Press

C

Scale in Feet

White was sacred to Winter, for the white of snow, red to Summer because of the sun's glow. But afterwards, as both pleasure and superstition gained pace, some dedicated red to Mars, others white to the Zephyrs, green to Mother Earth or Spring, blue to the sky and the sea, or to Autumn.[19]

Charax of Pergamon, who wrote a world history sometime between Nero's reign and the sixth century, states that either King Romus or Circe, Helios's daughter, installed circus games in Rome in honor of Helios.[20] He describes the circus as an image of the universe, in which the twelve doors corresponded to the twelve signs of the zodiac or the twelve months, the seven "spaces" to the seven planets. The sixth-century Byzantine writer Corippus adds that the four horses of the solar quadriga and the four parties represented the seasons, and each charioteer wore a color appropriate to his season.[21]

Exactly when the metaphor was conceived, or indeed when the association between sun and circus began, is hard to ascertain. John Humphrey notes that the association existed at least in Augustan times and probably well before, since Augustus planted Ramses II's obelisk from Heliopolis (now in Piazza del Popolo) on the Circus's *spina* in recognition of the sun's place there, and scenes of kings making offerings to the solar gods on its shaft emphasized its significance.[22] By the mid–first century A.C., the circus's form and the nature of the race were fully canonized, and George Hanfmann argues that by at least the second century they were conceived of as a vehicle for cosmic allegory, perhaps by Suetonius, in Hadrian's reign, in his lost treatise, *Ludicra Historia,* on Roman games and festivals.[23] Certainly archaeological and literary evidence accumulates more rapidly for the early second century, and in the Hadrianic period the chariot race became a popular motif for children's sarcophagi and for funerary reliefs (fig. 68).[24] Through depiction of the circus's circular motion, those who commissioned these works seem to have hoped to arrest the course of natural decay by symbolically harnessing the regenerative powers of the universe.[25]

Figure 68. Funerary relief from Ostia with a circus scene, late Trajanic or Hadrianic, Musei Vaticani. Photo: Courtesy of Musei Vaticani Archivio Fotografico Neg. N. XXXIV.5.85

Since by the Hadrianic period Romans appear to have interpreted anti-clockwise circular movement around a central solar symbol as an image of the cosmos in the circus, and since that image appears in a funerary context in his reign, it is conceivable that the Mausoleum, too, was a cosmic allegory, in which P. Aelius Hadrianus, at the very center of the tomb, was cast as the sun. Visitors who moved around the central chamber in an anti-clockwise direction played the parts of stars and animated the image.

The skeptic will not be swayed by such circumstantial evidence to allow the tomb a metaphorical role. Nor is it likely that it was that alone; the sheer mass and weight of its presence contradict an interpretation purely as a "celestial" building, even though its close connection with the Pantheon, discussed in Chapter 6, does suggest a strong similarity in ideological conception. Yet the select synopsis of the tradition of cosmic kingship that follows suggests that Hadrian was particularly inclined both to assign complex meanings to architectural form and to associate himself with the cosmos; although these poetic associations are not necessarily representative of his understanding of astronomy or the science of the universe, or proof of his deep-seated belief in a particular metaphysical system, he may have turned to them to transform his tomb from cold stone to architectural allegory.[26]

The subtlety of the cosmic allusions on the Columns of Trajan and Marcus Aurelius will become apparent only later in the chapter. Stock scenes of travel through distant lands signal the emperor's omnipresent command or *imperium,* which reminded Pliny of the swiftest star, *velocissimum sidus.*[27] What is more, when the emperor crosses a surging river at the beginning of the narrative on each column, the artist personifies the river as a monstrous, dripping giant and thereby transforms the act from a display of masterful engineering into a conquest of nature. In the famous "rain miracle" scene on the Aurelian Column (fig. 38), the emperor's command over nature saves the Roman army from overwhelming thirst and certain defeat; a sudden, god-given downpour is attributed to the emperor's agency, despite the fact that he was elsewhere when the event took place.[28]

COSMIC KINGSHIP

Taken as a group, the funerary monuments of the Roman emperors exhibit a pattern of cosmic allusions; in some cases they are explicit (the Horologium or the Column base of Antoninus Pius); in others (the Mausoleum of Hadrian, the sculpted columns), they are less obvious but emerge upon a contextual reading. Given this close tie with the emperor's person, the references suggest an association between emperor and prime mover in the universe. Sometimes Zeus-Jupiter (in his role as supreme god and especially as sky-god), the prime mover was identified with increasing frequency with the sun-god, Apollo, or Sol, whom, as chief of celestial bodies and regulator of the universe, Romans worshipped as Sol Indiges from at least the fourth century B.C., and with burgeoning enthusiasm in the last decades of the Republic.[29] Sharing such attributes as the eagle and radiate crown, Jupiter and Apollo-Sol and their patronage appear often to have been integrated or interchangeable.[30] The cult of Apollo came into dramatic prominence under Augustus and continued to flourish, while toward the end of the first century A.C., evidence for the cult of autochthonous Sol waned in favor of an Eastern form of solar worship centered around Sol Invictus, the unconquered sun. Developing gradually (Tacitus describes how, already in 69, "soldiers of the Third Legion saluted the rising sun, following Syrian custom"),[30] the cult was well established in Rome by the early second century as a result of continued eastern campaigns and through the influence of Syrian emigrants in Italy and Syrian soldiers enlisted in the Roman army. The trend toward sun worship accompanied a move away from a concept of distinctly individual gods and toward a more abstract idea of the divine that often approached monotheism.[31] Characteristics that had been peculiar to individual gods merged as different aspects of one supreme god to whom, as time passed, personifications of natural forces accrued; religious speculation transferred its focus from the interrelations of a pantheon of gods to the benefits a single god bestowed upon humans and his important role in the cosmic system. This cult characterized the sun as the *Basileos Helios,* a king surrounded by his servants who regulated the course of celestial bodies, a metaphor that Cicero had voiced long before in his Dream of Scipio, when he called the sun "leader, prince, and governor of the stars."[33] Significantly, when turned back upon itself, this anthropomorphism could not help but cast earthly rulers as the sun.[34]

The notion of cosmic kingship was not a Roman innovation, and neither was its signification in architectural or iconographical form; Babylonians, for instance, knew their king as the "Sun of Babylon," "King of the Universe," or

"King of the Four Quadrants of the World." Persians called their royal halls "heavens," and even if Herodotus does not explicitly state that there were cosmic undertones to the Median city of Ectabana, with its seven concentric walls of different colors surrounding the gilded royal palace, they may well have been there, as H. P. L'Orange suspects.[35] The metaphor of cosmic kingship was particularly popular in late classical and Hellenistic Greece. Plutarch recounts that when Alexander the Great assumed Darius's throne, he stepped beneath "the golden canopy of heaven (*ouraniskon*) on the royal throne"; and, according to the Severan writer Athenaios, the Athenians flattered Demetrius Poliorcetes with a hymn that described him as "majestic, all his friends encircling him, himself in their midst, his friends the stars, just as he is the Sun." A fragment of Duris relates that Demetrius Poliorcetes swathed himself in a dark robe embroidered with the poles of the sky, with golden stars and the twelve signs, and tells us that when the Athenians celebrated festivals, Demetrius was depicted on the proscenium, seated upon the orb of the earth. The metaphor found its way into coin portraits, such as those of Ptolemy III Euergetes (ca. 240 B.C.), with a diadem of alternating solar rays and horns, and prevailed in Rome in the first century B.C. even in the absence of monarchs. In Horace's *Satires,* for instance, Persius "praises Brutus and praises his men; he calls Brutus the Sun of Asia (*Solem Asiae*), and calls his friends his healthful stars (*stellae salubres)*."[36]

With Augustus's ascent to authority, the notion of cosmic kingship took hold, subtlely but firmly, among panegyrists (Caligula was the "New Sun," Claudius, the celestial star "that dispels the darkness over the world;" Domitian rose "with the rising sun and the great constellations, more radiant than they and shining more brilliantly than the Morning Star,") as among historians, who sometimes assigned him divine grace already as an infant, in a form of retrospective determinism; for instance, even Augustus's parentage was in question:

> When Atia [Augustus's mother] attended a solemn midnight rite at the Temple of Apollo, she had her litter set down, and when the rest of the married women slept, she too fell asleep. Suddenly a serpent glided into her, and later glided away again. On awakening, she purified herself, as if after intercourse with her husband. And immediately on her body there appeared a mark like a painted serpent, which she could never remove, so that soon she ceased ever going to the public baths. Augustus was born in the tenth month thereafter, and was thought to be Apollo's son. Before giving birth Atia herself dreamed that her intestines were carried up to the stars and spread out over the whole expanse of lands and skies; and his father, Octavius, dreamed that the radiance of the sun rose from her womb.[37]

Naturally, the "divine" newborn was drawn to his "parent," whom his actions mimicked:

> It is written by Gaius Drusus that, while still an infant, one evening Augustus was placed by his nurse in his cradle on the ground-floor, but by daybreak was nowhere to be seen; after a long search, he was finally discovered lying on top of a lofty tower, his face turned towards the rising sun.[38]

Despite a certain anxiety to keep the metaphor muted, at least in the early days of the empire, the emperors appear to have enjoyed its use: "[Augustus's] eyes were clear and radiant, and he liked people to believe that they shone with a sort of divine energy: it gave him profound pleasure if anyone at whom he looked promptly lowered his head as though dazzled by rays of sun."[39] Their personal behavior, moreover, did little to contradict the comparison. Augustus actively promoted his status as special protégé of Apollo, to whom, as god of victory, he attributed his Actian triumph, and whom (according to Mark Antony) he pretended to be during the scandalous "Feast of the Divine Twelve."[40]

The emperors do not seem to have been shy about giving artistic form to this panegyric characterization of themselves as the sun. For instance, a series of paintings in the Domus Aurea showing Phaethon receiving divine power from his radiate father, Apollo, unambiguously celebrates the solar father–son relationship. Recognizing Apollo as the god of his favorite pastimes, chariot racing and the lyre, Nero had an awning embroidered for Pompey's theater with golden stars on a deep-purple background and himself in a chariot at the center, in place of the sun; the theater itself he gilded for significant occasions. The colossal statue erected in the vestibule of his house depicted him with solar attributes, as do a number of reliefs and a gem perhaps reflecting its appearance. Coins bore his portrait wearing the radiate crown.[41] Hadrian issued coins throughout his reign with his own portrait, sometimes radiate, on the obverse and an image of Sol on the reverse.[42] He moved Nero's colossus, "and when he had consecrated this image to the Sun, after removing the face of Nero to whom it had previously been dedicated, he undertook to make another similar one for the Moon, with Apollodorus as architect."[43] After Antinous's death in October 130, the bereaved emperor erected a funerary monument for his beloved crowned by a small red granite obelisk. Now on the Pincio in Rome (fig. 69), its original whereabouts are a thorny issue: perhaps it stood in Antinoopolis, where Antinous was reportedly buried, and came to Rome only in Late Antiquity; perhaps it marked a tomb or a cenotaph at Hadrian's Villa at Tivoli, or in gardens on the Palatine. Alternatively, this small monolith may have replicated in Rome a larger monument erected in Antinoopolis. In any case, on its shaft a hieroglyphic inscription describes Hadrian as "The son of the Sun, the lord of the Diadems, Hadrian the ever-living," "[Hadrian] [the beloved] of the Nile and the Gods, the lord of Diadems who lives, is safe and healthy, who lives forever just like the Sun: [in] a fresh, beautiful youthful age. . . ."[44] Even though the monument is of an Egyptian type (which may have allowed for greater latitude) and even though relatively few Romans were fluently versed in hieroglyphs, the ruler's identification as son of Apollo is strikingly explicit.

Nowhere was there better opportunity for cosmocratic expression than in imperial architecture, and especially residential architecture, as ancient authors were quick to recognize. In building his house alongside Apollo's Temple on the Palatine, for instance, Augustus "cohabited" with Apollo; and in his golden palace, gleaming like Ovid's palace of the Sun, Nero clearly envisaged himself

Figure 69. Obelisk of Antinous on the Pincio, Rome, ca. 130. Photo: Penelope J. E. Davies

as cosmocrator at the heart of a man-made microcosm, complete with an enormous pool "as an image of a sea, ringed by buildings to resemble cities (*stagnum maris instar, circumsaeptum aedificiis ad urbium speciem*); more than that, there were different types of landscape – fields, pastures, and forests, with a multitude of every kind of domestic and wild animal."[45] In its famous octagonal room, Severus and Celer translated into architectural terms the self-appointed cosmocrator's inordinate fascination with the sun: on the two equinoxes and at solar midday, the luminous circle from its oculus exactly inscribed the north door onto a nymphaeum, uniting sun, earth, and water. In his main triclinium, of circular form, Nero dined beneath a roof that "revolved ceaselessly day and night, in time with the sky."[46] Even if the evidence for celestial symbols painted on the triclinium's dome is controversial,[47] the description of the dining room as a cosmic image by a contemporary author underlines a Roman propensity for assigning cosmic significance to certain forms of imperial architecture. Similarly, a few decades later Domitian ruled supreme in a Palatine heaven that "you would believe to be the golden ceiling of heaven," receiving ambassadors and administering justice enthroned in a majestic celestial apse.[48]

However, celestial imagery was particularly popular in Hadrianic architecture, as can be seen in the Pantheon and perhaps also in Hadrian's sprawling country residence at Tivoli. "He built up his villa at Tibur in an extraordinary way, applying to parts of it the renowned names of provinces and places, such as the Lyceum, the Academy, the *prytaneum,* the Canopus, the *Poecile,* and Tempe. And, so as to omit nothing, he even fashioned 'infernal regions,' " says the *Historia Augusta,* indicating at the least that Hadrian's purpose in building the villa was not simply to create structures in which to live.[49] Rather, with architectural symbols or with specific monuments chosen as ideograms, he recreated the lands he had visited and the places of his imagination in an architectural microcosm over which he, like Nero in his Golden House, was ruler.

One of these buildings is known as the Teatro Marittimo, or the Island Enclosure, and consists of an annular portico approached through a rectangular vestibule on the west side. Within the annular portico is a circular canal with an island at its center, to which two wooden swing bridges provided access. On the island a curvilinear vestibule opened on to an Ionic colonnaded atrium (figs. 70, 71). Scholars disagree over the building's function and prototype. Some characterize it as the temperamental emperor's retreat from the world, with a prototype in Plato's description of Poseidon's Atlantis; or Dionysius I's fortress on Ortygia; or Herod the Great's circular palace at Herodium.[50] Henri Stierlin reconstructs it along the lines of Varro's aviary at Casinum, with netting to contain birds, ducks in the canal, and on the island a domed pavilion, housing a triclinium with flowing water, a clock, and "a compass of eight winds, just as there is in the clock-tower at Athens."[51] He interprets both the aviary and the Island Enclosure through contemporary cosmographies such as Strabo's *Geography,* which envisaged the earth's disc at the center of a primordial ocean. The domes represented celestial equivalents for the earth's circles, and the Island En-

Figure 70. Island Enclosure at Hadrian's Villa, Tivoli, ca. 118–25, actual state. Photo: Penelope J. E. Davies

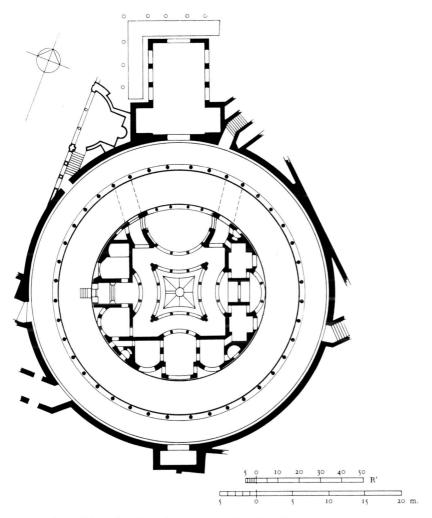

Figure 71. Plan of the Island Enclosure at Hadrian's Villa, Tivoli, ca. 118–25. From W. L. MacDonald and J. Pinto, *Hadrian's Villa and Its Legacy* (New Haven-London, 1995), fig. 95. Copyright Yale University Press

closure's ambulatory, conjoining the terrestrial and celestial zones, defined the turning motion that animated the *imago mundi*. Fish, birds, and plant life completed the cosmic image, and over this miniature cosmos, defined by his environment, the cosmocrator ruled supreme, dominating the elements at will and mastering time.[52]

This interpretation has experienced a mixed reception.[53] Indeed, there is no evidence for netting, and no reason to reconstruct the island suites (which seem to have included a lounge or library, a triclinium, and a bathroom) with the amenities Stierlin proposes. Steps leading into the canal suggest that it was used for swimming, and it is hard to imagine Hadrian swimming among ducks and geese. Yet even as a private retreat, the building was clearly a relative to the playful follies of later centuries, and it may well belong, in its basic form, to a tradition of "pleasure domes" identified by O. Grabar, including Nero's dining room and Varro's aviary.[54] Such rooms need not be interpreted as definitive manifestations of a theocratic politicoreligious scheme but as clever engineering feats with metaphorical cosmic undertones. In William MacDonald and John Pinto's words,

> [I]t is hard to resist the notion that some overriding meaning is expressed here symbolically; anything this original, indeed startling, provokes prolonged speculation. In view of Hadrianic and other monuments elsewhere it may be that a concept outside of purely Villa concerns inheres in the design, that part of the pleasure of using the place lay in knowing this. We leave questions of possible cosmological references to others but observe that this ingenious geometrical web and its circular government, with powers of implied radial expansion and convergence, could have had ideal connotations, could carry within it those strong implications of celestial shapes and paths found in other Roman art and architecture. . . . The Island Enclosure is a kind of built coin, with Hadrian the sentient man at its centre replacing the coin's image of Hadrian the all-powerful, the undeniable autocrat.[55]

It seems, then, that two separate but related motifs can be isolated as imperial idioms from the start of the empire: the panegyrical linkage of the ruler with the sun and his implicit relationship with and sometime portrayal as cosmocrator, often in the guise of the sun. An expression of absolutism, this association not only placed him at the summit of the human hierarchy but also imbued him with a celestial wisdom unavailable to other mortals and a power to read, and possibly influence, the workings of the cosmos. In all likelihood, attitudes imported from the East after Augustus's conquest of Mark Antony strengthened the concept, and even if political wariness cautioned the emperor not to explore the metaphor too fully, the reasons for its flourishing are easy to discern. Like the sun, which determined the length of the working day, Augustus regulated Roman existence; like the sun, he had visited and held sway over the farthest reaches of the known world, described, as today, by the sun's rising and setting. Like the sun, his peace brought fertility to the land through agriculture and, by restoring freedom of movement to the merchant, brought profit to traders. Shining forth after years of gloomy civil unrest, in short, the emperor had restored order and justice to a land in chaos, just as the all-seeing sun regulated the universe and caused the heavenly bodies to rotate in harmony. Likewise, it is easy to understand the continuing attraction of the metaphor for less self-effacing emperors such as Nero and Domitian, who enjoyed the idea of being the source of all administrative, judicial, and legislative power, of absolute terrestrial government and its poetical extension into the universe. Whereas under the Julio-Claudians and Flavians the association had been a more or less poetical one, under Hadrian it appears to have grown more determined and more philosophical. The reason for this directness should probably be sought in the personal predilections of the emperor, but also in a gradual change in religion in general, and especially in the cult of the sun.

Cosmic Motifs in a Funerary Context

The appeal of cosmic images can be readily understood as panegyric or as an expression of absolutism. Why, though, do they appear consistently on a type of monument that, by commemorating death, necessarily represents the emperor's relinquishment of absolute power?

A key to understanding the cosmic allegory in a funerary context lies in its capacity to signify rebirth and thus eternity. I suggested in Chapter 2 that imperial funerary monuments can just as easily be described as accession monuments, designed to counteract the problem of the emperor's mortality by emphasizing his apotheosis. Herein lies an advantage of the emperor's relationship to a solar deity: just as the sun, which appears every night to be forced into submission, emerges again every morning (whence its epithet, *aeternus,* without beginning and end), so the emperor, as the sun's associate, partakes in its immortality and at death rises to join in its unending cosmic status;[56] he does so with the assistance of one of the sun's agents, be it the solar eagle or the quadriga, as shown on the Antonine Monument of Ephesos, where the emperor (probably Trajan) rises in the sun's chariot, surrounded by cosmic deities such as Sol, Luna, and Tellus.[57] In the deceased emperor's divinity his successor found legitimation; but such legitimation necessarily relied upon an understanding that the new emperor was in some way imbued with the character of the old. This dominant imperial concern, to ensure the monarchy's survival, led in the funerary sphere to an attempt to create the impression of an eternity for the ruling family; in other words, images were used to imply that the emperor's death was less an ending than a transfer of power to a new generation, that the emperor did not die but was in some way eternally regenerated in his successors.

How did this "image of eternity" operate? In Augustus's funerary complex, the shadow of the Horologium's giant gnomon spun slowly and incessantly around, unendingly retracing its own course as days and seasons and years repeated themselves without end. Unlike most Westerners today who, largely as a result of Christian influence, think of time as a unilinear, irreversible progression from beginning to end, Romans, and Greeks before them, conceived of eternity as the ceaseless repetition of time already experienced, cosmological in nature, assuring continuity by the constant return of circular movement and, like a circle, knowing no beginning or end.[58] The circular zodiac and celestial bodies were therefore natural symbols for eternity (and appear as such framing portrait tondi on sarcophagi);[59] the Horologium seen through Roman eyes was not merely a gauge of time passing but also a reassuring confirmation of *eternal* time, reflected in the ordered movements of the cosmos. As commissioner of the instrument, Augustus in a sense regulated time himself.[60] Thus his subtle assimilation to Apollo the sun-god, regulator of daily time, was complete, implying the very apotheosis to which the obelisk's hieroglyphs refer.[61] The eternity implicit in the sundial's cosmic image signaled the regenerative quality of the Julian line, represented forcefully by the dynastic character of the Ara Pacis and the Mausoleum; the eternity to which it referred was not just Augustus's pure and simple, but Augustus's through the mediation of his family, under whose auspices Rome's potential chaos would be ordered, and to which Rome's own eternity had become inseparably linked in state propaganda.[62] The sundial literally demonstrated the unending, circular passage of time revolving around and governed by the omnipresent sun; and lest anyone should miss the connection between the sun and his favorite family, the smaller obelisks outside Augustus's Mausoleum echoed the sundial's gnomon.

In this way, the sundial's announcement of Augustus's immortality counteracted the Mausoleum's inevitable role as memento mori. The Ara Pacis as a whole summarizes the message: the theme of death (inherent in bucrania, sacrifice, and the thieving snake in the acanthus frieze) is balanced, and even outweighed, by motifs of regeneration and fecundity. Suckling females dominate two of the four panels flanking the enclosure doorways: the she-wolf nursing the infants Romulus and Remus (under the watchful eyes of their two "fathers") and a seated female figure with two infants on her lap (fig. 82). The two male infants in each scene, as scholars have been quick to recognize, are suggestive of Gaius and Lucius Caesar, Augustus's heirs at the time of the altar's construction. In the acanthus frieze, abundant vegetation teems with miniature forms of life such as birds, frogs, and scorpions (fig. 72), and some Romans might even have seen the meander motif between acanthus and procession friezes as a symbol of regeneration.[63] Eternal time is the context for the sacrificial procession frieze in honor of imperial peace that winds around the altar proper, and on the inside of the enclosure impossible garlands are fashioned out of plants from all seasons to conjure up the fullness of time. Wooden laths, bucrania, and gar-

Figure 72. Ara Pacis, detail of the acanthus frieze showing thieving snake and nest, Rome, 13–9 B.C. Photo: Penelope J. E. Davies

Figure 73. Ara Pacis, laths and bucrania on the enclosure interior, Rome, 13–9 B.C. Photo: Penelope J. E. Davies

lands translate into durable marble a temporary structure of perishable materials erected for the altar's dedication (fig. 73), offering a visual "eternalization" of the impermanent on one side of the marble slabs – in order to give instructions, as it were, for reading the other side, where the imperial family, apparently transitory, is also rendered immortal.[64] Thus, in solution to the crucial quandary of the monarch's mortality, Augustus's Campus Martius complex announces that his god-given qualities will not die with him but will be reborn in the next generation and the next, according to an Augustan eternity, *aeternitas Augusti,* that is celebrated on coins after his death.[65] The complex assures peace and order in Rome under Julian rule, and perhaps, by the implication of opposites, offers a cautionary reminder that without the sun's regulating hand, order – cosmos – turns to chaos.

A hypothesis that Hadrian designed his Mausoleum as an image of the cosmos to promote dynastic succession fits well with his concerns as manifested in numismatic images. His "accession" coins indicate that dynastic rebirth was well within his iconographic vocabulary: on the obverse of a gold coin minted in Rome in 117–18 is a laureate bust of Divus Trajanus, and on the reverse a radiate phoenix, mythical bird famed for its rebirth out of its father's ashes (fig. 74); Tacitus writes, "when the sum of its years is complete and death is at hand, [it is said] to make a nest in its own country and pour over it a procreative force – from which rises a young phoenix."[66] In the fourth century, Claudian elaborated

Figure 74. Hadrianic aureus showing a phoenix. Photo: Copyright The British Museum

further: "This bird never was conceived nor does it spring from any mortal seed, but is alike its own father and son, with none recreating it. It renews its outworn limbs with a regenerative death, and at each demise wins a fresh life."[67] King of birds to which others did obeisance, it was conceived not only as a bringer of prosperity but as a symbol of personal resurrection, since its dying day was also its birthday.[68] Already familiar to Romans in the first century, it was under Hadrian that the phoenix first emerged as a political symbol to suggest that the new emperor was in essence a reincarnation of the old, and the theme subsequently grew popular in Antonine propaganda.[69] More than that, though, the phoenix was the sun's bird, which accounted, in Claudian's mind, for its power of resurrection.[70] As there were those who viewed Hadrian's adoption with suspicion, believing that Trajan had intended to designate Neratius Priscus as his heir,[71] these hastily minted accession coins were especially appropriate; they declared Hadrian Trajan's successor through quasi reincarnation and implied his filial piety toward his father, since, by some accounts, the young phoenix transported its father's ashes to Heliopolis in an egg or an urn, just as Hadrian had arranged for Plotina, Matidia, and Attianus to transport Trajan's ashes carefully from Cilicia to Rome.[72] Hadrian's cosmic Pantheon belongs to these early days of his reign, and soon he would turn to designing his dynastic tomb. In later years, his concern to ensure his dynasty's perpetuation was such that it led him to try to control his succession through two generations, by requiring Antoninus Pius's adoption of his wife's nephew, Marcus Aurelius, and Aelius's son, Lucius Verus. A tomb that implied the rebirth of his charisma in his successor would therefore be entirely in keeping with his concerns as manifested in other media, as well as with other imperial funerary monuments.[73]

On the Antonine Column base, cosmic allusions articulate a message of apotheosis and dynastic rebirth, just as they do in the Augustan complex. On the one hand, the emperor's apotheosis, implicit in other funerary monuments, is the main subject of the Antonine pedestal. Yet, on the other, the prominent role of the personifications, and especially the winged figure, hints that there might be a subtheme hidden in the visual text; the winged figure appears to be the key to its decipherment. This has proven difficult, largely because the relief has been studied either in isolation or in juxtaposition with the Apotheosis of Sabina relief, and not in connection with earlier imperial funerary monuments, which might be expected to address similar ideological concerns. Some scholars recognize the figure as Zephyros, even though the wind god should have temple wings and is not usually associated with a globe; others see him as Ascensus, although this fails to account for his dominant role, or his youthfulness, seminudity, and globe. Most see him as a personification of a time-related concept, be it *Aeternitas,* Eternity (which should be female), *Saeculum Aureum,* Golden Age (which fails to explain his wings and the snake), or *Aion,* Eternity.[74]

A comparison with sculptural reliefs and mosaics makes Aion the most likely candidate. As a concept, in early Greek times *Aion* was roughly equivalent to "life" or "vital force" and quickly became synonymous with "eternity."[75] Further speculation on his nature in the works of Plato and Aristotle, in the magic papyri and the *Hermetica,* led to his identification with a "cosmic god," the "world soul," eternal and coextensive with the universe. An inscription from a statue base of the first century B.C., for instance, characterizes Aion as "the unique world, as it exists, has existed and will exist, which has no beginning, no middle, no end, partakes of no changes, who produces absolutely eternal divine nature."[76] By some accounts the son of Helios, from the Hellenistic period onward he was assimilated with a variety of traditional gods including Helios and Zeus, rapidly becoming a sort of *Aion Pantheos.* This was how he entered Roman thought in the second century B.C., and there he and his Latin derivatives, Saeculum and Aeternitas, were perceived as harbingers of a golden age. Envisaged as world governor, creator of natural phenomena, he was increasingly linked with the emperor's person and appeared on coins at times of accession, most notably in the Antonine period.[77] Often found in Mithraic contexts, he was not exclusively appropriated by one mystery cult but gave form to a general concept of eternity that was the focus of increasing interest as religious and philosophical thought became more cosmologically oriented.[78]

Aion was pictured in at least three guises in antiquity, reflecting the multiplicity of ideas he expressed in Greco-Roman thought and religion. Sometimes an aged bearded figure, in the second century A.C. he was a clean-shaven youth with a zodiac circle or wheel, usually accompanied by personified Seasons, representing Time Eternal that renews itself periodically and announcing the arrival of the golden age. On a Hadrianic or Antonine mosaic from the Isola Sacra Necropolis, for instance, he sits upon a rock, nude, holding a zodiac wheel through which the seasons are passing.[79] On a relief from Modena he is a nude, winged, and animal-hoofed youth entwined in a serpent's coils and holding a flame and scepter, standing inside a zodiac wheel, with busts of winds at the four corners. Here he resembles the Aion known to Mithrasts, an awe-inspiring, sometimes lion-headed figure with a snake coiled around him and zodiac signs around his person (fig. 75).[80]

The personification on the Antonine pedestal differs from other representations of Aion in that his attribute, the zodiac, takes the form of a globe, not a wheel. Indeed, the presence of a globe suggests that two iconographical traditions have merged in this relief in a form of visual shorthand. The globe alone,

Figure 75. Modena Relief, showing Aion, second century A.C. Photo: Deutsches Archäologisches Institut, Rom-InstNegNr 56-1391

even when stripped of cosmic symbols, had long been a sign of imperium or authority, as can be seen on Augustan capricorn coins and on the reverse of a bronze coin of 98 showing a globe and a rudder signifying Nerva's rule over land and sea (fig. 76). A legend describing Nerva as Augustus Restored, *Augustus Restitutus,* and an inscribed bust of Divus Augustus on the obverse indicate the origin of Nerva's imperial charisma.[81] In a more developed iconographical scheme found on accession issues beginning with Titus and on through the second century, the handing over or *traditio* of a globe symbolized investiture, and

Figure 76. Denarius showing a globe and a rudder, 98. Photo: Courtesy of the American Numismatic Society, New York

the donor represented the source of or claim to authority, chosen presumably according to propagandistic necessity. Thus Titus, receiving the globe from a personified *Providentia,* celebrates Vespasian's foresight in entrusting power to a worthy successor; anxious to be reconciled with the Senate, Nerva and Trajan portray it as bestower of power.[82]

The result of the iconographical fusion on the Antonine pedestal is a succinct visual statement. After cremation, Antoninus Pius and Faustina are transported to a place among the gods, thus providing Antoninus's heirs with the requisite divine parents. Upon dying, the emperor relinquishes his earthly power to Aion, Eternity, in the latter's capacity as cosmic deity and agent of the cosmocrator, keeper of terrestrial authority. In accordance with iconographical convention, Aion's identity justified the new emperors' claim to imperium; that is, the eternal nature of the ruling family authorizes their continuing rule, just as an imperial eternity had justified Julio-Claudian rule a century before. Pisces, the first sign on the globe's zodiac band, was the sign under which Antoninus Pius died and his heirs acceded to the throne, and together the three zodiac signs were the signs that Manilius used to designate spring.[83] Thus the symbols denote his death and a springlike regeneration of his authority in his sons, to whom Aion prepares to pass on the globe.

If this is a valid reading of the relief, it requires not only a transmitter of power, but also a recipient, and nowhere is there an explicit indication of who this might be. Yet, since accession is not the main subject but an implicit theme of the panel, an intimation might be sought in less obvious markers, and herein might lie the purpose of the monument's inherent duality. Not only are there two almost identical *decursio* scenes on east and west sides of the base, but in addition on the apotheosis relief two (tautologous) eagles accompany the imperial couple heavenward, and Roma sports an unusual shield device depicting the twin brothers Romulus and Remus suckled by the she-wolf (fig. 77).[84] As scholars have often noted, there is even a remarkable duality in sculptural style on the base: the apotheosis relief is carved in a classical style, while the decursio reliefs are closer to nonelite, Eastern, or late antique art.[85] Though the duality can be justified in various ways, the monument's importance lay not so much in its account of historical events (as there is little on the monument that is historical fact rather than symbol);[86] rather, the insistent duality appears to be a reference to the recipients of imperial authority following Antoninus Pius's death, his adoptive sons, Marcus Aurelius and Lucius Verus. They were remarkable precisely for being two, since Rome had been accustomed to a single ruler for almost two centuries. The decision to divide imperial power was made not by Antoninus Pius, who had primed Marcus Aurelius to be sole successor and recommended him as such on his deathbed, but by Marcus Aurelius and Lucius Verus shortly before they commissioned this monument, and they proclaimed their fraternal harmony widely on their accession coins and repeatedly thereafter.[87] As a whole, the Column base proclaims them Antoninus Pius's sons and rightful heirs to the imperial throne, spelling out in full the word FILII in the

Figure 77. Column of Antoninus Pius, detail of the apotheosis relief showing Romulus and Remus on Roma's shield, Rome, 161. Photo: Penelope J. E. Davies

inscription, rather than using the customary abbreviation, "F." Their right to rule is predicated upon Antoninus's divine status, signified by the statue on top of the shaft, to which he ascends in the apotheosis relief. The inscription as a whole makes the point clear in the positioning of DIVO at the beginning of the first line and FILII at the end of the last, the two most emphatic positions in a Latin sentence.

Cosmic allusions in the architecture and sculptural decoration of imperial funerary monuments align the emperor with the powers that regulate the universe and, specifically, with the sun-god. This association can be found in literature as well as in other art forms, where it has a panegyrical function or an absolutist significance. However, the allusions have a special meaning in a funerary context, where they create an image of eternity connected to the imperial family for the purpose of facilitating dynastic succession. In Chapter 2, I argued that the emperor's successors found legitimation in their divine parentage. This analysis of cosmic images reveals that, in their design, imperial funerary monuments – subtlely – made an even more audacious claim: the heir, son of a god, was tantamount to a god incarnate.

4

FIRE, FERTILITY, FICTION: THE ROLE OF THE EMPRESS

IN THE LAST two chapters, I proposed that in the design of their funerary monuments Roman emperors advertised their dynastic aspirations. The monuments, I argued, were not just funerary monuments but had a second role too, as accession monuments for the heir to the throne. Through the monument's design and decoration the emperor or his heir suggested that the emperor's death entailed a change of status from mortal to immortal and carefully implied his regeneration in his successor, imbued with the divine charisma that promised. This chapter takes as its starting point the surprising appearance of Faustina the Elder on the apotheosis relief on the Column base of Antoninus Pius, where she rises up to heaven on the back of a winged figure along with her husband (fig. 33). The image expresses the notion that upon dying and being publicly cremated on the Campus Martius the imperial couple experienced deification. It is remarkable for at least two reasons. First, by the time of the Column's construction, the empress had been dead for twenty years. Second, even though she is not named in the inscription, it is she, not Antoninus Pius, who is depicted at the center of the upper half of the relief. Why is her presence so crucial to this panel?

The image serves as a reminder that in some cases these funerary monuments were not just dedicated to the emperor but to his wife as well. This chapter explores how and why empresses were honored on commemorative monuments. I begin by tracing patterns of imperial female commemoration in Rome's visual record before focusing on three well-known sculptural reliefs to read as texts for such qualities as composition, syntax, and characterization. I make three simple points: (1) I contend (as others also have) that the empress's image is deployed primarily to suggest fertility; (2) I then comment on her prominence in these reliefs, in response to a tacit but still fairly widespread characterization of a Roman woman's role as a private one, the antithesis of her husband's role in the public domain; (3) I conclude that the empress's role (and the role of an ideal woman), as it is described in these reliefs, was a public one, upon which the very well-being of the state depended, especially at times of potential dynastic shift.

PATTERNS OF COMMEMORATION

In 29, fifteen years after Augustus's demise, Livia, the dowager empress, died at the age of eighty-seven. An arch was voted in her name (though never built), and her ashes were deposited in the Mausoleum of Augustus – probably, to judge by Livilla's alabaster urn in the Vatican Museums, inside a cinerary urn of some magnificence.[1] Even though it was a dynastic monument in which her burial could be anticipated, the tomb appears not to have recorded her memory in any way in its external form and decoration (or anyone else's except Augustus's), except, perhaps, in an inscription to one side of the entrance. Yet the Ara Pacis's intimate association with the Mausoleum tied it and its dynastic frieze closely to the tomb's commemorative role, recording those who would be buried in the Mausoleum and yet were not represented on the tomb itself.[2] Livia appears a little over halfway from the west end of the south processional frieze, and amid the crowd scholars also identify Antonia the Younger and Antonia the Elder, Julias the Elder and Younger, and Octavia (fig. 78).[3] The dedication of the Altar on Livia's birthday, January 30, went a long way toward suggesting that it would especially commemorate her,[4] for Romans honored the dead with sacrifices on their birthdays as well as the anniversaries of their death; the annual sacrifices at the Ara Pacis, depicted on the altar's small frieze, doubled as perpetual sacrifices to Livia.

Caligula's fourth wife, Milonia Caesonia, was ignominiously murdered by a centurion at the time of the emperor's assassination on 24 January 41.[5] Yet during his lifetime Caligula effected a significant change in the level of posthumous commemoration for female members of the imperial family. As new emperor in 37, one of his first acts was to brave stormy seas to retrieve his mother's ashes; Agrippina the Elder had starved to death in exile on the island of Pandateria in 33. With great pomp and circumstance he brought her remains to Rome for burial in Augustus's Mausoleum. He granted her the honor of having her image carried at the circus games in the *carpentum* (a covered wagon traditionally reserved for priestesses) and even struck coins featuring her portrait and full titles.[6] As for his sister, Drusilla, on Augustus's birthday in 38, the year of her death, she became the first Roman woman to be deified. Caligula entered into extravagant mourning, still within the bounds of Roman custom but on a scale unprecedented for a woman of such little political importance. Honors included an arch, a shrine attended by twenty male and female priests, and a statue in the Temple of Venus Genetrix in Julius Caesar's Forum.[7] After such extravagance, Livia's deification by Claudius's approval in 41, and the placement of her statue alongside the cult image in the Temple of Divus Augustus, must have seemed eminently appropriate.[8] Claudius's last wife, Agrippina, died at the hands of her son Nero's freedman, Anicetus, in Baiae, and her corpse was treated with less than filial respect (Suetonius recounts that Nero examined it and commented on its good and bad qualities between drinks).[9] Not so Nero's wife, Poppaea, who was deified in 65 after purportedly dying from a kick in the stomach from

Nero; she also received a shrine, inscribed to Sabina Poppaea, the Goddess Venus.[10] Vespasian's wife, Flavia Domitilla, mother of Titus and Domitian and a daughter with her own name, died before Vespasian became emperor; an inscription places the disposal of her remains near if not in Augustus's Mausoleum.[11] Less is known of Titus's second wife, Marcia Furnilla, whom he divorced in about 64, but their only child, Julia, was laid to rest in the Temple of the Flavian Dynasty;[12] judging by the fragmentary extant sculpture, she received no visual commemoration outside the tomb. Domitian's wife, Domitia Longina, lived long after her part in Domitian's assassination; when she died, between 126 and 140, one of her freedmen, Gnaeus Domitius Polycarpus, and his wife, Domitia Europe, dedicated a temple to her and her family in Gabii.[13]

The evidence weighs more heavily in the second century. After bestowing substantial funerary honors on his mother-in-law, Matidia, for instance, and deifying her in 119, Hadrian issued coins advertising her divine status.[14] He also commissioned an altar and a temple in her name on the Campus Martius, prestigious in location and large enough to vie with the later Hadrianeum. Basilicas attached to the temple commemorated Matidia and her mother, Trajan's sister, Diva Marciana, who had died in 112.[15] At Hadrian's instigation, moreover, the magnificent temple to Divine Trajan in Trajan's Forum was rededicated to include Trajan's wife, Plotina, after her apotheosis in 121/2; the temple he com-

Figure 78. Ara Pacis, south procession relief, Rome, 13–9 B.C. Photo: Michael Larvey

missioned in her honor at Nemausus (Nîmes) was probably also occasioned by her death. Coins honored her as Diva Augusta in 128.[16]

When his own wife, Sabina, died in 136/7, Hadrian erected a monumental altar in her honor, probably on the northern Campus Martius, to which a large marble relief panel, now in the Museo del Palazzo dei Conservatori, may have belonged (fig. 79).[17] In the relief a winged female figure, normally identified as *Aeternitas* (Eternity), soars aloft with the empress on her back.[18] Her torch and right leg create a diagonal division separating celestial from terrestrial space; a seated image of Hadrian dominates the latter with a standing man in attendance, and in the left corner reclines a seminude male figure, perhaps a personification of the Campus Martius, where the consecration took place. An accompanying panel of similar dimensions depicts Hadrian, mounted on a rostrum, reading from a scroll to two men and a child in front of a temple (fig. 80). Behind him are the Genius of the Senate and two attendants. Although this scene has long been identified as Hadrian's eulogy for Sabina or his declaration of her apotheosis, comparison with similar reliefs featuring children has led Eugenio La Rocca to reinterpret it as an *institutio alimentaria,* a public distribution of largesse.[19] Both panels were moved in late antiquity to the so-called Arco di Portogallo, spanning the Via Lata.[20]

Figure 79. Apotheosis of Sabina relief, Rome, 136–38, Museo del Palazzo dei Conservatori. Photo: Deutsches Archäologisches Institut, Rom-InstNegNr 1929.283.

Upon the completion of Hadrian's Mausoleum, after Hadrian's own death, Sabina's ashes were deposited there. As on Augustus's tomb, marble plaques affixed to the Mausoleum's podium commemorated those buried inside, including Sabina and other women of the imperial family, detailing their family ties and offices.[21] Sabina, however, occupied a privileged place, for when Antoninus

Figure 80. Hadrian's distribution of largesse relief, Rome, 136–38. Museo del Palazzo dei Conservatori. Photo: Deutsches Archäologisches Institut, Rom-InstNegNr 54.41

Pius dutifully completed the tomb for his adoptive father, he placed a dedicatory inscription above the entrance:

IMP. CAESARI DIVI TRAIANI PARTHICI FILIO DIVI NERVAE NEPOTI TRAIANO HADRIANO AUGUSTO PONT. MAX. TRIB. POT. XXII IMP. II COS. III P. P. ET DIVAE SABINAE IMP. CAESAR T. AELIUS HADRIANUS ANTONINUS AUG. PIUS PONTIFEX MAX. TRIBUN. POTEST. II COS. II DESIGN. III P. P. PARENTIBUS SUIS

(Imperator Caesar Titus Aelius Hadrian Antoninus Augustus Pius, Pontifex Maximus, twice holder of tribunician power, twice consul, three times consul designate, Father of his Country, [dedicates this] to his parents, Imperator Caesar Hadrian Augustus, son of Divine Trajan Parthicus, grandson of

Figure 81. Bronze peacock from Hadrian's Mausoleum, Rome, ca. 125–39, Musei Vaticani. Photo: Penelope J. E. Davies

Divine Nerva, Pontifex Maximus, with tribunician power twenty-two times, imperator twice, consul three times, Father of his Country, and the Divine Sabina).[22]

The year was 139; Sabina had already been deified and was termed *diva,* but the Senate had yet to decide on Hadrian's posthumous fate, and the title *divus* was conspicuously lacking from his nomenclature; as a result, in the inscription the empress enjoyed a higher status than the emperor.[23] Moreover travertine posts supporting the fence around the tomb bore bronze dolphins and peacocks, two of which are still preserved (fig. 81).[24] Since Romans conceived of the peacock as the primary vehicle for female apotheosis, the sculptures may have referred to the empress buried inside the tomb in her new divine status, just as numismatic images of her ascension to heaven seated on a peacock or an eagle celebrated her consecration.[25]

When Antoninus's wife, Faustina, died in 140/1, he established a charity in her name for young girls from the Italian countryside, the *puellae faustinianae,* and commemorated the institution on coins with reverse types showing the imperial couple on a dais receiving children.[26] He also erected a temple to the new *diva* in one of the most frequented and tradition-bound parts of the city, the Roman Forum, and commemorated it on gold, silver, and bronze coins. Impressive as the temple was, it would later suffice for his own cult as well.[27] Twenty years later, by Marcus Aurelius's and Lucius Verus's choice, she appeared in the relief with which we began. Faustina the Younger, for her part, was also honored with the institution of the *puellae faustinianae* when she died in 175 on the Eastern front with her husband, and her apotheosis was commemorated on coins.[28]

A brief examination of the types of commemoration afforded empresses yields an interesting pattern of ebbs and flows. Naturally accidents of survival may drastically affect the picture; we have no way of knowing, for instance, if the shrine of Poppaea outshone all earlier such buildings, or whether sculptural reliefs every bit as impressive as Sabina's embellished Matidia's altar. This caution aside, one might attempt to make some sense of the pattern as it appears.

A MIRROR OF POWER?

To be sure, it was a long established Roman custom to honor a deceased wife, as countless cinerary urns and inscriptions attest. This being so, what determined the extent of honors in the case of the imperial family?

Perhaps the honors reflect the emperor's genuine affection for his female relatives. This might explain Livia's prominence: literary sources describe a harmonious and mutually respectful relationship between her and Augustus, although his initial attraction to the beautiful (and married) Livia Drusilla was probably strategic. Livia accompanied her husband to the theater and on his travels, and patiently overlooked his sexual transgressions.[29] By all accounts, Caligula *was* unusually fond of Drusilla, and there is little cause to doubt the genuineness of his grief. Affection might also explain the respect Antoninus paid to Faustina's memory, since literary evidence suggests that theirs was a harmonious union.[30] Yet although Hadrian expressed personal grief at losing his mother-in-law Matidia in his oration at her funeral,[31] affection is hardly the emotion that characterized his relationship with Sabina. Admittedly, she did journey with him throughout the empire, but he was apparently more charmed by the attentions of Antinous, the young Bithynian upon whose death he openly wept "like a woman."[32] Gossips whispered that "He would have dismissed his wife too, for being morose and bitter – if he had been a private citizen," and when she died, it was "not without a rumour that she was killed by poison administered by Hadrian."[33]

A second possible explanation for the honors paid to an empress upon her demise is that the empress's visibility at specific moments reflects a commensurate increase in female power in elite circles; that is, the empress was more visible in commemorative relief sculpture at precisely those moments when she was more conspicuous in actuality. Again, this works for Livia, whose power and influence, both constitutional and otherwise, were far-reaching. In 35 B.C., both she and Octavia received financial independence and, more remarkably, tribunician sacrosanctity, a status usually reserved for select magistracies, which provided that anyone who did violence to the holder became an outlaw who could be slain.[34] In A.D. 9, Livia and other imperial women received the right to inherit beyond the stringent limits set out by the *lex Voconia* of 169 B.C., and she was bequeathed huge properties in Asia Minor, Gaul, and Palestine as well as many parts of Italy. Using her wealth freely on ambitious building projects in Rome, she also engaged in a wide variety of philanthropic activities.[35] She received senators in her house, rode in the prestigious *carpentum,* counseled Augustus on political decisions, and by some accounts her influence over him was such that she even obtained a pardon for Cornelius Cinna when he plotted against Augustus in 16–13 B.C. Indeed, Cassius Dio's humorous anecdote of an incident in the Senate house speaks volumes about Livia's freedom of rein: Augustus states, " 'You yourselves should guide and command your wives as you judge fit; that is what I do with mine.' On hearing this, [the senators] pressed Augustus still more eagerly, wanting to know what guidance he professed to give Livia. Though unwilling, Augustus uttered a few words about women's dress, their other ornaments, their going out and their modesty, quite untroubled by the fact that his words in no way conformed to his actions."[36]

This explanation, the visual record as a mirror of power, might also work for Hadrian's rededication of Trajan's temple to include Plotina and the temple at Nemausus; if we can believe the literary sources, she advised Trajan in matters of policy, manipulated Hadrian's succession to the throne by arranging his promotion to influential military posts and his marriage to Sabina, and maybe more besides: "There are those who have reported that Hadrian was adopted through Plotina's agency when Trajan was already dead; and that a substitute spoke on Trajan's behalf in a tired voice."[37] Yet we have noted that this was clearly not the case for Drusilla; nor is it alone a sufficient explanation for later in the second century, when empress commemoration became more common and more direct. Mary T. Boatwright has shown that there is no second-century evidence for the kind of financial independence exhibited by Livia, or for huge inheritances by empresses; she also notes a general absence of spectacularly generous acts on the part of Trajanic and Hadrianic women.[38]

AN IMAGE OF FERTILITY

Assuredly each of these motives was at work in some measure at different times. Yet a more powerful explanation for the patterns of empress commemoration in the first and second centuries may lie in perceiving the empress's image not so much as an index of affection or power, but as a symbol of fertility, in an age when "to conceive was not guaranteed, to miscarry was all too frequent, to die in childbirth was a high probability, and the survival of infants with or without their mothers was a cause for real rejoicing."[39]

A close examination of the empress's representation on the Ara Pacis, the Sabina relief, and the Column base of Antoninus Pius reveals just how her likeness was deployed for political ends. Clad in a tunic, with her long palla drawn up over her head, Livia appears on the Ara Pacis in a restful contrapposto, her body frontal to the viewer. Just as details of dress and stance intimate an assimilation between Augustus on the south side and Aeneas on the southwest (a visual parallel, as it were, for Virgil's Aeneas-Augustus), so here subtle details suggest a similarity between Livia (and, to a lesser extent, the other imperial women) and the problematic female figure on the southeast panel, variously identified as Tellus (Earth), Italia, Pax (Peace), Venus, and Ceres (fig. 82).[40] Livia's veil, her classicizing demeanor, and the children who accompany her establish the visual analogy with the panel figure; both women, too, glance away from a viewer as if to oversee one of the children. Most scholars now believe that, rather than representing a single deity or concept, "Tellus/Italia" is deliberately multivalent, and whatever her identity, the panel's primary message is one of newfound abundance and fertility.[41] Animals, water, and a background of oversized vegetation signify this fertility, as does the figure's very portrayal: her founded forms, accentuated by transparent clinging drapery, are visually likened to the smooth round fruits in her lap. The flanking figures with their billowing drapery, the apple that one child is offering to the female figure, and her slipping drapery remind one of Venus Genetrix, bearer of children and Trojan ancestress of all Romans and especially the Julian line.[42] On the other hand, her veil (of mourning), her vegetal crown, her rocky throne, the cow and sheep, and the two infants on her lap are decidedly reminiscent of Ceres' iconography,[43] and the vegetation in her

Figure 82. Ara Pacis, Venus/Tellus/Italia relief, Rome, 13–9 B.C. Photo: Penelope J. E. Davies

hair, like the cluster of plants to her right, includes ears of wheat (for which Ceres was metonymous), symbolic of growth, as well as opium poppy capsules (*Cereale papaver*) and pomegranates, symbolic of death.[44] Goddess of agricultural and, by extension, human fertility, Ceres also played an important role at liminal moments, when rituals enacted in her honor restored an individual's or a society's normative status. A family tainted by a member's death, for instance, would sacrifice a pig, *praesentanea porca,* to Ceres in order to regain purity and reentry into unsullied society, as well as to ensure rightful inheritance.[45] In the early empire, Ceres was closely tied to the imperial family; Augustus wears her distinctive *corona spicea* in a portrait dating to the late first century B.C. or early first century A.D., now in the Vatican, to emphasize Roman prosperity through trade. The empress, for her part, was often associated with Ceres, and was assimilated to her in the visual arts more frequently than to any other divinity. Barbette Spaeth argues that this reflects both a policy of moral renewal and a concern for dynastic continuity.[46] Appropriate in a commemorative context, then, the female figure on the Ara Pacis represents birth but also death; her image implies the whole cycle of life, birth after death, regeneration.

What was the purpose of this characterization? Diana Kleiner observes that the very presence of imperial women on the Ara Pacis friezes marks an abrupt change from earlier state relief, which focused almost exclusively on adult males. She explains this shift in terms of contemporary legislation: along with imperial children, these women form a visual embodiment of Augustus's laws policing irresponsible moral and sexual behavior and encouraging marriage and child-birth among the elite.[47] As well as referring to social policies, Kleiner suggests, "women and children are included . . . for the first time because for Augustus they were symbols of his dynastic ambitions."[48] Livia's association with the end panel's figure of abundance had the subtle power to rewrite the truth – that Livia's marriage to Augustus had proven barren, to his bitter disappointment, recreating her instead as signifier of fertility and regeneration.[49] Similarly, in 9 B.C., the year of the Altar's dedication, Augustus granted Livia the privileges of a mother of three in the face of the obvious fact that she had only two children, Tiberius and Drusus, thereby blatantly proclaiming her fictive fertility.[50] Though she was not directly related to Gaius and Lucius, Augustus's heirs at the time of the Altar's construction, and though by law she did not become their adoptive mother even after their adoption by Augustus, Livia was an essential component of a composite family image upon which the monarchy's continuity depended.[51]

Livia's position in respect to other figures in the frieze strengthens this reading. Although she stands at some distance from her husband, their laurel crowns distinguish them from the crowd and associate them closely with one another (fig. 78).[52] At the west end, Augustus supervises a religious procedure of some kind;[53] behind him are members of the college of priests, lictors, and Agrippa, who had died in 12. Next to Agrippa is Livia, and other imperial family members follow behind. For Mario Torelli, Agrippa's posthumous portrait stands at the head of the imperial household or *domus,* representing him as Augustus's heir, which he was in 13 B.C.[54] I suggest an alternative reading: with their mantles drawn over their heads as *pontifices,* Augustus and Agrippa visually frame the college of priests and the lictors, separating them from the ensuing section of the frieze and defining the religious domain. It is Livia who marks a thematic division in the frieze and stands at the head of the dynastic procession, grouped, significantly, with her son Tiberius.[55] Scholars have long recognized the dynastic character of the Ara Pacis friezes; yet the disposition of the imperial figures plainly implies that dynastic succession was Livia's realm. It was her image, the rewritten reproductive female, that introduced into the "historical" relief the further dimension of the future.

Despite the fact that Sabina and Hadrian bore no sons, the empress is cast in a similar fictive role in her apotheosis relief, where the visual metaphors become more explicit. The empress appears distinctly youthful (that is, capable of child-birth), even though she was probably at least forty-eight when she died.[56] She has drawn her veil up over her head and holds one end of it out to the side with her right hand. This gesture was characteristic of *Pudicitia,* a personification of the feminine virtues of modesty, purity, and chastity who, as early as the Augustan Age, had assumed the status of a goddess linked with the imperial house in an attempt to restore respect for the institution of marriage.[57] It was also characteristic of, and probably derived from, depictions of Hera, as seen in the assembly of gods on the Parthenon frieze, with whose Roman counterpart, Juno, the empress was associated upon deification; hence Faustina's scepter on the

Antonine apotheosis relief.[58] Hera was goddess of weddings and marriage, and the gesture probably refers to the consummation of her marriage to Jupiter, described in *Iliad* 14.153–353.[69] Yet the Greeks did not characterize her as a mother or represent her with children.[59] Romans, in marked contrast, syncretized Juno with the Earth Mother to represent the power of fertility in women, to the point of considering two *numina* to be present in the household during the whole period of childbearing: the man's Genius and the woman's Juno.[61] The empress's alignment with Juno therefore expressed more than the honor of apotheosis: like Livia on the Ara Pacis, the second-century empress became a symbol of wifedom but also of fictive fertility and regeneration. By honoring her in this image, an emperor could maneuver his successors into a position of advantage; by expressing filial piety (as Caligula did to his mother, Agrippina, great granddaughter of Augustus), he could play up those ties that bound him to power.

A Public Role

One of the startling aspects of these three reliefs is the sheer force of the empress's presence. Yet, for decades, when commenting on the reliefs, scholars at best underplayed the role of women in them, and at worst ignored it. For more recent scholars, such as Natalie Kampen, the appearance of imperial women in state art represents the "publicization" of the private; that is, women belong in the private sphere, and are brought out into the public at moments of political need.[62] To account for copious epigraphical, numismatic, and literary evidence that women were, inter alia, active patrons, public benefactresses, and priestesses, and able to exert influence over their male relatives, scholars see a gray area between public and private where elite women functioned, wielding power but having no authority.[63] The testimony of these three reliefs suggests that we should not relegate normative elite female behavior to a private world as we define it. On the Ara Pacis frieze, for instance, though the roles represented for women are solely those of wife and mother, their presence is not incidental; women do not simply accompany their respective male counterparts, standing behind or to one side of them;[64] instead, they are interspersed among the men to form marital units within the larger imperial family. Moreover, within those marital groups, with the exception of Livia, the wife stands ahead of her husband in the procession. The family units differ markedly from those represented on the Greek grave reliefs upon which they may be modeled, where the wife is often seated on a delicate chair, fingering her jewelry, her veil, or a mirror, in a picture that is decidedly more suggestive of cloistered domesticity (fig. 83). In other examples, she stands behind her husband, sometimes in lower relief.[65] Significantly, all but one of the female figures are depicted either in or close to a fully frontal position, even including the young daughter of Antonia the Elder and L. Domitius Ahenobarbus, an emphatic compositional device for establishing hierarchy that is more fully

Figure 83. Attic Funerary Stele, National Museum of Athens 3472. Photo: Hirmer Fotoarchiv, Hirmer Verlag München, Archiv-Nr 561.0443

exploited later in state art.[66] Moreover, as we have seen, both Augustus and Livia are identified with figures of the same sex on the end panels, embodying the proper conduct that will restore Rome's greatness, maintain the Pax Augusta, and ensure the dynasty's continuity: Augustus/Aeneas, by religious piety; Livia/ Venus-Ceres–and so on, by attention to procreation. Kleiner even characterizes the two ends of the altar as masculine (west) and feminine (east), signifying the masculine and feminine domains: the former defined as religious piety and, where needed, warfare (Mars, northwest panel); the latter as procreation and the maintenance of a Rome at peace (Roma seated on a pile of weapons, northeast panel).[67] This is exactly the division of responsibility according to gender that Horace outlines in *Odes* 3.6 for the public good. In short, the portrayal of women on the Ara Pacis suggests that the roles of wife and mother carry as much public weight as male roles, and that the existing distinction is simply one between female and male realms not starkly defined as private and public.[68]

Compositional choices in the Sabina relief render the empress's presence dramatically powerful there as well. In its present condition, the panel seems to privilege Hadrian's image over Sabina's, as the terrestrial zone is larger than the celestial, and Sabina is depicted on a smaller scale than the other figures. Yet judging by the differentiation in scale between the imperial couple and other figures on the Antonine apotheosis relief, it would seem that this device denoted distance rather than lesser status. The Sabina relief's present appearance differs from its original design in at least one important way. As part of an extensive restoration of both panels from the Arco di Portogallo in the seventeenth century, heavy marble frames were added around the slight Roman frames, which had incurred damage over time (fig. 84).[69] On the apotheosis panel, the modern frame effects a misleading visual distortion. In the second century, when the panel stood in its intended outdoor location, the sun provided a powerful overhead source of light. The panel's present location in the Palazzo dei Conservatori, by contrast, is relatively dark; and when photographers light the panel in such a way as to simulate the sun's effect, the heavy modern frame casts Sabina into a gloomy shadow that, given the small celestial space and her reduced scale, renders her all but invisible. In antiquity, her head broke the boundary of the lighter frame, and the strong overhead light, reflected back up by the deeply cut wings of Aeternitas, must have cast the empress into a celestial radiance appropriate for one experiencing apotheosis. Seen in this light, the balance of the scene changes: Hadrian is no longer the main focus, and the two imperial figures bear similar weight.

Similarly, Faustina the Elder occupies an emphatic position on the apotheosis relief. It is she, not the more recently deceased emperor, who sits at the center of the celestial zone, and a set of diagonal lines in the composition direct the viewer's gaze to her: she is positioned almost exactly in the center of the angle defined by Antoninus's scepter and the bold line of Aion's left wing and body, while Antoninus is framed in the angle of the obelisk and Aion's body.

The construction of these reliefs strongly suggests that the fertility and reproduction of which these women were symbolic were vital to the public good; that is, even though women's images were manipulated for propagandistic ends (as were men's), nevertheless, a designation of a male–female polarity in terms of the public and private is misleading; by tracing the "publicization" of the private

Figure 84. Apotheosis of Sabina relief, drawing by E. La Rocca showing restorations. By permission of Eugenio La Rocca

at moments of political need, scholars merely show that what they have characterized as private has a critical public role of its own.

THE EMPRESS IS DEAD, LONG LIVE THE EMPEROR!

Childless as she may have been, then, the empress could be recreated as an image of fertility and regeneration. This fact exposes the relatively high incidence of her representation in commemorative art and the uneven distribution of her image over the years as the results of a political strategy. As the previous chapters have discussed, it was precisely at the moment of the emperor's death, or when he made unequivocal reference to his mortality (as Augustus did by building a Mausoleum when still young), that the monarchy's safety was jeopardized. In this context, it was crucial to counteract potential political instability with images that somehow conveyed the notion of regeneration and, if possible, the emperor's quasi reincarnation in his descendants. Although each case is different, the images discussed in this chapter belong to periods when dynastic continuity could *not* be taken for granted, when the reigning or recently deceased emperor's heir was not immediately apparent: that is, the heir was not his biological son. Augustus, first emperor, author of a new monarchy, hoped that his nephew Marcellus would succeed him or provide him with an heir; in 23 B.C. Marcellus died. Enter Agrippa; when he died in 12 B.C., Augustus adopted his grandsons, Gaius and Lucius Caesar, as his own sons. Livia's characterization as a figure of fertility in 13–9 B.C. reflects Augustus's preoccupation with having no real son to appoint as heir. This concern was to plague him long after the Mausoleum's and the Altar's construction, as evidenced by his requiring Tiberius to adopt Germanicus (who nevertheless died before Tiberius in 19) in an attempt to guarantee succession through two generations.[70]

Similarly, over a century later, when Trajan died, Hadrian was anxious to ride the wave of his popularity and avoid the fate of many late-first-century rulers. Yet he was not Trajan's biological son, and recognized that suspicious rumors fast circulating about the circumstances of his adoption could discredit him in the eyes of the army and the Senate.[71] In response, he took propagandistic measures to strengthen his ties to his adoptive father, reinforcing his legitimacy with symbols of regeneration and resurrection, as discussed in Chapter 3. His public honorification of the women who bound him to Trajan – Matidia and Marciana – can be explained as just such a legitimizing device: by divinizing these female relatives, Hadrian took full advantage of a woman's potential to transmit family prestige both to her children and to her husband even in a patrilineal society. He thereby maintained the fiction of dynastic continuity and legitimized his rule.[72] When Plotina died in 121/2, her commemoration alongside Trajan in his temple established the late imperial couple in an idealized family image, and Hadrian as their dutiful son by his public devotion to their memory, an image that he reinforced by issuing coins with Divus Traianus on the obverse and Diva Plotina on the reverse.[73] When, in turn, Hadrian came to consider his own succession, he maneuvered vigorously to secure his dynasty through two consecutive generations. On Sabina's death, he took the opportunity to use her image in the apotheosis relief, attended by a pious husband, to propagate precisely the harmonious family image that, though fictitious, would promote his adoptive heir, Antoninus Pius, as his son.

Coming full circle to the Antonine Column base, a dual role as memorial and accession monument is now readily apparent. As we have seen, on his deathbed, Antoninus had entrusted the empire to Marcus Aurelius, whom he had primed as sole ruler. The subsequent (and dramatic) decision to divide imperial rule was made by Marcus Aurelius and Lucius Verus, neither of whom was Antoninus's real son. In the apotheosis relief, Aion takes the globe of imperial authority and prepares to pass it on to the new rulers, whose choice of joint rulership is implicit in the inscription and resonates in the monument's inherent duality. Faustina's appearance, with Juno's scepter, makes perfect sense: as signifier of family continuity through female fertility, her image was the essential dynastic link between the deceased Antoninus Pius and his successors, named in the inscription as FILII. That she was not their real mother was not important: emphasis on the empress's presence completed the fictive family unit.[74]

The empress's appearance in a commemorative context, then, rounded out a family image that reinforced the message of dynastic regeneration. As a symbol of fertility, she was central to imperial propaganda, guardian of the monarchy's future, who ensured that kingship did not die with the passing of the king. She did not need to be the heir's real mother to signify dynastic motherhood; on the contrary, the force of her image was mustered especially to promote *adoptive* ties by establishing a *fictive* family. The empress is dead – long live the emperor!

5

THE DYNAMICS OF FORM

For Romans, as countless ancient authors attest, remembrance by the living after death was no small concern.[1] In man's memory lay a form of immortality, even if the deceased did not participate in it actively. For a society whose beliefs about an afterlife were pessimistic if admittedly uncertain, this form of immortality may have offered the possibility of greater permanence than any gilded promise of a hereafter, and for many the most obvious way to construct a living memory was through a funerary monument. Thus, in Petronius's *Satyricon,* the arriviste Trimalchio, casting about for lighthearted dinner conversation, decides upon the design of his tomb, which he discusses with his friend and monumental mason, Habinnas. He concludes, "And, thanks to you, I'll be able to live on after my death."[2] Yet how exactly did a tomb function to promote perpetuation through memory? In this chapter, I argue that a phenomenological reading of the imperial funerary monuments reveals a concern to manipulate visitors both mentally and physically in the service of this aim.

A tomb may be monumental and unusual, but it acquires meaning only through those who look at it; it may speak, but it is always dependent on the passerby to read it aloud,[3] and it is in the glance or the voice of the living that perpetuation through memory lies. Disinterest or neglect means a true "death" for the deceased, for he or she no longer lives on in the minds of the living. Well aware of this, Romans often sought highly frequented locations for their sepulchers (such as the plot of land Eurysaces chose in the fork between two main arteries into Rome [fig. 85], the Via Labicana and the Via Praenestina,[4] or the spot Cicero selected for his daughter's tomb)[5] to ensure companionship and remembrance for the dead. Rites at the tomb, as well as its upkeep, were the oldest and most important ways of perpetuating memory, and Romans often made provisions to ensure that both would be maintained. Sometimes the tomb complex would include a garden, partly to encourage visitors to take their leisure nearby, and often to grow grapes for offerings of wine or fruit in order to raise money for the tomb's upkeep.[6] Frequently, moreover, the will would name the heir responsible for maintaining the tomb and allocate funds for the observance of rituals; Keith Hopkins draws attention, for instance, to a small-town ragman who left enough money for twelve fellow guild members to dine once a year at

Figure 85. Tomb of Eurysaces, Rome, late first century B.C., actual state. Photo: Alinari/Art Resource, New York, AN520

his tomb;[7] another man left a sum of money to a college of naval engineers so that they could celebrate annual festivals at his tomb.[8] As a rule, rites took place at a funerary monument on personal anniversaries and during the *dies Parentales* (or *Ferales*), also termed the *Parentalia* (13–21 February), when family and friends would visit the tomb with offerings of grain, salt, wine-soaked bread, and violets, and dine by the grave.[9] But how much better if the deceased could somehow be assured of daily attention from passersby! This issue, it seems, was one that tomb designers knowingly grappled with; as I argue below, they labored to exploit sculptural and architectural forms to reach out to those who had *not* come specifically to visit, but were merely passing by.

In pursuit of memory perpetuation, many Romans endeavored to engage a passerby through their tomb's design. Pleas for attention from the living exist, for instance, in epigraphy. Like an example from Ostia ("Be aware, traveler, that your voice is really mine"), epitaphs could be designed to be read aloud and, in quasi-magical fashion, to perpetuate the deceased through the spoken words of the living.[10] Besides encouraging speech, however, the tomb's design might effectively secure a visitor's attention by requiring his or her interaction with the monument, on either a cognitive-affective or a physical level. Intricate sculptural decoration of any kind, be it vegetal or figural, could evoke interest from a beholder, engaging his attention as it forced his eye to roam over cuts in the stone and experience lively movements of light and shadow, especially during nocturnal rites by the light of flickering lamps.[11] Figural decoration reliably piqued a viewer's curiosity; some, like Eurysaces the baker or the Haterii, provided a visual *res gestae,* or record of things achieved, for the viewer's entertainment, thus

Figure 86. Tomb of a wine merchant from Neumagen, Rheinisches Landesmuseum Trier. Photo: Rheinisches Landesmuseum Trier Foto-Nr. RD 56.47

perpetuating interest in their lives.[12] In the case of others (like, again, Eurysaces, or a Roman wine merchant from Neumagen, Germany, whose tomb is surmounted by a stone model of Moselle riverboats laden with casks of wine [fig. 86]),[13] the monument itself might be a huge sculpture denoting an aspect of their lives. This made it curious to behold, an invitation to interest. Freed persons of the Late Republican and Augustan periods used sculpture to address a passerby more directly still; groups of shoulder-length truncated busts, surrounded by a long, rectangular frame mounted windowlike on a roadside monument,[14] peered out, engaging passersby eye-to-eye with their frontal gaze, eerily reversing the usual hierarchy between viewer and viewed, living and dead, and forcing interest in their lives (fig. 87).

On a grander scale, however, an architect might choose to control a visitor's physical movement through a monument's architectonic design, thus bringing

Figure 87. Funerary relief of the Furii, Rome, 13 B.C.–A.D. 5, Musei Vaticani. Photo: Musei Vaticani Archivio Fotografico Neg. N. XXXIV.34.37

"life" to the sepulcher and promoting active memory perpetuation. An example of this might be the *exedra* monument, such as those of Cerrinius Restitutus, Aulus Veius, and Mamia on the Street of the Tombs outside the Herculanean Gate at Pompeii (fig. 88). This monument type consisted of a bench or vaulted niche lined with seats,[15] providing a resting place for a weary traveler to or from the city – on the unspoken condition that the visitor read the name of the deceased, featured prominently in the design; like the philosophers for whom such exedrae might be a meeting place, they might then contemplate man's fate and the life of the deceased. Accommodating for funerary banquets in honor of the dead, these monuments would entice banqueters to linger in the company of the deceased.

In the following pages, I argue that the architects of the imperial funerary monuments, likewise, appreciated the power of dynamics in architecture and sculpture, and learned to exploit its potential with increasing success, not only to engage a viewer, but also to draw him into a perpetual reenactment of funerary rituals.

Augustus's Mausoleum complex offers a ready example of cognitive manipulation through monument design. The huge Horologium functioned on a multitude of levels, but served, on the simplest, to draw a visitor into a daily dialogue with the complex. Petronius articulated just how it worked: the macabre Trimalchio asks Habinnas, "Are you building my monument in the way that I told you? . . . A clock (*horologium*) in the middle, so that anyone who looks at the time, whether he likes it or not, reads my name. . . ."[16] By offering the service

Figure 88. Exedra tomb, Pompeii. Photo: Stephen Petersen

of telling the time, Trimalchio's sundial would cast the visitor as an unwitting conspirator in Trimalchio's struggle for immortality in the minds of the living. In the same way, the incorporation of a sundial into Augustus's funerary complex ensured that, well after his death, every time anyone consulted the sundial he would, advertently or not, be reminded of its builder — and in that mental process lay Augustus's immortality. That immortality is itself alluded to in the very incorporation of the dimension of time into the tomb's design: the sundial stands as icon for the passage of time, through which Augustus's memory will survive.

Architectural design also forced a viewer's physical interaction with imperial funerary monuments, as is evidenced in the Mausolea of Augustus and Hadrian, where the architect manipulated a visitor's movement in prescribed directions. As we recall, inside the Mausoleum of Augustus, five concentric walls surrounded a central travertine pillar. Piercing the three outer walls, a vestibule led to an annular corridor between walls 3 and 2; two openings in this corridor granted access to a second annular corridor between walls 2 and 1. From this inner corridor one entered the burial chamber (fig. 5). The door in the south facade of Hadrian's Mausoleum opened into a vestibule, leading to an atrium, on the east side of which an annular corridor begins its anti-clockwise ascent through the tomb's interior. Spiraling 360 degrees, the ramp ended immediately above the vestibule, where a radial corridor led to the central burial chamber (figs. 26, 67).

In short, both imperial mausolea are circular in plan, and both incorporate annular corridors into their interior design, even though those corridors were not necessary for construction purposes.[17] For a visitor entering either mausoleum, the approach to the burial chamber is not in a straight line from the entrance; instead, he must move first through the ring corridors around the cella, in effect circumscribing the burial in the center of the tomb with his winding path. What was the purpose of such circumambulation?

An answer to this question appears to reside in magical properties that Romans, like many other people, ascribed both to the circle and to the act of circumscribing an object or person (even if the encircling action did not inscribe a perfect circle).[18] The circle's special quality could be harnessed for a variety of purposes. Often, it served to concentrate attention and power on its center, as was the case, presumably, in fertility rites ascribed by Pliny to the Phrygians and Lycaonians, who believed that the egg of a partridge or other bird, passed around (*circumductas*) a woman's breasts three times, would prevent them from sagging.[19] In his analysis of dreams, Artemidorus interprets the circle as a restrictive boundary, and indeed in the *Satyricon,* one of Trimalchio's fellow-freedmen threatens to use it for just such a purpose: he curses the young Ascyltos for laughing, and insists that if he were to urinate in a circle around him (*circumminxit*) he would prevent the boy from escaping.[21] Yet Artemidorus also sees it as a defensive device.[22] The boundary established through circular motion, then, both defined the area it enclosed and protected it; thus, according to Varro, circular movement took place during the creation of a town boundary,[22] and in the annual festivals of *amburbium* (the expiratory procession around Rome)[23] and *ambarvalia* (circumambulation of the fields).[24] The sanctity of this circular boundary was such that, according to legend, those who disrespected it might suffer deadly consequences; such indeed was the fate of Remus, who leaped over the foundation trench of Romulus's city wall in order to ridicule it.[25] In the *amburbium* and *ambarvalia,* circular movement also appears to have been conceived to effect a catharsis upon the area it enclosed, just as it did upon sacrificial victims when they were forced to circumambulate the altar before their slaughter.[26]

Circumambulation also played an important role in funerary rituals, where magic was omnipresent. Plutarch reports Varro's statement that when the living visited ancestral tombs they would "turn around" (περιστρέφονται) the graves, as they did the shrines of the gods.[27] Moreover, at a funeral, participants would circumambulate the pyre; Statius describes how seven squadrons of knights encircled the pyre of Opheltes to the left,[28] and several sources indicate that this type of ceremony was enacted with extravagant display at imperial funerals. Cassius Dio, for instance, recounts the procedure that took place during Augustus's funeral: "When the bier had been placed on the pyre in the Campus Martius, all the priests marched around it first, then came the knights, not only those who were to be senators but the others as well, and then the infantry of the Praetorian Guard circled it at a run and threw onto it all the triumphal decorations which any of them had ever received from the emperor for an act of valor."[29] Herodian describes a similar ritual during Pertinax's funeral nearly two centuries later: "When an enormous pile of these aromatic spices has been accumulated and the entire place has been filled, there is a cavalry procession around the pyre in which the whole equestrian order rides in a circle round and round in a fixed formation, following the movement and rhythm of the Pyrrhic dance. Chariots, too, circle round in the same formation, with their drivers dressed in purple-bordered togas."[30] It is this *decursio,* scholars believe, which is illustrated on the east and west sides of the base of Antoninus Pius's Column (fig. 89).[31] Moreover, Suetonius records that, after Drusus's death, the army erected a monument in his honor around which the soldiers made an annual ceremonial run; in subsequent years, in other words, the ritual *decursio* was repeated in a perpetual reenactment of the funerary ritual.[32]

It is in rituals of circumambulation of the kind described above that Windfeld-Hansen convincingly finds an explanation for the annular corridors in the imperial tombs, which accommodated encirclement of the central burial chamber by visitors before and after ingress.[33] Presumably the Mausolea were closed except at times of ritual activity, when officiating priests, family members, and those connected to the imperial house entered to pay their respects.[34] Judging by the nonfunerary examples cited above, the rituals of circumambulation that they enacted on these occasions may have been intended to confine or protect the dead inside the tomb. They may alternatively (or additionally) have been cathartic, since upon entering the tomb a visitor found himself moving dangerously between the realms

Figure 89. Column of Antoninus Pius, decursio relief, Rome, 161. Photo: Penelope J. E. Davies

of the living and the dead;[35] indeed, Statius describes the encircling action of the soldiers at Opheltes' pyre as a lustration, *lustrantque ex more sinistro orbe rogum.*[36] Perhaps, too, this rite of passage mirrored the soul's circuitous journey, as it moved, not directly from life to death, but instead through a tripartite change of state, from life to near-death and finally to death.[37] Needless to say, many an archaic ritual custom based upon principles of magic persisted long after its meaning had been lost or reinterpreted.[38] The ceremonial spectacle that took place at an imperial funeral, presumably in origin a response to and/or an expression of a concept of liminality,[39] nevertheless took on a further dimension: the cavalry's circular movement defined a central point or newel for its action and, in this way, focused attention on the pyre and the deceased leader; the *decursio* was therefore an honorific process. Inside the imperial mausolea, the visitor's circumambulation was certainly a ritualistic precaution, but it was probably also a perpetual reenactment of a gesture of piety and honor of precisely the kind that Suetonius records at Drusus's funerary monument.

In the first part of this chapter, I suggested that through both sculpture and architecture the designer of a funerary monument could manipulate a visitor, encouraging his participation in a dialogue with the monument, in order to maintain interest in its subject (and thereby perpetuate memory) as well as, in some cases, to carry on certain magical and honorific rituals. In the case of Trajan's Column, sculptural and architectural forms come together most successfully in the service of viewer manipulation, conspiring both to perpetuate Trajan's memory and to enforce reenactment of honorific rituals; at the same time, the visitor's experience of the Column was designed to culminate in a grand revelation regarding Trajan's illustrious career.

TRAJAN'S COLUMN

The Sculptural Frieze

It has often been charged that Trajan's Column's sculptural frieze, although stylistically of the highest caliber, is, in the final analysis, disappointing. In order to make sense of the narrative's continuity, scholars argue, a viewer is forced to walk around and around the column, head inclined sharply and uncomfortably upward. Richard Brilliant summarizes the problem as follows:

> Despite the grand scale of the concept and the height of the column, the numerous small figures were progressively difficult to see clearly, even if the low relief surface was once elaborately painted. Neither could they be easily comprehended from close by, because the proximity of the column to the libraries and to the Basilica Ulpia did not allow the viewer to step back sufficiently to gain a consistent, coherent perspective of the whole. Furthermore, the helical course of the relief band made it practically impossible to follow the path of the relief without losing one's place, especially as the figures became indistinct at the sides of the visual field. And it was and still is very difficult to understand the scenes in the higher elevations of the helix without undergoing the most taxing gyrations, complicated by lapses of memory, which conceal the narrative trail.[40]

Settis decries "the almost insurmountable difficulty of reading,"[41] which Lehmann-Hartleben passes off as a consequence of the design committee's disdain for the artist's wishes,[42] and Bianchi Bandinelli as the creation of an artist working only for himself.[43] Such criticisms have led to numerous readings of meaningful sequences on the main vertical axes of the shaft, in attempts to prove that a viewer did not *have* to move around the Column but could, in fact, understand its full message while standing still.[44] These studies shed valuable light upon the narrative and perceptive strategies of the frieze; yet the problematic encircling motion required of a visitor remains unexplained. How do we reconcile the outstanding quality of workmanship with such a seemingly poor design?

I believe that the solution to this problem lies in the Column's function as imperial tomb. Clearly, the encircling motion required of the viewer by the spiraling narrative cannot have taken the designer by surprise: it was a totally predictable effect that could have been abandoned at the drawing board. Moreover, if the ancients judged the Column's spiral to be disappointing, why then was it so carefully emulated in the Column of Marcus Aurelius?

The answer must be that it was not so judged, and that its effect, far from being a failure, was the desired effect, and one that its designer purposely accentuated; for not only did the narrative's format itself require a viewer to walk around the Column, but because it stood within a closed courtyard and because its sculpture was executed in relatively shallow relief, he was forced to do so in close proximity to the Column.[45] Might it be that our perception of the design is incorrect? Perhaps the idea was not first to illustrate the Dacian wars and then to find a way to fit them onto the column, but instead to create a spiral around the column (as illustrated on denarii minted between 112 and 117) and then to decorate it in such a way as to force a viewer to pursue it? Like the sculptor of Eurysaces' tomb, Trajan's master sculptor turned to a visual *res gestae* to engage the viewer, encouraging his mental interaction as he read the narrative, thereby forcing him to perpetuate Trajan's memory. Yet perhaps he also made use of decorative sculpture to promote movement in a certain direction, just as processional sculpture on monuments such as the Ara Pacis guided a viewer on a prescribed path;[46] that is, he hoped that by enticing the viewer to follow the narrative's trail, he could force him to walk around the column. When Trajan's Column is placed in its context with other imperial tombs, the reason for a manipulative frieze of this kind is readily apparent: like the annular corridors in the circular mausolea, the frieze encouraged the visitor to circumambulate the sacred burial spot, in order to commit the deceased to his resting place and to reenact and perpetuate rituals performed at the emperor's burial. Aptly, this respectful action took place before the Temple of the Divine Trajan, seat of the deceased emperor's cult. Given the Column's prominent location in one of Rome's most frequented areas, visitors would necessarily be constant and drawn from a wide cross-section of Roman society, for it was in the *Forum Traiani* that senators deposited their valuables, that lawyers tried their cases and (at least in late antiquity) learned of new laws; it was there also that large groups gathered for the emperor's *congiaria* or distribution of largesse and ex-slaves took their first steps of freedom.[47] Shoppers and merchants crossed the Forum on their way to the markets, and Rome's literati consulted books in the Bibliotheca Ulpia.[48] If the Column's design could engage them to follow the spiraling narrative, then at one and the same time their motion would perpetually honor and protect the ruler's mortal remains, after the example of Alexander the Great, who, with his companions, ran naked around Achilles' tomb near Troy before laying a crown upon the stele.[49]

When it is understood in the context of funerary monument design, the spiraling narrative of Trajan's Column is revealed to be anything but a conceptual miscalculation; rather, it was actively chosen and emphasized with the express purpose of manipulating a viewer. This dynamic quality has, for the most part, been obscured both by the Column's physical isolation from the modern viewer and by the different emphases of modern scholarship; yet recognition of this quality is of enormous consequence. When the Column is considered only as an object to be viewed, it demands nothing more from a beholder than the respect due to high-quality engineering and sculpture. When, on the other hand, it is considered as a dynamic force, it becomes an active work of architecture, encouraging and requiring the visitor's participation.

Internal Dynamics: Personal and Political Promotion

The exterior design of Trajan's Column functioned, I have argued, to perpetuate ritualistic and honorific behavior on a visitor's part. In the remainder of this chapter, I suggest that only through a similar experiential reading of the Column's interior design and its relation to surrounding buildings can we fully appreciate its intended purpose.

The most satisfactory reading of the Column's inscription indicates that its primary role was "to show how high was the mountain – the site for great works, after all – that was cleared away."[50] Just how it fulfilled this function has been the subject of no small debate. Until the early years of the twentieth century, scholars believed that Trajan's engineer, Apollodorus, had removed part of the Quirinal Hill in order to erect the Column in its present location, and that its height indicated the depth of earth removed. In 1906, however, Boni's excavations under the Column revealed Republican and early imperial strata where the supposed hillside would have been.[51] It is now thought that the Quirinal was indeed cut back, not beneath the Column but to prepare the ground for the Forum and the Markets. However, since Boni estimated the escarpment at roughly half the height of the Column, how can the Column's height have shown "how high was the mountain . . . that was cleared away"? The problem is solved when one reads the inscription in the light of the Column's dynamic function, as Amanda Claridge does: that is, if a viewer visited the Column properly, was willing to climb the spiral staircase inside the shaft and look out from its upper platform over the Forum and the place where once the Quirinal had protruded, he would, as the inscription promises, see how high a mountain had been cleared away adjacent to (but not underneath) the Column, and for what great works. The Column, in other words, was intended to function as a belvedere.[52] Its staircase, admittedly, is narrow and the platform small, and neither could have accommodated large groups from the busy forum at one time. Presumably, therefore, access to the Column's shaft was controlled; perhaps it was a privilege reserved for the powerful elite. Although a number of Trajanic coins appear to represent the doors of the base standing invitingly open (fig. 90), evidence dates mainly from late antiquity.[53] In the fourth century Constantius (or

Figure 90. Denarius showing Trajan's Column. Photo: Courtesy of the American Numismatic Society, New York

someone on his behalf) inscribed his name in the stairwell,[54] and in all likelihood Ammianus Marcellinus refers to the sculpted columns when he describes "the elevated heights which rise up, with platforms to which one can climb."[55] When, by the early fifth century, Cassiodorus commented, "The Forum of Trajan is a marvel to look upon, even after continual viewing,"[56] perhaps he meant as seen from the Column.

This adaptation of the tomb monument, from monument to be viewed to monument from which also to view, suggests that the architect was keenly aware of the potential failings of tomb architecture to engage a viewer, and equally of the power of kinetic design to overcome this problem. As we shall see, though, the solution he presented in Trajan's Column shows his ability not only to entice the privileged viewer into a dialogue but also to invest that dialogue with a powerful propagandistic content.

By the Trajanic period, Rome had its share of tall buildings; if one could gain access to their roofs, one might look out from them over the growing city. The seven hills of Rome, too, provided high points from which to survey lower ground. However, Trajan's Column was, it seems, the first public belvedere designed specifically as a viewing station.[57] What precisely was it that a visitor was supposed to see upon emerging from the Column, and why might it be important enough to merit a belvedere?

Two reasons might be suggested for the construction of a belvedere. The first, the more self-evident, was commemorative. In planning his tomb, Trajan hoped to be remembered as one of Rome's great benefactors through the magnificent forum–market complex he constructed. Architectural embellishment of a city was not an unusual means of securing a reputation, particularly in this period,[58] and memorials in the form of architectural gifts to the city had the added advantage of being assured maintenance regardless of monies set aside by the benefactor. The Column would provide a place from which a viewer could survey all that Trajan had built and, perhaps, have a reaction similar to Constantius's as it is described by Ammianus: "Indeed when he came to the Forum of Trajan, a structure that is unique beneath all of heaven, in my opinion, which even the divine gods agree is extraordinary, he stopped, astonished, while his mind took in the gigantic complex, which cannot be described by words and could never again be imitated by mortal men. Abandoning all hope of attempting anything like it, he said that he wanted – and was able – to copy only Trajan's horse, which was situated in the middle of the atrium and carried the emperor himself."[59]

It was not enough, though, that the emperor be remembered only for an architectural feat. Studies of late-first- and second-century fora throughout the empire reveal that in the Flavian period, and especially in Britain, the traditional Italic forum design, a rectangular piazza with the Capitol on a short end marking the long axis, began to give way to a square piazza with a basilica on one side.[60] These new developments appear to have influenced the design of Trajan's Forum. Yet, at the same time, as Rodenwaldt has convincingly argued, Apollodorus based its unusual layout upon the ground plan of a military camp such as the Praetorium of Vetera, in which the Column took the place of the army's standards.[61] The Romans were renowned for their swiftly constructed standardized camps, to which, Polybius implies, one might in part attribute their military success.[62] In designing the Forum as a military camp, Apollodorus intended a viewer not only to look down upon Trajan's munificence, but also to recognize his role as an accomplished general, the role that bespoke his virtue and upon which his authority, and ultimately his apotheosis, were predicated. Throughout the Forum, architecture and sculpture spoke of triumph. (For instance, the gate through which the visitor entered resembled a triumphal arch surmounted by a statuary group of a Victory crowning Trajan in a *seiugis;* and images of spoils and symbols of victory abound in the architectural sculpture.) Thus the whole Forum was characterized as a victory monument,[63] a visual form of *res gestae;* the disguise with which Trajan masked his tomb, within that Forum, was a celebration of the achievement of which he was proudest, and which would assure him immortality.

A second reason for the construction of a belvedere was that Trajan had an urgent message to impart during his lifetime. The empire he had inherited from Nerva and the Flavians was fraught with economic difficulties, partly as a result of Domitian's "rapacious devices,"[64] partly because of Nero's debasement of the currency in 64.[65] Trajan, the soldier-emperor, sought to remedy the situation through war, just as Augustus had done a century before. Many, though, perceived war differently from Trajan: they saw military activity not as a source of wealth but as an enormously costly undertaking, in terms of both manpower and money;[66] Domitian's recent wars against the Dacians, for instance, his most important foreign campaign, had not brought felicitous results[67] and must have lodged a less than optimistic conception of war in the Roman citizen's mind. Anxious to dissuade potential critics and, in particular, to appease the Senate, which met nearby, what Trajan needed to do, both to justify the wars he had already waged and to prepare for any others he planned, was demonstrate to civilian Rome the competence of the men who worked for him, so as to confirm the city's superiority in the world and fend off accusations of a needless and irresponsible waste of resources.[68] What better way to do this than to employ Apollodorus, his military engineer, to undertake an apparently impossible task ("could never again be imitated by mortal men") in the heart of Rome – to cut away the very ground upon which city-dwellers trod and erect in its place a new urban center for them? And, near the end of the Forum, what better idea than to have him (or another designer) create a powerful image of dominance, a hundred-foot column with a spiral staircase carved out of the very marble that held it up, from which a viewer could survey the Forum, designed as a symbol of army organization?[69] Trajan also needed to display as aggressively as possible the enormous quantities of booty he had won through war, sufficient to build the whole Forum *ex manubiis,* the first forum to be born of war and starkly opposed to the Flavian Templum Pacis on the other side of the Forum Transitorium.[70]

Captive Dacians in the attic of the portico recalled the influx of slave labor following the campaigns, and a richesse of colored marbles spoke of great new wealth from foreign sources. The Column towered above the Forum, a vantage point from which to experience the whole magnificent effect.

The importance of this message cannot be overestimated, for in 113, soon after dedicating the column, Trajan was to initiate another campaign, this time against the Parthians.[71] In later years, Cassius Dio was to suggest that the Parthian Wars were fought for glory, not necessity: the Parthians, he would claim, had been willing to negotiate Armenian sovereignty and were not a serious threat to Rome's eastern frontier;[72] the wars actually entailed the endurance of formidable toils and danger, the massacre of countless garrisons, and the loss of recent acquisitions in the East, all for little gain.[73] In all likelihood, while he was planning and embellishing the Forum, Trajan was also nurturing the thought of a new campaign as a means to acquire further military renown. Cassius Dio's criticisms were precisely those he must have anticipated and tried to preempt in the messages of his Forum, as he contrived to boost public support and troop morale.[74]

The subject matter of the Column's frieze played its part in expressing the required message. A comparison of the Trajanic Column with the later Aurelian imitation reveals an important characteristic of the earlier narrative: though it purports to illustrate Trajan's Dacian Wars, it contains very few actual battle scenes. Downplaying the gruesome realities of war, the Trajanic relief is made up, rather, of more peaceful themes, notably scenes of travel, construction, *adlocutio, submissio,* and sacrifice.[75] This can hardly be accidental. As suggested above, Trajan was anxious to prove the competence of his soldiers to dispel the city-dweller's resentment of the financial drain caused by war, and to display the wealth brought to Rome from foreign wars, perhaps with a view to promoting his planned Parthian campaign. Non-aggressive, constructive themes were opportunely chosen to represent his men in complete control rather than constantly pitting their strength against the Dacians. Compositional means were likewise exploited to this end: Roman soldiers struggle almost exclusively in the direction of the spiral, so a viewer inadvertently adds his movement – strength – to theirs. Meanwhile Roman calm is constantly opposed to Dacian panic,[76] and damage perpetrated against Rome is purposely minimized.[77] Sacrifice scenes periodically pepper the narrative to affirm that the campaigns were undertaken with the implied consent of the gods and with all due piety; Jupiter himself confirms this message by a sudden epiphany in scene XXIV, hurling his thunderbolt in support of the Romans, mirroring their gesture in an act of visual comradeship.[78] Scenes depicting Dacians dismantling their fortresses form an alternative means to slaughter or Dacian suicide to symbolize Roman supremacy,[79] and yet by contrasting its barbarity with the "civilization" of the Romans,[80] the designer justifies the need to tame the Dacian monster that lurks threateningly at the frontier. Moreover, none but the staunchest literalist can deny a metaphorical connection between the construction scenes on the Column (and especially the remarkable bridge over the Danube shown in scenes XCIX–C)[81] and the recently completed construction of the Forum, a connection that suggests a causal relationship between the campaigns and the resources resulting from them. The message: through the burden of war, this magnificence was made possible.

This, then, was Trajan's urgent message. Yet why did he insist on a column as belvedere? What made it so effective for his purpose? After all, he might have been content with allowing the visitor to view his works from the top of an-other great engineering feat, the market complex that now lined the Quirinal. The markets, even today, reach more or less to the height of the column and offer a spectacular view over the forum area.

Part of the reason must have been that from the top of the markets a viewer would not have seen the markets themselves so well; part also, that the column's role as belvedere encouraged visitors to mill around Trajan's tomb and temple area; but, more important, the felicitous combination of column and staircase was an exciting novelty that would enable Trajan to manipulate the visitor, to control and heighten the dramatic effect of his visual experience.[82]

From the moment a visitor stepped into Trajan's Forum through the triple archway on its southern side, he could see the column, raising Trajan's gilded statue high above and behind the Basilica Ulpia (fig. 91).[83] Indeed, his focus was directed there, since, along with the equestrian statue of Trajan and the basilica's main southern entrance, it marked the longitudinal axis of the open piazza, and the colonnades and rows of trees guided his attention to it. J. E. Packer surmises

Figure 91. Reconstruction drawing of Trajan's Forum, Rome, 100–112. From J. E. Packer, *The Forum of Trajan in Rome: A Study of the Monuments* (Berkeley, 1997). Courtesy of James E. Packer

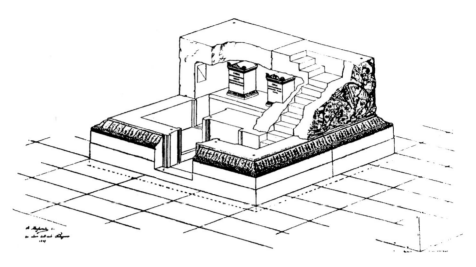

Figure 92. Reconstruction of the base of Trajan's Column, Rome, 113. From G. Boni, *Nsc* 1907, fig. 13

that as he moved through the forum the ancient viewer was "constantly surprised" by its columnar screens and hemicycles, offering shifting vistas enveloped in contrasts of light and shadow.[84] He reached the Column by passing into the basilica, where "the hemicycles and the orderly rows of columns . . . produced remote, mysterious vistas which receded into darkened interiors accented by daylight introduced from artfully concealed sources," and exiting it through the two small doors in its north wall. There, the porticoes of the basilica, the libraries, and the temple enclosed him and framed the Column as their focus. Even despite his foreknowledge of the Column's position and height, and even despite the Basilica's huge dimensions, the Column must have leapt up before him suddenly, its extreme verticality accentuated by the restricted courtyard.[85] Entering the Column through the door in its base, to his left was a passage to the chamber, sealed after 117 (fig. 92). To his right rose the helical staircase, a novelty in Trajan's time.[86] Once inside the shaft, he labored steeply upward, mindful, perhaps, of how his motion mirrored Trajan's ascent from mortal to god.[87] He climbed in a darkness alleviated only here and there by small slit windows in the thick encircling walls. Kevin Lynch notes that, in a city, a traveler's experience is heightened if the path tantalizingly reveals glimpses of other city elements, "hints and symbols of what is being passed by."[88] The Column's windows would have had a similar effect: through them small snatches of sky and cityscape were revealed, enticing to the eye, yet more disorienting in their disjointedness than useful in locating the visitor in his winding ascent.[89] The spiral staircase served, in effect, as a long, upward-leading corridor to the outside platform. As Arnheim illustrates, a corridor (like this one or those in the Mausolea of Augustus and Hadrian) creates a delaying effect that he terms "temporary retardation" in face of an ultimate goal: "Temporary retardation is known in the arts as a strong incentive toward forward movement. It is also a standard device of traditional drama, and is constantly used in music to dam the melodic flow before a new surge of power. Suspense derives from the temporary suspension of action. . . ."[90] Added to this effect, and to the general disorientation induced by circling, is the power of the spiral staircase to render the climber unable to judge either how far he has ascended or how much farther he has to go; this engenders a sense of spatial disorientation and, at the same time, anticipation. Moreover, an especially restrictive corridor such as the Column's staircase (which is only 0.74 meters wide at the base of the shaft and approximately two meters in height) contributes to the impact when the restriction is removed: "A temporary narrowing of the path can also act dynamically, by generating the tension of constriction, resolved into new expansion. There is furthermore the stimulating effect of the sudden surprise: the opening up of an unforeseen space. . . ."[91] In Trajan's Column, the "sudden surprise" was the visitor's abrupt emergence from the narrow, dark staircase into the dazzling sunlight, where he stood, blinded for a moment, surrounded on all sides by open air, released from total restriction to utter freedom.

This was the moment of revelation that the Column's designer planned as the extraordinary culmination of the viewer's experience. Harnessing all the force of that climactic moment, he engineered a chosen vista as the visitor's first sight on emerging into the light; in order to do so, he eschewed the expected, and typically classical, harmony of placing the door in relation to the lower entrance, either directly above it, due south and overlooking basilica and forum, or on the opposite side, due north, confronting the temple. Nor did he place it on the west side, to face respectfully toward the Capitol, with the Basilica Argentaria in the foreground. Instead, he located it on the east, facing out over the Quirinal;[92] there, the viewer's first sight when he emerged from the shaft was Apollodorus's remarkable and costly building feat lodged against the Quirinal where once there had been a hillside, a sight that epitomized Trajan's message to Rome, a message of competence, superiority, and enormous newfound wealth.[93]

A phenomenological reading of the funerary monuments reveals them to be purposely dynamic, designed to draw visitors into a dialogue involving them in an active process of commemoration. In particular, an experiential reading of Trajan's Column solves the problem of its spiraling frieze, unmasking the narrative as an instrument of manipulation that forced the viewer to reenact ritual and honorific procedures. Moreover, the dramatic potential of the novel combination of column and staircase is uncovered: it allowed the architect to orchestrate a viewer's experience as few other architectural forms could, creating disoriented suspense as he climbed the shaft in order, then, to create a surprising, and propagandistically loaded, climax when he emerged. Sculpture and architecture conspire in the Column to present the viewer with a dramatic propagandistic message concerning Trajan's life and afterlife. The following chapter explores a related problem: Where were the monuments located, and why?

6
∿

THE POWER OF PLACE

Here I lie by the chancel door,
They put me here because I was poor;
The further in the more you pay,
But here lie I as snug as they.[1]

THE PREVIOUS CHAPTER explored ways in which a Roman architect or sculptor might manipulate a viewer both mentally and physically through means of a monument's intrinsic design, sometimes channeling her in prescribed directions to provide selected, significant vistas. There was more that an architect could do to affect a viewer's experience of a monument, though; he could site it in such a way as to take advantage of preexisting landmarks, both natural and man-made. For the most part, such maneuvering was external to the monument's design, although in most cases design and location complemented one another.

Sites might be selected for a variety of reasons, which need not have been mutually exclusive. At perhaps the most basic level, a monument's location could greatly affect its visibility.[2] Yet an architect may also have hoped to harness the historical or social associations of a specific location. For Romans, topographical associations were extremely powerful; indeed, Piso suggests in Cicero's *De finibus* that they could be more impressive than verbal accounts of history: "Is it our nature or our fantasy, I wonder, that on seeing those places that tradition records to have been the favourite haunts of distinguished men, we are more moved than when we hear of their deeds or read something they have written?"[3] Catharine Edwards goes so far as to state: "Topography, for Romans, perhaps played a greater role than chronology in making sense of the past. Past time was conflated and places became vehicles for a kind of non-sequential history (we can have access to Romans' sense of place only through their narratives, but such narratives are often distinctive for their emphasis on the immediacy of the past as experienced through place)."[4] Such was the strength of these topographical associations that Romans used their physical surroundings as mnemonic aides; Piso continues, "Places have so forceful a power of suggestion that it is no wonder that the technical art of memory is based upon them."[5] This suggests that Romans visual memories were acute, and indeed, in the signless capital they appear to have oriented themselves through recollection of visual landmarks.[6]

Even more specifically, an architect could position a building in such a way as to conjure up a relationship with preexisting structures. Diane Favro's recent volume on the urban image of Augustan Rome gives numerous examples of alignments and juxtapositions, and shows how buildings gained prestige and meaning through these relationships. One obvious example would be Augustus's Temple of Apollo on the Palatine adjoining his own residence, which allowed him to express a subtle affiliation between himself and his patron god while at the same time avoiding direct identification.[7] Similarly, by locating his forum next to Julius Caesar's, which it openly imitated in form and function, Augustus promoted his highly publicized relationship with his adoptive father.[8] Sightlines could evoke connections between buildings and indeed played a sufficiently critical role in religious customs that in the first century B.C. the house of one Tiberius Claudius Centumalus on the Caelian had to be demolished because its height obscured the path of the auspices.[9] Advances in surveying techniques meant that relationships could be defined according to precise planimetrical calculations, and presumably the blossoming interest in cartography and planimetry evidenced in Ptolemy's work and Agrippa's map of the empire in the Porticus Vipsania further encouraged the practice.[10] Indeed, the intimate connection between mapping and conquest may even have imbued such planimetrical schemes with triumphal overtones, which feature in other ways, as we have seen, in imperial funerary art. In this chapter, I argue that the choice of location for an imperial funerary monument was not made casually; on the contrary, a site might offer maximum visibility and impact, in order to express an ideological statement specific to an emperor's claim to legitimation, often based upon dynastic premises.

THE MAUSOLEUM OF AUGUSTUS

The Campus Martius was an astute choice for the location of the Mausoleum of Augustus for a variety of reasons. A flat expanse of land beside the Tiber, it was an ideal site for construction, as large quantities of heavy building materials could easily be transported there by boat and Agrippa's drainage projects of 33 B.C. had rendered it more stable for building.[11] The flat, undeveloped northern Campus enabled an unobstructed view of the tomb from afar, and the Tiber's waters prevented later construction from marring primary views (fig. 93). As Favro puts it, "This floodplain to the northwest of the city center was ideally suited for maximum exposure. The Via Flaminia cut a wide swath along the eastern edge of the plain; this main northern highway into the city provided a well-defined path and

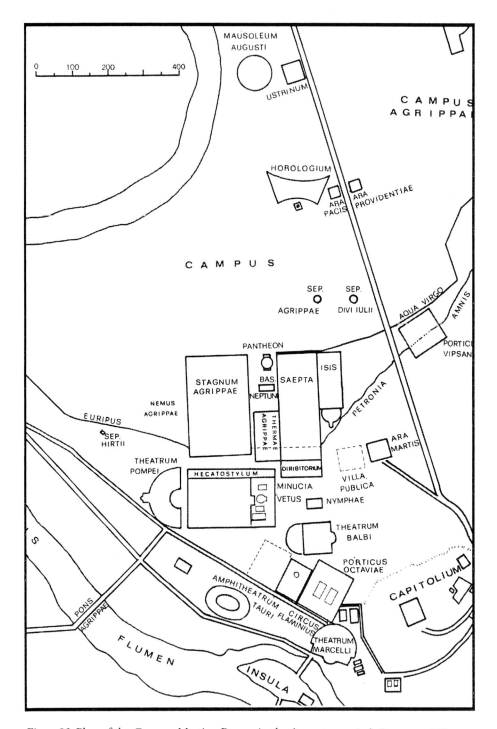

Figure 93. Plan of the Campus Martius, Rome, in the Augustan period. Constanze Witt

viewing platform. Spreading westward from the Via Flaminia, the ancient Campus was geographically distinct. To the East rose garden-covered hills; to the North and West, the turbulent Tiber formed a liquid border; to the South, a dominating closure was provided by the fortified escarpment of the Capitoline hill towering approximately 30 meters above the Campus."[12] Though it was outside the *pomerium,* throngs of people gathered regularly in the Campus Martius, where they might be exposed to the carefully worded text of Augustus's funerary complex. These crowds included visitors arriving from the north on the newly repaved Via Flaminia, foreigners awaiting approval to enter the city, armed troops (who were not permitted to cross the *pomerium*), people participating in or watching triumphal processions, and the tribal assembly, not to mention those who were visiting nearby recreational areas.[13]

The Campus was also rich in associations and civic memories. The implications of its decidedly military character were discussed in Chapter 2: Augustus's Mausoleum, doubling as a trophy, bespoke his military successes and justified Julian power, present and future. The Campus's early history also suggested links between Augustus and great men of Rome's past, since burial there was a privilege reserved for Rome's *summi viri.* In 78 B.C. the Senate had granted Sulla burial on the Campus, and two consuls, A. Hirtius and C. Vibius Pansa, who fought together against Antony and died in the battle of Mutina of 43 B.C., were also laid to rest there, as were Julius Caesar and his daughter Julia.[14] By building his dynastic tomb there, then, Augustus benefited from association with these historical figures, in much the same way as he did in the gallery of heroes in the porticoes of his Forum.[15] Prominent among these *summi viri* was Rome's legendary founder, Romulus, with whom Augustus promoted a well-documented parallel for himself, just as Caesar had, to style himself Rome's new founder.[16] As early as 36 B.C., for example, he began constructing a "humble" abode on the Palatine, "and his house gained an element of prestige from the [Palatine] hill as a whole, because Romulus had once resided there."[17] When, in 27 B.C., the Senate and People of Rome wanted to choose an honorary title for him, "Caesar had set his heart strongly on being called Romulus. But when he understood that this aroused suspicions that he aspired to kingship, he abandoned his efforts to obtain it and took the title Augustus."[18] Moreover, "As he was first taking the auspices as consul, twelve vultures appeared to him, as they had to Romulus."[19] Ernst Kornemann argues that this "Romulus Epoch" reaches its apogee in 29–28, manifesting itself in Augustus's new state order, his social reforms and return to the *mos maiorum,* and his restoration of early temples;[20] that is, by his calculation it peaked at the time of the Mausoleum's construction. This being so, the Mausoleum's location takes on new meaning, as Coarelli recognized, for, as Livy stresses, it was near the site of Augustus's later funerary complex that Romulus had mysteriously departed his life:

> While he was reviewing an assembly of his troops on the Campus near the Marsh of Capra, all of a sudden a storm broke with violent claps of thunder. It

engulfed the king in a cloud so thick that he was obscured from the assembly's view; from that moment Romulus was never seen again on earth. The Roman troops, who at length recovered from their fear when a calm and sunny light returned after such a turbulent day, saw that the royal seat was vacant, and although they readily believed the senators, who had been standing close to the king and now declared that he had been carried up on high by a whirlwind, still a silence reigned for some time, as if a fear of bereavement had struck. Then, first a few and then all voices in unison began to proclaim Romulus a god and son of a god, king and father of the city. . . .[21]

In choosing a site for his Mausoleum, Augustus appears to have purposely invoked Romulus's memory,[22] and to have done so in a specific and appropriate way, emphasizing the time of the latter's "death" and acclaimed apotheosis as Quirinus. Presumably, using Romulus as model, a Roman viewer was to impute Augustus's apotheosis as reward for his benefactions to Rome.

This anticipated change of status from mortal to immortal was rendered explicit by another building on the Campus Martius, the Agrippan Pantheon, which stood on the lowest point of the plain, perhaps on the very spot of the Marsh of Capra.[23] Its form and orientation are still the subject of debate; many scholars believe it to have been a rectangular building with an entrance on the long south side.[24] Yet William Loerke presents a compelling argument for a rectangular pedimented porch entered on the north side, leading to a circular hypaethral cella. Defining the cella was an annular portico with caryatids.[25] Assuming this is correct, the Mausoleum and the Pantheon, under construction contemporaneously, were united by their circular form (fig. 94).

Loerke notes that the concept of a pantheon, a building dedicated to all the gods, was a concept native to Egypt, where it would have included dynasts as well as heavenly deities.[26] The Agrippan Pantheon came as close to its Egyptian model as Roman custom would allow: a statue of the recently divinized Julius Caesar stood among the cult statues of Mars, Venus, and other gods inside the cella, and "Agrippa, for his part, wished to place a statue of Augustus there also and to bestow upon him the honor of having the structure named after him; but when the emperor would not accept either honor, he placed in the temple itself a statue of the former Caesar and in the porch statues of Augustus and himself. This was done, not out of any rivalry or ambition on Agrippa's part to make himself equal to Augustus, but from his hearty loyalty to him and his constant zeal for the public good; hence Augustus, so far from censuring him for it, honored him the more."[27] This arrangement of statues expressed the relationship between the new god and his adoptive son; more than that, it perhaps implied that upon his death Augustus too would join the Pantheon.[28] Moreover, as Castagnoli notes, if projected northward, the Pantheon's axis, 5 degrees west of north, drove straight to the Mausoleum, presenting a visitor with a direct sightline from the temple's door to the Mausoleum, with its southern entrance.[29] The axial connection between his Mausoleum and the Pantheon, two circular buildings, expressed the progression from mortal to immortal status: Augustus, like

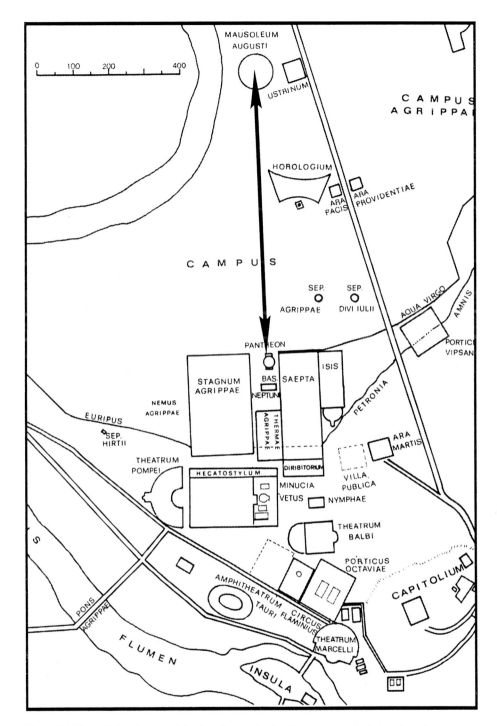

Figure 94. Plan of the Campus Martius, Rome, in the Augustan period, showing the sightline from the Pantheon to the Mausoleum of Augustus. Constanze Witt

Julius Caesar, and like Romulus on the very Marsh of Capra, would not die but achieve apotheosis. After 10–9 B.C., the Romulan quality of Augustus's projected apotheosis was further symbolized by the presence of the monumental sundial. It can scarcely be a coincidence that Rome's other monumental sundial, built by L. Papirius Cursor, was located in the precinct of the Temple of Quirinus/Romulus on the Quirinal, which Augustus himself had magnificently restored in 16–15 B.C. to mark his respect for Rome's first king.[30]

THE ARCH OF TITUS

The Arch of Titus stood in a prominent and fully visible site on the crest of the Velian, and probably spanned the Sacra Via on its way through the Forum (fig. 95).[31] If the Mausoleum of Augustus was located in such a way as to suggest affiliation with great men of history, the Arch's location both cemented a relationship between the Flavian dynasty and the early Julio-Claudians, on the one hand, and suggested Flavian improvements on Neronian policy, on the other.

By Mario Torelli's calculation, through its siting the Arch of Titus played its part in a program of carefully placed Flavian additions to the city center, a scheme designed to unify the "historic" (and distinctly Julio-Claudian) nucleus of the city within an architectural embrace that would exalt the Flavian name (fig. 96).[32] Centered around the Equus Domitiani in the Roman Forum and the

Figure 95. Plan of the east end of the Roman Forum, Rome. Constanze Witt

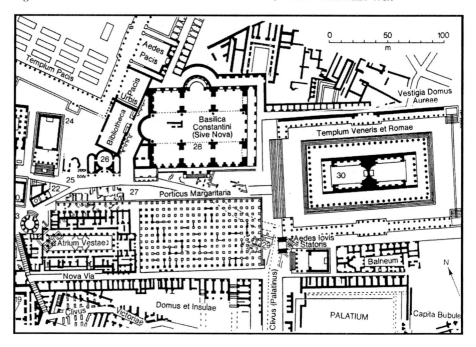

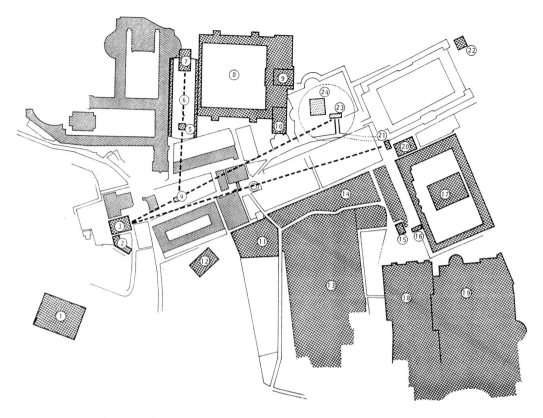

1. Temple of Capitoline Jupiter
2. Porticus of Dei Consenti
3. Temple of Divine Vespasian and Titus
4. Equus Domitiani
5. Janus Quadrifrons
6. Forum Transitorium
7. Temple of Minerva
8. Templum Pacis
9. Aedes Pacis
10. Bibliotheca and Forma Urbis
11. Athenaeum
12. Templum Novum Divi Augusti
13. Area of Domus Tiberiana
14. Domitianic facade of Palatium
15. Aedes Jovis Victoris
16. Arcus Domitiani
17. Templum Divi Augusti in Palatio
18. Domus Flavia
19. Domus Augustana
20. Aedes Jovis Propugnatoris
21. Arcus Divi Titi
22. Colossus Solis
23. Hypothetical location of Arcus Divi Vespasiani in Sacra Via Summa
24. Hypothetical location of Aedes Jovis Statoris

Figure 96. Plan showing the Flavian building program in the Roman Forum, Rome. By permission of Mario Torelli

Forum Transitorium, the program stretched over the slopes of the Capitoline, Velian, and Palatine hills, culminating in Domitian's restored Capitolium.[33] Its principle was, wherever possible, to juxtapose Flavian buildings with Augustan ones in order to establish a parallel between the dynasties: thus, the Temple of the Divine Vespasian and Titus on the lower slope of the Capitoline, along with the adjacent Portico of the Dei Consenti (fig. 96: 2–3), balanced the Augustan Temple of the Divine Julius at the opposite end of the Forum; the Flavian Forum of Peace and the Forum Transitorium (fig. 96: 6 and 8), next to Augustus's Forum, established the Roman Forum's northern boundary while echoing Augustus's architectural tradition.[34] To the south, Domitian restored the Templum Novum Divi Augusti (fig. 96: 12) and smothered the Palatine with his huge palace adjacent to the site of Augustus's house.[35] Finally, Torelli proposes, on the east side of the Forum, Domitian erected three arches to honor his *gens*, each in relation to a temple to Jupiter. The Arch of Titus was aligned with a temple on the podium to its southeast often considered the Temple of Jupiter Stator but identified by Torelli as the *aedes Iovis Propugnatoris* (Shrine of Jupiter the Vanguard), possibly raised on the location of Titus's birth (fig. 96: 20–21).[36] He conjectures that an arch to Divus Vespasianus (to be identified with the Haterii relief's *arcus in sacra via summa*) stood between the later Basilica of Maxentius and Temple of Venus and Roma, together with the actual Temple of Jupiter Stator (Stayer of Flight) (fig. 96: 23–24). Symmetrically arranged, the two arches and temples linked Vespasian with Jupiter in his capacity as suppressor of the Jews in revolt, and Titus with Jupiter as guide in the assault on Jerusalem.[37] The third arch, of which the foundations survive, formed a monumental gateway to Domitian's Palatine domicile (fig. 96: 16).[38] Together, this and the Arch of Titus framed the (so-called) Palatine Temple of Augustus (fig. 19: 17), defining it as part of Domitian's Palatine. This systematic grouping emphasized the ideological unity of the Arch of Titus, the aedes Iovis Propugnatoris, and the Templum Divi Augusti, and established them together as a nucleus of the imperial cult on the Palatine. Torelli further hypothesizes that a structure a few meters southwest of Domitian's arch, later incorporated into the huge fortress of the Frangipani, was the *aedes Iovis in Palatio* (Shrine of Jupiter on the Palatine), a temple vowed by Fabius Rullianus in 295 B.C. to Jupiter Victor (fig. 96: 15). This third temple, linked with the third arch, associated the third Flavian with Jupiter as Victor. The triple presence of Jupiter honored Domitian's predecessors as *divi* and simultaneously symbolically divinized him during his own lifetime.[39]

There is much in this scheme that is hypothetical, not least the identification of the podium in the area of the convent of San Bonaventura and the church of San Sebastiano (fig. 96: 16) as the remains of a Palatine Temple of Divine Augustus. However, it does have the advantage of arguing for careful calculation in the Arch's relationship to surrounding buildings.

What appears certain is that the Arch was intended to balance the Temple of the Deified Vespasian and Titus below the Capitoline.[40] Standing in a new public piazza, it also formed a monumental – albeit relatively small – gateway to the valley of Nero's Domus Aurea. One reading of its role there is that, against the backdrop of the Flavian amphitheater, symbol of a restored democratic ideal, it symbolized the Flavian policy of returning this land to the people; it declared a public entrance to land only recently held private, defining a dramatic contrast between the Flavians and their despotic predecessor (fig. 97).[41] Another suggests itself, however, and fits better with recent hypotheses on the use of the house and its fate after 68.

Figure 97. Arch of Titus, Rome, 81, view from the west. Photo: Deutsches Archäologisches Institut, Rom–InstNegNr 1936.507

The Golden House, discussed above, replaced the Domus Transitoria after the fire of 64 and filled the land between the imperial domus on the Palatine and the Horti of Maecenas on the Esquiline; its full extent is a matter of ongoing conjecture, though its central location, excessive size, and ostentation were all the subjects of severe criticism in antiquity.[42] Scholars now recognize that such charges, and vehement attacks to the effect that Nero evicted hoards of poor people from their homes in order to build his pleasure palace, are based upon a tradition of literary declamation aimed against a symbol of autocracy, and should not be allowed to overshadow archaeological and other literary evidence that presents a more moderate picture; in fact, magnificent though it was, the Domus Aurea belonged to an established tradition of such villas, and Vitellius's wife, Galeria, would later decline to live there on account of its relative austerity. Moreover, by the time of Nero's accession much of the area occupied by the Domus Aurea was already imperial property in imperial or public use. In the area of the Esquiline Wing, owners of profitable commercial properties may have had reason to complain: masonry analyses show that it rose on top of commercial buildings and structures possibly associated with guilds. In the valley of the later amphitheater, and on the Velian, the Oppian, the Esquiline, and the lower slopes of the Caelian, residential areas do appear to have been affected; those who were ousted, though, certainly included members of the vociferous elite most likely to have left record of their annoyance.[43]

Nor is it clear, as Martial implies, whether Nero denied the general public access to his magnificent park and lake. To be sure, one ought probably to envisage some sort of enclosure to confine the animals Suetonius describes, but this could have been localized. E. Champlin argues that, in his golden palace, nestled like a glittering stage set on the edge of the hillside, Nero's posturing would have been wasted without an audience. The estate incorporated at least two major arteries through the city, a north–south road linking the saddle between the Palatine and the Caelian to the Colosseum valley, and an east–west road uniting the valley with the Palatine (including part of the Via Triumphalis along its route); the roads met at the point of the later Meta Sudans.[44] If the Domus cut off these roads, then public complaint would have been justified; yet the attacks could just as easily reflect the displeasure of those who were forced to cross the new imperial estate to reach the Forum, thus becoming part of Nero's audience. His practice of entertaining the masses regularly in lavish style at the Stagnum Agrippae and Naumachia on the Campus Martius is known from Tacitus:

> He gave feasts in public places as if the whole city were his own home. But the most prodigal and notorious banquet was given by Tigellinus. To avoid repetitious accounts of extravagance, I shall describe it, as a model of its kind. The entertainment took place on a raft constructed on Marcus Agrippa's lake. It was towed about by other vessels, with gold and ivory fittings. Their rowers were degenerates, assorted according to age and vice. Tigellinus had also collected birds and animals from remote countries, and even the products of the ocean. On the quays were brothels stocked with high-ranking ladies. Opposite them could be seen naked prostitutes, indecently posturing and gesturing.[45]

His description of this and other similar events leads Champlin to suggest that Nero was purposely subverting Roman customs, as if engaging in an extended Saturnalia through which he sought to win popularity. There is a good likelihood that he did – or planned to do – the same at his luxury estate;[46] whether these public revels, however frequent, entail that the state was permanently accessible remains to be seen.

It may initially seem surprising that there is little to suggest that his villa was systematically destroyed when, after Nero's suicide and formal *damnatio memoriae,* his image was erased from visual memory;[47] archaeological evidence for the fate of the Esquiline Wing meshes well with literary accounts that Otho allotted fifty million sesterces to complete construction, and that Vitellius had enough experience of it as a dwelling for Galeria to decide that it was inadequate to her tastes.[48] Pliny's mention of a Domus Titi (where the Laocoön was on view) may suggest that Titus used the east block of the Esquiline Wing as his residence; perhaps he lived there until the fire of 80, or perhaps, as Warden suggests, construction stopped with his death, when Domitian turned his attention to grander designs on the Palatine.[49]

All the same, the Flavians seem to have been intent on "rehabilitating" the area; draining the lake, Vespasian began construction on the Flavian amphitheater, dedicated to the entertainment of the masses:

> Here where the glittering solar colossus views the stars more closely and where in the central road lofty machines grow up, the hateful hall of the beastly king used to radiate its beams, at the time when a single house used to occupy the whole city. Here where the mass of the conspicuous and revered amphitheater rises up, the pools of Nero once stood. Here where we marvel at that swiftly built donation, the baths, an arrogant field had deprived the poor of their homes. Where the Claudian portico spreads its shade afar, the farthest part of the palace came to an end. Rome is restored to herself, and under your direction, O Caesar, those delights now belong to the people which once belonged to the master.[50]

Out of reverence for the earlier Julio-Claudians, Vespasian completed the temple of Divine Claudius; Titus built a bath complex. The unfinished Domus Aurea became a source of material for Flavian projects: removing works of art for display at his Temple of Peace, Vespasian gradually stripped it of fine revetment, and the rooms of the Esquiline Wing were relegated to use as storage space or barracks, presumably because of the nearby amenities.[51] Early in his reign, Domitian completed buildings begun by his predecessors; at the same time, along with the Senate and People of Rome, he built the Arch of Titus where Nero had constructed a pair of porticoes leading up to a monumental propylon, a huge golden portal to his residence.[52] What was the significance of these Flavian buildings?

The extravagant entertainment that Nero provided his subjects, so distasteful to some, must at least in part account for his popularity with less privileged sectors of the populace, who had begun to enjoy the pleasures hitherto reserved for the few.[53] From early in his reign he had courted and won public opinion with his care for the corn supply, entertainments (often with a Greek character), and lavish generosity in his distribution of largesse; he had even housed the homeless on the Campus Martius and in his imperial gardens after the great fire. His popularity with the nonelite was enduring; there were those, after all, who continued to tend his grave and offer prayers for his return when his memory had been officially condemned by the Senate.[54] Anxious, presumably, to please Nero's detractors, Vespasian would have been ill-advised all the same to alienate those who had enjoyed his largesse. Seen in this light, his amphitheater was a masterpiece of diplomacy. In its construction, he accommodated architecturally those types of activity that the public had enjoyed or expected to enjoy on Nero's land, but conspicuously elevated and controlled them, reinforcing their Roman character and making them morally acceptable. Indeed, the amphitheater's staunchly Roman architectonic form, and the strict seating arrangements for the crowd within the amphitheater according to social hierarchy, must have appeared to reassert the very Roman values and social order that Nero's revels had subverted.[55] The Arch, then, was a gateway to a Flavian Domus Aurea, where the masses were still entertained, but in a fashion more acceptable to all. Perhaps this accounts for the Arch's diminutive size and understated decoration, which signaled a new (though short-lived) moderation.

What the Arch lacked in size, however, it made up for in another fashion: it gained emphasis through a process of seriation as one of three arches on the Sacra Via within the short distance of approximately 320 meters, the other two being Augustus's Parthian Arch of 19 B.C. and the Fornix Fabiorum, the first triumphal arch of Rome, erected in 121 B.C. by Q. Fabius Maximus Allobrogisius in celebration of his victories over the Allobroges.[56] For a visitor leaving the Forum, the three arches in sequence must have marched in a rhythmic crescendo, with the Arch of Titus on the brow of the Velian Hill as the sonorous climax.

THE TEMPLUM GENTIS FLAVIAE

In 1966, Jean-Claude Richard remarked upon the unusual status of an imperial tomb such as the Mausoleum of Augustus or Hadrian. On the one hand, the monument was a tomb (*sepulchrum, sema*) where dynast and family were laid to rest and where, subsequently, funerary rituals took place on anniversaries of their deaths. Yet, on the other, since the deceased emperor was worshipped there in his divinity, it was almost tantamount to a temple, even while remaining separate from the straightforward temple where his cult was celebrated.[57] As a result of this ambiguity, burial inside an imperial tomb inherently implied a sort of apotheosis even for the undeified, who, in death, basked in the reflected glory of their divine relatives. The Temple of the Flavian Dynasty stands apart in this respect, for it unabashedly conflated the functions of tomb and temple, the natural architectural resolution, perhaps, of this ambiguity. More than that, the Templum Gentis Flaviae was birthplace too, as Suetonius records. Burial within a private estate is attested as early as the Republic, when many a landowner was interred on his own property,[58] and the posthumous conversion of a lifetime domicile into a temple found a precedent in the Temple to Divus Augustus on the site of the young Octavian's house *iuxta Romanum Forum supra scalas anularias* (next to the Roman Forum at the top of the ring maker's stairs).[59] The combination of a tomb and a temple on the site of birth recalls honors that Livia accorded Augustus when after his death she erected a shrine or *sacrarium* on the site of his birthplace *ad Capita Bubula* in Regio X.[60] Her action symbolically linked Augustus's entrance to mortal life with his entrance to the company of the gods, implying a causal progression between his earthly deeds and his apotheosis, just as Augustus himself had done in the design of his tomb. Also implicit in her gesture was the notion that Augustus's birth and greatness were divinely ordained, a concept that was widely expounded in Augustan literature. Yet, for his Flavian heaven, Domitian pointedly chose his own birthplace, not the birthplace of Vespasian or Titus, the formally decreed Flavian *divi;* a self-appointed second Augustus, in doing so he chose not to wait for others to grant him posthumous honors but to reap the benefits of implied divinization while still alive.[61] Although Vespasian's famous dying words, "Alas, I think I am becoming a god,"[62] show that emperors had come to perceive deification as a formality, until Domitian's reign that formality had been respected. Domitian defiantly enrolled himself among the gods while still alive, choosing the title "Master and God," *Dominus et deus,* for written communications and conversation, and sitting during the games between the priests of Capitoline Jupiter and the Deified Flavians, whose crowns bore engraved golden images of the Capitoline triad and Domitian.[63] The temple of the Flavian Dynasty celebrated this fact: as a god on earth, it declared, his birth had been divinely ordained, and his death was merely a change of state from god on earth to god in the heavens. In one building he celebrated the whole cycle of his birth, death, and apotheosis,[64] much as Augustus had done more subtly in his funerary complex.

The comparison with Augustus extends further. Like Augustus, when Domitian came to power in 81, he faced a capital in urgent need of care as a result of the devastating effects of fires in 64 and 80 and the civil war of 68–69.[65] To be sure, Nero had initiated a farsighted rebuilding program, characterized by good architectural sense,[66] and his Flavian predecessors had begun construction on baths, an amphitheater, and a forum dedicated to peace, but much remained to be completed. Taking charge promptly, Domitian energetically restored and rebuilt the city, thereby becoming the most prolific builder in the history of imperial Rome except for Augustus.[67] Indeed, in *Epigrams* 8.80.5–6, Martial states: *sic nova dum condis, revocas, Auguste, priora: debentur quae sunt quaeque fuere tibi* ("so while you found new things, Augustus, you evoke things of old: what is and what was are due to you"). Inevitably, his architectural policy and program of moral renewal must have cast Domitian as a new city founder, a second Augustus, a third Romulus, and it is in this image, as refounder of Rome, that he appears to have presented himself to the public in his Templum Gentis Flaviae.

In case the implicit message of his mausoleum was not clear enough to a Roman viewer, Domitian seems to have selected Romulus as a legendary counterpart for himself, whose earthly and heavenly careers in his judgment mirrored his own, and he explored the parallel in the Temple precinct's iconography. The dominant structure on the Quirinal was the Temple of Quirinus, for which

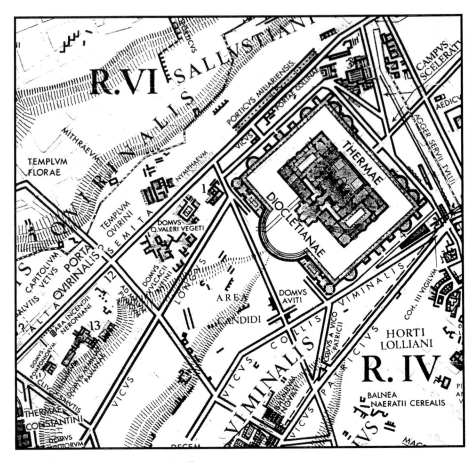

Figure 98. Plan of the Quirinal Hill

the hill was probably named (fig. 98).[68] Tradition told that Iulius Proculus had founded this temple after Romulus appeared to him and commanded him to construct a temple in his honor as the god Quirinus. The earliest building on the site for which there is evidence was vowed in 325 B.C. by L. Papirius Cursor, dictator during the Samnite War, and dedicated by his son in 293.[69] Damaged by lightning in 206 and by fire in 49, the temple was restored by Julius Caesar, of whom a statue was placed there in 45, "to the unconquered god."[70] Vitruvius and Cassius Dio record, as we have seen, that in 16 B.C. Augustus sumptuously rebuilt the temple as a huge peripteral octastyle building, surrounded on all sides by porticoes and set within a shady grove.[71] Ancient sources indicate that it stood in the vicinity of Santa Susanna,[72] so the Temple of the Flavian Dynasty and the Temple of Romulus were in close proximity to one another.[73]

Domitian appears to have deliberately emphasized the proximity of his temple/tomb to the hallowed Temple of Quirinus in the former's sculptural embellishment. In 1901, Paul Hartwig purchased a group of sculptural fragments on the art market in Rome and donated them to the Museo Nazionale delle Terme. He recorded that they were discovered "during the construction of the large semicircular palazzo on the northern side of the exedra of the baths of Diocletian . . . not in organized excavations but in the process of digging a foundation trench for a private building."[74] Also in 1901, Francis W. Kelsey bought a set of relief fragments, now in the Kelsey Museum in Ann Arbor, Michigan. Two of them, records indicate, came from the Baths of Diocletian, a third from the foreman of a construction site near the baths, and a fourth from a dealer "at the school" (presumably the British or the American School in Rome); no provenance is recorded for a fifth fragment. Köppel supposes that all the fragments came from a single construction site.[75]

The Hartwig and Kelsey fragments are all sculpted in a similar style. All are fashioned of Pentelic marble, with veins of mica, and the proportions of the figures represented in them are close.[76] Taken together, they can be classed in three groups. One group belonged to an entablature crowning a wall, supported by free-standing columns shaped as stylized palm trees, with male figures leaning against them (figs. 99, 100). The second group includes the head of Vespasian; the torso of an armored soldier; the idealized, youthful head of the Genius Populi Romani; the head and neck of a sacrificial bull; the head of a helmeted soldier in front of an ashlar wall, and a *flamen* in front of a portion of a temple facade (figs. 101–3). A fragment with the helmeted head of a soldier stands alone, on account of its larger scale. Gerhard Köppel and Rita Paris distribute the fragments of the second group between two hypothetical relief panels, one depicting the emperor sacrificing before a temple (as seen in the Villa Medici sacrifice scene from the Ara Pietatis or the Louvre's Mattei relief), the other an *adventus* or *reditus Augusti* (figs. 104, 5).[77] Stylistically, the fragments belong in the late first or early second century. Pentelic marble was popular in Domitian's reign, and the palm tree columns and capitals accord well with the imagery used in reliefs and on coins to celebrate the subjugation of Judaea in 70, making a Flavian date highly probable.[78] The presence of Vespasian's head, and the high quality of the sculpture, suggest that they belonged to a major Flavian building, and the only Flavian building listed in the Regionary Catalogues for Regio VI is the Templum Gentis Flaviae.[79] The presence of griffins, *thymiateria,* and *baityloi* on the sima decoration, standard motifs in a context of apotheosis, support this conjecture.[80] Köppel suggests that the fragments may have belonged to a small arch with two panel reliefs in the passage, similar to the Arch of Titus, but smaller and more ornate.[81] The sestertius die identified by Torelli as the Templum Gentis Flaviae shows just such an arch at the entrance to the building's enclosure (fig. 17).[82] Paris has more recently argued for his alternative suggestion of a precinct wall within the complex for the architectural fragments, similar to the Ara Pacis enclosure wall, with male caryatids leaning against palm trees on the facade (fig. 106).[83]

Scholars identify the building in the background of the *flamen* fragment (fig. 103) as the Temple of Quirinus, and the sacrifice as part of the ceremony that took place for the *sacrum* or founding of the Templum Gentis Flaviae. Initially, Hartwig identified the scene shown in the temple's pediment as the *augurium augustum,* the taking of auspices at the foundation of the city of Rome, watched

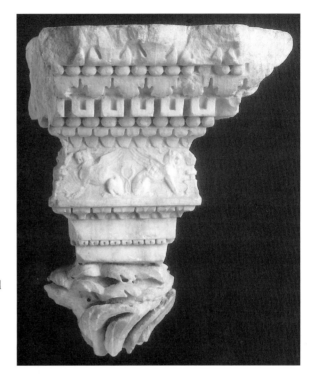

Figure 99. Fragment of architectural sculpture, Hartwig fragment, Domitianic, Museo Nazionale Romano. Photo: Museo Nazionale Romano, Archivio Fotografico Neg. 407146

Figure 100. Male torso, Hartwig fragment, Domitianic, Museo Nazionale Romano. Photo: Museo Nazionale Romano, Archivio Fotografico Neg. 407137

Figure 101. Head of Vespasian, Domitianic, Kelsey Museum of Archaeology, Ann Arbor, Michigan. Photo: Kelsey Museum of Archaeology, University of Michigan, KM 2430

Figure 102. Head of the Genius Populi Romani, Hartwig fragment, Domitianic, Museo Nazionale Romano. Photo: Museo Nazionale Romano, Archivio Fotografico Neg. 407143

153

Figure 103. Relief showing the head of a flamen in front of a temple, Domitianic, Museo Nazionale Romano. Photo: Museo Nazionale Romano, Archivio Fotografico Neg. 407133

Figure 104. Reconstruction of a relief belonging to the Templum Gentis Flaviae. By permission of Rita Paris

Figure 105. Reconstruction of a relief belonging to the Templum Gentis Flaviae. By permission of Rita Paris

by Romulus and Remus.[84] However, Rita Paris has convincingly reinterpreted it as the apotheosis of Romulus, shown frontally, bare-chested, and crowned by Victory at the left side of the pediment; Aeneas, Mercury, Hercules, Faustulus, and his wife, Acca Larentia, are all present as witnesses.[85] As Paris states, the attraction of both Romulus and Hercules lay in their status as descendants of gods who were accepted among the immortals in the heavens after death, the perfect prototypes for imperial apotheosis.[86] It was perhaps inevitable that Domitian, the more competitive and the survivor of two brothers in command of Rome, should perceive an equivalence between himself and Romulus (with whom he

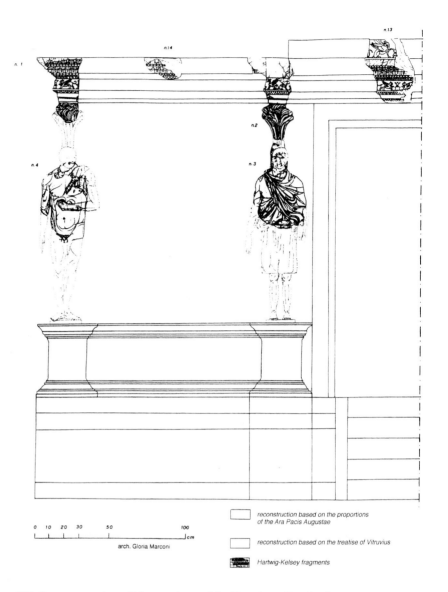

reconstruction based on the proportions
of the Ara Pacis Augustae

reconstruction based on the treatise of Vitruvius

Hartwig-Kelsey fragments

0 10 20 30   50   100
                              ⌐cm
        arch. Gloria Marconi

Figure 106. Reconstruction of the precinct of the Templum Gentis Flaviae. By permission of Rita Paris

also shared a much celebrated Sabine heritage), just as Augustus had approximately a century before. Choosing, like Augustus, to reside upon the Palatine, like Augustus he restored Romulus's hut there,[87] and archaeological evidence suggests that he also restored Augustus's sundial on the Campus Martius, with its distinctly Romulan associations. Like Augustus, too, he opted in the design of his tomb to associate himself with Rome's first founder specifically at the moment of his apotheosis.[88]

This relatively subtle allusion to Romulus assumes a more vivid hue when a second fragmentary relief is brought to bear, half of which is presently in the

Vatican's Museo Gregoriano Profano, half in the Palazzo Massimo alle Terme (fig. 107). The relief shows the emperor (whom Thorwaldsen restored as Trajan) accompanied by lictors and standing in front of a decastyle temple.[89] Long identified as the Temple of Venus and Roma, this building has suggested a Hadrianic date after 135 for the relief. On stylistic grounds, however, the relief better belongs in the Flavian period, and Torelli argues that the building is none other than the Templum Gentis Flaviae.[90]

Figure 107. Relief of the emperor and lictors before a temple, probably Flavian, Musei Vaticani and Museo Nazionale delle Terme. Photo: Penelope J. E. Davies

If this is correct, its pedimental sculpture suggests a forceful iconographic program for the temple. The subject of the pediment is the birth of Romulus and Remus. In the center reclines the sleeping Vestal Virgin, Rhea Silvia; above her, hovering in the heavens, was Mars, of whom only the legs and a spear survive. To the left the she-wolf suckles the infant twins Romulus and Remus, issue of the couple's union. Entranced by the spectacle, two shepherds stand nearby, their flocks (denoted by a single ram and sheep) in the pediment corner. Clearly there was little subtlety to Domitian's alliance with Romulus: in the pediment of the temple erected on the location of his birth, he depicted the birth of Romulus; within the complex decoration, perhaps on the gateway leading into the temple that implied his own deification, he represented Romulus's apotheosis as Quirinus. The cycle of life, death, and apotheosis that is implicit in the choice of location is rendered explicit in the temple's decoration. The correspondence with Augustus's choice of location for his mausoleum is self-evident: both sites are directly linked with Romulus at the moment of his apotheosis, establishing him as an exemplum of divinization through benefaction to Rome.

THE MAUSOLEUM OF HADRIAN

Hadrian's Mausoleum stood on the west bank of the Tiber on the Ager Vaticanus (fig. 108).[91] Since the plain was marshland prone to flooding, it was not a salubrious place and was barely inhabited; even in the late first century, according to Tacitus, a pestilence decimated Vitellius's troops when they set up camp there. Cicero tells us that it was farming ground in early times, and poor land at that; Martial and Juvenal add that it produced pottery and wine of rather inferior quality.[92] All the same, the plain was the location of luxurious *horti* from the first century B.C. on, and though hard to define, these private gardens appear to have covered most of the area. Among them was an estate belonging to Agrippina, daughter of Agrippa, and as her son Caligula reportedly received Jewish ambassadors in the property, there must have been a palace there.[93] Archaeological finds suggest that the buildings were magnificently decorated, and that the lifestyle they witnessed was extravagant. The Horti Agrippinae may have encompassed the Horti Domitiae, associated either with Nero's aunt, Domitia Lepida, or with Domitian's wife, Domitia Longina, daughter of Corbulo; it was in this estate that the Mausoleum was located.[94]

Construction in the area may have fallen within these imperial gardens: a large building behind the later Mausoleum identified as a *Naumachia*;[95] and Nero's infamous stadium, the Circus Gaii at Neronis, which appears initially to have been in private use but housed Nero's public races and displays by 59, including his own games, the *Neronia*.[96] Public access to the circus must have been along the Via Recta, carried across the Tiber from the Campus Martius on the Pons Neronianus, built either by Nero or Caligula.[97] Scattered burials lined a network of other roads: the Via Triumphalis leading north from Nero's circus

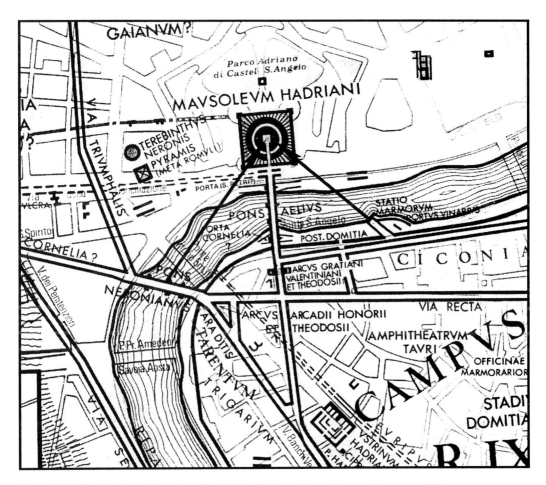

Figure 108. Plan showing viewpoints for Hadrian's Mausoleum, Rome. Constanze Witt

and the Via Cornelia, which extended the Via Recta.[98] The construction of the Mausoleum spurred further burials in the area, as well as greater development: an embankment road between the tomb and the Tiber continued east up the riverbank and west to join the Via Cornelia near the circus.[99]

Romans often situated their tombs in their gardens.[100] In Hadrian's case, scholars concur that the emperor intended his tomb to sit in a private extension of the Campus Martius, where he could build at will without needing the Senate's posthumous decision for public burial. Indeed, the new Pons Aelius and Mausoleum changed the orientation of the plain to match that of the Campus Martius. Perhaps by situating his tomb across the river Hadrian hoped to evoke thoughts of the soul's journey across the Styx or the Acheron to the Underworld in mythology, or the Egyptian custom of burying the dead across the Nile, an image that a nearby pyramidal tomb, the Meta Romuli, similar to but larger than the pyramid of Gaius Cestius (fig. 49), must have conjured readily to mind, to say nothing of the Isiac cult center in the region.[101] As for the Mausoleum's precise

Figure 109. View of Hadrian's Mausoleum from the Pons Neronianus, Rome. Photo: Michael Larvey

location within the estate, however, Boatwright comments, "So far no one has satisfactorily explained the unusual location of the Mausoleum, nor related Hadrian's tomb and bridge to the rest of the Hadrianic city."[102]

An analysis of the tomb's relationship to its surroundings, and to buildings elsewhere in Rome, reveals that its site was not haphazardly chosen. The Mausoleum stood almost equidistant from two busy points for traffic on and across the river. One of these was the Pons Neronianus. As he crossed the familiar Neronian bridge, and especially when he stood at its midpoint on the river, a passerby had an unencumbered view of Hadrian's entire funerary complex, bridge and tomb, which was must less easily obtained from either shore (figs. 108, 9). On the north side of the Pons Aelius a similar view presented itself (fig. 110): work on the Tiber embankments in 1890 uncovered a substantial tufa and travertine jetty, which scholars identify with the Ciconiae mentioned in literary sources.[103] A principal stopping point for Tiber traffic beyond the Forum Boarium dock area, this jetty was probably used for unloading cargo such as marble and wine from other parts of Italy and the empire, or as a waiting dock. It was certainly a focus of activity on the right bank and may have been the first port of entry to Rome for visitors from elsewhere. If so, it was from here that they received their first impressions of the empire's capital.

Either of the scripted views presented a viewer with a sort of dynastic narrative. On the one hand, the very act of building a new mausoleum marked a break from Hadrian's adoptive father, Trajan, and first-century predecessors; this separation was effected quite literally by the tomb's location across the Tiber. Yet, while claiming a fresh dynastic start in this way, Hadrian was still fully conscious

Figure 110. View of Hadrian's Mausoleum from the Ciconiae, Rome. Photo: Michael Larvey

of the value of legitimizing devices and the legitimizing power of his institutional antecedents. In his choice of a circular dynastic monument, and in its proportions (both 300 feet at the base), he visually acknowledged Augustus, whose mausoleum stood, conspicuously, farther up the Tiber on the east bank.

From the Pons Neronianus or the Ciconiae, a viewer saw an inscription running along either side of the bridge similar to the inscription still visible on the Pons Fabricius, downstream from the Pons Aelius.[104] The Pons Aelius and the Temple of Divine Trajan and Plotina were the only two buildings that Hadrian signed with his name.[105] In the former case, his dynastic ambitions speak for themselves: Hadrian is heir to the now divine emperor, legitimate descendant of Trajan's and Plotina's "fictive family." The bridge's inscription had a similar purpose, as his choice of titles reveals:

IMP. CAESAR DIVI TRAIANI PARTHICI FILIUS DIVI NERVAE NEPOS TRAIANUS HADRIANUS AUGUSTUS PONTIFEX MAXIMUS TRIBUNIC. POT XVIII COS. III FECIT

[The Emperor Caesar Trajanus Hadrianus Augustus, son of Divine Trajanus Parthicus, grandson of Divine Nerva, with tribunician power for the 18th time, in his third consulship made this][106]

Heir to Trajan the Divine, he also claims descent from the Divine Nerva, establishing his legitimacy through two generations of *divi*;[107] thus legitimized, he becomes the founder, like Augustus, of his own dynasty, embodied by his tomb, modeled after that of Augustus.

An even grander planimetrical scheme inscribed Hadrian's descent from the deified Trajan into the cityscape. I argued in the previous chapter that by

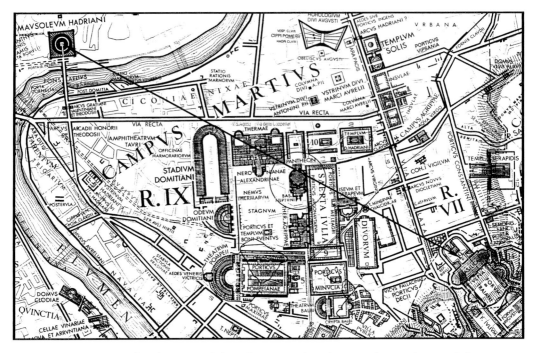

Figure 111. Plan showing sightlines from Trajan's Column to the Pantheon and the Mausoleum of Hadrian, Rome. Constanze Witt

Hadrian's time Rome had a spectacular new belvedere in the form of Trajan's Column, from which a viewer could survey the city as a massive architectural stage. I also suggested that vistas from the column were carefully managed, and dramatically enhanced by the long, dark climb to reach the platform. Looking northwest from the top of the Column, a viewer would have recognized the Pantheon, a vast reflecting dome amid the gabled roofs of the city. Directly behind the Pantheon, she would have seen another circular building, Hadrian's Mausoleum, and its crowning statue or tempietto rising above the Pantheon's dome as if emerging from it – for a perfectly straight line unites the Column with temple and tomb (fig. 111). This planimetrical relationship must have implied a thematic link between the two circular buildings – just as sightlines had bound Agrippa's Pantheon to Augustus's Mausoleum a century and a half before – and that theme, I argued in Chapter 3, was the cosmos and Hadrian's implicit role within them as cosmocrator.[108] A celestial building, the Pantheon celebrated all the gods, old and new. Hadrian moved within it during his lifetime as a quasi cosmocrator; in death he joined its gods, his image rising in the distance above its dome to express his newly divine status. If one were to look out from Hadrian's Mausoleum, in turn – and the staircase inside suggests that one could – one would see the vast dome of the Pantheon in the mid-ground and, behind it, the Column of Trajan with its gleaming apotheosized statue of Trajan, an architectural metaphor, perhaps, for Hadrian's descent from Trajan, the new god, and his association with the sun – Hadrian as a sunlike quasi reincarnation of Trajan.

In the form of his Mausoleum, then, Hadrian bracketed himself with Augustus. Yet, through careful siting of the tomb, he was also able to identify himself with Nerva and Trajan, and to imply his connection with the sun-god. The entire Mausoleum complex thus expressed his dynastic heritage while still establishing him as the founder of a separate line of rulers.

The Column of Antoninus Pius

For the column in honor of their father, Antoninus Pius, Marcus Aurelius, and Lucius Verus turned back to the Campus Martius, where a series of recent buildings – the Temples of Divine Hadrian and Matidia and the basilicas dedicated to Matidia and Marciana – formed a commemorative district for the Antonines to the south of that of Augustus (fig. 112).[109] Standing between these complexes, the Column was deliberately aligned on a northwest–southeast axis with a second monumental structure twenty-five meters away, discovered in 1703 under Via degli Uffici del Vicario: a colossal altar standing within a peperino enclosure wall with a door and two lateral niches; around the enclosure was a 100-foot (30 m.) square precinct marked by travertine cippi and iron chains or bronze grilles. The proximity and alignment of the two structures suggest that this altar was Antoninus Pius's consecration altar, raised on the site of his cremation to commemorate his change

Figure 112. Plan of the Antonine commemorative district on the Campus Martius, Rome

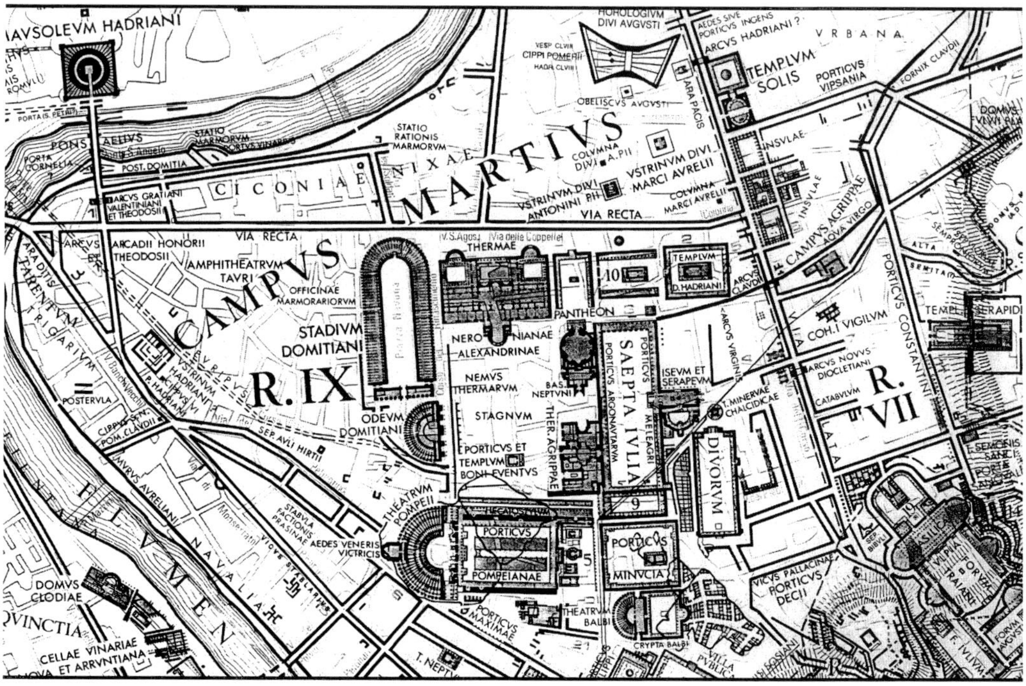

Figure 113. Drawing of the Column of Antoninus Pius showing its relationship to the Solarium Augusti. Drawing: Penelope J. E. Davies

of state from mortal to immortal.[110] The orientation of the Column and Altar set them apart from the Hadrianic buildings with their east–west orientation and suggests an effort to establish a visual link with the Augustan funerary complex to the north, specifically with the gnomon of the sundial, fashioned, like the Column's shaft, of a single piece of red granite. The Column's iconography worked in synergy with the planimetrical scheme. When a viewer looked at the Column from the Altar, she faced the apotheosis relief on its pedestal.[111] In the relief, the reclining personification of Campus Martius holds a representation of the obelisk of Augustus's sundial to indicate the location of Antoninus Pius's cremation. A viewer would witness Antoninus Pius and Faustina rising in perpetual apotheosis between two obelisks, the actual obelisk to the right of the base, and its sculpted image at the left (fig. 113). The matching monoliths, markers of apotheosis in their original context, framed the new divinities in shafts of gleaming red tapering to the sky, echoing the symmetrical obelisks outside Augustus's Mausoleum and the long tradition of paired obelisks outside Egyptian mortuary complexes where divinized monarchs were commemorated.

THE COLUMN OF MARCUS AURELIUS

In antiquity, the Column of Marcus Aurelius stood at the center of a precinct similar to the court surrounding Trajan's Column but substantially larger. Nestled between the Via Lata/Flaminia to the east and the Via Recta to the south, the precinct opened on to the Via Flaminia, at a level approximately three meters higher than the road.[112] A monumental arch demarcating the entry may have borne the Aurelian relief panels on the Arch of Constantine and in the Palazzo dei Conservatori.[113] Reconstructions place porticoes on the east, north, and south sides of the precinct, and on the west side, under the nineteenth-century Palazzo Wedekind, a Temple to Divine Marcus, featured in the Regionary Catalogues.[114]

None would dispute that the Column of Marcus Aurelius replicates Trajan's Column in more abstract form. Sonia Maffei's recent commentary encapsulates the sculptural changes that had occurred in the years that separated them:

> From the art-historical point of view, the striking comparison with the compositional richness of the Trajanic model has for years relegated the extreme essential quality of the Column's iconographic schemes to the reductive status of a poor-quality imitation. Its vivid "expressionism" has been read and analyzed essentially as a critical point in Roman art's progression toward a complete dissolution of "classicism," in the name of the change of style termed "Stilwandel" that introduces a new late antique sensibility. More recent studies, starting with an interest in narrative mechanisms and problems of visibility on Trajan's Column (Brilliant) have recognized a precise creative purpose in the radical compositional schematism of the scenes of Marcus Aurelius's Column, which exploits its new formal language in the service of greater legibility of content and an increasingly intense effectiveness in communication, skilfully calibrated to the needs of the viewer.[115]

Heightened abstraction – deeper carving, fewer spirals, intensified schematic scene placement – also increases the frieze's impact in the service of legibility.[116] In many ways, in terms of sculpture the Column is a more succinct version of its predecessor. The same is true in terms of architecture. Architectural setting and sculpture are more fluidly integrated, for instance; at the beginning of the frieze, ships' prows and huts (scenes I–III) simulate column flutes to smooth the transition from torus to frieze. The added base height serves a purpose too, for the Column appears sturdier against the sky than its predecessor.[117] Like Trajan's Column, this one was a belvedere, and its powerful impact resided in a visitor's experience of the dark, turning shaft contrasting with the dazzling view from the summit. With its greater height, that view reached far beyond the confines of the surrounding precinct to present a schematic dynastic narrative.

If the architect's dominant concern had been to create a formal copy of Trajan's Column, he would have placed the door onto the viewing platform on the north side, 90 degrees anti-clockwise from the lower door, which faced east (just as, on Trajan's Column, the lower door faces south and the upper door east). As a visitor emerged, his view would have extended parallel to the Via Flaminia, taking in the Mausoleum of Augustus, the Sundial, and the Ara Pacis. Implicitly, the vista would have aligned Marcus Aurelius with Rome's first emperor, an identification that most rulers were anxious to perpetuate. Yet this was not the architect's choice.

Other possibilities presented themselves. A door on the east, above the lower door, had little to recommend it, offering a view across the Via Flaminia to Regio VII, a residential area composed mostly of *insulae*.[118] To the south, far beyond the Via Recta, were the Capitol and Trajan's Column, and, closer at hand and slightly southwest, the Temples of Divine Hadrian and Matidia and the Basilicas of Matidia and Marciana.[119] Such a view might have forcefully acknowledged the conceptual model for the Column and placed a visitor in a suggestive context of commemorative Antonine architecture. A view to the west led, in the foreground, to the Temple of Marcus Aurelius; the Via Recta might then have drawn the eye to the spectacular silhouette of Hadrian's Mausoleum in the distance. Burial place of the Antonines, symbol of the man who had so generously promoted the young Marcus Aurelius, the tomb bespoke another important dynastic connection to the founder of Rome's third dynasty.

Remarkably, though, the architect altogether disregarded the four cardinal points. Instead, he set the door on the northwest angle of the viewing platform (fig. 114). A concern for safety may have partially motivated the design, as the corner of the platform offered more space than the sides. All the same, the dramatic effect of the choice was to offer an emerging visitor a striking panorama: a comprehensive view of Augustus's and Hadrian's Mausolea within a single eye-span (calculated at approximately 110 degrees). With their similar form and dimensions, these two monuments formed the outer visual boundaries for a visitor's gaze, and together they evoked two illustrious dynasties (fig. 115). As he surveyed the horizon, the two tombs defined a visual frame within which his focus would fall (fig. 116). There, in the near-ground just beyond the Column's precinct, stood Antoninus Pius's Column and consecration altar, an overt acknowledgment of Marcus Aurelius's adoptive father, predecessor, and political mentor.[120] Slightly to the east of the altar were two more altars, dubbed Altars "A" and "B." Altar B came to light during the construction of a new Camera dei Deputati in 1907–10. Lanciani considered its lavish ornamentation (now in the Museo Nazionale Romano, Aula VIII) to date to Marcus Aurelius's reign, although it was not aligned with his Column but was oriented northwest–southeast like the Altar of Antoninus Pius.[121] The square marble altar (10.5 × 10.5 m.), with its high molded socle and crowning cornice, stood inside an enclosure wall (24.45 m.) with a door on one side flanked by fenestrated

Figure 114. Viewing platform on the Column of Marcus Aurelius, Rome, ca. 180–93. Photo: Penelope J. E. Davies

niches and acroteria at the corners; an iron railing enclosed the precinct.[122] Altar A, discovered in 1910–11 beneath the Palazzo di Montecitorio, stood between this altar and that of Antoninus Pius and shared a party precinct fence with Altar B. Similar in form to Altar B, its east precinct wall was curvilinear.[123]

By Vincent Jolivet's calculation, a careful scheme dictated the location of these altars. He argues that they stood around a central point (now more or less beneath the entrance to the Palazzo di Montecitorio) that lay along an imaginary line extending from the center of Augustus's Mausoleum through the sundial's gnomon to the cella of the Temple of Divine Hadrian (fig. 117).[124] At this point, he contends, was the *ustrinum* of Augustus, mentioned in Strabo's description of the Campus Martius.[125] He suggests that Hadrian conceived a grand

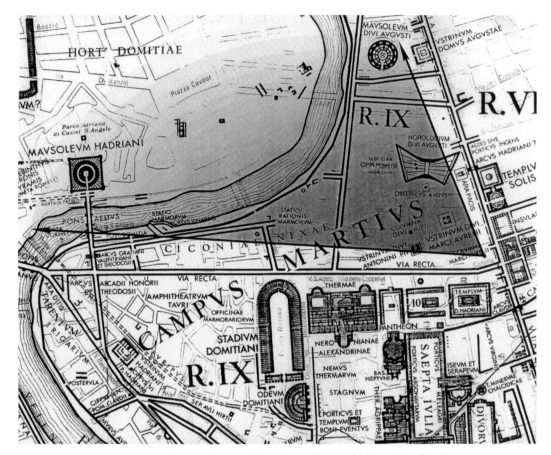

Figure 115. Plan showing the vista from the Column of Marcus Aurelius, Rome.
Constanze Witt

commemorative complex centered around Augustus's monuments, celebrating the principal themes of the emperor as Sol, and peace.[126] Regardless of the *ustrinum*'s location, Altars A and B do fall precisely astride Jolivet's imagined line from the Mausoleum through the gnomon to Hadrian's Temple. Moreover, though aligned with the Altar of Antoninus Pius, Altar A stood exactly in front of a visitor as he emerged onto the viewing platform on Marcus Aurelius's Column. These sight-lines, and the unconventional location of the upper door at an angle, intimate ongoing planimetrical schemes in the layout of the central and northern Campus Martius.

This being correct, the matter of Altar A's identification takes on a new significance. The post settings on the travertine blocks of the party fence indicate that it was constructed before Altar B, and in Pensabene's judgment, Altar B's acroteria belong stylistically to Aurelius's reign or soon thereafter.[127] Two scenarios might be imagined. On the one hand, Altar A may have commemorated Marcus Aurelius's consecration; perhaps Commodus erected both Column and Altar in his late father's honor in 180. An attractive hypothesis would then name a close member of

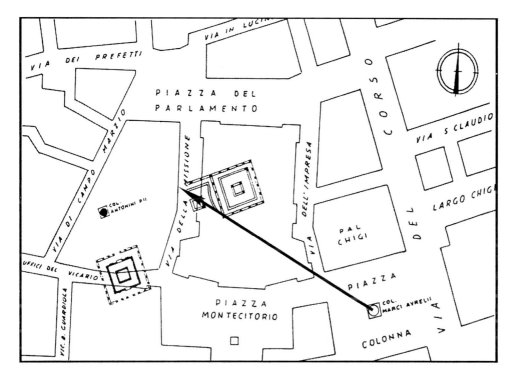

Figure 116. Plan of ustrina on the Campus Martius, Rome. Constanze Witt

Marcus Aurelius's family for Altar B, since both altars appear to be the product of a single plan; perhaps it honored Lucius Verus very belatedly, or perhaps when building a consecration altar (A) for his father, Commodus mapped out or even built a twin altar (B) for himself, which Severus put to its intended use when, despite Commodus's *damnatio memoriae,* he "enrolled [him] among the gods, with the grant of a Herculean-Commodian *flamen* (which Commodus had planned to have for himself while still alive)."[128] Alternatively, the Altar could have honored Pertinax, whom the Senate and People of Rome also "enrolled among the gods,"[129] or Septimius Severus, who though cremated in York may have had a consecration altar in Rome as part of his ongoing effort to associate himself with Marcus Aurelius through posthumous adoption.[130]

On the other hand, if Lanciani was correct in assigning the later altar, Altar B, to Marcus Aurelius, the earlier altar may have honored a close member of his family who predeceased him, perhaps Lucius Verus, who died in 169, or his wife, Faustina Minor. The latter is a strong candidate, for coins minted in her honor represent a consecration altar resembling these structures on the Campus Martius.[131] Her death in 176 coincided roughly with the end of the first campaign depicted on the Column, and upon her demise, "[Marcus Aurelius] asked the Senate to bestow honors and a temple for Faustina, and he praised her. . . . He instituted new Faustinian girls in his dead wife's honor, and gave thanks that Faustina had been deified as well, by the Senate."[132]

169

Figure 117. Schematic plan showing a commemorative scheme on the Campus Martius, Rome, by V. Jolivet

An analysis of the Column's role in its architectural context leads to a richer understanding of its purpose. If Altar A honored Marcus Aurelius, the panorama presented to a visitor reinforced the Column's sculptural message: the frieze's *res gestae* justify the emperor's apotheosis (in the statue), and the view commemorates the actual moment of its happening (the altar). In its entirety, the Column establishes Marcus Aurelius as the worthy successor of Rome's "good" emperors: of Augustus and the Antonines by manipulation of a viewer's panorama; and of Trajan, Optimus Princeps, by the very choice of a sculpted column.

It remained only for Commodus to identify himself, in turn, as next in line for the throne. This was not a difficult task, as Marcus Aurelius had granted him extraordinary powers from an early age, and made him joint ruler in 177.[133] His appearance in the spiraling frieze, like Hadrian's on Trajan's Column, is unemphatic and disputed. It is probable, though, that the relief decorating the Column's base known from prerestoration drawings represented the heir designate alongside his father (fig. 36).[134] On the far right side of the relief stood a horse, and secondary figures were sketchily rendered in the background. On the left, four barbarians wearing animal pelts and long-sleeved garments subjected themselves to the mercy of a group of Roman soldiers at the center, the most prominent of whom, holding a spear and dressed in a cuirass and mantle, is identified as Marcus Aurelius.[135] The figure beside him, also in a cuirass, may be Commodus.[136] Commodus had joined the front in 177 and celebrated triumphs for the northern wars along with his father. The dying emperor grudgingly entrusted the campaigns' conclusion to his son, who chose not to pursue an aggressive military policy.[137] If he did stand at his father's side in the base frieze, Commodus's position as heir would have been explicit, and his legitimation implied through the dynastic heritage expressed in the column's topographical ties.

Similar in form and function, then, the Columns of Trajan and Marcus Aurelius nevertheless imparted messages of very different content. Trajan, a Spaniard of obscure birth, adopted heir of a competent but unremarkable emperor, sought renown and immortal recompense through his own achievements. Smarting as it was from decades of instability, the imperial tradition offered a shaky foundation upon which to found any expectations. Trajan's fame and apotheosis rested, therefore, upon his successful foreign and domestic policies, signified respectively by the Column frieze and his Forum. By Marcus Aurelius's time, the service of several "good" emperors had redeemed the monarchy, and apotheosis was the expected reward for a term well served. Dynastic succession, through blood ties or adoption, was once more the norm, and as Marcus Aurelius's biological son Commodus had a better claim to power than most heirs.[138]

Substantial landowners and, for the most part, men of enormous wealth, the Roman emperors were spoilt in the latitude of available choices for the location of their tombs. They appear to have selected sites to align their monuments with select preexisting structures, and the alignments seem uniformly to have stressed dynamic ties, both with the emperor's immediate dynasty and with earlier rulers; on the whole, they appear to have been designed to encourage association rather than rivalrous comparison.[139] In some cases, similarities in form emphasized the planimetrical ties. The links exposed in the foregoing pages establish the late or the new emperor as heir to a long line of select rulers, underscoring the concept of regeneration discussed in earlier chapters.

CONCLUSION

IN THE FOREGOING PAGES, I have offered interpretations of the funerary monuments of the Roman emperors based upon commonalities I perceived between them when analyzing them as a genre. I offer these interpretations in the spirit of speculation, not in the hope of ousting prevailing opinion but in order to explore avenues opened up by applying a variety of methodologies to well-known material.

After a brief overview of the monuments in the first chapter, in the second I explored their architectural and decorative multivalency. Paying close attention to its place in architectural history, I recast the Mausoleum of Augustus in a dual role, as both tomb and war trophy, and argued that this and subsequent funerary monuments were designed to illustrate or embody the lifetime achievements of the deceased (primarily military), thus constituting a form of visual *res gestae* to complement information given in inscriptions. The *res gestae,* I contend, performed as an immediate justification for the emperor's apotheosis, which was often denoted in the monument's decoration, either implicitly or explicitly. Quite apart from ensuring the emperor's continued existence after death, his apotheosis was a vital means of guaranteeing his descendants divine patronage, and thus setting them above potential pretenders to the throne.

These conclusions led me to consider a pattern of cosmic allusions that emerges when the imperial funerary monuments are seen as a cohesive group. Sometimes these allusions are explicit; at other times I believe they exist in architectural metaphor, an immensely powerful visual language whose elusive quality, perhaps, has discouraged scholars from probing deeply. These allusions associate the emperor with the cosmocrator, a problematic characterization that I explored in panegyrical literature and in the visual arts. I propose an additional meaning for cosmic metaphors in the funerary realm, where they served to imply the emperor's eternal nature and his regeneration in his successors; not only deified, these images imply, he was eternally reborn. By this means, his successors were introduced into the funerary context and this, in turn, facilitated dynastic succession.

In the fourth chapter, I examined the occurrence of the empress's image on imperial funerary monuments in the light of current scholarship on Roman women's roles. The modes of her representation on the Ara Pacis Augustae, the Antonine Column base, and the relief in the Palazzo dei Conservatori commemorating the apotheosis of Hadrian's wife, Sabina, strongly suggest that the empress's image was deployed as a symbol of fertility. With her husband, she completed an image of family unity and, through her implied fertility, of family regeneration, even, and especially, when she was childless. Her individual commemoration occurred specifically at times when dynastic succession could not be guaranteed, and thus she played a central part in the fictive "imperial eternity" suggested by the monuments' cosmic allusions.

In the penultimate chapter, I considered how these propagandistic images might have worked upon a Roman viewer. Surprisingly little attention has been focused on the interaction between work of art and viewer in the Roman world; even though Frank Brown's seminal text on Roman architecture begins by exhorting his reader to recognize that "the architecture of the Romans was, from first to last, an art of shaping space around ritual," and even though scholars of ancient art and architecture admit movement within sculpture or eccentricities in architectural form, they rarely afford a work of art an intended active role in manipulating a viewer or visitor, perhaps because of the dangers inherent in attempting to understand the response to a work of art of another age or culture.[1] I argue that the imperial funerary monuments exhibit an increasingly compelling tendency to maneuver a visitor in specific directions, through both architectural and sculptural means. The visitor's mental and/or physical participation in a scripted dialogue with the monument assured heightened interest in the sepulcher and thus in the life of the deceased. Through such means, architects and sculptors helped to keep the dead ever present in the memory of the living.

In the final chapter, I explored choices made in placing the funerary monuments within the urban topography of Rome, bringing into question the interrelationships between buildings and other topographical features. This type of study is gradually gaining ground in scholarship on Roman architecture, and with promising results.[2] In these pages I moved beyond general observations made by G. Waurick on the locations of imperial funerary monuments, to suggest that choice of site was determined, not only for maximum visibility or by traditions ascribed to certain districts, but more specifically according to carefully thought-out planimetric ties with other landmarks, both in the immediate vicinity and farther afield.[3] Often these ties promoted forceful dynastic links between rulers.

Taking these conclusions together, I propose that we might characterize these structures less as funerary monuments than as magnificent accession monuments, whose message spoke to the living about the living as well as the dead – and the reborn. This vital propagandistic role might account for the extraordinary workmanship lavished upon them and for the curiously central place a group of funerary monuments continues to occupy in the history of Roman art.

Abbreviations Used
in Notes

A list of standard abbreviations for ancient texts is to be found in *The Oxford Classical Dictionary* (Oxford, 1996).

AA	*Archäologischer Anzeiger*
ActaAArtHist	*Acta ad archaeologiam et artium historium pertinentia*
AIIN	*Annali Istituto italiano di numismatica*
AJA	*American Journal of Archaeology*
AJP	*American Journal of Philology*
AnnPerugia	*Annali della Facoltà di lettere e filosofia, Università degli studi di Perugia*
AnnPisa	*Annali della Scuola normale superiore di Pisa*
ANRW	H. Temporini, ed., *Aufstieg und Niedergang der römischen Welt* (Berlin, 1972–)
AntCl	*L'Antiquité Classique*
AntJ	*The Antiquaries Journal. The Journal of the Society of Antiquaries of London*
AntW	*Antike Welt. Zeitschrift für Archäologie und Kulturgeschichte*
AquilNost	*Aquileia Nostra*
ArchCl	*Archeologia classica*
ArchJ	*Archaeological Journal*
ArchRW	*Archiv für Religionswissenschaft*
ArtB	*The Art Bulletin*
ArtJ	*Art Journal*
BAntFr	*Bulletin de la Société nationale des antiquaires de France*
BCH	*Bulletin de correspondance hellénique*
BCSSA	*Bollettino del Centro di studi per la storia dell'architettura*
BdA	*Bollettino d'arte*
BJb	*Bonner Jahrbücher des Rheinischen Landesmuseums in Bonn und des Vereins von Altertumsfreunden im Rheinlande*
BMCRE	*Coins of the Roman Empire in the British Museum* (London 1923–)
BSR	*Papers of the British School at Rome*
BullCom	*Bullettino della Commissione archeologica del Governatorato di Roma*
CAH	*Cambridge Ancient History*

CEFR	*Collection de l'Ecole française de Rome*
CIL	*Corpus inscriptionum latinarum*
CJ	*Classical Journal*
ClAnt	*Classical Antiquity*
ClMed	*Classica et Mediaevalia. Revue danoise de philologie et d'histoire*
CP	*Classical Philology*
CQ	*Classical Quarterly*
CR	*Classical Review*
CRAI	*Comptes Rendus des séances de l'Académie des inscriptions et belles-lettres* (Paris)
CSCA	*California Studies in Classical Antiquity*
DialArch	*Dialoghi di archeologia*
DOP	*Dumbarton Oaks Papers*
DOS	*Dumbarton Oaks Studies*
EAA	*Enciclopedia dell'arte antica, classica e orientale*
EchCL	*Echoes du monde classique. Classical Views*
EtTrav	*Etudes et Travaux. Studia i prace. Travaux du Centre d'archéologie méditerranéene de l'Académie des sciences polonaise*
GaR	*Greece and Rome*
GCS	*Griechische christliche Schriftsteller der ersten drei Jahrhunderte*
HAC	*Historia-Augusta-Colloquium* (Bonn)
HSCP	*Harvard Studies in Classical Philology*
HThR	*Harvard Theological Review*
JdI	*Jahrbuch des Deutschen Archäologischen Instituts*
JEA	*The Journal of Egyptian Archaeology*
JIES	*Journal of Indo-European Studies*
JRA	*Journal of Roman Archaeology*
JRGZM	*Jahrbuch des Römisch-Germanischen Zentralmuseums, Mainz*
JRS	*The Journal of Roman Studies*
JSAH	*Journal of the Society of Architectural Historians*
JWarb	*Journal of the Warburg and Courtauld Institutes*
LibAnt	*Libya Antiqua*
LIMC	*Lexikon Iconographicum Mythologiae Classicae* (Zurich and Munich 1974–)
LTUR	*Lexicon Topographicum Urbis Romae* (Rome 1993–)
MAAR	*Memoirs of the American Academy in Rome*
Meded	*Mededeelingen van het Nederlands Historisch Istituut te Rome*
MEFR	*Mélanges d'archéologie et d'histoire de l'Ecole française de Rome*
MEFRA	*Mélanges de l'Ecole française de Rome, Antiquité*
MemLinc	*Memorie. Atti della Accademia nazionale dei Lincei, Classe di scienze morali, storiche e filologiche*
MemPontAcc	*Memorie. Atti della Pontificia Accademia romana di archeologia*
MonAnt	*Monumenti antichi*
MonPiot	*Monuments et mémoires. Fondation E. Piot*

NC	*Numismatic Chronicle*
NR	*Numismatic Review*
NSc	*Notizie degli scavi di antichità*
ÖJh	*Jahreschefte des Österreichischen archäologischen Instituts in Wien*
OpArch	*Opuscula Archaeologica*
OpRom	*Opuscula Romana*
PCPS	*Proceedings of the Cambridge Philological Society*
PIR	*Prosopographia imperii romani*
PP	*La parola del passato*
ProcBritAc	*Proceedings of the British Academy*
QArchEtr	*Quaderni del Centro di studio per l'archeologia etrusco-italica*
QITA	*Quaderni dell'Istituto di topografia antica dell'Università di Roma*
RA	*Revue archéologique*
RE	Pauly-Wissowa, *Real-Encyclopädie der klassischen Altertumswissenschaft*
REA	*Revue des études anciennes*
REG	*Revue des études grecques*
REL	*Revue des études latines*
RendLinc	*Atti dell'Accademia nazionale dei Lincei. Rendiconti*
RendPontAcc	*Atti della Pontificia Accademia romana di archeologia. Rendiconti*
RHLR	*Revue d'histoire et de littérature religieuse*
RHR	*Revue de l'histoire des religions*
RIC	*The Roman Imperial Coinage* (London 1923–)
RIN	*Rivista italiana di numismatica e scienze affini*
RivStorAnt	*Rivista storica dell'antichità*
RM	*Mitteilungen des Deutschen Archäologischen Instituts, Römische Abteilungen*
RN	*Revue numismatique*
RPhil	*Revue de philologie, de littérature et d'histoire anciennes*
SMSR	*Studi e materiali di storia della religione*
StMisc	*Studi miscellanei. Seminario di archeologia e storia dell'arte greca e romana dell'Università di Roma*
TAPA	*Transactions of the American Philological Association*
TAPS	*Transactions of the American Philosophical Society*
TrWPr	*Trierer Zeitschrift für Geschichte und Kunst des Trierer Landes und seiner Nachbargebiete*
ZPE	*Zeitschrift für Papyrologie und Epigraphik*

NOTES

INTRODUCTION

1. J. Arce, *Funus imperatorum: Los funerales de los emperadores romanos* (Madrid, 1988), 59–124, brings the tombs together and writes, "No existe un trattamento completo del tema que abordo en este capitulo" (59).

2. See H. Daniel-Lacombe, *Le Droit Funéraire à Rome* (Paris, 1886), 26; L. Vogel, *The Column of Antoninus Pius* (Cambridge, Mass., 1973), 30. There is little reason to object to this term. A cenotaph is normally defined as a burial monument lacking a burial on account of the body's unavailability, due, for instance, to its loss at sea. The distinction, then, between the cenotaph and the commemorative monument described here is the simple one between being unable to bury the deceased in the cenotaph and being unwilling to do so (because of a desire to bury it in a dynastic tomb).

3. B. Frischer, "*Monumenta et arae honoris virtutisque causa:* Evidence of memorials for Roman civic heroes," *BullCom* (1983): 51–86, esp. 75, for whom the closest relative to these monuments is the Greek heroön. He insists that the memorial must be set apart from tombs and cenotaphs because it honored the life, not the death, of the honoree. The distinction is hard to accept, since most Roman tombs commemorated the life of the deceased on the occasion of his/ her death. See also E. Panofsky, *Tomb Sculpture* (London, 1964), 16, on retrospective and prospective commemoration.

4. See G. Mansuelli, "Il monumento commemorativo romano," *BCSSA* 12 (1958): 3–23, esp. 3–4.

5. For examples, see: R. Brilliant, *Visual Narratives: Storytelling in Etruscan and Roman Art* (Ithaca, N.Y., 1984); M. Eisner, *Zur Typologie der Grabbauten in Suburbium Roms* (Mainz, 1986); H. Colvin, *Architecture and the Afterlife* (New Haven-London, 1991); H. von Hesberg, *Römische Grabbauten* (Darmstadt, 1992); J. B. Ward-Perkins, *Roman Imperial Archtecture*[2] (Harmondsworth, 1981); and D. E. E. Kleiner, *Roman Sculpture* (New Haven-London, 1992).

6. Petr. *Sat.* 65.

7. On later imperial tombs, see M. J. Johnson, *Late Antique Imperial Mausolea* (Ph.D. diss., Princeton University, 1988).

8. W. L. MacDonald, "Sorting Out Roman Architecture," *AJA* 102 (1998): 614–17, esp. 616.

9. On Augustus: J. C. Reeder, "Typology and Ideology in the Mausoleum of Augustus," *Cl Ant* 11.2 (1992): 265–304. On Hadrian: W. L. MacDonald and J. Pinto, *Hadrian's Villa and Its Legacy* (New Haven, Conn., 1995), 132–33; A. R. Birley, *Hadrian: The Restless Emperor* (London and New York, 1997), 175–77.

10. On Plutarch's mention of initiation ceremonies, R. MacMullen, *Paganism in the Roman Empire* (New Haven, Conn., 1981), writes: "If [initiations] had conferred immortality, surely they would not have received so casual a mention, added by afterthought to such agreeable diversions as one might find at a church picnic. Initiations, *teletai,* can have meant nothing more soul-shaking than . . . big, open spectacles . . . " (56).

11. H. Bardon, *Les empereurs et les lettres latines d'Auguste à Hadrien* (Paris, 1968), 10, 23. Stoics believed man to be a microcosm who reproduced in his person the constitution of the universe. Just as the world's mass is animated by the Divine Fire, so man is animated by a detached particle of it. The soul, as a portion of the universe, is reabsorbed into the fiery ether after separation from the body and avoids disintegration until the great conflagration ending each cosmic age, after which a palingenesis returns the soul to the same body. For the true Stoic, man's purpose was not to prepare for death but to achieve perfect virtue in this life. In first-century Rome, however, Stoicism combined with the Pythagorean doctrine of celestial immortality to promise an afterlife that contrasted in its tranquillity with life's tribulations.

12. Cass. Dio 69.11.4. See Bardon (1968), 428; J. Prieur, *La mort dans l'antiquité romaine* (Rennes, 1986), 132–35; M. Guarducci, "La religione di Adriano," in *Les empereurs d'Espagne* (Paris, 1965), 209–21, esp. 215; R. Lambert, *Beloved and God: The Story of Hadrian and Antinous* (New York, 1992), 143–54. There was surprisingly little speculation about where the divinized emperor resided, whether among the stars or among the state gods. See F. Cumont, *Lux Perpetua* (Paris, 1949), 115–19; idem, *After Life in Roman Paganism*[2] (New York, 1959), 12–13.

13. Marcus Aurelius's writings reveal a man determined not to concern himself with thoughts of a heavenly afterlife or immortality through earthly fame, insisting instead on the value of lifetime virtue. He writes (trans. A. S. L. Farquharson):

> On death: either dispersal, if we are composed of atoms; or if we are a living unity, either extinction or a change of abode. (7.32)
> On fame: neither memorial nor fame nor anything else at all is worth a thought. (9.30)
> All things quickly fade and then turn to fable, and quickly, too, utter oblivion covers them like sand. And this I say of those who shone like stars to wonder at; the rest, as soon as the breath was out of their bodies, were

> "unnoticed and unwept." And what after all is everlasting remembrance? Utter vanity. (4.33)

See also A. Birley, *Marcus Aurelius: A Biography* (New Haven, Conn., 1987), 211–23.

14. Cumont (1949), 132–33; see also K. Hopkins, *Death and Renewal* (Cambridge, 1983), 226–35.

15. Suet. *Ner.* 49.4; Tac. *Hist.* 2.49; Arce (1988), 37–40.

16. Tab. Siar. 1.6–8; C. B. Rose, *Dynastic Commemoration and Imperial Portraiture in the Julio-Claudian Period* (Cambridge, 1997), 26.

17. Petr. *Sat.* 71.5–12.

18. Suet. *Aug.* 100; Tac. *Ann.* 1.8.4; Arce (1988), 39.

19. Gaius Licinianus 36.25–26; Cic. *Leg.* 2.22, 57; Pliny *HN* 7.187; Arce (1988), 18.

20. F. Lepper and S. Frere, *Trajan's Column: A New Edition of the Cichorius Plates* (Gloucester, 1988). See also R. Bianchi-Bandinelli, "Un problema di arte romana: Il 'Maestro delle imprese di Traiano,'" *Le Arti* 1 (1938–39): 325ff.; C. Agosti, "Ranuccio Bianchi-Bandinelli dall'invenzione del 'Maestro delle imprese di Traiano' alla scoperta dell'arte 'plebea,'" *AnnPisa*, s. 3.16 (1986): 307–29; K. Lehmann-Hartleben, *Die Traianssäule, ein römisches Kunstwerke zu Beginn der Spätantike* (Berlin-Leipzig, 1926).

21. See, for instance, P. Zanker, *The Power of Images in the Age of Augustus,* trans. A. Shapiro (Ann Arbor, Mich., 1988).

22. S.H.A., *Hadr.* 14.8–9; 16; 20.

23. Cass. Dio 49.4.1–5. See also S.H.A. *Hadr.* 15.10; Aur. Vict. *Caesares* 14.2; R. Syme, "Hadrian the Intellectual," in *Les empereurs d'Espagne* (Paris, 1965), 243–53; T. Rivoira, "Di Adriano architetto e dei monumenti Adrianei," *RendLinc* 18 (1909): 172–77; C. F. Giuliani, "La rivoluzione adriana, revisione archeologica I," *L'architettura, cronache e storia* 279.1 (1979): 45–51; G. Gullini, "Apollodoro e Adriano. Ellenismo e classicismo nell'architettura romana," *BdA* 53 (1968) [1971]: 63–80; W. L. MacDonald, *The Architecture of the Roman Empire, I: An Introductory Study*[2] (New Haven, Conn., 1982), 129–37; MacDonald and Pinto (1995), 22–23; J. C. Anderson, *Roman Architecture and Society* (Baltimore, 1997), 64–65.

24. S.H.A., *Hadr.* 19.11.

25. The *Scriptores Historiae Augustae* (S.H.A., *Hadr.* 16) even suggest that he ghostwrote it,

"for indeed Phlegon's writings, it is said, are Hadrian's in reality"; Suda, s.v. Phlegon 4 745 (Adler); M. T. Boatwright, *Hadrian and the City of Rome* (Princeton, N.J., 1987), 27.

26. Suet. *Dom.* 13.

27. See MacDonald (1982), 127–29; Anderson (1997), 55–59. The extant sculptural fragments do not, however, manifest the "signature" feature of Rabirius's work, two small rings between the dentils.

28. G. Martines, "La struttura della Colonna Traiana. Un esercitazione di meccanica alessandrina," *Prospettiva* 32 (1983): 60–71; M. Wilson Jones, "One Hundred Feet and a Spiral Stair: The Problem of Designing Trajan's Column," *JRA* (1993): 23–38; L. Lancaster, "Building Trajan's Column," *AJA* 103 (1999): 419–39. On the identity of Trajan's architect, see Cass. Dio 69.4. 1–6; Proc. *Aed.* 4.6.13; Bianchi-Bandinelli (1938–39); Agosti (1986); Lehmann-Hartleben (1926); J. E. Packer, "Trajan's Forum Again: The Column and the Temple of Trajan in the Master Plan Attributed to Apollodorus (?)," *JRA* 7 (1994): 163–82; W. L. MacDonald, *The Architecture of the Roman Empire, 1: An Introductory Study* (New Haven, Conn., 1982), 129–36; idem, "Roman Architects," in S. Kostof, ed., *The Architect: Chapters in the History of the Profession* (Oxford, 1982), 44–51; idem, "Apollodorus," in the *Macmillan Encyclopedia of Architects* (New York, 1982), 1:91–94; Lepper and Frere (1988), 187–93; Anderson (1997), 59–63.

29. See Anderson (1997), 65. For the designation of workshops, see most recently D. A. Conlin, *The Artists of the Ara Pacis: The Process of Hellenization in Roman Relief Sculpture* (Chapel Hill, N.C., 1997). See also M. K. Thornton and R. L. Thornton, *Julio-Claudian Building Programs: A Quantitative Study in Political Management* (Wauconda, Ill., 1989).

30. Von Hesberg (1992), 19. See also F. Coarelli, "Il sepolcro degli Scipioni," *DialArch* 6 (1972): 36–106; Frischer (1983), 51–86.

31. See G. Colonna, "Un aspetto oscuro del Lazio antico. Le tombe del VI–V secolo a.C.," *PP* 32 (1977): 160–61.

32. F. Coarelli, *Il sepolcro degli Scipioni a Roma* (Rome, 1988).

33. Von Hesberg (1992), 20.

34. Ibid. (1992), 22–26; Coarelli (1988).

35. Von Hesberg (1992), 27–36, 94–99, 171; L. Quilici, *Via Appia da Porta Capena ai colli Albani* (Rome, 1989), 70; Mansuelli (1958), 12.

36. See below, Chapter 6.

37. See A. Kuttner, "Some New Grounds for Narrative: Marcus Antonius's Base (*The Ara Domitii Ahenobarbi*) and Republican Biographies," in *Narrative and Event in Ancient Art,* ed. P. Holliday (Cambridge, 1993), 198–229.

38. *LTUR* 1:309 s.v. Columna Rostrata C. Duilii (Forum) (L. Chioffi); L. Pietilä-Castrén, *Magnificentia Publica. The Victory Monuments of the Roman Generals in the Era of the Punic Wars* (Helsinki, 1987), 30.

39. *LTUR* 2:267 s.v. Fornices Stertinii (F. Coarelli); Pietilä-Castrén (1987), 71–72.

40. Mansuelli (1958), 12.

41. See Kuttner (1993).

42. See C. Picard, *Les trophées romains. Contribution à l'histoire de la religion et de l'art triomphale de Rome* (Paris, 1957), 185–86; F. Coarelli, *Il Campo Marzio dalle origini alla fine della repubblica* (Rome, 1997), 539–80.

43. See Arce (1988), 37–38.

44. Livy 2.16.7, 3.43.7; Dion. Hal. 6.96.3; S. Weinstock, *Divus Julius* (Oxford, 1971), 348–49; Arce (1988), 17.

45. App. *BCiv.* 1.105.493–500; Plut. *Vit. Sull.* 38.3; Weinstock (1971), 349; Arce (1988), 19–21, 30–31.

46. Plut. *Vit. Sull.* 38.4; App. *BCiv.* 1.106.500.

47. Arce (1988), 19, 28, 34.

48. Suet. *Caes.* 84.1–3; App. *BCiv.* 2.143.599; Cic. *Phil.* 2.90; Weinstock (1971), 350–51.

49. Pliny *HN* 18.16; Suet. *Iul.* 84.3–4; App. *BCiv.* 2.148.615–16; Cass. Dio 44.50.2; Cic. *Phil.* 2.91; *Att.* 14.101; Weinstock (1971), 355; Arce (1988), 33–34. For funerals in general, see J. Scheid, "*Contraria facere:* Renversements et déplacements dans les rites funéraires," *Archeologia e storia antica* 6 (1984): 117–39.

50. S. R. F. Price, "From Noble Funerals to Divine Cult: The Consecration of Roman Emperors," in *Rituals and Royalty: Power and Ceremonial in Traditional Societies* (Cambridge, 1987), 59.

51. Cass. Dio 74.4.2; Diod. 18.26; Weinstock (1971), 361–62.

52. Cass. Dio 56.34.1, 74.4.3; Weinstock (1971), 361.

53. Arce (1988), 41–43, 53. Anomalies in Augustus's procession are described in Chapter 2.

54. A. Frazer, "The Roman Imperial Funeral Pyre," *JSAH* 27 (1968): 209; idem, "The Pyre of Faustina Senior," in *Studies in Classical Art and Archaeology. A Tribute to P. H. von Blanckenhagen,* ed. G. Kopcke and M. B. Moore (New York, 1979), 271–74; P. N. Schulten, *Die Typologie der römische Konsekrationsprägungen* (Frankfurt, 1974), 21–22.

55. See Weinstock (1971), 356–58.

56. Ov. *Met.* 15.843; *Fast.* 3.701.

57. Suet. *Iul.* 88; Weinstock (1971), 370–84.

58. Cass. Dio 56.46.2; Suet. *Aug.* 100; Arce (1988), 140–51.

59. Cass. Dio 56.42.3, 75.4.5; Herod. 4.2.11; Price (1987), 95; Arce (1988), 131–33.

60. Tac. *Ann.* 1.8.1–4; Suet. *Aug.* 101.1.4; Cass. Dio 56.33.1; Tert. *Apol.* 13.3; Weinstock (1971), 388; Arce (1988), 126, 129. Herodian (4.2) states that the Romans deified emperors who left sons as successors.

61. Suet. *Calig.* 59, *Claud.* 11.3; Cass. Dio 60.4.1. See E. R. Varner, "*Damnatio Memoriae* and Roman Imperial Portraiture" (Ph.D. diss., Yale University, 1993).

62. Price (1987), 54, 91–92, 96.

63. Cass. Dio 47.18.3; Weinstock (1971), 391–98.

64. App. *BCiv.* 2.148.616; Cass. Dio 47.18.3–4; Weinstock (1971), 364–67, 386–91, 399–401; see below, Chapter 5.

65. Suet. *Vesp.* 9; Aur. Vict. *Caesares* 9.7; *LTUR* 1:277–78, s.v. Claudius, Divus, Templum (Reg. II) (C. Buzzetti).

66. E. D'Ambra, *Private Lives, Imperial Virtues: The Frieze of the Forum Transitorium in Rome* (Princeton, N.J., 1993), 19–46; M. Torelli, "Culto imperiale e spazi urbani in età flavia dai rilievi Hartwig all'arco di Tito," in *Urbs: Espace urbain et histoire, Ier siècle avant J.-C. - Ier siècle après J.-C. CEFR* 98 (Rome, 1987): 563–82; R. Darwell-Smith, *Emperors and Architecture: A Study of Flavian Rome* (Brussels, 1996).

67. See. J. E. Packer, *The Forum of Trajan in Rome: A Study of the Monuments* (Berkeley, 1997), 131–35.

68. *LTUR* 3:7–8, s.v. Hadrianus, Divus, Templum; Hadrianeum (M. Cipollone).

69. See below, Chapter 4.

70. S.H.A. *M. Ant.* 6; *LTUR* 1:46–47 s.v. Antoninus, Divus et Faustina, Diva, Aedes, Templum (A. Cassatella).

71. *LTUR* 3:212 s.v. Marcus, Divus, Templum (F. De Caprariis).

72. Cass. Dio 47.8.5; Weinstock (1971), 397.

73. E. Beurlier, *Essai sur le culte rendu aux empereurs romains* (Paris, 1890), 69–73; Arce (1988), 125–27.

74. Cass. Dio 47.19.2, 56.34.2; Weinstock (1971), 393–94; Price (1987), 79; F. Dupont, "The Emperor-God's Other Body," in *Fragments for a History of the Human Body* (New York, 1989), 397–419, esp. 415.

CHAPTER ONE

1. For Augustus's building program, see most recently D. Favro, *The Urban Image of Augustan Rome* (Cambridge, 1996).

2. *LTUR* 3:237–39 s.v. Mausoleum Augusti: le sepolture (Macciocca).

3. See most recently H. von Hesberg and S. Panciera, *Das Mausoleum des Augustus. Der Bau and seine Inschriften* (Munich, 1994); R. T. Ridley, "*Augusti Manes Volitant per Auras:* The Archaeology of Rome under the Fascists," *Xenia* 11 (1986): 19–46.

4. Strab. 5.3.9. Excavations unearthed two cippi with iron rings under the Church of San Rocco, suggesting that bronze chains delimited a paved area around the Mausoleum: G. Q. Giglioli, "Il sepolcreto imperiale," *Capitolium* 6 (1930): 532–67, esp. 563. The garden probably extended behind the tomb to the north; no physical evidence of the ustrinum has been found. For hypotheses, see V. Jolivet, "Les cendres d'Auguste. Note sur la topographie monumentale du Champ de Mars septentrionale," *Archeologia Laziale* 9 (1988): 90–96; F. Coarelli, *Il Campo Marzio dalle origini alla fine della repubblica* (Rome, 1997), 599–601.

5. In the following description the walls are numbered from the outside (5) inward, following G. Gatti, "Nuove osservazioni sul Mausoleo di Augusto," *L'Urbe* 3.8 (1938): 1ff. See R. A. Cordingley and I. A. Richmond, "The Mausoleum of Augustus," *BSR* 10 (1927): 25–26, for earlier reconstructions. Restorations must satisfy four criteria. They must: (1) agree with Strabo's description; (2) incorporate surviving fragments of architectural decoration; (3) make sensible use of a substantial load-bearing wall (wall 3); (4) include architectural details recorded in notes and sketches by Bal-

dassare Peruzzi in 1519 during excavations undertaken by Leo X for the opening of Via Ripetta (at that time called Via Leonina): see A. Bartoli, *I monumenti antichi di Roma nei disegni degli Uffizi di Firenze* (Rome, 1914–22), CXI.197, CXII.199–200, CIX.204, CXV.205, CLIV.285, CCXII.355. These indicate a circular base with a small attic; travertine facing over a section of *opus caementicum,* presumably belonging to an exterior wall; and a cornice with a Doric frieze.

6. See Bartoli (1927), 30–46; Giglioli (1930); E. Fiorilli, "A proposito del Mausoleo di Augusto," *BdA* 7 (1927): 214–19; L. Richardson, Jr., *A New Topographical Dictionary of Ancient Rome* (Baltimore, 1992), 248.

7. See Cordingley and Richmond (1927); von Hesberg and Panciera (1994). For a variant reconstruction, see G. Gatti, "Il Mausoleo di Augusto. Studio di ricostruzione," *Capitolium* 10 (1934): 457–64; idem (1938).

8. Giglioli (1930), 551, 557. The pillar measured 12 feet in width, and with the concrete coating 30 feet in diameter. Its removal before the mid-sixteenth century caused the Mausoleum's collapse. See A. M. Colini and C. Q. Giglioli, "Relazione della prima campagna di scavo nel Mausoleo di Augusto," *BullCom* 54 (1926) [1927]: 191–234, esp. 233.

9. Colini and Giglioli (1926); von Hesberg and Panciera (1994).

10. Suet. *Aug.* 101. See most recently S. Güven, "Displaying the *Res Gestae* of Augustus: A Monument of Imperial Image for All," *JSAH* 57 (1998): 30–45; J. Elsner, "Inventing Imperium: Texts and the Propaganda of Monuments in Augustan Rome," in *Art and Text in Roman Culture,* ed. J. Elsner, 32–53 (Cambridge, 1996); Z. Yavetz, "The *Res Gestae* and Augustus' Public Image," in *Caesar Augustus: Seven Aspects,* 1–36 (Oxford, 1984). See also F. W. Shipley, *Res Gestae Divi Augusti* (London, 1924). The tablets were melted down for coinage in the Middle Ages.

11. See most recently E. Buchner, "Ein Kanal für Obelisken. Neues vom Mausoleum des Augustus in Rom," *AntW* 27 (1996), 161–68. One was moved to Piazza dell'Esquilino in 1587 by Sixtus V, the other to Piazza del Quirinale by Pius VI in

1782; see C. D'Onofrio, *Gli obelischi di Roma,*[2] 155–59 and 256–67 (Rome, 1967); A. Roullet, *The Egyptian and Egyptianising Monuments of Imperial Rome,* 78–79 (Leiden, 1972); L. Habachi and E. Buchner, *Die unsterblichen Obelisken* (Mainz, 1982). Some scholars have viewed them as a later addition to the Mausoleum, perhaps Domitianic, since Ammianus Marcellinus, writing in ca. A.D. 360, states that Augustus brought only two obelisks to Rome (those in the Campus Martius and Circus Maximus) and that subsequent generations transported the Mausoleum pair (17.4.12, 16) and because Pliny did not record them earlier in his description of Roman obelisks (*HN* 36.69–74). D. Boschung, "Tumulus Iuliorum – Mausoleum Augusti," *Hefte des Berner Archaeol. Seminars* 6 (1980): 38–41, esp. 39, maintains, however, that Ammianus Marcellinus is not wholly reliable in such details (the Vatican obelisk was brought to Rome under Caligula, not Constantius II, as Ammianus asserts), and that Pliny's was not an inventory of all Roman obelisks but a selection of outstanding examples in which these small, uninscribed obelisks had no place.

12. See D. E. E. Kleiner, *Roman Sculpture* (New Haven, Conn., -London, 1992), 90–99, and bibliography on 119; most recently, D. A. Conlin, *The Artists of the Ara Pacis: The Process of Hellenization in Roman Relief Sculpture* (Chapel Hill, N.C., 1997).

13. E. Buchner, *Die Sonnenuhr des Augustus: Nachdruck aus RM 1976 und 1980 und Nachtrag über die Ausgrabung 1980/1981* (Mainz, 1982); see below, Chapter 3.

14. M. Schütz, "Zur Sonnenuhr des Augustus auf dem Marsfeld," *Gymnasium* 97 (1990): 432–57. For the isolation of the monuments from other buildings, see D. Favro, "Reading the Augustan City," in *Narrative and Event in Ancient Art,* ed. P. J. Holliday (Cambridge, 1993), 230–57. See also Jolivet (1988), 90–96 on the development of the northern Campus Martius as an imperial funerary district from Augustan times on.

15. See J. Arce, *Funus imperatorum: Los funerales de los emperadores romanos* (Madrid, 1988), 74–75; von Hesberg and Panciera (1994); *LTUR* 3:237–39.

16. Suet. *Calig.* 59; see Arce (1988), 73–74.

17. Eutropius, *Breviarum ab urbe condita,* 7.18.4; Suet. *Vit.* 11; Tac. *Hist.* 2.95. See Arce (1988), 75–76; R. Krautheimer, *Rome, Profile of a City, 312–1308* (Princeton, N.J., 1980).

18. Galba: Suet. *Galba* 20; Eutropius, *Breviarum ab urbe condita* 7.16.3; Plut. *Galba* 27.1, 28.4; Tac. *Hist.* 1.49.1. Otho: Suet. *Otho* 11–12; Tac. *Hist.* 2.49; Plut. *Ot.* 18.1. Vitellius: Suet. *Vit.* 17; Eutropius 7.11.5. Vespasian: *CIL* 6.893, on which the single word *Vespasiani* may refer to Vespasian's burial in the Mausoleum, or to his cremation nearby, or to the wife or son of Flavius Clemens: see Arce (1988), 77–78; O. Hirschfeld, "Die kaiserlichen Grabstätten in Rom," in *Kleine Schriften,* 462–63 (Berlin, 1913).

19. Suet. *Dom.* 2. On the Flavian building programs, see R. Darwell-Smith, *Emperors and Architecture: A Study of Flavian Rome* (Brussels, 1996); E. D'Ambra, *Private Lives, Imperial Virtues: The Frieze of the Forum Transitorium in Rome* (Princeton, N.J., 1993), 19–46; M. Torelli, "Culto imperiale e spazi urbani in età flavia dai rilievi Hartwig all'arco di Tito," in *Urbs: Espace urbaine et Histoire, Ier siècle avant J.-C. – Ier siècle après J.-C., CEFR* 98 (Rome, 1987): 563–82.

20. See M. Pfanner, *Der Titusbogen, Beitrage zur Erschliessung Hellenistischer und Kaiserzeitlicher Skulptur und Architektur 2* (Mainz, 1983) 4–11; J. B. de Rossi, *Inscriptiones Christianae Urbis Romae* (Rome, 1888), 48; R. Valentini and G. Zucchetti, *Codice topografico della città di Roma* (Rome, 1940–53), II–IV; P. P. Lugano, *Santa Maria Nova* (Rome, 1923), 7; E. Rodocanachi, *Les monuments de Rome après la chute de l'empire* (Paris, 1914), 136; G. Valadier, *Narrazione artistica dell'operato finora nel ristauro dell'Arco di Tito letta nell'Accademia Romana di Archeologia* (1822), 8; E. Brües, "Raffaele Stern. Ein Beitrag zur Architekturgeschichte in Rom zwischen 1790 und 1830" (diss., University of Bonn, 1958), 128 ff.

21. Pfanner (1983), 19. The arch measures 13.50 (width) × 4.75 (depth) × 15.40 m. (height), with an archway of 8.30 (height) × 5.36 m. (width): Richardson (1992), 30.

22. Pfanner (1983), 44, suggests that there may have been sculpture to left and right of the inscription as well.

23. Ibid., 79–90. For the triumph: Suet. *Vesp.* 8.1, 12; *Tit.* 6.1; *Dom.* 2.1; Cass. Dio 65.12.

The surviving figures include ministrants, a *victimarius,* and a sacrificial stier.

24. See Pfanner (1983), 44–76; Kleiner (1992), 185–91.

25. See F. Cumont, "L'aigle funéraire d'Hierapolis et l'apothéose des empereurs," *Etudes syriennes* (1917); A. Roes, "L'aigle du culte solaire syrien," *RA,* ser. 6. 36 (1950): 129–46; idem, "L'aigle psychopompe de l'époque impériale," *Mél. Ch. Picard* 2 (Paris, 1949) II.881–91; U. Geyer, "Der Adlerflug im römischen Konsekrationszeremoniell" (diss., University of Bonn, 1967).

26. Cassiod. *Var.* 10.30.1.

27. *CIL* 6.945. On the west side, a nineteenth-century inscription records Valadier's restoration. F. Magi, "L'iscrizione perduta dell'Arco di Tito: Una ipotesi," *RM* 82 (1975): 99–116, proposes an inscription in the Vatican Museums (*CIL* 6.946) as the original inscription.

28. J. M. C. Toynbee, review of F. Magi, *I rilievi flavi del Palazzo della Cancelleria* (Rome, 1945), *JRS* 37 (1947): 187–91, esp. 190; M. E. Blake, *Roman Construction in Italy from Tiberius through the Flavians* (Washington, D.C., 1959), 111ff.; J. B. Ward-Perkins, *Roman Imperial Architecture*[2] (Harmondsworth, 1981), 72; M. Spannagel, "Wiedergefundene Antiken: Zu vier Dal-Pozzo-Zeichnungen in Windsor Castle," *AA* (1979): 348–77. The similarity of the arch to the later Arch of Trajan at Benevento has led other scholars to believe that both monuments were the product of a single workshop and has also provoked a redating of the Arch of Titus to Trajan's reign; see D. McFayden, "The Date of the Arch of Titus," *CJ* 11 (1915–16): 131–41; A. Bonanno, *Portraits and Other Heads on Roman Historical Relief up to the Age of Septimius Severus* (Oxford, 1976), 319.

29. Pfanner (1983), 91: Titus is celebrated as a *divus* on coins dating to 81/2, e.g., *BMC* 2, pl. 69.9.

30. F. S. Kleiner, "The Arches of Vespasian in Rome," *RM* 97 (1990): 127–36, argues that the groups on the panel's arch represent Vespasian and Titus in their triumphal quadrigas, and Domitian on horseback accompanied by Minerva, his patron goddess. The arch must celebrate the triumph and date between the triumph and the con-

struction of the Arch of Titus. It must also predate Vespasian's death, since Titus is represented as sole triumphator once he becomes emperor. Kleiner proposes that the arch is one of the monuments mentioned by Cassius Dio (65.7.2), voted by the Senate in the year before the triumph, and that it was under construction at the time of the procession but its attic sculpture was unfinished. Pfanner identifies it as the Porta Triumphalis, as shown in the Codex Coburgensis: "Codex Coburgensis Nr. 88: Die Entdeckung der porta triumphalis," *RM* 87 (1980): 327ff.; idem (1983): 91–92.

31. K. Lehmann-Hartleben, "L'Arco di Tito," *BullCom* 62 (1934): 89–122.

32. *CIL* 6.944. Lehmann-Hartleben (1934), 107–9.

33. Lehmann-Hartleben (1934), 109–11.

34. Pfanner (1983), 98–99. Contra: S. De Maria, *Gli archi onorari di Roma e dell'Italia romana* (Rome, 1988), 120.

35. Suet. *Dom.* 1.

36. Mart. *Epigr.* 9.1.6–10, 9.35.8; Suet. *Dom.* 17; E. K. Gazda and A. E. Haeckl, *Images of Empire: Flavian Fragments in Rome and Ann Arbor Rejoined* (Ann Arbor, Mich., 1996). F. Coarelli, *Roma sepolta* (Milan, 1984), 153, expresses doubt about Vespasian's and Titus's burial there.

37. Suet. *Dom.* 17.

38. Mart. *Epigr.* 9.1.8–9, 9.3.12, 9.3.18–19, 9.8.3, 9.20.1–2, 9.34, 9.35.8; Stat. *Silv.* 4.3.18–19, 5.1.240–41; Suet. *Dom.* 15.2. See H. Erkell, "Statius' Silvae 1.1 und das Templum Gentis Flaviae," *Eranos* 56 (1958): 173–82; H. Sauter, "Der römische Kaiserkult bei Martial und Statius," *Tübinger Beiträge zur Altertumswissenschaft* 21 (1934): 150–52; R. Helm, "Eusebius Werke: Chronik des Hieronymus," *GCS* 7 (1956): 191; J. C. Anderson, "A Topographical Tradition in Fourth Century Chronicles: Domitian's Building Program," *Historia* 32 (1983): 93–105.

39. Suet. *Dom.* 5; B. W. Jones, *The Emperor Domitian* (London, 1992), 79–81.

40. H. Gsell. *Essai sur le règne de l'empereur Domitien* (Paris, 1894), 114–15, places its completion as early as 89; K. Scott, *The Imperial Cult under the Flavians* (Stuttgart-Berlin, 1936), 66, argues that it was probably not begun before 94 and was finished in 95, the presumed publication date of

Martial's ninth book of *Epigrams,* in which the poet expresses his admiration for the Temple. Torelli (1987), 563–64, prefers a date after 89 for the initiation of construction, and 95/96 for its completion.

41. R. Paris, ed., *Dono Hartwig: Originali ricongiunti e copie tra Ann Arbor e Roma. Ipotesi per il Templum Gentis Flaviae* (Rome, 1994), 16. See also M. Santangelo, "Il Quirinale nell'età classica," *MemPontAcc* 5 (1941): 77–214, esp. 143; D'Ambra (1993), 38.

42. Coarelli (1984), 151; Torelli (1987), 568–69; Paris (1994), 24–25. See also Anderson (1983), 97; S. B. Platner and T. Ashby, *A Topographical Dictionary of Ancient Rome* (London, 1929), 247.

43. *CIL* 6.29788, 15.7451; Suet. *Vesp.* 4; Tac. *Hist.* 3.69; Coarelli (1984), 151–53; Torelli (1987), 567–68; Paris (1994), 23. The Vigna Sadoleto has not been definitively located.

44. Mart. *Epigr.* 9.34.1–2, 67.

45. *Silv.* 4.3.18–19.

46. W. Altmann, *Die Italischen Rundbauten* (Berlin, 1906), 88; Anderson (1983), 97; D'Ambra (1993), 39–40. The sketches of a peripteral tempietto and a circular porch by Flaminio Vacca and Pirro Ligorio, respectively, were reportedly based on ruins still visible at the time. See Santangelo (1945), 152; Torelli (1987), 563.

47. Only two such coins are known: one in a private collection in Switzerland, the other inserted into a medallion in Bonn; see Paris (1994), 26.

48. Torelli (1987), 564–68. For other identifications of the building represented on the coin, see E. Nash, "Suggerimenti intorno ad alcuni problemi topografici del Foro e del Palatino," *ArchCl* 11 (1959): 227–36; C. F. Giuliani, "Domus Flavia: Una nuova lettura," *RM* 84 (1977): 91–106.

49. Eutropius, *Breviarum ab urbe condita* 8.2; Aur. Vict. *Caesares* 12.12; *Chr.* 354 (Mommsen, *Chr. Min.* 1.146. 21); Hier. *Chr.* 193; Arce (1988), 83.

50. *CIL* 6.960; *Fasti Ostienses* 48, A. Degrassi, *Inscr. Ital.* 13.1.203. For the Forum, see J. E. Packer, *The Forum of Trajan in Rome: A Study of the Monuments* (Berkeley, 1997); idem, "Trajan's Forum Again: The Column and the Temple of Trajan in the Master Plan Attributed to Apollodorus (?)," *JRA* 7 (1994): 163–82; idem, "Report from Rome: The Imperial Fora, a Retrospective," *AJA* 101

(1997): 307–30. Opinion differs on two major issues concerning the temple. (1) On the basis of finds from past excavations and new corings in and around the presumed location of the temple podium, R. Meneghini, "L'architettura del Foro di Traiano attraverso i ritrovimenti archeologici più recenti," *RM* 105 (1998): 127–48, insists that there is no evidence for a traditional temple at the northwest end of the forum. Extant monolithic columns and foundations there lead him to reconstruct a propylon instead, serving as a monumental entrance to the forum from the Campus Martius. While this propylon may have housed an aedicular temple in Trajan's honor, he prefers to place a temple similar to the nearby Temple of Mars Ultor at the southeast end of the forum, flanked by halls on the design later evidenced in the Severan Forum at Lepcis Magna. I am grateful to J. E. Packer for allowing me to read his forthcoming response to these hypotheses, which would suggest that the traditional reconstruction should stand. Meneghini's reconstruction would reverse the orientation of the forum, with the effect that a visitor confronted the column upon first entering. This presents a problem, as Michael Larvey points out to me, because the column's dedicatory inscription and door face the basilica. (2) Scholars have long been divided on whether the temple formed part of the Forum's original design, since it is unlikely that Trajan would have openly professed his own divinity while alive. Brickstamps indicate that it was not completed until Hadrian's reign. As a passage of the H.A. states that Hadrian dedicated the temple to the Divine Trajan after his death, later rededicating it to Trajan and Plotina (as an inscription traditionally associated with the temple appears to confirm), some scholars contend that it was entirely a Hadrianic building (see, e.g., Richardson [1992], 175). It is more likely that the temple was part of the plan, as Settis argues (1988, 75–82); either the Forum complex was purposely left unfinished, so that his successor could finish it and dedicate the temple to the divinized Trajan, or Trajan planned to dedicate it to his real father, Divus Traianus Pater, whom he had di-

vinized. The Temple of Faustina in the Roman Forum offers an excellent example of a temple built in a prominent location in honor of one divinized person in full expectation that another more important dedicatee (Antoninus Pius) could join her once he was divinized himself. In the event that Meneghini's hypothesis of a temple on the southeast end is correct, the latter scenario is most likely, because, by Lynne Lancaster's deduction, building materials were brought into the forum area from the northwest side, where the portico substructures were greatly reinforced with brick ribbing, and construction in the forum probably began on the southeast side and progressed northwest; on this assumption, Meneghini's temple would have been built before the Basilica Ulpia. See L. Lancaster, "Building Trajan's Column," *AJA* 103 (1999): 419–39.

51. Packer (1994), 167–68 n. 15, 171. Sixtus V replaced the statue in 1588 with Giacomo della Porta's figure of Saint Peter. Numismatic representations of the Column show a cuirassed male figure holding a spear and an orb.

52. Eutropius *Breviarum ab urbe condita* 8.5.2: "[Traianus] inter divos relatus est solusque omnium intra urbem sepultus est. Ossa conlata in urnam auream in foro, quod aedificavit, sub columna posita sunt." A. Claridge, "Hadrian's Column of Trajan," *JRA* 6 (1993): 5–22, esp. 11, notes that this need not mean that the ashes were buried in the base itself, and that a cavity under the Column, explored by Boni, could feasibly have contained them.

53. Cic. *Leg.* 2.23.58; *Dig.* 47.12.5; S.H.A. *M. Ant.* 12.3; Paulus Sent. 1.21.2–3. See Arce (1988), 88.

54. Claridge (1993). For the unlikely proposal that the Column initially stood in the eastern hemicycle of Trajan's Forum, see V. Groh, "La Colonna di Traiano," *Rend-Linc*, s. 6.1 (1925): 40–57; Richardson (1992), 101–7. See also J. C. Anderson, *The Historical Topography of the Imperial Fora* (Brussels, 1984), 155–59.

55. For which, see G. Martines, "La struttura della Colonna Traiana. Un esercitazione di meccanica alessandrina," *Prospettiva* 32 (1983): 60–71; M. Wilson Jones, "One Hundred Feet and a Spiral Stair: The Prob-

lem of Designing Trajan's Column," *JRA* 6 (1993): 23–28.

56. G. Lugli, "La tomba di Traiano," *Omagiu lui Constantin Daicoviciu* (Bucharest, 1960), 337–38; F. Lepper and S. Frere, *Trajan's Column: A New Edition of the Cichorius Plates* (Gloucester, 1988), 21; Claridge (1993), 5–22; G. Boni, "Esplorazione del Forum Ulpium," *NSc* 4 (1907): 361–427, esp. 368. When Trajan's ashes were in place, the room was sealed with a thick wall of cement and brick, not, Lugli notes, part of the original plan, since it obstructs the access corridor. The present hole in the wall dates from the medieval theft of Trajan's urn.

57. Lugli (1960), 338; Claridge (1993), 11–13; G. Rodenwaldt, review of H. Lehner, *Das Römerlager Vetera bei Xanten. Ein Führer durch die Ausgrabungen des Bonner Provinzialmuseums* (Bonn, 1926), *Gnomon* 2 (1926): 338–39; S. Stucchi, "*Tantis viribus:* L'area della Colonna nella concezione generale del Foro di Traiano," *ArchCl* 41 (1989): 237–91, esp. 255–57.

58. Lepper and Frere (1988), 22.

59. G. Becatti, *La colonna coclide istoriata* (Rome, 1960), 30–31; B. Haarlov, *The Half-Open Door. A Common Symbolic Motif within Roman Sepulchral Sculpture* (Odense, 1977); P. Zanker, "Das Trajansforum in Rom," *AA* (1970): 499–544; D. Boschung, *Antike Grabaltäre aus den Nekropolen Roms, Acta Bernensia* 10 (Berne, 1987), passim.

60. E. P. McGowan, "Tomb Marker and Turning Post: Funerary Columns in the Archaic Period," *AJA* 99 (1995): 615–32. Lugli (1960) traces the origin of the sepulchral column to its use as support for a sacred object. Either the cinerary urn took the sacred object's place or the column served as a stele over the burial. This practice is best documented in Asia Minor, but also in Greece, the Greek colonies, Sicily, and Italy. In the Hellenistic period huge sepulchral columns supporting statues of the deceased appeared in Syria (see K. Humann and O. Puchstein, *Reisen in Kleinasien und Nordsyrien* [Berlin, 1890]; L. Vogel, *The Column of Antoninus Pius* [Cambridge, Mass., 1973], 25). See also J. Prieur, *La mort dans l'antiquité romaine* (Rennes, 1986), 98.

61. B. Frischer, "*Monumenta et Arae Honoris Virtutisque Causa:* Evidence of Memorials for Roman Civic Heroes," *BullCom* (1983): 51–86, esp. 73.

62. Zanker (1970); S. Settis, A. La Regina, G. Agosti, and V. Farinella, *La Colonna Traiana* (Turin, 1988), 53–56; Packer (1994), 163–82.

63. Schol. Vet. (in Pind. *Car.*), ed. A. B. Drachman (Leipzig, 1903), 149b; J. Rykwert, *The Idea of a Town* (Princeton, N.J., 1976), 34. See also Frischer (1983).

64. Zanker (1970), 531 and 536; see also R. Martin, *Recherches sur l'agora grecque* (Paris, 1951), 48 and 194–201; A. Brelich, *Gli eroi greci. Un problema storico-religioso* (Rome, 1958), 129; G. Waurick, "Untersuchungen zur Lage der römischen Kaisergräber in der Zeit von Augustus bis Constantin," *JRGZM* 20 (1973): 107–46, esp. 118; H. Thiersch, "Die Alexandrinische Königsnekropole," *JdI* 25 (1910): 55–97. This fashion was experiencing a revival in Trajan's time (at least in Asia Minor), as evidenced by Celsus's burial in a cella beneath his library at Ephesus: see *Forschungen in Ephesos* 5.1 (Vienna, 1953); C. Callmer, "Antike Bibliotheken," *OpArch* 3 (1944): 144–93, esp. 170.

65. Zanker (1970), 539. The libraries may have held some eschatological meaning as well: funerary imagery suggests that intellectualism gradually came to be perceived as a vehicle for apotheosis: see H.-I. Marrou, *Mousikos aner. Etudes sur les scènes de la vie intellectuelle figurant sur les monuments funéraires romains* (Grenoble, 1938); Settis et al. (1988), 60–74; *LTUR* 2:358 s.v. Forum Traiani (S. Maffei).

66. Seen, for instance, in the naming of the Basilica Ulpia (using Trajan's family name in the style of the Basilicae Julia and Aemilia) and the Forum's construction *ex manubiis;* it reflected Trajan's determination to settle the conflict between *princeps* and Senate: Zanker (1970), 531.

67. Suet. *Iul.* 85. See also Cass. Dio 44.51; Cic. *Att.* 14.15, *Phil.* 1.5; Frischer (1983), 68–69 and 73; S. Weinstock, *Divus Julius* (Oxford, 1971), 364–67. The evidence on the column is difficult to piece together. Weinstock surmises that Amatius began an altar in Caesar's name, which Dolabella destroyed within two weeks. Subsequently a column (with or without a statue) was erected to mark the unofficial beginnings

of the new cult to Divus Julius, probably by Octavian. It may have been replaced the following year by a consecration altar. For other parallels between Trajan and Julius Caesar, see D. Nardoni, *La Colonna Ulpia Traiana* (Rome, 1986), 125–28.

68. Cass. Dio. 44.3–7.

69. See K. A. Waters, "Traianus Domitiani Continuator," *AJP* 90 (1969): 385–405. Still, if the Column was designed as a burial monument, it may have been Trajan's presumption that led Hadrian to confirm the interdiction against burial within the *pomerium* (*Dig.* 47.12.3.5).

70. Zanker (1970).

71. Mercati di Traiano inv. no. 3197; L. Ungaro and M. Millela, *I luoghi del consenso imperiale. Il Foro di Augusto, il Foro di Traiano* (Rome, 1995), 216–17; Packer (1997), 217–44; G. Piazzesi, "Gli edifici: Ipotesi ricostruttive," *ArchCl* 41 (1989): 125–96, esp. 177; Zanker (1970), 522 and fig. 44. For the commemorative context, see Altmann (1905), passim; F. Cumont, "Les lampes et les cierges allumés sur les tombeaux," *Miscellanea G. Mercati* 5 (Vatican City, 1946); G. Rushford, "Funeral Lights in Roman Sepulchral Monuments," *JRS* 5 (1915): 149–64; J. Scheid, "*Contraria facere*: Renversements et déplacements dans les rites funéraires," *Archeologia e storia antica* 6 (1984): 117–39.

72. Ungaro and Millela (1995), 196–97; Packer (1997), 127.

73. Mercati di Traiano inv. no. 4000; Ungaro and Millela (1995), 220–24; Piazzesi (1989), 134 and fig. 36; Packer (1997); 279.

74. Apul. *de Mundo* 38; E. Simon, "Zur Bedeutung des Greifen in der Kunst des Kaiserzeit," *Latomus* 21 (1962): 749–80, esp. 770.

75. Ungaro and Milella (1995), 220; Packer (1994), 171. Its association with Apollo dates to the sixth century, and developed more fully from the fourth century B.C., particularly with the burgeoning popularity of Pythagoreanism and Orphism and a concomitant belief in the transmigration of the soul. The griffin is mostly associated with Dionysos as Sabazios, master of plants and animals, god of rebirth, who, like Apollo, guaranteed immortality to his adherents. Simon (1962) remarks "ist der bacchische Charakter des Frieses unverkennbar," and

notes the added Dionysiac touch of a silenus and maenads depicted on the volute krater shown in the frieze. See also R. Turcan, *Les sarcophages romains à représentations dionysiaques: Essai de chronologie et d'histoire religieuse* (Paris, 1966), 368–77, who documents a "réveil du Dionysisme romain sous Trajan," which manifested itself particularly strongly in funerary art. "Dans le cas précis des frises de ce Forum, nous ne pensons pas que le griffon "solaire" du Levant nous réfère précisément à la politique orientale de Trajan: c'est un symbole de *puissance* valable pour toute espèce d'impérialisme romain. Comme tel aussi et comme tous les motifs de la symbolique triomphale, il pourra représenter la victoire sur la mort de l'âme, qu'il arrache aux miasmes du monde et qu'il véhicule au-dessus de la matière jusqu'aux splendeurs etherées" (371–72, n. 7).

76. Putti accompany the griffin in both Dionysiac and Apolline iconography: see R. Stuveras, *Le putto dans l'art romain* (Brussels, 1969), 33–63. Frequently represented in its own right in a funerary context, a putto often holds a downward-facing torch to symbolize extinction of life and is characterized as guide of the dead or *psychopompos*: see D. Delplace, *Le griffon, de l'archaïsme à l'epoque impériale. Etude iconographique et essai d'interprétation symbolique* (Brussels-Rome, 1980), 365–75, 416–18; Simon (1962), 763–72.

77. "Quest'ultimo connesso con la sua funzione di guardiana della tomba": Ungaro and Millela (1995), 222; Packer (1979), 279.

78. *P.Fay.* 19, in *Fayum Towns and Their Papyri*, ed. B. P. Grenfell and A. S. Hunt (London, 1900), 112–16. See also P. Alexander, "Letters and Speeches of the Emperor Hadrian," *HSCP* 49 (1938): 141–77, esp. 170.

79. "Animula vagula blandula / hospes comesque corporis / quae nunc abibis in loca / pallidula rigida nudula / nec ut soles dabis iocos," S.H.A. *Hadr.* 25.9, trans. Birley. See H. Bardon, *Les empereurs et les lettres latines d'Auguste à Hadrien* (Paris, 1968), 417–18; M. Guarducci, "La religione di Adriano," in *Les empereurs d'Espagne* (Paris, 1965), 209–21, esp. 219.

80. S. Aurigemma, *Villa Adriana* (Rome, 1984), 146–47; W. L. MacDonald and J. Pinto,

Hadrian's Villa and Its Legacy (New Haven, Conn., 1995), 131–38.

81. S.H.A. *Hadr.* 14.8–9; Cass. Dio 49.4.1–5. See also S.H.A. *Hadr.* 15.10; Aur. Vict. *Caesares* 14.2; R. Syme, "Hadrian the Intellectual," in *Les empereurs d'Espagne* (Paris, 1965), 243–53; T. Rivoira, "Di Adriano architetto e dei monumenti Adrianei," *Rend-Linc* 18 (1909): 172–77; C. F. Giuliani, "La rivoluzione adriana, revisione archeologica I," *L'architettura, cronache e storia* 279.1 (1979): 45–51; G. Gullini, "Apollodoro e Adriano. Ellenismo e classicismo nell'architettura romana," *BdA* 53 (1968) [1971]: 63–80; W. L. MacDonald, *The Architecture of the Roman Empire, I: An Introductory Study* (New Haven, Conn., 1982), 129–37; M. T. Boatwright, *Hadrian and the City of Rome* (Princeton, N.J., 1987); F. Rakob, "Adriano – Imperatore e architetto," in *Adriano e il suo mausoleo*, M. Mercalli, ed. (Milan, 1998), 7–19.

82. The date construction began is unknown. Brick stamps dating from 123 provide a terminus ante quem: see H. Bloch, *I bolli laterizi e la storia edilizia romana. Contributi all'archeologia e alla storia romana* (Rome, 1947) 253–56; J. R. Pierce, "The Mausoleum of Hadrian and the Pons Aelius," *JRS* 15 (1925): 75–103, esp. 83 n. 4, 97 n. 2.

83. S.H.A. *Hadr.* 25.7–26. *Invisus omnibus* could also mean "unseen by all" or "envied by all." See A. R. Birley, *Hadrian: The Restless Emperor* (London, 1997), 279–307.

84. For the complex history of the Mausoleum, see M. Borgatti, *Castel Sant'Angelo in Roma* (Rome, 1931); C. D'Onofrio, *Castel Sant'Angelo: Images and History* (Rome, 1984); Pierce (1925), 78–81; Mercalli, *Adriano e il suo Mausoleo*.

85. *CIL* 6.973. Boatwright (1987), 176–77; J. Le Gall, *Le Tibre, fleuve de Rome dans l'antiquité* (Paris, 1953), 211–15; C. Mocchegiani Carpano, "Indagini archeologiche nel Tevere," *QArchEtr* 5 (1981): 144; Pierce (1925), 96–97; P. Gazzola, *Ponti romani. Contributo ad un indice sistematico con studio critico bibliografico* (Florence, 1963), 2:132–32. Statues of unknown identity decorated the bridge, as recorded on a series of gold medallions minted to celebrate its opening. M. Pensa, "Rappresentazioni di monumenti sulle monete di Adriano," *RIN* 80 (1978): 27–78, esp. 66–68, tentatively identifies them as male figures, possibly herms. C. C. Vermeule, *Greek Sculpture and Roman Taste* (Ann Arbor, Mich., 1977), 104, suggests statues of provinces and regions of the empire or members of the imperial family. See also J. M. C. Toynbee, *Roman Medallions* (New York, 1944), 146 n. 196, 232; A. Donini, *Ponti su monete e medaglie* (Rome, 1959); P. Serafin, "La moneta al tempo di Adriano," in Mercalli, *Adriano e il suo Mausoleo*, 187–225, esp. 224, no. 10.

86. F. Coarelli, *Roma* (Rome, 1980), 367. The enclosure measured 115 m. on a side, possibly standing out 15.60 m. from the square base. This part of the complex may have been built by Antoninus Pius. See T. Squadrilli, "Il Mausoleo di Adriano," *Capitolium* 50.7–8 (1975): 20–31, esp. 21; Pierce (1925), 76–77, 97; M. A. Tomei, "Il Mausoleo di Adriano: La decorazione scultorea," in Mercalli, *Adriano e il suo Mausoleo*, 101–47, esp. 103, 106.

87. M. Squadrilli (1975) and De'Spagnolis, "Contributi per una nuova lettura del Mausoleo di Adriano," *BdA* 61 (1976): 62–68, propose a fourth tier as well.

88. For the inscription, see Tomei (1998), 105–6; *CIL* 6:984–95. On the sculptures, see Procop. *Goth.* 1.22.14. G. Alberti, *Codici Borgo San Sepolcro* (1579), 25.26; R. Lanciani, *The Ruins and Excavations of Ancient Rome* (Boston-New York, 1897), 557. For the decoration: D. E. Strong, "Late Hadrianic Architectural Ornament in Rome," *BSR* 21 (1953): 118–51, esp. 129–47; Borgatti (1931), 38–40; Tomei (1998). Three marble fragments of horse tails and one fragment of a mane found near the tomb suggest that, as Procopius states, they may have been marble, although the *Mirabilia* describes them as bronze. Rivet holes in the corner blocks have yet to be analyzed (G. Angeletti, conversation, Rome, 1992). Ficorini believed that the groups resembled those from the Baths of Constantine, now in Piazza del Quirinale: Borgatti (200 n. K). R. Artioli, *Castel Sant'Angelo* (Rome, 1923), 23, identifies the horses of San Marco, Venice, as the sculptures from the Mausoleum, but with no substantive evidence: Pierce (1925), 83 n. 1. A. Manodori, "Memorie sparse del Mausoleo di Adriano," in Mercalli, *Adriano e il suo Mausoleo*, 149–59, also entertains this possibility.

89. Pierce (1925), 82; Angeletti, conversation, Rome, 1992. There is no substantive evidence for the summit decoration. John of Antioch (eighth century), *Codex Palatin. Graec.* 93 f. 47, states that there was a colossal quadriga on the tomb, placed there after Hadrian's death, and Borgatti (1931), 49, notes that a solar image would suit Hadrian's name, Aelius, and the quadriga surmounting Pertinax's pyre (see Introduction) might support such a notion. See Manodori (1998), 153–54; Tomei (1998). G. Angeletti, "Esito delle indagini attuate nel secondo tratto della rampa elicoidale," *Studi su Castel Sant'Angelo: Archivum arcis* 3 (1991): 158–60, prefers a tempietto. See also M. Mercalli, "The Angel of the Castle, Its Iconography, Its Significance," *The Angel and Rome* (Rome, 1987), 67–93.

90. G. N. Rushforth, "Magister Gregorius de Mirabilibus Urbis Romae: A New Description of Rome in the 12th Century," *JRS* 9 (1919): 14–58; Helbig, 2:382–83, no. 1067.

91. L. Abbondanza, "Osservazioni su alcuni rinvenimenti dell'area di Castel Sant'Angelo," in Mercalli, *Adriano e il suo Mausoleo* (1998), 39–44; Tomei (1998), 109; eadem, "Nuovi elementi di recenti acquisiti," in Mercalli, *Adriano e il suo Mausoleo,* 55–61. See also B. S. Ridgway, *Hellenistic Sculpture I. The Styles of ca. 331–200 B.C.* (Madison, Wisc., 1990), 313–14 and 340–41 n. 1; E. Rodocanachi, *Les monuments de Rome après la chute de l'empire* (Paris, 1914), 5; Borgatti (1931), 40; Squadrilli (1975), 21, 27.

92. Borgatti (1931), 18; De'Spagnolis (1975), 62; Pierce (1925), 86. See also G. Angeletti, "Mausoleo di Adriano. Atrio: restauro superfici lapidee," *Studi su Castel Sant'Angelo: Archivum arcis* 3 (1991): 155–57; idem, "1987–1990: Scavi e restauri nel Mausoleo di Adriano," in Mercalli, *Adriano e il suo Mausoleo,* 57–61. The head of the statue was moved to the Vatican Museums in 1788: inv. 543, and the door was carried off by Alexander VI: see Tomei (1998).

93. Six meters high and 3 meters wide, the corridor was paved with monochrome mosaic and lit by pyramidal light wells; the walls were finished with skirting, pilasters, and a cornice. All interior walls were faced with brick and covered with marble or stucco: Pierce (1925), 86; Tomei (1998), 103.

94. The cella measured 10.20 m. in height and 8 m. on a side. A fragment of yellow marble and a series of plug holes reveal that the walls were revetted up to the springing, where they were probably decorated with painted stucco. See Pierce (1925), 87; De'Spagnolis (1975), 63; Angeletti (1991), 161–66; idem (1998). The porphyry sarcophagus was taken to the Vatican in 1139 and reused by Innocent II in 1143; small fragments with warriors' heads now in the cloister at San Giovanni in Laterano and the Archeological Museum and Palazzo Riccardi in Florence may be all that survive of the chest after the Lateran fire of 1308: R. Delbrück, *Die antike Porphyrwerke* (Berlin, 1932), 212–18. Its ruined lid was reused for Otto II's burial in 983, and now serves as a baptismal font in Saint Peter's: see F. Gregorovius, *Die Gräbmaler der römischen Päpste* (Leipzig, 1857), 33; H. Grisar, "Il sepolcro dell'imperatore Ottone II nel paradiso dell'antica Basilica Vaticana," *Civiltà cattolica* 55 (1904): 463–73; Borgatti (1931), 28–29; C. Cecchelli, "Le chiese della Colonna Traiana e la leggenda di Traiano," *Studi e documenti sulla Roma sacra I (Miscellanea della R. Deputazione Romana di Storia Patria)* (Rome, 1938), 95–125; J. Deer, *The Dynastic Porphyry Tombs of the Norman Period in Sicily, DOS* 5 (Cambridge, Mass., 1959), 150–51; Krautheimer (1980), 212–13; M. Greenhalgh, *The Survival of Roman Antiquities in the Middle Ages* (London, 1989), 131; Manodori (1998); Tomei (1998), 104.

95. See Angeletti (1991), 158–60. The upper rooms are the present Sala della Giustizia and the Sala del Tesoro, which originally incorporated the modern Sala della Rotonda as well. They may have been used for less important burials: Borgatti (1931), 28.

96. "Se al primo piano abbiamo un percorso periferico circolare, rieccheggiante l'esterno, unito alla camera sepolcrale da un asse ortogonale a questa, al secondo la camera centrale e il perno di una serie di ambienti che con andamento stellare uniscono volumetricamente centro e periferia assolvendo inoltre alla necessaria funzione di passaggio per il piano superiore che nella pianta si rifà al primo;" Angeletti (1991), 159.

97. S.H.A., M. Ant. 12.4.

98. *CIL* 6.986.

99. E.g., *BMCRE* 4:528, no. 893. Marble fragments of the balustrade came to light in excavations of 1703: see F. Posterla in C.

Fontana, *Discorso sopra l'antico Monte Citatorio situato nel Campo Marzio . . .* (Rome, 1708).

100. Cod. Vat. Lat. 9023, f. 221v. (Vatican Library, 1704); most recently Vogel (1973), 5–22.

101. C. Fea. *Miscellanea filologica, critica e antiquaria* 1 (Rome, 1790) 1:123; Vogel (1973), 5–6.

102. *IG* 14.2421.1; Vogel (1973), 6. J. B. Ward-Perkins, "Columna divi Antonini," *Mélanges d'histoire ancienne et d'archéologie offerts à Paul Collart* (Lausanne, 1976), 345–52, suggests that it was left over after the completion of the Temple of Trajan and Plotina.

103. For details of restorations, see Vogel (1973), 5–6, 10–12. The pedestal measures 2.47 × 3.38 × 3.38 m., including cornice and foot molding. Eighteenth-century sketches reveal that it was crowned on all sides by an astragal molding, a cyma reversa, and a narrow fillet. See I. Vignoli, *De Columna Imperatoris Antonini Pii Dissertatio* (Rome, 1705), plates between 12 and 13; F. Bianchini, *De Kalendario et Cyclo Caesaris ac de Paschali Canone S. Hippolyti Martyris. Dissertationes duae . . . Quibus Inseritur Descriptio, et Explanatio Basis, in Campo Martio Nuper Detectae Sub Columna Antonino Pio Olim Dicata* (Rome, 1703), plates between 72 and 73. The lower moldings, an astragal, and a cyma were extremely fragmentary by the time the drawings were executed.

104. *CIL* 6.1004; Vogel (1973), 18. Cardinal points refer to the base's original location.

105. Vogel (1973), 56–68; see also M. L. Hadzi's review, *ArtB* 57 (1975): 123–25. The subject is unique in Roman art. Both scenes suffered considerable damage in the Middle Ages and the Renaissance: see drawings by Bianchini (1703) and Vignoli (1705). The restoration betrays a misunderstanding of the subject; the infantrymen's modern faces express a surprise and fear more suitable to an ambush than to a military exercise.

106. S.H.A. *Ver.* 10–11.

107. *CIL* 984–95; Aur. Vict. *Caesares* 16: *soli omnia decrevere templa, columnas sacerdotes.* See also S.H.A. *M. Ant.* 18, 27.11–12; Cass. Dio 71.33.4–71.34; Aur. Vict. *Caesares* 17.2; Tert. *Apol.* 25; Notitia, Regio 9; C. Caprino, A. M. Colini, G. Gatti, M. Pallottino, and P. Romanelli, *La Colonna di Marco Aurelio* (Rome, 1955), 18; A. R. Bir-

ley, *Marcus Aurelius: A Biography* (New Haven, Conn., 1987), 149, 209–10.

108. E. Petersen, A. von Domaszewski, and G. Calderini, *Die Marcussäule auf Piazza Colonna in Rom* (Munich, 1896), 6, 30; Caprino et al. (1955), 19. 26.

109. M. Jordan-Ruwe, "Zur Rekonstruktion und Datierung der Marcussäule," *Boreas* 13 (1990): 53–69, esp. 57; see also Petersen et al. (1896), 30; Caprino et al. (1955), pl. 2, fig. 3.

110. Jordan-Ruwe (1990), with earlier reconstructions. Jordan-Ruwe contends that a two-part base is unattested for any other Roman column monument, and that its tapering design would make the base undistinguishable from the column shaft from a distance, destroying its harmonious proportions; moreover, a cornice should be expected at the top of the base. She assigns two fragments of sculptural decoration in the foreground of Vico's sketch to the base: a sima block and a fragment of a long rectangular block decorated with a garland and an eagle. On Arcadius's Column, see E. H. Freshfield, "Notes on a Vellum Album Containing some Original Sketches of Public Buildings and Monuments, Drawn by a German Artist who Visited Constantinople in 1574," *Archaeologia* 72 (1921–22): 87–104.

111. Equivalent to 29.601 m. Its lower diameter measured 3.80 m, the upper 3.66. See Petersen et al. (1896), 29–30, 34.

112. Petersen et al. (1896), 3, suggests that Marcus Aurelius was accompanied by his wife, Faustina, but the only evidence to support this hypothesis is a reference to the column as the Column of Marcus Aurelius and Faustina (*CIL* 6.1585). Lanciani (*BC* [1873] 94; *CAR* IIG. 196) linked a colossal bronze finger found in Palazzo Ferrajoli, south of Piazza Colonna, and now in the Palazzo dei Conservatori, with the Column statue.

113. See Caprino et al. (1955), 61–117; Kleiner (1992), 295–301.

114. *CIL* 6.1585; Caprino et al. (1955), 32, 38–40.

115. See J. Morris, "The Dating of the Column of Marcus Aurelius," *JWarb* 15 (1952): 33–47, esp. 38; H. Wolff, "Welchen Zeitraum stellt der Bilderfries der Marcus-Säule dar?" *Ostbairische Grenzmarken. Passauer Jahrbuch für Geschichte, Kunst und Volkskunde* 32 (1990): 9–29, esp. 20–22. The earlier

years of the war, Wolff argues, are omitted from the frieze because they consisted mainly of skirmishes; the Column focuses upon the emperor's performance in the war rather than on the war itself, and it was not until 174 that Marcus Aurelius committed himself for prolonged periods to the front. Petersen et al. (1896) argued that the narrative begins in 171, with the start of Roman campaigns against Germanic tribes. See also J. Guey, "La date de la 'pluie miraculeuse' (172 après J.C.) et la colonne Aurelienne I," *MEFR* 60 (1948): 105–28; idem, "Encore la 'pluie miraculeuse,' mage et dieu," *RPhil* 22 (1948): 16–62; idem, "La date de la pluie miraculeuse (172 après J.C.) et la colonne Aurelienne II," *MEFR* 61 (1949): 93–118.

116. Cassius Dio, 71.10.4, explicitly indicates that as a result of the miracle Marcus Aurelius's troops hailed him as *Imperator* for the seventh time, and coins celebrate this salutation in summer and early autumn of 174. Moreover, he links the event with Faustina's assumption of the title of *Mater Castrorum,* which occurred at the earliest in 174–75. See Wolff (1990), 11–12; *RIC* III.236, nos. 299–309; 301, nos. 1109–21. These dates pose an obvious problem for Von Domaszewski's beginning date of 171: if scene XVI represents the rain miracle of 174, and the frieze as a whole, as he thinks, narrates the events of only 171–75, then the first four spirals cover three to four years, and the remaining 245 meters of the frieze narrate only one or two years; moreover, the victory appears out of sequence. These problems forced Petersen et al. (1896), 105–7, to accept a faulty date of 171 for the rain miracle and led H. Stuart Jones, "Notes on Roman Historical Sculptures," *BSR* 3 (1906): 213–71, esp. 254–57, and others to contend that the narrative did not progress chronologically: see J. Dobias, "Le monnayage de l'empereur Marc-Aurèle et les bas-reliefs historiques contemporains," *RN* 4.35 (1932): 127–61, esp. 150–54; A. G. Roos, "Het Regenwonder op de zuil can Marcus Aurelius," *Meded* 6.1 (1943): 30ff. Contra: W. Zwikker, *Studien zur Markussäule I* (Amsterdam, 1941).

117. Wolff (1990), 12, agrees with Morris (1952), 40, that the Victory, which can be paralleled on coins from 175–76, probably represents the end of the first Marcomannic war and the triumph of December 23, 176. Jurdan-Ruwe (1990), 67–69, posits an early date for the Column; since Commodus was harshly criticized by the Senate for his peaceful policy, he is unlikely, she contests, to have publicly called attention to his late father's offensives.

118. The campaign represented on the Column ends victoriously. Cassius Dio states that the wars of 178 began with the Quintilii and were not concluded successfully, forcing Marcus Aurelius to intervene in the autumn of 178. Since he died before the beginning of the campaign season of 180, scenes LVI–CXVI probably show at least the start of 179, possibly even reaching autumn: Wolff (1990), 22. In Von Domaszewski's view (1896), as Marcus Aurelius is always depicted as sole commander, the frieze cannot represent events taking place after 177, when Commodus assumed joint emperorship with his father; moreover, as Marcus Aurelius did not take part in the war between the revolt of Cassius in 175 and Commodus's arrival in 177, the frieze must represent the campaigns of 171–75. Morris (1952), 40–43, recognizes Commodus in a number of scenes on the upper section of the shaft and argues that the frieze represents events taking place after his assumption of joint emperorship in 177; even if Commodus cannot be identified, his portrait could well have been removed or recarved after his *damnatio memoriae.* See, e.g., scenes XLII, LVI, and LXX. As heir to the throne, Commodus may have been confined to an administrative post for the sake of security: Wolff (1990), 17–18.

119. Perhaps decorated with the reliefs now in Palazzo dei Conservatori and on the Arch of Constantine. See M. Wegner, "Bemerkungen zu den Ehrendenkmälern des Marcus Aurelius," *AA* 53 (1938): 157–95, esp. 195; E. Angelicoussis, "The Panel Reliefs of Marcus Aurelius," *RM* 91 (1984): 140–205; E. La Rocca, *Rilievi storici capitolini: Il restauro dei pannelli di Adriano e di Marco Aurelio nel Palazzo dei Conservatori*

(Rome, 1986), 38–52; Kleiner (1992), 228–95.

120. See Jolivet (1988), 90–96.

CHAPTER TWO

1. Plut. *Vit. C. Gracchus* 3.1; Plut. *Vit. Pomp.* 40.5, 44.3; Cic. *Rab. Perd.* 11; Plin. *Paneg.* 63.7; Cic. *Leg.* 2.23.58. For the Campus Martius, see F. Coarelli, *Il Campo Marzio dalle origini alla fine della repubblica* (Rome, 1997); J. R. Patterson, "Survey Article: The City of Rome: From Republic to Empire," *JRS* 82 (1992): 186–215, esp. 194–200; *LTUR* 1:222, s.v. Campus Martius (T. P. Wiseman); G. Waurick, "Untersuchungen zur Lage der römischen Kaisergräber in der Zeit von Augustus bis Constantin," *JRGZM* 20 (1973): 107–46; C. L. Visconti, "Delle scoperte avenute per la demolizione delle Torri della Porta Flaminia," *BullCom* (1877): 184–252; H. Jordan and C. Hülsen, *Topographie der Stadt Rom im Altertum* (Berlin, 1871–1907), 463, 491, 621; D. Favro, *The Urban Image of Augustan Rome* (Cambridge, 1996), 206–7.

2. Cass. Dio 44.3: "[Caesar's] death occurred for the following reason. He had aroused envy that was not entirely unjustified, except inasmuch as it was the senators themselves who, by their novel and excessive honors, had encouraged him and inflated his vanity, only to criticize him on this very account." There follows an account of the privileges accorded Caesar, which concludes at 44.7: "At the same time as these, they passed another resolution, which explicitly revealed their disposition: it gave him the right to build his tomb within the pomerium; and they inscribed the decrees regarding this issue in golden letters on silver slabs and placed them beneath the feet of Jupiter Capitolinus. . . ."

3. Strab. 5.3.8. See Waurick (1973), 116; L. Richardson, Jr., *A New Topographical Dictionary of Ancient Rome* (Baltimore, 1992), 65–67. Wiseman places the Campus's northern boundary in the vicinity of the modern Via Tomacelli: "[S]uetonius mentions Augustus's funeral in the Campus, but described the *Mausoleum* as *inter Flaminiam viam ripamque Tiberis* (Aug. 100.3–4). It is true that Strabo includes the *Mausoleum* in his description of the *Campus* area, but since

he also includes the *theatrum Marcelli,* that cannot be pressed as a technical description. The site of the *Mausoleum* was certainly chosen in order to dominate the *Campus* to the north, but it was probably not in the *campo* itself" (*LTUR* 1:221). But see now Coarelli (1997), 3–10, 591–602.

4. Suet. *Aug.* 100.4; Verg. *Aen.* 6.874; Cass. Dio 53.30.5. K. Kraft, "Der Sinn des Mausoleums des Augustus," *Historia* 16 (1967): 189–206, esp. 191, takes Suetonius's use of the pluperfect *exstruxerat* in 28 B.C. to mean that the tomb was finished, while conceding that its ornamentation may not have been. Cassius Dio's use of the imperfect when discussing Marcellus's burial may indicate that it was still not complete at this time.

5. Kraft (1967), 190.

6. See, for instance, V. Gardthausen, *Augustus und seine Zeit* 1 (1891): 980. Suetonius (*Aug.* 81.1) sets his worse illness later, and it would be many years before the onset of a sickness that Augustus believed would kill him. Sources imply that even though his health was poor in his youth, he recovered quickly; see Kraft (1967), 189–90.

7. O. Hirschfeld, "Die kaiserlichen Grabstätten in Rom," *Kleine Schriften* (Berlin, 1913), 449; E. Kornemann, "Zum Augustusjahr. 1. Octavians Romulusgrab. 2. Der Princeps als Hegemon im Ostem," *Klio* 31 (1938): 94.

8. Kraft (1967), 195–96. Suet. *Aug.* 17; Plut. *Vit. Ant.* 58.3–8: "[This will] had been deposited with the Vestal Virgins, and they would not give it to [Caesar] when he asked for it; but if he wanted to get hold of it, they told him to come and do so. So he went and took it; and at first he perused its contents in private, and marked certain discreditable passages; then he read it to an assembly of the Senate, though most of them were displeased to hear him do so." Mark Antony had declared Caesarion Julius Caesar's son in 34 and coregent over the Roman sphere of influence; bequests to Cleopatra and her children had been publicized in 36–34: Cass. Dio 49.41.1–3; Plut. *Vit. Ant.* 54.6.

9. Kraft (1967), 197.

10. Kraft (1967), 200; see also C. Edwards, *Writing Rome: Textual Approaches to the City* (Cambridge, 1996), 47–48.

11. A. Bartoli, "L'architettura del mausoleo di Augusto," *BdA* 7 (1927): 30–46; E. Fiorilli, "A proposito del Mausoleo di Augusto," *BdA* 7 (1927): 214–19; G. Q. Giglioli, "Il sepolcreto imperiale," *Capitolium* 6 (1930): 532–67. For Etruscan tombs, see A. Akerstrom, *Studien über die Etruskischen Gräber* (Uppsala, 1934); M. Demus-Quatember, *Etruskischer Grabarchitektur* (Baden-Baden, 1958); F. Prayon, "Architecture," in *Etruscan Life and Afterlife,* ed. L. Bonfante (Detroit, 1986), 174–201.

12. R. R. Holloway, "The Tomb of Augustus and the Princes of Troy," *AJA* 70 (1966): 171–73.

13. M. Eisner, "Zur Typologie der Mausoleen des Augustus und des Hadrian," *RM* (1979): 319–24; idem, *Zur Typologie der Grabbauten in Suburbium Roms* (Mainz, 1986). For the Republican tombs, I follow H. von Hesberg's dating as set out in *Römische Grabbauten* (Darmstadt, 1992), 94–100: tumuli come to the fore in the first century B.C. and increase in size and interior articulation as the century progresses, lasting until the Late Republic and early Augustan period.

14. R. A. Cordingley and I. A. Richmond, "The Mausoleum of Augustus," *BSR* 10 (1927): 23–25; J.-C. Richard, "'Mausoleum': d'Halicarnasse à Rome, puis à Aléxandrie," *Latomus* 29 (1970): 370–88. On Halicarnassos, see G. Kleiner, *Diadochen-Gräber* (Wiesbaden, 1963); K. Jeppesen, F. Hojland, and K. Aaris-Sorensen, *The Mausolleion at Halikarnassos,* 1: *The Sacrificial Deposit* (Copenhagen, 1981); K. Jeppesen and A. Luttrell, *The Mausolleion at Halikarnassos,* 2: *The Written Sources and the Archaeological Background* (Aarhus, 1986); P. Clayton and M. J. Price, *The Seven Wonders of the Ancient World* (London, 1989), 100–123; H. Colvin, *Architecture and the Afterlife* (New Haven-London, 1991), 30–42. For other possible sources of inspiration for Augustus's Mausoleum, see J. C. Reeder, "Typology and Ideology in the Mausoleum of Augustus," *ClAnt* 11.2 (1992): 265–304, who argues that the Mausoleum is a tower tomb, with individually traceable components: the tumulus to Macedonia, the "tempietto" to the Greek tholos exemplified by the Arsinoeion at Samothrace; its mazelike interior to the tholos at Epidauros; and its role as heroön to the Philippeion at Olym-

pia. V. Kockel, *Die Grabbauten vor dem Herkulaner Tor in Pompeii* (Mainz, 1983), 15–41; W. K. Kovacsovics, *Römische Grabdenkmäler* (Waldsassen-Bayern, 1983), 63, and W. von Sydow, "Ein Rundmonument in Pietrabbondante," *RM* 84 (1977): 294–96, derive the tumulus from Hellenistic examples in Greece and the East.

15. Cass. Dio 51.16. See P. M. Fraser, *Ptolemaic Alexandria* (Oxford, 1972), 2:32; H. Thiersch, "Die Alexandrinische Königsnekropole," 3 *JdI* 25 (1910): 55–97; G. Fiaccadori, "The Tomb of Alexander the Great," *PP* 263 (1992): 128–31. This mausoleum was the final resting place for Alexander's body, after Ptolemy Soter or Philadelphus had "snatched" it en route from Babylon to Vergina and possibly deposited it briefly in a mausoleum in Memphis. It was probably destroyed in the late-third-century Aurelian wars.

16. Luc. 8.694, 10.19; Strab. 18.1.7–10; Zenobius 3.94. M. L. Bernhard, "Topographie d'Aléxandrie: Le tombeau d'Aléxandre et le mausoleum d'Auguste," *RA* 47 (1956): 129–56, isolates a tholos-type building in cityscapes on terra-cotta lamps from Italy, which she dates to the first half of the first century A.C. Contra: D. M. Bailey, "Alexandria, Carthage and Ostia (Not to Mention Naples)," in *Alessandria e il mondo ellenistico-romano. Studi in onore di A. Adriani II* (Rome, 1984), 265–72; K. Lehmann-Hartleben, *Die antiken Hafenanlagen des Mittelmeers* (Leipzig, 1923), 227; J. de Wit, "Vergilius Vaticanus und die nord-afrikanische Mosaiken," *Mnemosyne* 3.1 (1934): 29–31; M. Bertacchi, "Elementi per una revisione della topografia ostiense," *RendLinc,* s. 8.15 (1960): 8–32; E. Joly, "Nuove lucerne con vedute di porto nell'Antiquarium di Sabratha," *LibAnt* 5 (1968): 35–54. See also Reeder (1992), 277; Fraser (1972), 2.17 n. 31.

17. F. Coarelli and Y. Thébert, "Architecture funéraire et pouvoir: Réflexions sur l'hellénisme numide," *MEFRA* 100.2 (1988): 761–818; see also Eisner (1979), 322; Kockel (1983), 35 n. 293; F. Castagnoli, "Influenze alessandrine nell'urbanistica della Roma augustea," in *Alessandria e il mondo ellenistico-romano. Studi in onore di A. Adriani* 3 (Rome, 1984), 520–26. On Cyrus's tomb: C. Nylander, *Ionians in Pasargadae. Studies in Old Persian Architecture* (Uppsala, 1970), 91–102. For the

Nereid Monument: P. Coupelle and P. Demargne, *Fouilles de Xanthos, III, Le monument des Néréides (l'architecture)* (Paris, 1958); R. Martin, "Le monument des Néréides et l'architecture funéraire," *RA* (1971): 327–37; G. Roux, "Un chef-d'oeuvre d'architecture gréco-lycienne: Le 'monument des Néréides,' " *REG* 88 (1975): 182–89; J. M. Barringer, *Divine Escorts: Nereids in Archaic and Classical Greek Art* (Ann Arbor, 1994), chap. 3.

18. Coarelli and Thébert (1988), 762–66; M. Christofle, *Le tombeau de la Chrétienne* (Paris, 1951); G. Camps, "Nouvelles observations sur l'architecture et l'âge du Medracen, mausolée royal de numide," *CRAI* (1973): 470–516; S. Gsell, *Histoire ancienne de l'Afrique du Nord* (Paris, 1913–20), 261–73; F. Rakob, "Architecture royale numide," in *Architecture et société de l'archaisme grec à la fin de la république romaine, Rome 1980* (Rome, 1983), 326ff.; C. Picard and G. Picard, "Recherches sur l'architecture numide," *Karthago* 19 (1977–78): 15–33; J. Fedak, *Monumental Tombs of the Hellenistic Age: A Study of Selected Tombs from the Pre-Classical to the Early Imperial Era* (Toronto, 1990), 137–39. Medracen's base measures over 63 m. on a side and accommodates the access to the funerary chamber. The Tomb of the Christian measures nearly 59 m. in diameter and 18.50 m. in height. The cone covers a central chamber, entered through a corridor opening onto the cone's third and fourth steps.

19. Kraft (1967), 190.

20. See M. E. Blake, *Ancient Roman Construction in Italy from the Prehistoric Period to Augustus* (Washington, D.C., 1947), 69; F. T. Bertocchi, "Un nuovo mausoleo a Canosa," *Palladio* 11 (1961): 86–91; A. W. Clapham, "Roman Mausolea of the Cartwheel Type," *ArchJ* 79 (1922): 93–100; Eisner (1986), passim; von Hesberg (1992), passim. Chambers and corridors existed only in the concrete examples.

21. Giglioli (1930), 552.

22. Reeder (1992). For tombs in Asia Minor, see Fedak (1990). The "Tomb of the Curatii" at the Via Appia's sixth milestone consists of a central cement tower and a single wall encircling it: see Eisner (1986), 201; von Hesberg (1992), 95.

23. A varient of this technique may have been used for the fourth-dynasty pyramids; see

D. Arnold, *Building in Egypt: Pharaonic Stone Masonry* (Oxford, 1991); S. Clarke and R. Engelbach, *Ancient Egyptian Construction and Architecture* (New York, 1990), 117–29; L. Grinsell, *Egyptian Pyramids* (Gloucester, 1947), 70–72, 133–37, fig. 18, 101–8, fig. 9; I. E. S. Edwards, *The Pyramids of Egypt* (London, 1949). The later method, developed in the Middle Kingdom and evidenced in the pyramid of Sesostris I at Lisht, involved surrounding a series of internal walls radiating from the center with a rubble fill.

24. Only sparse remains survive beneath the fort of Sultan Qayt-Bay; see H. Thiersch, *Pharos, Antike und Islam* (Leipzig, 1909). The most informative account comes from Ibn al-Sayj, who traveled from Spain to Alexandria in 1166 and took notes and measurements while compiling an encyclopaedia for his son (*Kitab Alif Ba* [1287], 2:537–38); see M. de Asin and M. L. Otero, "The Pharos of Alexandria," *ProcBritAc* 19 (1933): 277–92. See also R. Bedon, "Les phares antiques," *Archeologia* 231 (1988): 54–66; *The Seven Wonders of the Ancient World,* ed P. Clayton and M. Price (London, 1989), 138–57; G. C. Picard, "Sur quelques représentations nouvelles du phare d'Aléxandrie, et sur l'origine aléxandrine des paysages portuaires," *BCH* 76 (1952): 61–95; M. Reddé, "La représentation des phares à l'époque romaine," *MEFRA* 91.2 (1979): 845–72; M.-H. Quet, "Pharus," *MEFRA* 96 (1984): 789–845; J.-Y. Empereur, *Alexandria Rediscovered* (London, 1998), 63–87.

25. The striking parallel between the Pharos and the Mausolea is readily apparent in a scale section drawing, even allowing for the Pharos's greater verticality. Augustus's architect may have wished the tomb to be taller but been constrained by the location; even today there are few tall buildings on the Campus Martius. I owe this observation to Pieter Broucke.

26. These buttressing techniques are frequently seen in Roman circular buildings, and Vitruvius advocated similar devices for earth-filled foundations to counteract the thrust of fill against the outer wall; he also advised leaving chambers open to allow drainage from the tumulus (*De Archit.* 6.8). For recumbent arches, see Eisner (1986), 30–33, A2; Colvin (1992), 47, fig. 39.

27. Eisner (1986), R6 25–27 and passim.

28. H. Windfeld-Hansen, "Les couloirs annulaires dans l'architecture funéraire antique," *Acta Instituti Romani Norvegiae* 2 (1962): 35–63; R. Fellmann, *Das Grab des Lucius Munatius Plancus bei Gaeta* (Basel, 1957).

29. H. von Hesberg and S. Panciera, *Das Mausoleum des Augustus. Der Bau and seine Inschriften* (Munich, 1994), 5.

30. Reeder (1992). If it was intentional, it was not the only manifestation of the labyrinth in Augustan art and literature. Its hieroglyphic form, the meander pattern (developed from the Egyptian "palace sign," more correctly the sign for a tomb: see W. H. Matthews, *Mazes and Labyrinths: A General Account of Their History and Developments* [London, 1922], 31–35; C. N. Deedes, "The Labyrinth," in *The Labyrinth,* ed S. H. Hooke [London, 1935], 4–11) runs around the exterior of the Ara Pacis enclosure above the acanthus frieze, tying mausoleum and altar together in a thematic unity. It also decorates the portico coffers and the projecting course capping the socle of orthostats on the Temple of Mars Ultor in the Augustan Forum and on the Temple of Augustus and Rome at Ankara: P. Zanker, *Forum Augustum. Das Bildprogramm* (Tübingen, 1968); J. B. Ward-Perkins, *Roman Imperial Architecture* (Harmondsworth, 1981), 32–33; D. Krencker and M. Schede, *Der Tempel in Ankara Denkmäler Antiker Architektur, III* (Berlin-Leipzig, 1936). A labyrinth is the metaphor that comes to Virgil's mind for the *Lusus Troiae,* or Trojan Ride, that Ascanius invents for Anchises' funeral (5.588–95); and in Book 6.27ff., written shortly after Marcellus's death and burial in the Mausoleum in 23 (mentioned at 6.874), Virgil describes a labyrinth that Daedalus fashioned in bronze for the doors of the Temple of Apollo at Cumae, which Aeneas had to visit before penetrating the Underworld. If, as some scholars suggest, Icarus (whom Daedalus's grief prevented him from depicting) was a veiled reference to Marcellus (W. Fitzgerald, "Aeneas, Daedalus and the Labyrinth," *Arethusa* 17 [1984]: 51–65; H. C. Rutledge "Virgil's Daedalus," *CJ* 62 [1967]: 309–11), the labyrinth may refer to the mausoleum that Marcellus inaugurated. Literary treatments of the labyrinth are casual, assuming prior knowledge of the Minotaur myth on the audience's part: see Ov. *Her.* 10.71, 10.128; *Met.* 8.1–262.

31. Deedes (1935), 3–42; H. Kern, *Labyrinthe. Erscheinungsformen und Deutung 5000 Jahre Gegenwart eines Urbilds* (Munich, 1982), 69–84. The mid-fourth-century Tholos at Epidauros incorporated a labyrinthine crypt in which to keep the sacred snakes of Asclepios, or to protect the fictive tomb of Asclepios: F. Robert, *Thymélé, recherches sur la signification et la destination des monuments circulaires dans l'architecture religieuse de la Grèce* (Paris, 1939); G. Roux, *L'architecture de l'Argolide aux IVe et IIIe siècles avant J.-C.* (Paris, 1961) 134; Reeder (1992), 294ff. The labyrinthine cellar is echoed in hieroglyphic form on the entablature both inside and out as a meander pattern, and in the coffers as a running spiral.

32. Herod. 2.148. Built by the Egyptians next to a vast lake, he writes, the labyrinth comprised three thousand rooms arranged in courts above and below ground; closed to visitors, the lower level housed tombs of the kings who had built it and of sacred crocodiles. He describes colonnades, roofs built from single slabs of stone, a pyramid, and an underground passage. Strabo's (17.1.37) maze consists of winding, intercommunicating passages that concealed entrances to countless courts and prevented strangers from finding their way in or out without a guide. See also Diod. Sic. 1.66; Pompon. 1.8.9.

33. Pliny *HN* 36.19.

34. Indications of attempts to hide the dead king's body within his tomb date from the Second Dynasty: Deedes (1922), 11–14; W. F. M. Petrie, *Royal Tombs of the Earliest Dynasties* (London, 1900–1901), 1:11.

35. Suet. *Aug.* 18. "About the same time he had the sarcophagus and Alexander the Great's body brought out from the inner shrine and, after gazing at its features, venerated it by crowning it with a golden diadem and scattering it with flowers. When asked if he would like to visit the Mausoleum of the Ptolemies, he replied that he wished to see a king, not corpses."

36. Cass. Dio 51.16; Tac. *Ann.* 2.59; Suet. *Aug.* 50.1. On Augustus's *imitatio Alexandri,* see the extensive bibliography in Reeder (1992), and Coarelli and Thébert (1988), 788–89.

37. Coarelli and Thébert (1988), 790–91. See also M. Malaise, *Les conditions de pénétration et de diffusion des cultes egyptiens en Italie* (Leiden, 1972); A. Roullet, *The Egyptian and Egyptianising Monuments of Imperial Rome* (Leiden, 1972); M. de Vos, *L'Egittomania in pitture e mosaici romano-campani della prima età imperiale* (Leiden, 1980).

38. R. Ling, *Roman Painting* (Cambridge, 1991), 142–43; E. Buchner, *Die Sonnenuhr des Augustus: Nachdruck aus RM 1976 und 1980 und Nachtrag über die Ausgrabung 1980/1981* (Mainz, 1982); F. Coarelli, "L'apoteosi di Augusto e l'apoteosi di Romolo," *AnalRom* Suppl. 10 (1983): 41–46; Coarelli and Thébert (1988), 790.

39. *LTUR* 3:234 (von Hesberg). De Vos (1980), frontispiece, 60 n. 137, 74, assigned it to the Mausoleum itself.

40. F. Coarelli, *Roma sepolta* (Milan, 1984); R. Bedon, "Les obélisques de Rome," *Archeologia* 216 (1986): 63, 57.

41. See, in general, Robert (1939); S. Stucchi, "Fari, campanili e mausolei," *AquilNost* 30 (1959): 15–32; F. Richard, "Les dieux des phares," *Sefunim* 6 (1981): 37–45; Picard (1952); Fedak (1990), passim. As did people in many other societies, Greeks and Romans conceived of death as entailing a journey over water (the river Styx or Acheron before reaching the Underworld, or the seas on the way to the Isles of the Blessed), which A. van Gennep, *Les rites de passage* (Paris, 1909), and others understood to represent a liminal state between life and death. A more straightforward metaphor also existed in literature: just as, among pagan poets, a tempest at sea was a vivid metaphor for life's tumultuous adversities, so the harbor represented death, a refuge from those troubles: Pl. *Leg.* 803B; Marcus Aurelius *Medit.* 3.3.6; C. Bonner, "Desired Haven," *HThR* 34 (1941): 49–67; W. Vollgraff, "Le péan delphique à Dionysos," *BCH* 48 (1924): 97–208. See also B. Andreae, "Studien zur römischen Grabkunst," *RM,* Suppl. 9 (Heidelberg, 1963): 136; Quet (1984); Bedon (1988), 35. A lighthouse was a natural visual symbol for death's haven of safety, as seen in a monochrome mosaic in front of Tomb 34 at Isola Sacra, inscribed "Here an end to pain": G. Calza, *La necropoli del Porto di Roma nell'Isola Sacra* (Rome, 1940), 169–70, fig. 83.

In early Christian iconography, a lighthouse bore the flame to which the faithful looked as a sign of salvation (e.g., Vatican, Galleria Lapidaria inv. 5985; G. Stuhlfauth, "Der Leuchtturm von Ostia," *RM* 53 [1938]: 139–63, esp. 145–47, fig. 4). Tombs were often placed near water; e.g., the Mausoleum at Halicarnassos and the tomb of L. Munatius Plancus at Gaeta: N. Purcell, "Tomb and Suburb," in *Römische Gräberstrasse* (Munich, 1987), 31, n. 33, and a fifth-century B.C. inscription (*IG* 12.8.683) describing the tower tomb of Akeratos in the Bay of Potamia on Thasos as "the sign of a safe harbour for ships and sailors" suggests a functional affiliation between lighthouse and tomb: L.-H. Jeffrey, *The Local Scripts of Archaic Greece* (Oxford, 1961), 301–2, 307, no. 67. See also Plut. *Vit. Them.* 32.5. In Taposiris Magna (Abusir) a Ptolemaic sepulcher consisting of a square base surmounted by an octagon and a cylinder bears a drawing of a lighthouse labeled "Pharos": see Fraser (1972), 1:18, 144; 2:253–54, n. 96. The tomb's role as a marker for navigators enhanced its efficacy as memorial; see *Od.* 24.80–84. Even inland Roman tombs resembled the Pharos – e.g., the monument of the Gens Julia at Boville and "La Conocchia" at Santa Maria in Capua Vetere. Stucchi writes: "Anche in Italia penso che si sia imitato in qualche costruzione sepolcrale romana il faro famoso. Altre imitazioni egiziane in Italia sono ben note, dalla piramide sepolcrale di Caio Cestio, ad un'altra piramide di Borgo, di cui rimane soltanto la parte inferiore, monumenti che imitano direttamente le famose piramidi faraoniche, ai monumenti "a piramide" post-augustei, che oppongono alla semplicità delle linee delle piramidi dell'ultimo secolo avanti Cristo un elaborato gioco di linee e di volumi." M. Wilson Jones, "One Hundred Feet and a Spiral Stair: The Problem of Designing Trajan's Column," *JRA* 6 (1993): 23–38, also surmises that lighthouse design may have been a source of inspiration for Trajan's Column. Interestingly, when discussing funerary pyres, which scholars have long noted were probably combustible imitations of tombs, Herodian (4.2) comments that, "One might compare the form of the structure to lighthouses." The appearance of light-houses on sarcophagi and in funerary reliefs suggests that, at least by the Trajanic period, the association was not simply due to similarities in construction. For many scholars, a lighthouse in a harbor relief is a locating device representing the haven at which the honoree, a seafarer, habitually came to port (e.g., L. Casson, *The Ancient Mariners: Seafarers and Sea Fighters of the Mediterranean in Ancient Times* [Princeton, N.J., 1991], 214); thus harbor sarcophagi are biographical, showing scenes from the life of the deceased; see L. Berczelly, "A Sepulchral Monument from the Via Portuense and the Origin of the Roman Biographical Cycle," *ActaAArtHist* 8 (1978): 49–74; N. B. Kampen, *Image and Status: Roman Working Women in Ostia* (Berlin, 1981); G. Zimmer, *Römische Berufdarstellungen* (Berlin, 1982); J. Whitehead, "Biography and Formula in Roman Sarcophagi," (Ph.D. diss., Yale University, 1984). Yet of twenty-four lighthouse sarcophagi known to Andreae (1963), 135–36, only four were found at Ostia or Porto and can reliably be considered to have belonged to seafarers; others depict not Ostia but Alexandria (where the Roman sea merchant was *not* at home). As for lighthouse tombs, Stucchi contends that the sheer visibility of a lighthouse is reason to appropriate its form for a memorial. Robert writes of Greek lighthouses in general, "Les noms de certains phares ou semaphores, comme la *tour de Neoptolème* à l'embouchure du Tyras, évoquent des légendes cultuelles et donnent à penser qu'en plus de leur destination pratique, ces monuments durent avoir quelque importance religieuse" (200–201). Indeed, the Pharos itself stood close to or on the very location of an earlier tomb once connected with the worship of Proteus, a local sea-god, and then associated with the hero cult of Hephaestion, Alexander's friend.

42. Despite Pliny's assertion that labyrinths were not always sepulchral (*HN* 36.19), it was in association with the dead that they were frequently adopted in Italy as well, e.g., Diodorus Siculus 1.66.1–4. The Etruscan king Porsenna built a huge tomb with a maze at Chiusi, "so that the vanity of foreign kings should be surpassed by Italian kings." Pliny quotes Varro's description: inside a square base surmounted by towering pyramids was an inextricable labyrinth, "and if one entered it without a ball of thread, one would not find an exit." See R. De Launay, "Les fallacieux détours du labyrinthe," *RA* 2 (1915): 114–25, 348–63, (1916): 3: 116–26, 387–98, 4: 119–28, 286–94, 413–21, 114–25, and 348–63; Kern (1982) 78–81. During the Roman Empire, in humbler sepulchers in Africa such as a tomb at Hadrumetum (Sousse), a two-dimensional version in mosaic substituted for the monumental labyrinth; see G. Doublet, "Communications: Lettre à M. Héron de Villefosse sur la mosaïque d'Hadrumète qui représentait Thesée, le Minotaure et le labyrinthe," *CRAI* (1892): 318–29. The same is true of the meander pattern, which runs as a band around a monumental *pulvinus* from a substantial funerary altar of the turn of the era in the courtyard of the Palazzo dei Conservatori (inv. 797), and which frames the inscription on a funerary altar in the Museo Nazionale delle Terme (inv. 72456). See E. La Rocca, *La riva a mezzaluna: Culti, agoni, monumenti funerari presso il Tevere nel Campo Marzio occidentale* (Rome, 1984), 91–92; D. Boschung, *Antike Grabaltäre aus den Nekropolen Roms, Acta Bernensia* 10 (Berne, 1987), 112, no. 927. Penelope Reed Doob, *The Idea of the Labyrinth from Classical Antiquity through the Middle Ages* (Ithaca, N.Y., 1990), 52, suggests that in antiquity a labyrinth had a dual, paradoxical nature, a positive and a negative significance. On the one hand, it could be a formidable and intricate work of art, worthy of admiration; on the other, a bewildering and frightening place of interminable wandering. It embodies both order and chaos, depending on one's perspective (on whether one sees it from above or from within) or on one's state of knowledge (whether or not one knows the way through it). When used as a metaphor, literary or architectural, both facets may come into play, and in its context in the imperial tomb both aspects of the paradox are apparent. Its magnificence glorified Augustus's wisdom and the tomb's splendor, yet the gloomy, multicursal approach to the burial chamber also performed as a symbolic protective device

for the ruler's physical remains, just as it had more literally for Egyptian kings and for Porsenna. Centuries later, a labyrinth embroidered on imperial robes alluded to the emperor's sagacity: "Let there be represented on [the emperor's robe] a labyrinth of gold and pearls, in which is the Minotaur, made of emerald, holding his finger to his mouth, thus signifying that, just as none may know the secret of the labyrinth, so none may reveal the monarch's counsels": *Graphia Aurea Urbis Romae,* Bibl. Laur. Pluteus, infer., cod. 41, trans. Doob, 80. See also Pliny *HN* 36.19, who associated the labyrinth with the Sun-God; later writers have seen it as a symbol of the world and life, life and death, rebirth, the course of the sun and souls, and the Underworld: see Deedes (1935), 42; G. de Launay 2 (1915), 123; W. F. J. Knight, "Virgil and the Maze," *CR* 93 (1929): 212–13; M. de Verrall, "Two Instances of Symbolism in the Sixth *Aeneid,*" *CR* 24 (1910): 43–46; H. C. Rutledge, "The Opening of *Aeneid* 6," *CJ* 67 (1972): 110–15.

43. J. Grafton Milne, "Greek and Roman Tourists in Egypt," *JEA* 3 (1916): 76–80; L. Casson, *Travel in the Ancient World* (Baltimore, 1994), 257–58.

44. See Thiersch (1909), passim; Quet (1984).

45. W. W. Tarn, "The Battle of Actium," *JRS* (1931): 173–99.

46. Such a conflation is not unknown in Greece: see C. Picard, *Les trophées romains. Contribution à l'histoire de la religion et de l'art triomphale de Rome* (Paris, 1957), 21, on the cenotaph of Pyrrhus in the Argive agora.

47. W. M. Murray and P. M. Petsas, *Octavian's Campsite Memorial for the Actian War* (Philadelphia, 1989). Marine motifs consistently decorated monuments commemorating Actium and the Sicilian victory of 36 B.C., to signify the character of the battle, e.g., the Basilica Neptuni and the Portico of the Argonauts: Castagnoli (1984), 520–22. Augustus pointedly rebuilt the Porticus Octavia, originally erected by Cn. Octavius shortly after 168 to commemorate a naval triumph over Perses, and Octavia's new Porticus Metelli had a frieze of marine motifs: Vell. Pat. 2.1.2; Pliny *HN* 34.13; Festus 178M.188L; T. Hölscher, "Actium und Salamis," *JdI* 99 (1984): 205–14; Richardson (1992), 317–18.

48. See J. J. Pollitt, *Art in the Hellenistic Age* (Cambridge, 1986), 41–46, 83–97.

49. Pliny *HN* 34.64; Plut. *Vit. Aem.* 28; H. Kähler, *Der Fries vom Reiterdenkmal des Aemilius Paullus in Delphi* (Berlin, 1965); T. Hölscher, *Monumenti statali e pubblico* (Rome, 1994), 23–24.

50. Amm. Marc. 17.4.6. See the inscription on the sundial's obelisk; *CIL* 6.702, and below, Chap. 3. See also Edwards (1996), 100. On the use of spoils as part of a victory monument, see Hölscher (1994), 20–24; A. L. Kuttner, "Some New Grounds for Narrative. Marcus Antonius's Base (*The Ara Domitii Ahenobarbi*) and Republican Biographies," in *Narrative and Event in Ancient Art,* ed. P. Holliday (Cambridge, 1993), 198–229.

51. On the visual impact of the written *res gestae,* see S. Güven, "Displaying the *Res Gestae* of Augustus: A Monument of Imperial Image for All," *JSAH* 57 (1998): 30–45.

52. Cass. Dio 51.10. On Cleopatra's Mausoleum, see Plut. *Vit. Ant.* 74, 86; Fraser (1972), 2:33–34, n. 81.

53. Cass. Dio 51.15; Suet. *Aug.* 17; Kraft (1967), 198–99.

54. J. Formigé, *Le trophée des Alpes (La Turbie)* (Paris, 1949), suggests that the trophy was inspired by the Mausoleum at Halicarnassos. Significantly, in the thirteenth-century Song of St. Honorat, Raymond Feraud took the trophy to be the Tomb of Apollo: Picard (1957), 295.

55. See F. B. Florescu, *Das Siegesdenkmal von Adamklissi: Tropaeum Traiani* (Bucharest-Bonn, 1965); C. Picard, "Le Trophée de Trajan à Adam Klissi," *RA* (1962): 91–94.

56. A decorative similarity between tomb and trophy was already in place when Augustus was designing his tomb and provided a context in which a purposeful blurring of the distinction between the two monument types would have been simple. The usual trophy sported weapons and spolia; so, too, did the tomb, as is seen, for instance, in the Hellenistic period in the painted tombs of Lefkhadia; see S. G. Miller, "Macedonian Tombs: Their Architecture and Architectural Decoration," *Studies in the History of Art* 10: *Macedonia and Greece in Late Classical and Early Hellenistic Times,* ed. E. N. Borza and B. Barr-Sharrar (Washington, D.C., 1982). Whether Augustus

exploited this common iconographical theme is difficult to assess, since most of the Mausoleum's sculptural decoration has perished. Like the Mausoleum, moreover, a trophy was often accompanied by an altar (here, notably, an altar to peace) and was surrounded by a planted *temenos:* Picard (1957), 134, 184, 261.

57. The trophy was decorated with spoils taken during the campaign, similar in concept to the mass of spoils that Germanicus heaped up and abandoned on his battle site in A.D. 16. See Tac. *Ann.* 2.18; Florus 2.30; Picard (1957), 302, 318–19. See also Livy 5.29.1; Formigé (1949), 80; Richard (1939), 284.

58. Picard (1957), 294, 302.

59. Cass. Dio 56.34; Tac. *Ann.* 1.8; Suet. *Aug.* 100; H. S. Versnel, *Triumphus. An Inquiry into the Origin, Development and Nature of the Roman Triumph* (Leiden, 1970), 122–23. Another innovation was the presence of people at the head of his funerary procession carrying boards indicating the names of peoples he had subjugated.

60. Intrigued by Seneca's comment in ca. A.D. 40 that *funus triumpho simillimum* (*Consol. ad Marc.* 3.1), scholars have attempted to document commonalities in Roman modes of funeral and triumphal celebration, perceiving similarities in paraphernalia such as wreaths and torches, activities such as banquets and games, the use of arches and other insignia such as the quadriga, the *corona Etrusca,* red lead paint, the *bulla,* and the phallus: see A. Brelich, "Trionfo e morte," *SMSR* 14 (1938): 189–93; R. Heidenreich, "Tod und Triumph in der römischen Kunst," *Gymnasium* 58 (1951): 326–40; Richard (1966). Versnel (1970), 115–31, dismisses most of the similarities on the grounds that they are objects or usages found in religious ceremonies or *pompae* in general, or that comparisons are made without proper respect for the different periods from which data are taken.

61. D. Boschung, "Tumulus Iuliorum— Mausoleum Augusti," *Hefte des Berner Archaeol. Seminars* 6 (1980): 38–41; H. von Hesberg, "Das Mausoleum des Augustus," *Kaiser Augustus und die verlorene Republik* (Mainz, 1988), 244–51, esp. 248. See also P. Zanker, *The Power of Images in the Age of Augustus,* trans. A. Shapiro (Ann Arbor,

Mich., 1988), 76. Picard (1957), 208–11, proposes a similar ambiguity for the trophy at Kbor Klib. For other instances of dual valency, consider the dedication of the Temple of Concord, rebuilt by Tiberius to commemorate his triumph over Germany and to perpetuate the memory of his brother Drusus. See also F. W. Shipley, "Chronology of the Building Operations in Rome from the Death of Caesar to the Death of Augustus," *MAAR* 9 (1931): 7– 60, esp. 12; Coarelli (1983), 44.

62. For the altar: Liv. 2.5.2; Plut. *Vit. Poplic.* 8.1; Florus 1.3.9.1 It may have stood between the modern Piazza Venezia, Via del Corso, and Piazza del Collegio Romano: see L. Attilia, "Il mausoleo di Augusto," *Roma repubblicana dal 270 a.C. all'età augustea* (Rome, 1987), 29–34, esp. 29. On military exercises: Liv. 1.16.1; Dion. Hal. 2.56.2. Tarquinius Superbus expropriated the Campus for his own purposes in the sixth century, but upon his expulsion it was solemnly rededicated to Mars: Dion. Hal. 5.13.2; Serv. *Aen.* 9.272; Liv. 2.5.2; Plut. *Vit. Publ.* 8.1. See *LTUR* 1:222 s.v. Campus Martius (T. P. Wiseman); Coarelli (1997).

63. L. Pietilä-Castrén, *Magnificentia Publica. The Victory Monuments of the Roman Generals in the Era of the Punic Wars* (Helsinki, 1987); Richardson (1992), 67. See also Coarelli (1984), 86; idem (1997).

64. Coarelli (1984), 88.

65. See Picard (1957), 185–86; Coarelli (1997), 539–80.

66. Tert. *Spect.* 10; Richardson (1992), 384.

67. In the Palazzo dei Conservatori: Helbig 2.1600; F. Coarelli, *Il sepolcro degli Scipioni a Roma* (Rome, 1988), pls. 2–3. See also P. J. Holliday, " 'Ad Triumphum Excolendum': The Political Significance of Roman Historical Painting," *Oxford Art Journal* 3.2 (1980): 3–8; idem, "Roman Triumphal Painting: Its Function, Development and Reception," *ArtB* 79 (1997): 130–47; H. I. Flower, *Ancestor Masks and Aristocratic Power in Roman Culture* (Oxford, 1996), 160–66.

68. *BJ* 7.121ff.

69. M. Pfanner, *Der Titusbogen, Beitrage zur Erschliessung Hellenistischer und Kaiserzeitlicher Skulptur und Architektur* (Mainz, 1983), 2:67–71, 76; I. A. Richmond, *Roman Archaeology and Art* (London, 1969), 228; Hölscher (1967), 94.

70. On the spoils, see L. Yarden, *The Spoils of Jerusalem on the Arch of Titus: A Reinvestigation* (Stockholm, 1991), 71–106.

71. S. De Maria, *Gli archi onorari di Roma e dell'Italia romana* (Rome, 1988), 120. If there were bronze elephants atop the arch, they too would have been a reference to apotheosis. See H. H. Scullard, *The Elephant in the Greek and Roman World* (London, 1974), 254–59.

72. See G. Traversari, *L'Arco dei Sergii* (Padua, 1971); K. Lehmann-Hartleben, "L'Arco di Tito," *BullCom* 62 (1934): 89–122; Pfanner (1983), 77–78; De Maria (1988); F. S. Kleiner, *The Arch of Nero in Rome: A Study of the Roman Honorary Arch before and under Nero* (Rome, 1985); C. B. Rose, *Dynastic Commemoration and Imperial Portraiture in the Julio-Claudian Period* (Cambridge, 1997), 19.

73. See below, Chapter 6.

74. See D. E. E. Kleiner, *Roman Sculpture* (New Haven-London, 1992), 102–3. Another motif in the Arch's decoration, the wax personification of the River Jordan in the small frieze, carried on a *ferculum* by four soldiers (see J. A. Ostrowski, "Personifications of Rivers as an Element of Roman Political Propaganda," *EtTrav* 15 [1990]: 309–19), is also ambiguous: at a glance, the motif has much in common with the iconography for the deceased being carried on a funerary bed, as seen, for instance, on the Amiternum relief: see Kleiner 103–5, figs. 88–89; L. Franchi, "Rilievo con pompa funebre e rilievo con gladiatori al museo dell'Aquila," in *Sculture municipali dell'area sabellica tra l'età di Cesare e quella di Nerone, StMisc* 10 (1963–64), ed. R. Bianchi-Bandinelli, 23–32.

75. Trajan's Column, scene LXXVIII; Marcus Aurelius' Column, scene LV.

76. T. Birt, *Die Buchrolle in der Kunst* (Leipzig, 1907). Contra: K. Weitzmann, *Illustrations in Roll and Codex* (Princeton, N.J., 1970), who contests the existence of continuous illustrated rotuli before the tenth-century Joshua Roll. A mosaic from a basilica or synagogue in Mopsuestia showing the Old Testament Samson cycle, with continuous narrative illustration set below verses from the Book of Judges, strengthens the case for the existence of continuous illustrated rotuli as early as the fifth century; see E. Kitzinger, "Observations on the Samson Floor at Mopsuestia," *DOP* 27 (1973): 133–44. S. Settis et al., *La Colonna Traiana* (Turin, 1988), 86–93; *EAA,* Suppl. 2 (1996): 230–34, s.v. Colonna coclide istoriata, and Colonna Traiana (S. Settis).

77. Prisc. *Inst.* 6.13 (Keil's *Grammatici Latini* 2.205); see F. Lepper and S. Frere, *Trajan's Column: A New Edition of the Cichorius Plates* (Gloucester, 1988), 211–29; S. Settis et al. (1988), 7. Cassius Dio's *Roman History* in eighty books, written under the Severans, covered the reigns of Nerva and Trajan in Book 68; what little survives of this comes from Xiphilinus's eleventh-century *Epitome* and the *Excerpta* for the Encyclopedia of Constantine VII Porphyrogenitos (912–59). There must also have been a medical officer's journal from the campaigns.

78. R. Brilliant, *Visual Narratives: Storytelling in Etruscan and Roman Art* (Ithaca, N.Y., 1984), 90–123; P. G. Hamberg, *Studies in Roman Imperial Art* (Copenhagen, 1945), 104–19, 149–60. These traditional Roman virtues were to appear in standardized form on sarcophagi; see G. Rodenwaldt, "Über den Stilwandel in der antoninischen Kunst," *Abhandlungen der Preussischen Akademie der Wissenschaft zu Berlin, Phil.-Hist. Klasse* 3 (1935). On imperial virtues, see A. Wallace-Hadrill, "The Emperor and his Virtues," *Historia* 30 (1981): 298–323.

79. E. Condurachi, "Riflessi della propaganda politica e della strategia militare sui rilievi della Colonna di Traiano," in *L'esame storico-artistico della Colonna Traiana. Colloquio italo-romano, Roma 25 Ottobre 1978* (Rome, 1982), 7–19; H. Wolff, "Welchen Zeitraum stellt der Bilderfries der Marcus-Säule dar?" *Ostbairische Grenzmarken. Passauer Jahrbuch für Geschichte, Kunst und Volkskunde* 32 (1990): 9–29.

80. See other examples in Pietilä-Castrén (1987), 30; Serv. *Commentary on Virgil's Georgics* 3.29 (ed. Thilo, 3.277); W. Haftmann, *Das italienische Saülenmonument* (Leipzig, 1939), 27–28.

81. See above, Chapter 1.

82. P. Schmitt-Pantel, "Evergétisme et mémoire du mort," in *Le mort, les morts dans les sociétés anciennes,* ed. G. Gnoli and J. P. Vernant (Cambridge, 1982), 177–88, esp. 179; F. Dupont, "The Emperor-God's Other Body," in *Fragments for a History of the*

Human Body (New York, 1989), 397–419, esp. 413; Hölscher (1994), 43.

83. Polyb. 6.54.2. See O. C. Crawford, "Laudatio funebris," CJ 37 (1941–42): 17–29; S. G. MacCormack, Art and Ceremony in Late Antiquity (Berkeley, 1981), 97. As Tacitus (Agric. 46) puts it, when remembering Agricola, "Let us show our reverence rather with admiration, and praise, and if strength suffice, with imitation: this is true honor, this kinship's piety. . . . Many of the ancients oblivion will eclipse, as though they had neither fame nor family. Agricola, whose story will be handed down to future generations, will live on."

84. Flower (1996); J. A. North, "These He Cannot Take," JRS 73 (1983): 169–74, esp. 170; B. Frischer, "Monumenta et Arae Honoris Virtutisque Causa: Evidence of Memorials for Roman Civic Heroes," BullCom (1983): 51–86, esp. 65; Hölscher (1994), 144.

85. See Cic. Rep. 6.13: "There is indeed a place set apart in heaven for all who preserved, aided and increased their fatherland, and there the blessed enjoy eternity; for there is nothing on this earth more welcome to the supreme god who rules the entire world than councils and federations of men united by law. These are called states, and their governors and preservers descend from here, and return hither."

86. E.g., Hor. C. 3; Ov. Met. 868–70; Verg. G. 1. See J. Bayet, "L'immortalité astrale d'Auguste, ou Manilius commentateur de Virgile," REL 17 (1939): 141–71; P. Boyance, "Le sens cosmique chez Virgile," REL 32 (1954): 220–49, esp. 243; D. Fishwick, "Ovid and Divus Augustus," CP 86 (1991): 36–41; S. R. F. Price, "From Noble Funerals to Divine Cult: The Consecration of Roman Emperors," in Rituals and Royalty: Power and Ceremonial in Traditional Societies (Cambridge, 1987), 80. K. Hopkins, Conquerors and Slaves (Cambridge, 1978), 200–21, notes that the cult established as a result of a dead ruler's apotheosis had the power to unify the far-flung regions of the empire. Ironically, though granted by human decree, apotheosis gave the appearance of confirming that the ruler had reigned by divine election.

87. Suet. Iul. 6.1.

88. Suet. Iul. 88. See S. Weinstock, Divus Julius (Oxford, 1971), 370–84.

89. G. K. Galinsky, Augustan Culture (Princeton, N.J., 1996), 17.

90. See Kleiner (1992), 61; Galinsky (1996), 17.

91. See also MacCormack (1991), 95–99, 105.

92. See Price (1987), 82–89.

93. "L'imperator romain . . . n'est que candidat à l'apothéose et son regne constitue l'examen de ses capacités:" L. Cerfaux and J. Tondriau, Le culte des souverains dans la civilisation Gréco-Romaine (Tournai, 1957), 311.

94. See E. H. Kantorowicz, The King's Two Bodies: A Study in Medieval Political Theology (Princeton, N.J., 1957); E. Bickermann, "Die römische Kaiserapotheose," ArchRW 27 (1929): 1–34; idem, "Consecratio," Le culte des souverains dans l'empire romain, Entr. Fond. Hardt 19 (Geneva, 1973): 3–25; G. Feeley-Harnik, "Issues in Divine Kingship," Annual Review of Anthropology 14 (1985): 273–313; Dupont (1989).

CHAPTER THREE

1. E. Plowden, Commentaries or Reports (London, 1816), 233a, in E. H. Kantorowicz, The King's Two Bodies: A Study in Medieval Political Theology (Princeton, N.J., 1957), 13.

2. CIL 6.702. The sphere in the Capitoline Museum may belong on this obelisk: Kaiser Augustus und der Verlorene Republik (Mainz, 1988), 244–45; Helbig⁴ 2.1581.

3. Amm. Marc. 17.4.7; Pliny HN 36.14.64; Tert. Spect. 8, "The massive obelisk is put up for the sun . . ."; Isid. Etym. 18.31. See E. Iversen, Obelisks in Exile, 1: The Obelisks of Rome (Copenhagen, 1968), 11–17; A. Roullet, The Egyptian and Egyptianising Monuments of Imperial Rome (Leiden, 1972), 13–15; contra: E. Nash, "Obelisk and Circus," RM 64 (1957): 232–59.

4. "In angulis quatuor venti ex opere musivo cum inscriptione ut Boreas spirat; efossum horologium, quod habebat septem gradus circum" (1484, described in 1515 as "gradibus de auratis"). "Invenisse varia signa caelestia ex aere artificio mirabili, quae in pavimento circa gnomonem hunc erant" (1502): G. B. De Rossi, "Note di topografia romana," in Studi e documenti di storia e diritto (1882), 3:56–60; R. Lanciani, Storia degli Scavi 1 (1902): 83, 136, 169; Buchner (1982), 42. S. L. Gibbs, Greek and Roman Sundials (New Haven, Conn., 1976), 46–48;

M. Schütz, "Zur Sonnenuhr des Augustus auf dem Marsfeld," *Gymnasium* 97 (1990): 432–57, with an important critique of E. Buchner, *Die Sonnenuhr des Augustus: Nachdruck aus RM 1976 und 1980 und Nachtrag über die Ausgrabung 1980/1981* (Mainz, 1982); idem, "*Horologium Augusti.* Neue Ausgrabungen in Rom," *Gymnasium* 90 (1983): 494–508; idem, "Ein Kanal für Obelisken. Neues vom Mausoleum des Augustus in Rom," *AntW* 27 (1996): 161–68. For the sundial's subsequent history, see M. T. Boatwright, *Hadrian and the City of Rome* (Princeton, N.J., 1987), 67–73. See N. De Grummond, "Pax Augusta and the Horae on the Ara Pacis," *AJA* 94 (1990): 663–77, for allusions to seasons and constellations in the Ara Pacis "Tellus" relief.

5. S. Abercrombie, *Architecture as Art* (New York, 1984), 127.

6. *Silv.* 4.3.18–19. Principal manuscripts have *lumina* (in which case there is no mention of the Temple), but later manuscripts have *limina,* for which H. Sauter, "Der römische Kaiserkult bei Martial and Statius," *Tübinger Beiträge zur Altertumswissenschaft* 21 (1934): 150–52, convincingly argues; see also K. Scott, *The Imperial Cult under the Flavians* (Stuttgart-Berlin, 1936), 64–65.

7. W. Loerke, "A Rereading of the Interior Elevation of Hadrian's Rotunda," *JSAH* 49 (1990): 22–43, esp. 41. See W. L. Mac-Donald, *The Pantheon: Design, Meaning and Progeny* (Cambridge, Mass., 1976), 34 and 88: "In a very real sense, the Pantheon rotunda is a metaphor in architecture for the ecumenical pretensions of the Roman Empire, the girdling cornices a statement in architectural form of the nine-thousand-mile boundary that surrounded the later Greco-Roman world. . . ."; K. de Fine Licht, *The Rotunda in Rome: A Study of Hadrian's Pantheon* (Copenhagen, 1968), 198–202; D. Keinast, "Zur Baupolitik Hadrians in Rom," *Chiron* 10 (1980): 391–412.

8. Vitr. *De Archit.* 1.2.5: "Statione, cum Iovi Fulguri et Caelo et Soli et Lunae aedificia sub divo hypaethraque constituentur; horum enim deorum et species et effectus in aperto mundo atque lucenti praesentes vidimus."

9. MacDonald (1976), 77, 89. See also I. Kagis McEwen, "Hadrian's Rhetoric I. The Pantheon," *Res* 24 (1993): 55–66.

10. Loerke (1990), 38, 42, and Manilius *Astronomica* 1.563–602. Loerke notes that four of the ribs that frame the coffers tie the dome to the floor patterning, dividing the 28 vertical rows of coffers (a lunar month) into four groups of seven (the days of the week); these ribs fall directly over the axes of the diagonal exedrae to inscribe an ideal square within the circular plan, the sides of which run through seven squares in the floor. The five circles are reflected also in the five files of floor squares from the center to the sides of the inscribed square. See also MacDonald (1976), 72. Khristaan D. Villela, "Notes on the Sundial of Augustus on the Campus Martius, Rome," unpublished seminar paper, University of Texas at Austin, 1998, suggests that the Pantheon is a vast adaptation of a type of sundial well known to Romans: a roofed spherical dial, in which the gnomon is a hole, sometimes surrounded by a metal plate to enhance precision, through which a shaft of light passed to illuminate markings on the inner surface of a cutaway sphere. (See Gibbs [1976], 23–27, 71.) Correspondences with the Sundial of Augustus would then be self-evident.

11. Cass. Dio 27.2; 69.7.1: "[Hadrian] conducted all the important and most pressing business with the aid of the Senate and he passed judgment with the guidance of the foremost men in the palace, the Forum, or the Pantheon, or in various other places."

12. M. De'Spagnolis, "Contributi per una nuova lettura del Mausoleo di Adriano," *BdA* 61 (1976): 62–68, esp. 66–67.

13. "In sembianze solari"; "non solo come tomba imperiale ma quasi come un tempio dedicato ad una deità solare": T. Squadrilli, "Il Mausoleo di Adriano," *Capitolium* 50.7–8 (1975): 20–31, esp. 29.

14. S.H.A., *Hadr.* 23.10: "Tunc Ceionium Commodum . . . adoptare constituit. Adoptavit ergo Ceionium Commodum Verum invitis omnibus eumque Helium Verum Caesarem appellavit"; S.H.A., *Ael.* 3.1–6; 2.2; "Ceionius Commodus qui et Helius Verus appellatus est"; S.H.A., *Ver.:* "Huic naturalis pater fuit Lucius Helius Verus." See A. S. L. Farquharson, "On the Names of Aelius Caesar, Adopted Son of Hadrian," *CQ* 2 (1908): 1–8; M. Hammond, "The Transmission of the Powers of the Roman

Emperor from the Death of Nero in A.D. 68 to that of Alexander Severus in A.D. 235," *MAAR* 24 (1956): 61–133, esp. 93–95. For Antoninus Pius's coins, see *BMCRE* 3:152, 369–72, 549–52.

15. Prudentius calls the bridge the Pons Hadriani in the fourth century (*Peristeph.* 12.61), as does the author of the *Mirabilia*: L. Richardson, Jr., *A New Topographical Dictionary of Ancient Rome* (Baltimore, 1992), 296. His villa at Tivoli was known in antiquity as the Villa Tiburs (*CIL* 14.3635–3637), the Villa Tiburtina (S.H.A., *Had.* 26.5) and the Aelia Vil[l]a (*CIL* 14.3911), but not the Villa Hadriana: Boatwright (1987), 138.

16. See also M. Basso, *Guide to the Vatican Necropolis* (Vatican City, 1986). On Hadrian and sunrises witnessed from Mount Etna and Mount Casius, see S.H.A., *Hadr.* 13.3, 14.3. On the Archonship, see Guarducci (1965), 216. See, in general, A. Manodori, "Memorie sparse del Mausoleo di Adriano," in M. Mercalli, *Adriano e il suo Mausoleo* (Milan, 1998), 149–59; M. Borgatti, *Castel Sant'Angelo in Roma* (Rome, 1931), 61.

17. For Borgatti (1931), 12, and Stierlin (1984), 205, the spiral ambulatory recalls the pyramids.

18. Squadrilli (1975), 21. I am grateful to John Clarke for drawing my attention to a parallel with the perspective design of the coffers in the Pantheon's dome, which force a visitor to the center of the temple, directly beneath the oculus; see W. L. MacDonald, *The Architecture of the Roman Empire, I: An Introductory Study*[2] (New Haven, Conn., 1982), 115.

19. *Spect.* 9. See also Stierlin (1984), 153–59.

20. F. Jacoby, *Fragmente der griechischen Historiker* (Berlin, 1926), 489–90, no. 34; G. M. A. Hanfmann, *The Seasons Sarcophagus in Dumbarton Oaks* (Cambridge, Mass., 1951), 1:160, 2:76 n. 114.

21. Corippus, *In laudem Iustini* 1.314–17 (*Monumenta Germaniae Historica,* 3:2 [Berlin, 1879]); A. Bachrens, *Poetae Latini Minores* (Leipzig, 1881), 4:320–21, n. 377; Hanfmann (1951), 1:60. See also P. Wuilleumier, "Cirque et astrologie," *MEFR* 44 (1927): 184–209; A. Frazer, "The Cologne Circus Bowl: Basileos Helios and the Cosmic Hippodrome," in *Essays in Memory of Karl Lehmann* (New York, 1964), 105–13.

22. Tac. *Ann.* 15.74.1; Pliny *HN* 36.71; Amm. Marc. 17.4.12. J. Humphrey, *Roman Circuses: Arenas for Chariot Racing* (Berkeley-Los Angeles, 1986), 91–92, 269–72; M. Turcan, " 'Aedes Solis' au Grand Cirque," *REL* 36 (1958): 255–62. Following the example set in the Circus Maximus, the Vatican circus, and circuses in Sessorian, Tyre, Caesarea, Antioch, and elsewhere were all endowed with a central obelisk.

23. This document is known from the *Suda* and is alluded to by Tertullian *De Spect.* 5: "It is written in Suetonius Tranquillus for which idols they established the games, or in the works of the authors from whom Suetonius borrowed." His earlier sources may have included Varro, whom Tertullian also names as an etymological source. See Hanfmann (1951), 2:75, n. 112.

24. As exemplified by, for instance, the well-known commemorative relief from Ostia: D. E. E. Kleiner, *Roman Sculpture* (New Haven, Conn., 1992), 236, dated to the Trajanic or early Hadrianic period; A. Aymard, "Relief funéraire romain représentant les jeux du cirque," *BAntFr* (1957): 71–72, and a sarcophagus in the Vatican Museums' Sala della Biga, inv. 613. Helbig, 1:393–95, no. 497. The chariot race appears on adult sarcophagi beginning in ca. 200: Humphrey (1986), 196–203. See also G. Koch and H. Sichtermann, *Römische Sarkophage* (Munich, 1982), 210; M. Turcan-Deleani, "Les monuments représentés sur la Colonne Trajane, schématisme et réalisme," *MEFR* 70 (1958): 149–76; C. Belting-Ihm, "Ein römischer Circus-Sarkophag," *JRGZM* 8 (1961): 195–208. Tacitus mentions an ancient hypaethral shrine, *aedes vetus,* to the solar god, located near or in the Circus Maximus, and by the Trajanic period, numismatic images of the Circus Maximus show a temple-like building on the Aventine side, with an acroterion that seems to represent the radiate sun or its beams.

25. For interpretations of the sarcophagi, see Hanfmann (1951); Humphrey (1986), 196; A. Piganiol, *Recherches sur les jeux romains* (Paris, 1923), 144; A. Merlin and A. Poinssot, "Factions du cirque et saisons sur des mosaïques de Tunisie," in *Mélanges Ch. Picard* (Paris, 1949): 2:732–45, esp. 734; Turcan-Deleani (1958); P. Veyne, "Les idéaux collectifs dans l'art funéraire," *REL*

37 (1959): 43–45; L. Vogel, "Circus Race Scenes in the Early Roman Empire," *ArtB* 51 (1969): 155–60.

26. The tomb's opposition of square to octagon to circle opens itself to further tentative speculation. On the circle or sphere as symbol of the heavens, see O. Grabar, "From Dome of Heaven to Pleasure Dome," *JSAH* 49 (1990): 15–21; L. Hautecoeur, *Mystique et Architecture. Symbolisme du Cercle et de la Coupole* (Paris, 1954), 61– 173; K. Lehmann, "The Dome of Heaven," *ArtB* 27 (March 1945): 1–17; G. Bachelard, *The Poetics of Space* (Boston, 1969), 232–41. In imperial times, cosmographers also viewed the earth as a sphere, as did some poets, e.g., Ov. *Met.* 2.1–30; R. Brown, "The Palace of the Sun in Ovid's *Metamorphoses*," in *Homo Viator,* ed. M. Whitby, P. Hardie, and M. Whitby (Bristol, 1987), 211–20. Yet Plato and the pre-Socratics assigned cubical particles to earth, and archaic Romans understood the world as a square, which it remained in poetry: Pl. *Ti.* 23; G. Hersey, *Pythagorean Palaces: Magic and Architecture in the Italian Renaissance* (Ithaca, N.Y., 1976), 19–27; P. Kranz, *Jahreszeiten-Sarkophag: Entwicklung und Ikonographie des Motivs der Vier Jahreszeiten auf Kaiserzeitlichen Sarkophagen und Sarkophagdeckeln* (Berlin, 1984), 1:345, 403; P. L. Couchoud and A. Audin, "Le carré magique," *Latomus* 17 (1958): 518–27. The most unusual aspect of the tomb is the polygonal interior of the upper half of the first drum, which may or may not have been visible. By Glauco Angeletti's calculations, the angle at the meeting of two wedge-shaped rooms at the drum wall measured about 140 degrees ("Esito delle indagini attuate nel secondo tratto della rampa elicoidale," *Studi su Castel Sant'Angelo: Archivum arcis* 3 [1991]: 158–60, 159), which would produce a nonagon. One hundred and thirty-five degrees, still "circa 140," would produce an octagon, which is more probable on account of its ease of construction and its known presence in Hadrianic architecture: see W. L. MacDonald and J. Pinto, *Hadrian's Villa and Its Legacy* (New Haven, Conn., 1995), 94–101. Plato considered the air to be composed of octahedra, and octagons appear often to have been associated with the elements in ancient art (*Ti.* 22–23; Plut. *Quaest. Plat.*

5.1003). The most renowned octagonal building in imperial times was the Tower of the Winds in Athens, and Angeletti supposes that it influenced the design of Hadrian's tomb (conversation, Rome, 1992); the emperor was certainly familiar with it, for he chose an adjacent site for his library. This scenario would create an interesting thematic parallel with Augustus's funerary complex. In the early empire, the winds were an integral part of cosmic images such as Augustus's Horoloqium or Mithraic reliefs and were conceived, in a general simplification of diverse philosophical systems, as vehicles for astral ascension: see L. Musso, "Ascensione ad astra e iconografia funeraria sulla composizione di due sarcofagi romani del III secolo," *Scienze dell'antiquità. Storia, archeologia, anthropologia* 1 (1987): 319–38; F. Cumont, *Recherches sur le symbolisme funéraire des romains* (Paris, 1942), 104–76. They appear on sarcophagi, sometimes in the marine voyage to the Isles of the Blessed, and on funerary reliefs and monuments such as the Tomb of the Secundii at Igel, where four winds blow Hercules' quadriga to heaven, to be received by Athena within a zodiac circle: see Musso (1987); ead. (1990), 182–83, no. 99, 242–43, no. 130; H. Steinmetz, "Windgötter," *JdI* 25 (1910): 1–55; K. Nueser, *Anemoi. Studien zur Darstellung der Winde und Windgottheiten in der Antike* (Rome, 1982); H. Dragendorff and E. Krüger, *Das Grabmal von Igel* (Trier, 1924), 70–73; E. Zahn, *Die Igeler Säule bei Trier, Rheinische Kunststätten* 6–7 (1968). As a result, one might tentatively venture to read in the tomb's forms a geometrical representation of the cosmos where, perhaps, the square earth is surmounted by the circle of the skies, dwelling place of the winds. Through the skies, perhaps transported by the winds, the soul rises to a state of apotheosis.

27. Hanfmann (1951), 1:164.

28. S. Maffei, "La 'felicitas imperatoris' e il dominio sugli elementi," *Studi classici e orientali* 40 (1990): 329–67.

29. G. H. Halsberghe, *The Cult of Sol Invictus* (Leiden, 1972), 26–29; J. Ferguson, *The Religions of the Roman Empire* (Ithaca, N.Y., 1970), 44–47.

30. As an anecdote recorded by Suetonius illustrates: ". . . [Octavius] dreamed that his

son appeared in superhuman majesty, with a thunderbolt, sceptre, and the insignia of Jupiter Optimus Maximus, crowned with a solar diadem, and riding in a chariot wreathed with laurel and drawn by twelve dazzlingly white horses," *Aug.* 94. See Hanfmann (1951), 1:121; Halsberghe (1972), 27.

31. Tac. *Hist.* 3.24.

32. See Halsberghe (1972), 35–49; T. Barton, *Ancient Astrology* (London, 1994), 203; J. R. Fears, *Princeps a Diis Electus: The Divine Election of the Emperor as a Political Concept in Rome* (Rome, 1977), 92–97.

33. *Somnium Scipionis* 4: "Dux et princeps et moderator luminum reliquorum, mens mundi et temperatio." See O. Brendel, "The Shield of Achilles," *The Visible Idea: Interpretations of Classical Art* (Washington, D.C., 1980), 67–82; Halsberghe (1972), 37.

34. The shift toward a single cosmic deity drew strength from a grounded tradition of astrology, in which many Romans placed great faith (with notable exceptions such as Cicero *Div.* and Juvenal, "What shall I do at Rome, ignorant of the motion of the stars?" 3.41–43). Pythagoreanism, Platonism, and especially Stoicism all had a place for astrology, the Stoics adopting and conferring their authority upon the art of apotelesmatism (casting horoscopes): Cumont (1949), 123, 304; Hanfmann (1951), 1:122–24; R. Turcan, "Littérature astrologique et astrologie littéraire dans l'antiquité classique," *Latomus* 27 (1968): 329–405; J. Soubiran, "L'astronomie à Rome," *L'astronomie dans l'antiquité classique* (Paris, 1979), 167–83; A. M. Tupet, "La mentalité superstitieuse à l'époque des Julio-Claudiens," *REL* 62 (1984): 206–35. As for astronomy, its influence is seen in Virgil's *Georgics,* in Vitruvius (9.3–5), Manilius, Hyginus, etc.; Aratos's *Phenomena* was translated into Latin more often than any other Greek work. At the start of the Empire (though recorded by Suetonius), Augustus's predestined role as leader of Rome manifested itself through the workings of the universe (Suet. *Aug.* 94), and on his coinage Augustus placed the globe of his command between the front legs of a capricorn, the position of the moon in the zodiac at the time of his birth, showing that a cosmic power greater than humanity had foreordained his rule: *BMCRE* 1:48; Fears

(1977), 209–10; Schütz (1990), 446–49. See also T. Barton, "Augustus and Capricorn: Astrological Polyvalency and Imperial Rhetoric," *JRS* 85 (1995): 33–51. If the *Historia Augusta* can be believed, Hadrian's gift for reading the stars astonished his contemporaries: "In astrology he regarded himself as such an expert that late on the Kalends of January he would write down what might happen to him during the whole year. In fact, he wrote down for the year when he died what he was going to do up to the very hour of his death" (trans. Birley). See also H. Bardon, *Les empereurs et les lettres latines d'Auguste à Hadrien* (Paris, 1968), 394; J. Gagé, *Basileia. Les Césars, les rois d'Orient et les mages* (Paris, 1968); contra R. Syme, "Astrology in the *Historia Augusta,*" *HAC* 1972–74 (1976): 291–390.

35. H. P. L'Orange, *Studies in the Iconography of Cosmic Kingship in the Ancient World* (Oslo, 1953), 10, 22. Hesych. s.v. *Ouranos;* Herod. 1.98: μεμηχάνηται δὲ οὕτω τοῦτο τὸ τεῖχος ὥστε ὁ ἕτερος τοῦ ἑτέρου κύκλος τοῖσι προμαχεῶσι μούνοισι ἐστι ὑψηλότερος. τὸ μέν κού τι καὶ τὸ χωρίον συμμαχέει κολωνὸς ἐὼν ὥστε τοιοῦτο εἶναι, τὸ δὲ καὶ μᾶλλόν τι ἐπετηδεύθη. Κύκλων δ᾽ ἐόντων τῶν συναπάντων ἑπτά, ἐν δὴ τῷ τελευταίῳ τὰ βασιλήια ἔνεστι καὶ οἱ θησαυροί. τὸ δ᾽ αὐτῶν μέγιστων ἐστὶ τεῖχος κατὰ τὸν Ἀθηνέων κύκλον μάλιστά κη τὸ μέγαθος. τοῦ μὲν δὴ πρώτου κύκλου οἱ προμαχεῶνες εἰσὶ λευκοί, τοῦ δὲ δευτέρου μέλανες, τρίτου δὲ κύκλου φοινίκεοι, τετάρτου δὲ κυάνεοι, πέμπτου δὲ σανδαράκινοι. οὕτω τῶν πέντε κύκλων οἱ προμαχεῶνες ἠνθισμένοι εἰσὶ φαρμάκοισι· δύο δὲ οἱ τελευταῖοι εἰσὶ ὁ μὲν καταργυρωμένους ὁ δὲ κατακεχρυσωμένους ἔχων τοὺς προμαχεῶνας.

36. Plut. *Vit. Alex.* 37.4: λέγεται δὲ καθίσαντος αὐτοῦ τὸ πρώτοω ὑπὸ τὸν χρυσοῦν οὐρανίσκον ἐν τῷ βασιλικῷ θρόνῳ τὸν Κορίνθιον Δημάρατον εὔνουν ὄντα ἄνδρα καὶ πατρῷον φίλον Ἀλεξάνδρου πρεσβυτικῶς ἐπιδακρῦσαι . . . ; Athenaios 6.253d: σεμνόν τι φαίνεθ᾽, οἱ φίλοι πάντες κύκλῳ, ἐν μέσοισι δ᾽ αὐτός, ὅμοιον ὥσπερ οἱ φίλοι μὲν ἀστέρες, ἥλιος δ᾽ ἐνεῖκος; *FHG* II.477: τὴν μὲν γὰρ ὑπόθεσιν, ἥν εἶχε, κατεσκεύαζεν ἐκ

πολλοῦ δαπανήματος· ἦν γὰρ κατὰ μὲν τὸ σχῆμα τῆς ἐργασίας σχεδὸν ἐμβάτης, πίλημα λαμβάνων τῆς πολυτελεστάτης πορφύρας· τούτῳ δὲ χρυσοῦ πολλὴν ἐνύφαινον ποικιλίαν ὀπίσω καὶ ἔμπροσθεν ἐνιέντες οἱ τεχνῖται. αἱ δὲ χλαμύδες αὐτοῦ ἦσαν ὄρφνινον ἔχουσαι τὸ φέγγος τῆς χρόας, τὸ δὲ πᾶν ὁ πόλος ἐνύφαντο, χρυσοῦς ἀστέρας ἔχων καὶ τὰ δώδεκα ζῴδια. μίτρα δὲ χρυσόπαστος ἦν, ἢ καυσίαν ἀλουργῆ οὖσαν ἔσφιγγεν, ἐπὶ τὸ νῶτον φέρουσα τὰ τελευταῖα καταβλήματα τῶν ὑφασμάτων. γινομένων δὲ τῶν Δημητρίων Ἀθήνησιν, ἐγράφετο ἐπὶ τοῦ προσκηνίου ἐπὶ τῆς οἰκουμένος ὀχούμενος. C. M. Kraay and M. Hirmer, *Greek Coins* (New York, 1966), 243; J. J. Pollitt, *Art in the Hellenistic Age* (Cambridge, 1986), 32, 27, fig. 15d; L'Orange (1953), 28; Hor. *Sat.* 1.7.24: "laudat Brutum laudatque cohortem; / solem Asiae Brutum appellat, stellasque salubris / appellat comites. . . ." On Alexander as Helios, see "Apoteosi," *EAA* 1:492 s. v. Apoteosi (H. P. L'Orange).

37. Suet. *Aug.* 94. Sen. *Cons. Ad Polyb.* 13.1; *IGR* IV. 145; Stat. *Silv.* 4.1.2–4. See S. Weinstock, *Divus Julius* (1971): 383–84; Tupet (1984), 222. In Egypt, Heptakomians hailed Hadrian as the son of Apollo upon his accession: "With Trajan in my chariot of white horses I have just climbed aloft to heaven; and now I come to you, o people, I Phoebus, by no means an unknown god to proclaim the new ruler Hadrian. All things serve him on account of his virtue and the genius of his Divine Father"; *P. Giss* 3, adapted from the translation by P. J. Alexander, *HSCP* 49 (1938): 143–44, by K. Hopkins, *Conquerors and Slaves* (Cambridge, 1978), 210. See J. R. Fears, "Jupiter and Roman Imperial Ideology," *ANRW* 2.17.1 (1981): 3–141, esp. 85–89; M. Guarducci, "La religione di Adriano," in *Les empereurs d'Espagne* (Paris, 1965), 209–21, 213; F. R. Walton, "Religious Thought in the Age of Hadrian," *Numen* 4 (1957): 165–70; A. R. Birley, *Hadrian: The Restless Emperor* (London, 1997), 82.

38. Suet. *Aug.* 94.

39. Ibid. 79.

40. See Suet. *Aug.* 70: "Cena quoque eius secretior in fabulis fuit, quae vulgo dodekathos vocabatur; in qua deorum dearumque

habitu discubuisse convivas et ipsum pro Apolline ornatum." See also Hor. *C.* 3.9.21–25; Brendel (1980), 73; K. Galinsky, *Augustan Culture* (Princeton, N.J., 1996), 213–14 and passim. He sits in a cosmic setting on the Gemma Augustea: C. Küthmann, "Zur Gemma Augustea," *AA* 65–66 (1950–51): 89–103; E. Simon, *Augustus, Kunst und Leben in Rom um die Zeitenwende* (Munich, 1986), 156–61. In imitation of the sun, "by night [Caligula] would repeatedly invite the full radiant moon into his embrace and his bed"; he even had a temple built to himself, where birds sacred to the sun were sacrificed: Suet *Calig.* 22. See Hanfmann (1951), 1:164; J. R. Fears, "The Solar Monarchy of Nero and the Imperial Panegyric of Q. Curtius Rufus," *Historia* 25 (1976): 494–96.

41. For an extensive treatment of this problematic issue, see E. Champlin, "God and Man in the Golden House," in *Horti Romani: Atti del convegno internazionale, Roma,* ed. M. Cima and E. La Rocca (Rome, 1998), 333–44. See also J. M. C. Toynbee, "Ruler Apotheosis in Ancient Rome," *NC* 7 (1947): 126–49. The nature of Nero's association with the sun-god is much debated; see, e.g., Cumont (1933), 157; Fears (1976); M. T. Griffin, *Nero, the End of a Dynasty* (New Haven, Conn., 1985), 216–20; L. Duret, "Néron-Phaéton ou la témérité sublime," *REL* 66 (1988): 139–55; M. Bergmann, *Der Koloss Neros, die Domus Aurea und der Mentalitätswandel im Rom der frühen Kaiserzeit, TrWPr* 13 (1993): 3–37.

42. E.g., *BMCRE* 2.340, no. 16, 345, no. 43; Kantorowicz (1963); Halsberghe (1972), 35, 44. The legend *Oriens* emphasized the Eastern origin of the assimilation.

43. S.H.A., *Hadr.* 19.13.

44. Trans. Erman (1917), 3–47, and O. Wintermute, in Boatwright (1987), 244, who contends that the obelisk was "too out of harmony with Hadrian's known religious policy in Rome" and must originally have been erected in Antinoopolis. For its location in Tivoli, see most recently R. Lambert, *Beloved and God: The Story of Hadrian and Antinous* (New York, 1992), 155–60; in the Gardens of Adonis on the Palatine, see J.-C. Grenier, "La tomb d'Antinous à Rome," *MEFRA* 98.1 (1986): 217–29, and F. Coarelli, "Porticus adonaea, aedes

heliogabali, aedes iovis ultoris. La tomba di Antinoo?" *MEFRA* 98.1 (1986): 230–53 (with other hypotheses).

45. Ov. *Fast.* 4.949–54/4.9–54: "Phoebus habet partem, Vestae pars altera cessit; quod superest illis, tertius ipse tenet. State Palatinae laurus, praetextaque quercu stet domus: aeternos tres habet una deos." Suet. *Ner.* 31. On Augustus and Apollo, see also D. Favro, *The Urban Image of Augustan Rome* (Cambridge, 1996), 100. On the Domus Aurea: *LTUR* 2:49–64 s.v. Domus Aurea (A. Cassatella, S. Panella, E. Papi, L. Fabbrini); I. Iacopi, *Domus Aurea* (Milan, 1999); Champlin (1998).

46. Suet. *Ner.* 31: "parecipua cenationeum rotunda, quae perpetuo diebus ac noctibus vice mundi circumageretur." See J. Le Gall, "Les romains et l'orientation solaire," *MEFRA* 87 (1975): 287–320; J.-L. Voisin, "*Exoriente sole* (Suetone, Nér. 6). D'Aléxandrie à la Domus Aurea," in *Urbs: Espace Urbain et histoire, Ier siècle avant J.-C.–Ier siècle après J.-C., CEFR* 98 (1987): 509–43; Y. Perrin, "D'Alexandre à Néron. Le motif de la tente d'apparat. La salle 29 de la Domus Aurea," in *Neronia 4. Alejandro Magno, Modelo de los emperadores romanos* (Brussels, 1990), 211–29. The whole palace was designed astronomically and exactly oriented by the cardinal points. L'Orange (1953), 18–27, compares this room with the later Sassanian Throne of Khosro II (624 C.E.), which moved beneath a revolving vault of heaven in which the king and courtiers, as sun and stars, determined the course of the universe. If the two are not related directly, they do appear to share a common ancestor, to be sought in an Eastern, probably Parthian prototype. See also J. B. Ward-Perkins, "Nero's Golden House," *Antiquity* 30 (1956): 209–19; contra A. Boethius, "Nero's Golden House," *Eranos* 44 (1946): 442–59; idem, "*Et crescunt media pegmata celsa via* (Martial's *De Spectaculis* 2.2)," *Eranos* 50 (1952): 129–37.

47. Y. Perrin, "Nicolas Ponce et la Domus Aurea de Néron. Une documentation inédite," *MEFRA* 94 (1982): 843–91; H. Joyce, "Hadrian's Villa and the 'Dome of Heaven,'" *RM* 97 (1990): 347–81. For numerous other instances, see Champlin (1998).

48. Stat. *Silv.* 4.2.18–31: "Tectum augustum, ingens, non centum insigne columnis / sed

quantae superos caelumque Atlante remisso / sustentare queant. Stupet hoc vicina Tonantis / regia, teque pari laetantur sede locatum / numina. Nec magnum properes escendere caelum; / tanta patet moles effusaeque impetus aulae / liberior campo multumque amplexus operti / aetheros et tantum domino minor; ille penates / implet et ingenti genio iuvat. Aemulus illic / mons Libys Iliacusque nitens et multa Syene / et Chios et glaucae certantia Doridi saxa / Lunaque portandis tantum suffecta columnis. / Longa supra species: fessis vix culmina prendas / visibus auratique putes laquearia caeli." On the *Domus Flavia,* see MacDonald (1982), 47–74.

49. S.H.A., *Hadr.* 26.5. See MacDonald and Pinto (1995) on this tradition.

50. See M. Üblacker, *Das Teatro Marittimo in der Villa Hadriana* (Mainz, 1985); MacDonald and Pinto (1995), 81–89; Herter, "Die Rundform in Platons Atlantis und ihre Nachwirkung in der Villa Hadriani," *Rheinisches Museum für Philologie* 96 (1953): 1–20; J. Ferguson, *Utopias of the Classical World* (London, 1975), 73–75.

51. Varro, *Rust.* 3, 4.2, 5.8–17; H. Stierlin *Hadrien et l'architecture romaine* (Fribourg, 1984); A. W. van Buren and R. M. Kennedy, "Varro's Aviary at Casinum," *JRS* 9 (1919): 134–41; G. Fuchs, "Varros Vogelhaus bei Casinum," *RM* 69 (1962): 22. Stierlin believes the aviary may have been inspired by a structure in the park at the royal palace at Pergamon.

52. Hanfmann (1951), 1:172, and Lehmann (1945) use antiquarian sketches of ceiling paintings at Tivoli showing the seasons and Helios to argue for Hadrian's fascination with the cosmos. Joyce (1990) dismisses them as antiquarian fantasies.

53. M. T. Boatwright *JSAH* 45 (1986): 408–10, warns that it should be read "with caution"; P. Grimal, *REL* (1984): 541–42, admires its brilliant audacity.

54. Grabar (1990).

55. MacDonald and Pinto (1995), 89.

56. F. Cumont, "L'éternité des empereurs romains," *RHLR* 1 (1896): 435–52, esp. 443. Hautecoeur (1954), 164; Halsberghe (1972), 36. *Aeternus* was initially applied to Syrian deities in Italy, nominally Jupiter-Baal, and especially the stars. On assimilation to a

divinity, usually chosen through association with one's profession, as a means to enter immortality, see H. Wrede, *Consecratio in Forman Deorum: Vergöttlichte Privatpersonen in der römischen Kaiserzeit* (Mainz, 1981).

57. U. Geyer, *Der Adlerflug im römischen Konsekrationszeremoniell* (diss., University of Bonn, 1967). See also F. Cumont, *Lux Perpetua* (Paris, 1949), 291–93; O. Brendel, "Classical Ariels," *The Visible Idea: Interpretations of Classical Art* (Washington, D.C., 1980), 49–66; S. G. MacCormack, *Art and Ceremony in Late Antiquity* (Berkeley, 1981), 102. This image was not restricted to the imperial family: see D. Boschung, *Antike Grabaltäre aus den Nekropolen Roms* (Berne, 1987), passim.

58. H.-C. Puech, "Le gnose et le temps," in *En quête de la gnose* (1978), 1:215–70; Hanfmann (1951), 1:122–24. For Plato, time, determined and measured by the revolution of the celestial spheres, was the mobile image of immobile eternity (*Ti.* 37c–38a), while Pythagoreans, Stoics, and Neoplatonists defined eternity as the repetition of events within ages, *anakuklosis.* See also *Corp. Herm.* (*Asklepios* 30–31); J. Annequin, *Recherches sur l'action magique et ses représentations (Ier–IIe siècles après J.C.)* (Paris, 1973), 136–37: for the Roman magician, time was a length of repetitions, risings, and settings of moon and sun; he tried to harness the powers of the universe by imitating astral rhythms.

59. Dumbarton Oaks inv. 36.65; Campo Santo, Pisa, inv. 31; Mus. Naz., Sassari. See Kranz (1984), 193–94, 196–97, 205. On the zodiac, see J.-P. Martin, "Hadrien et le phénix: propagande numismatique," in *Mélanges d'histoire ancienne offerts à William Seston* (Paris, 1974), 336. On sun and moon: Boatwright (1987), 128; Brown (1987).

60. In doing so, he was undoubtedly aware of Ovid's words concerning Julius Caesar's reorganization of the calendar, which suggest that he was acquainting himself with the heavens that he would later inhabit. *Fast.* 3.155–60: "Sed tamen errabant etiam nunc tempora, donec / Caesaris in multis haec quoque cura fuit. / non haec ille deus tantaeque propaginis auctor / credidit officiis esse minora suis / promissumque sibi voluit praenoscere caelum / nec deus ig-

notus hospes inire domos." See K. Allen, "The *Fasti* of Ovid and Imperial Propaganda," *AJP* 43 (1922): 250–66.

61. Villela (1998), 29.

62. When Augustus became Pontifex Maximus in 12 B.C., he consecrated in his Palatine house a new sanctuary of Vesta, whose eternal flame was a symbol of Rome's eternity. See Cumont (1896); Gagé (1968); C. Edwards, *Writing Rome: Textual Approaches to the City* (Cambridge, 1996), 87. See also G. Feeley-Harnik, "Issues in Divine Kingship," *Annual Review of Anthropology* 14 (1985): 273–313, esp. 300, on reconstruction of the king (death and rebirth) and the recreation of time; and P. Hardie, *Virgil's Aeneid: Cosmos and Imperium* (1986), 368–69.

63. C. N. Deedes, "The Labyrinth," in *The Labyrinth,* ed. S. H. Hooke (London, 1935), 1–44, esp. 24, 42. On the acanthus frieze, see D. Castriota, *The Ara Pacis Augustae and the Imagery of Abundance in Later Greek and Early Roman Imperial Art* (Princeton, N.J., 1995).

64. In Augustus's time, temporary wooden stage sets were immortalized in paint in rooms such as Augustus's Hall of the Masks: G. Carettoni, "Due nuovi ambienti dipinti sul Palatino," *BdA* 46 (1961): 189–99. A well-attested device in the funerary realm, the transformation of the transitory into a permanent medium is seen in facade monuments such as the Midas Monument in Phrygia (C. H. E. Haspels, *The Highlands of Phrygia: Sites and Monuments* [Princeton, N.J., 1971], 1:73–76), and in Etruscan tomb paintings and reliefs that imitate houses (e.g., Tomb of the Hut or Thatched Roof) or hunting tents (Tomb of the Hunter): F. Prayon, "Architecture," in *Etruscan Life and Afterlife,* ed. L. Bonfante (Detroit, 1986), 174–201, esp. 180–82; M. Moretti, *New Monuments of Etruscan Painting* (University Park, Pa., 1970), 147–68. On the Ara Pacis the device has been considered simply artistic convention (e.g., A. Borbein, "Die Ara Pacis Augustae. Geschichtliche Wirklichkeit und Programm," *JdI* 90 [1975]: 242–66, esp. 246).

65. After the horror of 69, for instance, when the house once proclaimed eternal was cut down, Titus and Domitian again minted coins declaring the *aeternitas Augusti:* see

M. Charlesworth, "Providentia and Aeternitas," *HThR* 29 (1936): 124; Cumont (1896), 438–39.

66. Tac. *Ann.* 6.28. *RIC* 2:343, no. 27, pl. XII, no. 220. See Kantorowicz (1957), 388–413; R. Van den Broek, *The Myth of the Phoenix according to Classical and Early Christian Traditions* (Leiden, 1972), 233–303; Annequin (1987), 192ff. In 119–21, an issue with Hadrian's head on the obverse showed on the reverse a male figure, nude to the waist, holding a globe surmounted by a phoenix, all framed by an oval held in his left hand. The legend, *Saec. Aur. P.M. Tr. P. Cos. III,* has led Vogel (1973), 33–38, to identify him as *Saeculum Aureum,* while Martin (1974) sees him as Trajan contemplating the globe and his successor. A third type from Alexandria represents *Pronoia* holding a radiate phoenix and a sceptre. For this and other issues emphasizing the succession, see Birley (1997), 81–83.

67. Claud. *Phoenix* 23–26.

68. Ibid. 76–82; Martin (1974), 333. See also A. J. Festugière, "Le symbole du phénix et le mysticisme hermétique," *MonPiot* 38 (1941): 147–51.

69. E.g., Ov. *Am.* 2.6.54, *Met.* 15.392–402; Luc. 6.680; Mart. *Epig.* 5.7; Stat. *Silv.* 2.4.36–37, 3.2; Pliny *HN* 10.2; Tac. *Ann.* 6.28. See Martin (1974), 330.

70. Claud. *Phoenix* 51–54: "[Phoebus consoles his child] . . . , 'You whose death means but the renewal of life and who by self-destruction regains lost youth, receive back your life' "; Tac. *Ann.* 6.28: "[The phoenix] is sacred to the sun." Hadrian's coins may be the first representations of the phoenix with a nimbus, suggesting that Hadrian particularly emphasized its solar aspect.

71. S.H.A., *Hadr.* 4.9; Eutrop. 8.6.1; Aur. Vict. *Caesares* 13.13. See Hammond (1956), 61–133; Birley (1997), 50–51, 77–92.

72. Van den Broek (1972), 146; Martin (1974), 335.

73. S.H.A., *Hadr.* 24.1, *M.Ant* 4.5; Cass. Dio 69.2.1. See also P. Gerade, "Le règlement successorial d'Hadrien," *REA* 52 (1950): 258–77; H.-G. Pflaum, "Le règlement successorial d'Hadrien," *HAC* (1963): 95–122; E. Champlin, "Hadrian's Heir," *ZPE* 1 (1976): 79–89.

74. Zephyros: Steinmetz (1910), 55; F. Brommer, "Aion," *Marburger Winckelmann-Programm* (1967): 1–5. Ascensus; Brendel (1980). Aeternitas: E. Q. Visconti, *Il Museo Pio Clementino* V (Rome, 1796), VII (Milan, 1822), 55. Saeculum Aureum: Vogel (1973), 35–38, and reviews by M. L. Hadzi, *ArtB* 57 (1975): 123–25, and D. L. Thompson, *AJA* 78 (1974): 208. Aion: L. Deubner, "Die Apotheose des Antoninus Pius," *RM* 27 (1912): 1–20; D. Levi, "Aion," *Hesperia* 13 (1944): 269–314; R. Turcan, "Le piédéstal de la Colonne Antonine à propos d'un livre récent," *RA* 2 (1975): 305–18. Alternative identifications include a generic *Genius Alatus* (F. Bianchini, *De Kalendario et Cyclo Caesaris ac de Paschali Canone S. Hippolyti Martyris. Dissertationes duae . . . Quibus Inseritur Descriptio, et Explanatio Basis, in Campo Martio Nuper Detectae Sub Columna Antonino Pio Olim Dicata* [Rome, 1703]) or the Genius of the World (I. Vignoli, *De Columna Imperatoris Antonini Pii Dissertatio* [Rome, 1705]).

75. *Homeric Hymn to Hermes* 42, 119; Hom. *Il.* 19.27; *LIMC,* 1:400–402 s.v. Aion (M. Le Glay), esp. 409.

76. *LIMC,* 1:409; A. Alföldi, "*Aiôn Plutonios – Saeculum Frugiferum,*" in *Greece and the Eastern Mediterranean in Ancient History and Prehistory: Studies Presented to F. Schachermeyr* (1977) 25, no. 103.

77. Pl. *Ti.* 37D; Turcan (1975), 314; Festugière (1941), 2:142, 152, 181; Alföldi (1972); idem (1977) 3.23; *LIMC,* 1:404–5, 409–10.

78. See Levi (1944), 269–314.

79. G. Calza, *La necropoli del Porto di Roma nell'Isola Sacra* (Rome, 1940), 183, fig. 92; F. Gury, "Aion juvénile et l'anneau zodiacal: L'apparition du motif," *MEFRA* 96.1 (1984): 7–28. See L. Foucher, *Découvertes archéologiques à Thysdrus en 1961* (Tunis, 1961), 25, pls. IX–X; idem, "Annus et Aion," in *Le temps chez les Romains* (1976), 197–203, for an aged Aion. For other examples, see *LIMC,* 400–5.

80. *LIMC,* 405–9, no. 17. On the snake's circularity and eternity, see W. Amelung, *Die Skulpturen des Vaticanischen Museums* (Berlin, 1903–56), 1:889; as an emblem for Aion, Festugière (1941), 150.

81. *RIC,* 2:232, no. 131, pl. VIII, no. 129. See P. Arnaud, "L'image du globe dans le monde romain: Iconographie, symbolique," *MEFRA* 96.1 (1984): 53–116; S. Guye and

H. Michel, *Mesures du temps et de l'espace horloges, montres et instruments anciens* (Fribourg, 1970), 207–22. C. Nicolet, *Space, Geography, and Politics in the Early Roman Empire* (Ann Arbor, Mich., 1991), 35–37, insists upon the futility of attempting to distinguish terrestrial from celestial globes; coins are too small to allow for representation of celestial details on the globe and, conversely, the geographical sphere was rare and cumbersome. "For all that, the distinction is of little importance, for the globe is less the sign of concrete domination of space easily located on the surface of the earth than of a sovereignty the more recognizable for being general and 'cosmic,' even more than geographic."

82. Fears (1977), 245. See also Charlesworth (1936).

83. Vignoli (1705); Visconti (1822); Astronomica1 2.265–68; "Temporibus quoque sunt propriis pollentia signa: aestas a Geminis, autumnus Virgine surgit, bruma Sagittifero, ver Piscibus incipit esse. Quattuor in partes scribuntur sidera terna...." See R. Hannah, "Praevolante Nescio Qua Ingenti Humana Specie.... A Reassessment of the Winged Genius on the Base of the Antonine Column," *BSR* 57 (1989): 90–105, esp. 97, who suggests that a reference to spring indicates Antoninus's personal apotheosis. In later systems Aries announced the start of spring: Turcan (1975), 307–8.

84. Romulus and Remus are not commonly found on Roma's shield; see C. C. Vermeule, *The Goddess Roma in the Art of the Roman Empire* (Cambridge, Mass., 1959). On the she-wolf as a symbol of Rome's eternity, see A. D. Nock, "Sarcophagi and Symbolism," *AJA* 50 (1946): 140, n. 2. The cloth of Roma's mantle is finished with tassles in the shape of acorns, symbolic of regeneration: see Vignoli (1705), 151–53; Visconti (1877), 57; Vogel (1973), 32–33.

85. Vogel (1973), 3. For meanings inherent in different styles, see A. L. Kuttner, "Some New Grounds for Narrative: Marcus Antonius' Base (The *Ara Domitii Ahenobarbi*) and Republican Biographies," in P. Holliday, *Narrative and Event in Ancient Art* (Cambridge, 1993), 198–229.

86. For some, the two decursio reliefs represent separate events following Faustina's death in 141 and Antoninus Pius's in 161;

for others, two contemporaneous events, each hosted by one of the heirs, Marcus Aurelius and Lucius Verus, in their parents' honor. L. Curtius, *Das antike Rom* (Vienna, 1944), 56; J.-C. Richard, "Les aspects militaires des funérailles impériales," *Mél-Rome* 78 (1966): 313–25; T. Kraus, *Das römische Weltreich* (Berlin, 1967), 234; D. E. E. Kleiner and F. S. Kleiner, "The Apotheosis of Antoninus and Faustina," *RendPontAcc* 51–52 (1978–80): 389–400. See also Turcan (1975), 317; J. B. Ward-Perkins, "Columna divi Antonini," in *Mélanges d'histoire ancienne et d'archéologie offerts à Paul Collart* (Lausanne, 1976), 345–52, 346; Vogel (1973), 66–67; Hadzi (1975), 124.

87. S.H.A., *M. Ant.* 6.6–7.3. See Hammond (1956), 99–102. The coins featured the legend *Concordia* almost exclusively in the first year of their reign, illustrated by a seated personification of Concordia or the brothers standing with clasped hands: *RIC*, 3:214–19, 250–53. A second recurrent legend is *Providentia Deorum*, with the personified Providentia: *RIC*, 3:215, nos. 18–25, 251, no. 460.

CHAPTER FOUR

1. Cass. Dio 58.2.2; *PIR* L.301; C. B. Rose, *Dynastic Commemoration and Imperial Portraiture in the Julio-Claudian Period* (Cambridge, 1997), 35. Livilla's urn: Braccio Nuovo, inv. 2302; Helbig, 1:324–45, no. 420.

2. The representation in the friezes of those who were not present at the time of the altar's dedication supports such a contention.

3. For identification of figures, see E. Petersen, *Ara Pacis Augustae* (Vienna, 1902); M. Torelli, *Typology and Structure of Roman Historical Reliefs* (Ann Arbor, Mich., 1982), 43–54. On problems of identification, see most recently D. A. Conlin, "The Reconstruction of Antonia Minor on the Ara Pacis," *JRA* 5 (1992): 209–15.

4. See D. E. E. Kleiner, *Roman Sculpture* (New Haven, Conn.,-London, 1992, 90, 98; P. Gros, *Aurea templa: Recherches sur l'architecture religieuse de Rome à l'epoque d'Auguste* (Rome, 1976), 31–34.

5. Suet. *Calig.* 59.

6. Suet. *Calig.* 15; A. R. Barrett, *Caligula: The Corruption of Power* (London, 1989), 60–61;

A. Ferrill, *Caligula, Emperor of Rome* (London, 1991), 97; Rose (1997), 35–36.

7. Barrett (1989), 86–89; Ferrill (1991), 109–11; Rose (1997), 32, 35–36. On empress deification, see also S. B. Matheson, "The Divine Claudia: Women as Goddesses in Roman Art," in *I, Claudia: Women in Ancient Rome,* ed. D. E. E. Kleiner and S. B. Matheson (New Haven, Conn., 1996), 182–93.

8. Suet., *Claud.* 11.2; Cass. Dio 60.5.2; *CIL* 6.4222.

9. Suet. *Ner.* 34.

10. Cass. Dio 62.28.1–2, 59.11.2–3; Tac. *Ann.* 16.6, 21; Suet. *Ner.* 35; Rose (1997), 49.

11. *CIL* 6.893; *LTUR,* 3:238.

12. R. Paris, ed., *Dono Hartwig: Originali ricongiunti e copie tra Ann Arbor e Roma. Ipotesi per il Templum Gentis Flaviae* (Rome, 1994), 75–76; S. Gsell, *Essai sur le règne de l'empereur Domitien* (Paris, 1894), 113; E. Rodríguez Almeida, "Alcune note topografiche sul Quirinale di epoca domizianea," *BullCom* 91.1 (1986): 49–60.

13. *CIL* 14.2795=*ILS* 272; E. R. Varner, "Domitia Longina and the Politics of Portraiture," *AJA* 99 (1995): 187–206.

14. S.H.A., *Hadr.* 9; E. Fantham, H. P. Foley, N. B. Kampen, S. B. Pomeroy, and A. L. Shapiro, eds., *Women in the Classical World* (Oxford, 1994), 351.

15. Evidence for the altar comes from a fragment of the edict of Tarracius Bassus (*CIL* 6.318893); see L. Richardson, Jr., *A New Topographical Dictionary of Ancient Rome* (Baltimore, 1992), 246. On the temple, see H. Dressel, "Der Matidiatempel auf einem Medallion des Hadrianus," in *Corolla Numismatica in Honour of Barclay Head* (Oxford, 1906), 16–28; C. Hülsen, "Trajanische und hadrianische Bauten im Marsfelde in Rom," *ÖJh* 15 (1912): 124–42; E. Lissi Caronna, "Roma. Rinvenimenti in Piazza Capranica 78," *NSc* (1972): 398–403. On the *Basilica Matidiae et Marcianae,* see M. T. Boatwright, *Hadrian and the City of Rome* (Princeton, N.J., 1987), 58–62; Richardson (1992), 53–54; *LTUR,* 1:182 s.v. Basilica Marciana, Basilica Matidia (E. Rodrìguez Almeida).

16. S.H.A., *Hadr.* 12.1–2. See A. R. Birley, *Hadrian: The Restless Emperor* (London, 1997), 144; Fantham et al. (1994), 351. Bracket marks set to one side in the burial chamber wall in the base of Trajan's Column might imply that a second bracket for Plotina's urn complemented Trajan's, but the wall surface has perished: G. Boni, "Esplorazione del Forum Ulpium," *NSc* 4 (1907): 361–427. Perhaps the joint dedication of the adjacent temple suggests that both were buried in the Column. Prohibitions against burial within the *pomerium* may have been waived for Plotina to allow husband and wife to be buried together. In any case, the Column in no way records Plotina's presence in its appearance. Former imperial women such as Agrippina were depicted in the Forum's sculpture in the form of *imagines clipeatae,* but there is no evidence for Plotina's representation: S. Wood, "Agrippina the Elder in Julio-Claudian Art and Propaganda," *AJA* 92 (1988): 409–26; R. Winkes, "Pliny's Chapter on Roman Funerary Customs in Light of *Clipeatae Imagines,*" *AJA* 83 (1979): 481–84; K. Fittschen and P. Zanker, *Katalog der römischen Porträts in den Capitolinischen Museen und den anderen kommunalen Sammlungen der Stadt Rom III, Kaiserinnen und Prinzessinbildnisse, Frauenporträts* (Mainz, 1983), 5–6. F. Lepper and S. Frere, *Trajan's Column: A New Edition of the Cichorius Plates* (Gloucester, 1988), 202, suggest that the temple's flanking colonnades provided niches for family memorials.

17. Inv. 1213: Helbig[4] 2:569–70, no. 1800; G. Köppel, "Die historischen Reliefs der römischen Kaiserzeit IV: Stadtrömischen Denkmäler unbekannter Bauzugehörigkeit aus hadrianischer bis konstantinischer Zeit," *BJb* 186 (1986): 7–8, 39–43; E. La Rocca, *Rilievi storici capitolini: Il restauro dei pannelli di Adriano e di Marco Aurelio nel Palazzo dei Conservatori* (Rome, 1986), 21–37; Boatwright (1987), 226–29, 231–34; Kleiner (1992), 253–55; Richardson (1992), 338; D. E. E. Kleiner and S. B. Matheson, *I Claudia: Women in Ancient Rome* (New Haven, Conn., 1996), 70.

18. For the winged figure's identification, see L. Deubner, "Die Apotheose des Antoninus Pius," (*RM* 1912): 1–20, esp. 13.

19. Inv. 832. Helbig, 2:264–65, no. 1447. See La Rocca (1986), 24–28. On the relief as a eulogy: A. J. B. Wace, "Studies in Roman Historical Reliefs," *BSR* 4 (1907): 258–63; as a declaration of apotheosis: R. Bianchi Bandinelli and M. Torelli, *L'arte dell'antichità classica, 2: Etruria, Roma* (Turin, 1976), no. 140.

20. Wace (1907) suggests that the reliefs belonged to a monument similar to Antoninus Pius's Column. On the Arco di Portogallo, see Richardson (1992), 21–22; S. Stucchi, "L'Arco detto 'di Portogallo' sulla Via Flaminia," *BullCom* 73 (1949–50): 101–22; *LTUR*, 1:77–79 s.v. Arco di Portogallo (M. Torelli).

21. *CIL* 6.984–95. The last of the inscriptions was removed by Gregory in 1579 for the marble decoration of the Cappella Gregoriana in St. Peter's: see R. Lanciani, *The Destruction of Ancient Rome* (1899), 151; J. R. Pierce, "The Mausoleum of Hadrian and the Pons Aelius," *JRS* 15 (1925): 75–103, esp. 78; M. A. Tomei, "Il Mausoleo di Adriano: La decorazione scultorea," in *Adriano e il suo Mausoleo,* ed. M. Mercalli (Milan, 1998), 106.

22. *CIL* 6.984.

23. I thank Eric Varner for pointing this out to me.

24. Inv. nos. 5117, 5120. See Pierce (1925), 76–77, 97; also J.-C. Richard, "Tombeaux des empereurs et temples des 'Divi': Notes sur la signification religieuse des sépultures impériales à Rome," *RHR* 170 (1966): 127–42, esp. 132.

25. See e.g., *BMCRE* 3:362; G. Camozzi, "La consecratio nelle monete da Cesare ad Adriano," *RIN* 14 (1901): 27–53; M. Bernhart, "*Consecratio:* Ein numismatischer Beitrag zur römischen Kaiserkonsekration," in *Festschrift F. Hommel* 2 (1917): 136–67.

26. Kleiner and Matheson (1996), 76, with coins declaring her apotheosis.

27. S.H.A., *M. Ant.* 8.1; A. Bartoli, "Il tempio di Antonino e Faustina," *MonAnt* 23 (1914): 949–74: Richardson (1992), 11–12; Fantham et al. (1994), 351–52; Kleiner and Matheson (1996), 80.

28. For coins showing her funerary pyre, see Kleiner and Matheson (1996), 80.

29. Tac. *Ann.* 3.34, 5.1.5; Cass. Dio 55.16–20, 169; Suet. *Aug.* 71.1.

30. Barrett (1989), 86; H. Mattingley, "The Consecration of Faustina the Elder and her Daughter," *HThR* 41 (1948): 147–51.

31. *CIL* 14.3579; Fantham et al. (1994), 350–51.

32. S.H.A., *Hadr.* 11.7, 14.5–6. See H. Halfmann, *Itinera Principum* (Stuttgart, 1986), 91; Boatwright (1987), 529; R. Syme, "Journeys of Hadrian," *ZPE* 73 (1988): 162–68.

33. S.H.A., *Hadr.* 11.3, 23.9. F. S. Kleiner writes: "However estranged Hadrian and Sabina might have been, there is no suggestion of any discord either on the Roman coinage or in monumental relief sculpture" (Kleiner and Matheson [1996], 70).

34. Cass. Dio 49.38.1. See N. Purcell, "Livia and the Womanhood of Rome," *PCPS,* n.s. 32 (1986): 78–105, esp. 85–86 and n. 41. A. Bauman, *Women and Politics in Ancient Rome* (London-New York, 1992), 93–98, sees the grant of sacrosanctity as a result of Antony's repeated insults to Octavia, and as a *casus belli.* For Livia's power, see also Kleiner and Matheson (1996).

35. Cass. Dio 56.10.2. The *Lex Voconia* prohibited women from inheriting more than 100,000 sesterces at a time. See Purcell (1986), 85–89; Boatwright (1987), 519; M. B. Flory, "*Sic Exempla Parantur:* Livia's Shrine to Concordia and the Porticus Liviae," *Historia* 33 (1984): 309–30. On the inscription of the Temple of Fortuna Muliebris, she even used a nomenclature that reveals her independence from Augustus, naming an alternative filiation before her husband: *Drusi f. uxor [Caesar Augusti].*

36. Cass. Dio 54.16, trans. I. Scott Kilvert; see also idem 55.14–22, 57.12.2, 60.22.2; Sen. *Clem.* 1.9; Purcell (1986), 86–87.

37. S.H.A., *Hadr.* 4.10; 4.1, 4.4, 4.10; Aur. Vict. *Caesares* 42.21. Cassius Dio (69.1.2) even alleges Plotina's infidelity with Hadrian. See H.-C. Pflaum, "Les Impératrices de l'époque des Antonins dans l'*Historia Augusti,*" *HAC* 4 (1979/81): 245–46, who discerns Plotina's influence over Hadrian in his favorable response to her letter on behalf of the Epicureans in Athens; M. T. Boatwright, "The Imperial Women of the Early Second Century A.C.," *AJP* 112 (1991): 513–40, esp. 530–36; Birley (1997), passim.

38. Boatwright (1991), 520, attributes this absence not to poverty or parsimony but to a reluctance to accrue gratia by public liberality. She notes also that these empresses did not come from long-standing influential families. See M. Corbier, "Divorce and Adoption as Roman Familial Strategies," *Marriage, Divorce, and Children in Ancient Rome,* ed. B. Rawson (Oxford, 1991), 61, on imperial women as "power-brokers"; idem, "Male Power and Legitimacy through

Women: The *Domus Augusta* under the Julio-Claudians," in *Women in Antiquity: New Assessments,* ed. R. Hawley and B. Levick (London, 1995), 178–93.

39. Fantham et al. (1994), 304.

40. See M. Fullerton, "The *Domus Augusti* in Imperial Iconography of 13–12 B.C.," *AJA* 89 (1985): 473–83, esp. 480.

41. See G. K. Galinsky, "Venus, Polysemy, and the Ara Pacis Augustae," *AJA* 96 (1992): 457–75. Tellus and Italia: Petersen (1902), 49–54; E. Strong, "Terra Mater or Italia?" *JRS* 27 (1937): 114–26; A. W. van Buren, "The Ara Pacis Augustae," *JRS* 3 (1913): 134–41; G. Moretti, *Ara Pacis Augustae* (Rome, 1948). Pax: V. Gardthausen, *Der Altar des Kaiserfriedens, Ara Pacis Augustae* (Leipzig, 1908), 14–16; N. de Grummond, "Pax Augusta and the Horae on the Ara Pacis," *AJA* 94 (1990): 663–77. Ceres: K. Hanell, "Das Opfer des Augustus an der Ara Pacis," *OpRom* 2 (1960): 31–123; B. S. Spaeth, "The Goddess Ceres in the Ara Pacis Augustae and the Carthage Relief," *AJA* 98 (1994): 65–100; eadem, *The Roman Goddess Ceres* (Austin, 1996).

42. G. K. Galinsky, "Venus in a Relief on the Ara Pacis Augustae," *AJA* 70 (1966): 223–43.

43. Spaeth (1994), 73–74; S. B. Pomeroy, *Goddesses, Whores, Wives, and Slaves: Women in Classical Antiquity* (New York, 1975), 184.

44. Verg. *G.* 1.212; Spaeth (1994), 69–71; ead. (1996), 38, 128; Pomeroy (1975), 214–15.

45. For Ceres' connection with death rituals, see Aulus Gellius, *NA* 4.6.8; Stat. *Theb.* 4.460, 5.156; Spaeth (1996), 26–27, 33–49, 53–56.

46. Vat. Mus. inv. 715; Spaeth (1996), 23, 119. Livia's portraiture changed after Augustus's death and apotheosis, when a cult was established in his name of which Livia was chief priestess. When depicted in this role, she was portrayed in the guise of Ceres, epitomizing perpetuation of the genius of Augustus through procreation. See G. Grether, "Livia and the Roman Imperial Cult," *AJP* 67 (1947): 222–52; Purcell (1986), 92; R. Calza, *Scavi di Ostia, 5. I Ritratti* (Rome, 1964), 1:78–80, no. 127; *BMC,* 2:476, 3:70–71. See also T. Mikocki, "Les impératrices et les princesses en déesses dans l'art romain," *Eos* 78 (1990): 209–18; idem, *Sub specie deae: Les impératrices et princesses romaines assimilées à des*

déeesses. Etude iconologique (Rome, 1995), 18–21.

47. D. E. E. Kleiner, "The Great Friezes of the Ara Pacis Augustae: Greek Sources, Roman Derivatives and Augustan Social Policy," *MEFRA* 90 (1978): 753–85; ead. (1992): 92–93. Upon restoring peace to Rome in 31 B.C.,, Augustus addressed domestic policy with a vigor that aroused bitter unpopularity. The *lex Julia de maritandis ordinibus* of 18 B.C., modified after protest by the *lex Papia Poppaea* in A.D. 9, removed restrictions on marriage but prohibited the marriage of senators to freedwomen or actresses. The laws penalized the unmarried and the childless, male and female, by curtailing inheritance rights, and offered special privileges to freeborn women with three children and freedwomen with four. They also imposed obstructions to divorce. The *lex Julia de adulteriis coercendis* of 18–17 B.C. established severe penalties for adulterers (who were by legal definition female). See Dio Cass. 55.2; G. K. Galinsky, "Augustus' Legislation on Morals and Marriage," *Philologus* 125 (1981): 124–44; A. Rousselle, "Personal Status and Sexual Practice in the Roman Empire," *Fragments in the History of the Human Body* (New York, 1989), 3:300–333; A. Richlin, "Approaches to the Sources on Adultery at Rome," in *Reflections of Women in Antiquity,* ed. H. P. Foley (New York, 1980), 379–404; R. I. Frank, "Augustus' Legislation Concerning Marriage and Children," *CSCA* 8 (1975): 41–52; P. Csillag, *The Augustan Laws on Family Relations* (Budapest, 1976); L. Raditsa, "Augustus' Legislation Concerning Marriage, Procreation, Love Affairs and Adultery," *ANRW* 11.13 (1980): 278–339; S. Treggiari, "*Digna Condicio:* Betrothals in the Roman Upper Class," *EchCl* 28 (1984): 419–51; ead., *Roman Marriage* (Oxford, 1991), 277–98; E. Badian, "A Phantom Marriage Law," *Philologus* 129 (1985): 82–98.

48. D. E. E. Kleiner, "Women and Family Life on Roman Imperial Altars," *Latomus* 46 (1987): 545–54, esp. 545.

49. Suet. *Aug.* 63. See also Kleiner (1992), 98.

50. Cass. Dio 55.2.

51. J. H. Corbett, "The Succession Policy of Augustus," *Latomus* 33 (1974): 87–97, argues that Tiberius was Augustus's heir at

this time. See Kleiner (1992), 98, on Livia the "doubly abundant"; Corbier (1991), 63; Rose (1997); A. L. Kuttner, *Dynasty and Empire in the Age of Augustus: The Case of the Boscoreale Cups* (Berkeley, 1995).

52. J. Pollini, "Studies in Augustan 'Historical' Reliefs" (Ph.D. diss., University of California, Berkeley, 1978), 100.

53. See Hanell (1960), 88–89; R. Billows, "The Religious Procession of the Ara Pacis Augustae: Augustus' *supplicatio* in 13 B.C.," *JRA* 6 (1993): 80–92.

54. Torelli (1982), 49.

55. Torelli (1982), 50, writes, "On the same side, immediately after Agrippa, but with a significant compositional staccato, we see Livia. . . . To her the second rank undoubtedly was due, and her posture and compositional conception emphasize her stand in the sequence."

56. Sabina's date of birth is not known. She married Hadrian in 100; the average age for girls at marriage was the late teens or early twenties, although senatorial women probably married several years earlier: P. Garnsey and R. Saller, *The Roman Empire: Economy, Society and Culture* (Berkeley, 1987), 131. If Sabina had married Hadrian at the early age of twelve, she would have been forty-eight at death. On Sabina's portraiture, see M. Wegner, *Hadrian, Plotina, Marciana, Matidia, Sabina* (Berlin, 1956); A. Carandini, *Vibia Sabina* (Florence, 1969); Calza (1964), 79–80. Birley (1997), 16, estimates that she was born in about 86, which would make her fifty at her death.

57. See E. D'Ambra, "Pudicitia in the Frieze of the Forum Transitorium," *RM* 98 (1991): 243–48, esp. 245; ead., *Private Lives, Imperial Virtues: The Frieze of the Forum Transitorium in Rome* (Princeton, N.J., 1993), 36ff.

58. See Mikocki (1995), 62.

59. Deubner (1912), 15–16; A. Alföldi, "Insignien und Tracht der römischen Kaiser," *RM* 50 (1935): 1–171, esp. 95–110; J. Beaujeu, *La religion romaine à l'apogée de l'empire, I: La politique religieuse des Antonins (96–192)* (Paris, 1955), 69–80. W. Roscher, *Ausführliches Lexikon der griechischen und römischen Mythologie* (Leipzig, 1892), II. 1. 600–601; L. Vogel, *The Column of Antoninus Pius* (Cambridge, Mass., 1973), 39. See also M. Wegner, *Die Herrscherbildnisse in Antoninischer Zeit* (Berlin, 1939), 29–30;

LIMC, V.1. 814–56, V.2. 537; Mikocki (1995), 23–25, 160–63; E. Corbaud, *Le bas-relief romain à représentations historiques* (Paris, 1899), 84. On Hera, see *LIMC,* IV.1. 659–719, IV.2. 415–16; E. Simon, *Die Götter der Griechen*[2] (Munich, 1980), 35–65.

60. W. Burkert, *Greek Religion* (Oxford-Cambridge, Mass., 1985), 131–35. She was invoked in wedding prayers and linked with the act of consummation. Although Alcaeus does refer to her as *panton genethla,* generation of all (129.7), Ares was her only legitimate child fathered by Zeus, who hated him most of all the gods (*Il.* 5.890).

61. E. Simon, *Die Götter der Römer* (Munich, 1990), 94–106. Moreover, the minor deities Lucina (who made the child see the light of day) and Opigena (who brought help to women in childbirth) were either assimilated to Juno or were titles of hers that sometimes took on independent existence. On Faustina the Younger's lifetime affiliation with Juno Lucina, see Kleiner and Matheson (1996), 71.

62. N. B. Kampen, "Between Public and Private: Women as Historical Subjects in Roman Art," in *Women's History and Ancient History,* ed. S. B. Pomeroy (Chapel Hill-London, 1991), 218–48. See also ead., "The Muted Other," *ArtJ* (1988): 15–19; ead., "The Muted Other: Gender and Morality in Augustan Rome and Eighteenth-Century Europe," in *The Expanding Discourse: Feminism and Art History,* ed. N. Broude and M. D. Garrard (New York, 1992), 160–69. J. P. Hallett, *Fathers and Daughters in Roman Society: Women and the Elite Family* (Princeton, N.J., 1984), 29, perceives a fusion between public and private despite the ancients' sometime use of the terms.

63. N. B. Kampen, "Gender Theory in Roman Art," in *I Claudia: Women in Ancient Rome* (1996), 14–25. See also R. MacMullen, "Women in Public in the Roman Empire," *Historia* 29 (1980): 208–18; idem, "Women's Power in the Principate," *Klio* 68 (1986): 434–43; J. P. Hallett, "The Role of Women in Roman Elegy: Counter-Cultural Feminism," in *Women in the Ancient World: The Arethusa Papers* (Albany, 1984), 241–44. On the public role of women in the Republic, see S. Dixon, "A Family Business: Women's Role in Patronage and Politics at Rome,

80–44 B.C.," *ClMed* 34 (1983): 91–112; M. R. Lefkowitz, "Wives and Husbands," *GaR* 30 (1983): 31–47; M. Arthur, " 'Liberated' Women: The Classical Era," in *Becoming Visible: Women in European History*, ed. R. Bridenthal and C. Koonz (Boston, 1987), 96–104; J. A. McNamara, "*Matres Patriae/Matres Ecclesiae*: Women of the Roman Empire," in Bridenthal and Koonz, *Becoming Visible*, 107–29; D. E. E. Kleiner, "Imperial Women as Patrons of the Arts in the Early Empire," in Kleiner and Matheson, *I, Claudia*, 28–53. The only women depicted on the Ara Pacis in their professional capacity are the Vestal Virgins on the altar frieze, who were forbidden to marry. Even so, their role was to guard the hearth, heart of the home and the state. See M. Beard, "The Sexual Status of the Vestal Virgins," *JRS* 70 (1980): 12–27; "Rereading (Vestal) Virginity," in *Women in Antiquity: New Assessments*, ed. R. Hawley and B. Levick (London, 1995), 166–77; S. B. Pomeroy, *Goddesses, Whores, Wives, and Slaves: Women in Classical Antiquity* (New York, 1975), 210–14. Equally, men are represented on the friezes almost exclusively in a religious role, with the exception of Drusus the Elder, who is shown in military dress. At the time of the dedication, he was on campaign in Germany: Torelli (1982), 48.

64. Or at the beginning of the file, since the emphatic position in a Roman procession was at the end: R. MacMullen, communication.

65. Kleiner (1978), 757–66. See, e.g., stele of Dion and Mika, Athens NM C157: K. F. Johansen, *The Attic Grave-Reliefs of the Classical Period: An Essay in Interpretation* (Copenhagen, 1951), 38, fig. 19, and passim. Moreover, on the Parthenon frieze, women appear in groups on the north side, not dispersed among the men.

66. R. Brilliant, *Gesture and Rank in Roman Art: The Use of Gesture to Denote Status in Roman Sculpture* (New Haven, Conn., 1963), 105–61; P. G. Hamberg, *Studies in Roman Imperial Art* (Copenhagen, 1945), passim; G. Rodenwaldt, "Römische Reliefs: Vorstufen zur Spätantike," *JdI* 55 (1940): 43.

67. Kleiner (1992), 98.

68. See A. Wallace-Hadrill, "The Social Structure of the Roman House," *BSR* 56 (1988): 43–97, for a discussion of the public and private areas of the Roman house, which are not gender-specific; idem, "Engendering the Roman House," in Kleiner and Matheson, *I, Claudia*, 104–15. See also G. Pollock, "Modernity and the Spaces of Femininity," *Vision and Difference: Femininity, Feminism and the Histories of Art* (London, 1988), 50–90; Spaeth (1996), 67, 69; G. K. Galinsky, *Augustan Culture* (Princeton, N.J., 1996), 128–40.

69. La Rocca (1986), pl. 7.

70. Kleiner and Matheson (1996), 64.

71. Hadrian's eagerness to please the Senate at the start of his reign is demonstrated by his sending a letter to them to apologize for the army's haste in acclaiming him emperor, a decision that should rightfully be made by the Senate (S.H.A., *Hadr.* 6.2).

72. On the woman as the agent of transmission of family prestige and possessions, see M. Corbier, "Male Power and Legitimacy through Women: The *Domus Augusta* under the Julio-Claudians," in *Women in Antiquity: New Assessments*, ed. R. Hawley and B. Levick (London, 1995), 178–93, esp. 53–55. On the continued link between woman and blood family after her marriage, see Pomeroy (1976), 215–27. The prevalence in the imperial period of marriage without *manus* certainly enhanced such potential. See also J. F. Gardner, *Women in Roman Law and Society* (Bloomington-Indianapolis, 1986), 31–65; M. Murray, "Royal Marriage and Matrilineal Descent," *Journal of the Royal Anthropological Institute of Great Britain and Ireland* 45 (1915): 317–25; A. C. Bush and J. J. McHugh, "Succession to the Throne of Rome through 192 A.D.," *JIES* 2 (1974): 259–77; Fantham et al. (1994), 351; Boatwright (1991).

73. By law, the heir was responsible for performing burial rites, unless the deceased had specified otherwise. See J. M. C. Toynbee, *Death and Burial in the Roman World* (London, 1971), 54; Fantham et al. (1994), 351.

74. Compare C. R. Sherman's findings for the French monarchy in the fourteenth century, "Taking a Second Look: Observations on the Iconography of a French Queen, Jeanne de Bourbon (1338–1378)," in *Feminism and Art History: Questioning the Litany,*

ed. N. Broude and M. D. Garrard (New York, 1982), 100–17.

CHAPTER FIVE

1. See, for instance, Polyb. 6.53; Tac. *Agr.* 46; O. C. Crawford, *"Laudatio funebris,"* *CJ* 37 (1941–42): 17–29.

2. *"Ut mihi contingat tuo beneficio post mortem vivere"*: Petron. *Sat.* 71.6. See also Cic. *Leg.* 2.22.55–57, on the tomb's crucial role in rendering the burial spot sacred.

3. H. Lavagne, "Le tombeau, mémoire du mort," in *La mort, les morts et l'au-delà dans le monde romain* (Caen, 1987), 61; J. A. North, "These He Cannot Take," *JRS* 73 (1983): 169–74, esp. 171. See also P. Veyne, *A History of Private Life, I: From Pagan Rome to Byzantium,* ed. P. Veyne, trans. A. Goldhammer (Cambridge, Mass.-London, 1987), 169–71.

4. P. Ciancio Rossetto, *Il sepolcro del fornaio Marco Virgilio Eurisace a Porta Maggiore* (Rome, 1973); O. Brandt, "Recent Research on the Tomb of Eurysaces," *OpRom* 19 (1993): 13–17.

5. Cic. *Att.* 12.12, 12.18; see also Lavagne (1987), 61; H. von Hesberg, *Römische Grabbauten* (Darmstadt, 1992), 5–6.

6. E.g., *CIL* 13.5708. See P. Schmitt-Pantel, "Evergétisme et mémoire du mort," in *Le mort, les morts dans les sociétés anciennes,* ed. G. Gnoli and J. P. Vernant (Cambridge, 1982), 177–88, esp. 178. For gardens, see P. Grimal, *Les jardins romains* (Paris, 1943); J. Stevens Curl, *A Celebration of Death. An Introduction to Some of the Buildings, Monuments and Settings of Funerary Architecture in the Western European Tradition* (London, 1980), 52–54; M. Basso, *Guide to the Vatican Necropolis* (Vatican City, 1986), passim; L. Farrar, *Ancient Roman Gardens* (Stroud, Glos., 1998), 177–79.

7. *CIL* 11.5047; K. Hopkins, *Death and Renewal* (Cambridge, 1983), 233. See also the documents collected by M. Amelotti. *Il testamento romano attraverso la prassi documentale* (Florence, 1966).

8. H. Dessau, *ILS* 7258; see also *ILS* 8370, 8373.

9. Ov. *Fast.* 2.533–42. On the closing of temples, banning of marriage, and other measures in force during the *Parentalia,* see *Fast.*

2.557–71; Plut. *QR* 34. See also A. Bouche-Leclerq, *Manuel des institutions romaines* (Paris, 1886), 466; J. M. C. Toynbee, *Death and Burial in the Roman World* (London, 1971), 63–64; R. Schilling, "Roman Festivals and Their Significance," *Acta Classica* 7 (1964): 44–56; Hopkins (1983), 233; von Hesberg (1992), 16–17.

10. *CIL* 14.356; S. Walker, *Memorials to the Roman Dead* (London, 1985), 62. See also inscription from Tomb 23, Porta Nocera, Pompeii: *Hospes paullisper morare si non est molestum, et quid evites cognosce. Amicum hunc quem speraveram mi esse abeo mihi accusato res subiecti et iudicia instaurata deis gratias ago et meae innocentiae omni molestia liberatus sum; qui nostrum mentitur eum nec di penates nec inferi recipiant* (A. de Vos and M. de Vos, *Pompei, Ercolaneo, Stabia. Guida archeologiche laterza* [Rome, 1982], 159–60). I am grateful to John Clarke for drawing my attention to this inscription. The very utterance of a name could have special magical significance: see J. Annequin, *Recherches sur l'action magique et ses représentations (Ier–IIe siècles après. J.C.* (Paris, 1973), 28–29. See also Prop. 4.7.79–86.

11. See J. Scheid, *"Contraria facere:* Renversements et déplacements dans les rites funéraires," *Archeologia e storia antica* 6 (1984): 117–39.

12. On the former, a frieze detailing breadmaking (see Ciancio Rossetto [1973]), and on the latter a relief perhaps referring to Haterius's career as a building contractor (see W. Jensen, *The Sculptures from the Tomb of the Haterii* [Ph.D. diss., University of Michigan, 1978]).

13. W. Von Massow, *Die Grabmäler von Neumagen* (Berlin-Leipzig, 1932); H. Colvin, *Architecture and the Afterlife* (New Haven-London, 1991), 99.

14. D. E. E. Kleiner, *Roman Group Portraiture: The Funerary Reliefs of the Late Republic and Early Empire* (New York, 1977); ead., *Roman Sculpture* (New Haven, Conn., 1992), 78–80.

15. See Toynbee (1971), 122; V. Kockel, *Die Grabbauten vor dem Herkulaner Tor in Pompeii* (Mainz, 1983), 47–52, 57–59; W. L. MacDonald, *The Architecture of the Roman Empire, 2: An Urban Appraisal* (New Haven-London, 1986), 151; L. Vogel, *The Column of Antoninus Pius* (Cambridge, Mass., 1973), 25 and

110–11; L. Borrelli, *Le tombe di Pompei a schola semicircolare* (Naples, 1937); M. Eisner, *Zur Typologie der Grabbauten in Suburbium Roms* (Mainz, 1986), 66–67 A39, 227–28; von Hesberg (1992), 164–70.

16. Petron. *Sat.* 71. On Trimalchio's tomb, see T. Mommsen, "Trimalchios Heimath und Grabschrift," *Hermes* 13 (1878): 106–21; E. Hübner "Zum Denkmal des Trimalchio," *Hermes* 13 (1878): 414–22; L. Pepe, "Sul monumento sepolchrale di Trimalchione," *Giornale italiano di filologia* 10 (1957): 293–300; R. Bianchi-Bandinelli, "Introduzione," *StMisc* 10 (1966): 9–20; J. Whitehead, "The 'Cena Trimalchionis' and Biographical Narration in Roman Middle Class Art," in P. J. Holliday, ed., *Narrative and Event in Ancient Art* (Cambridge, 1993), 299–325.

17. For Roman circular tombs, see Eisner (1986), passim. Examples with rectilinear corridors indicate that circular corridors were not simply due to construction technique; moreover, circular walls required for construction need not house accessible corridors.

18. For evidence of belief in special properties inherent in the circle, an almost universal phenomenon, see L. Hautecoeur, *Mystique et Architecture. Symbolisme du Cercle et de la Coupole* (Paris, 1954), 34; S. Eitrem, *Opferritus und Voropfer der Griechischen und Römer* (Kristiania, 1915), 8 and passim. The circle's power persists in contemporary Western witchcraft: see T. M. Luhrmann, *Persuasions of the Witch's Craft: Ritual Magic and Witchcraft in Present-Day England* (Oxford-Cambridge, Mass., 1989), 224–26.

19. Pliny *HN* 30.131. See also Claud. *Cons. Hon.* 324–27; Pliny *HN* 28.23; Petron. *Sat.* 62; Annequin (1973), 136–40.

20. Petron. *Sat.* 57. See also Hom. *Od.* 11.26–28, where Odysseus makes a sacrifice of three libations around a sacred pit as he prepares to invoke the dead and thus, as F. Robert, *Thymélé, recherches sur la signification et al destination des monuments circulaires dans l'architecture religieuse de la Grèce* (Paris, 1939), 321, puts it, delimits the terrain that will be soiled by infernal contact and prevents the soiling from spreading beyond the *bothros.*

21. Artem. 2.24.

22. Varro *Ling.* 5.143; Eitrem (1915), 17–18, 20, 28; H. Winfeld-Hansen, "Les couloirs annulaires dans l'architecture funéraire antique," *Acta Instituti Romani Norvegiae* 2 (1962): 35–63, esp. 59; H. Cancik, "Rome as Sacred Landscape and the End of Republican Religion in Rome," *Visible Religion: Annual for Religious Iconography* 4 (1985): 250–65; J. Rykwert, *The Idea of a Town* (Princeton, N.J., 1976), 45–49 and passim, who suggests that the *templum,* or piece of land designated as sacred for augury or for state and religious functions, was carefully defined by a circular boundary; Varro *Ling.* 7.7; Aul. Gell. 14.7. Contra: J. Linderski, "The Augural Law," *ANRW* II.16.3 (1968): 2–146. On the relationship between Roman magic and religion, see Annequin (1973), 140.

23. S.H.A., *M. Ant.* 20.3: "lustrata urbs, cantata carmina, amburbium celebratum, ambarvalia promissa"; Paulus Fest. p. 17M.

24. Macrob. *Sat.* 3.5.7: "Ambarvalis hostia est, ut ait Pompeius Festus, quae rei divinae causa circum arva ducitur ab his qui pro frugibus faciunt." Paul. Fest. p. 5; Serv. *G.* 1.345. See Serv. *Aen.* 1.283 on the *ambilustrum*; Polyb. 4.21.8 on the how Mantineans enacted a solemn purification of their city with piacular sacrifices, carried around the city and all their territory in a circle: Μαντινεῖς δὲ μετὰ τὴν μεταλλαγὴν αὐτῶν καὶ καθαρμὸν ἐποιήσαντο καὶ σφάγια περιήνεγκαν τῆς τε πόλεως κύκλῳ καὶ τῆς χώρας πάσης; Cato *Agr.* 141: "Agrum lustrare sic oportet. Impera suovetaurilia circumagi: 'Cum divis volentibus quodque bene eveniat, mando tibi, Mani, uti illace suovetaurilia fundum agrum terramque meam quota ex parte sive circumagi sive circumferenda censeas, uti cures lustrare' "; Luc. 1.592.

25. Plut. *Vit. Rom.* 10; Apollodorus (1.18) describes how Oeneus, Calydonian wine-god, killed his own son Toxeus for leaping across the ditch surrounding his vineyard, and according to Plutarch (*Quaest. Graec.* 37) Poimander tried to kill Polycrithos for jumping over the walls of his new fortress; See Rykwert (1976), 27–28.

26. See Serv. *Aen.* 4.62: "Spatiatur ad aras matronae enim sacrificaturae circa aras faculas tenentes ferebantur cum quodam gestu . . . ; quidam genus sacrificii appellant quo veteres, cum aras circumirent et rursus cum reverterentur et deinde consisterent, dicebant

minusculum sacrum. an hoc ad impatientiam amoris referendum est, quo iactata Dido loco stare non poterat, iuxta illud"; Porph. *Abst.* 2.54 (a human sacrificial victim was compelled to run three times around the altar); Valerius Flaccus 245–46. See also Schol. Ar. *Pax* 957 (when Trygeus sacrifices to Peace, he orders his slave to encircle the altar with a vessel and lustral water); for other Greek examples, see Robert (1939), 319–20 (who notes that, in mockery of this practice, Hector is chased three times around the walls of Troy before being killed, and then dragged three times around his pyre [*Il.* 22.165; 24.16, 417]); Eitrem (1915), 25–26.

27. Plut. *Quaest. Rom.* 14. On turning during prayer, see Plut. *Num.* 14: καὶ τὸ προσκυνεῖν περιστρεφομένους καὶ τὸ καθῆσθαι προσκυνήσαντας; idem *Cam.* 5.

28. Stat. *Theb.* 6.213–16. See also Valerius Flaccus 3.347–50; "inde ter armatos Minyis referentibus orbes / concussi tremuere rogi, ter inhorruit aether / luctificum clangente tuba"; Eitrem (1915), 43.

29. Cass. Dio 56.42, trans. I. Scott-Kilvert.

30. Hdn. 4.2.9 (trans. C. R. Whittaker); Cass. Dio 75.5.5: οἱ δέ ἄρχοντες καὶ ἡ ἱππὰς τὸ τέλος προσφόρως σφίσιν ἐσκευασμενοι, οἵ τε ἱππεῖς οἱ στρατιῶται καὶ οἱ πεζοὶ περὶ τὴν πυρὰν πολιτικὰς τε ἅμα καὶ πολεμικὰςδιεξόδους διελίττουτες διεξῆλθον; *Declamationes Pseudo-Quintilianeae* 329: "funus publicum: ducatur ingens funeris pompa, eat primus senatus . . . , universus denique populus lustret atque ambiat rogus." See Robert (1939), 321; J.-C. Richard, "Les aspects militaires des funérailles impériales," *MélRome* 78 (1966): 313–25, esp. 314; J. Arce, *Funus imperatorum: Los funerales de los emperadores romanos* (Madrid, 1988), 53 and 171.

31. See F. Bianchini, *De Kalendario et Cyclo Caesaris ac de Paschali Canone S. Hippolyti Martyris. Dissertationes duae . . . Quibus Inseritur Descriptio, et Explanatio Basis, in Campo Martio Nuper Detectae Sub Columna Antonino Pio Olim Dicata* (Rome, 1703); Vogel (1973), 56–67.

32. Suet. *Claud.* 1: "Ceterum exercitus honorarium ei tumulum excitavit, circa quem deinceps stato die quotannis miles decurreret Galliarumque civitates publice supplicarent."

33. Windfeld-Hansen (1962), 58; G. Welter, "Zwei vorrömische Grabbauten in Nordafrika," *RM* 42 (1927): 113–15; Eitrem (1915), 6; B. Göttze, *Ein römisches Rundgrab in Falerii, Baugeschichte des römischen Adels- und Kaisergrabes* (Stuttgart, 1939), 11; R. Fellmann, *Das Grab des Lucius Munatius Plancus bei Gaeta* (Basel, 1957), 87–89. A. Fleming, "Vision and Design: Approaches to Ceremonial Monument Typology," *Man* 7 (1972): 57–73, argues that the circle is a preferable form for monuments that accommodate ceremonies, since it affords maximum visibility to all participants.

34. There is little evidence on this subject. However, according to Suetonius (*Vesp.* 23), Vespasian dreamed that Augustus's Mausoleum opened, which he took as a presage of another's death: "nam cum inter cetera prodigia mausoleum derepente patuisset et stella crinita in caelo apparuisset, alterum ad Iuniam Calvinam e gente Augusti pertinere, alterum ad Parthorum regem qui capellatus esset." Judging by this anecdote, we may assume that it was usually closed.

35. Eitrem (1915), 61.

36. *Theb.* 6.215–16.

37. See R. Hertz, "Contribution à une étude sur la représentation collective de la mort," *Année sociologique* (1907): 48–137; A. Van Gennep, *Les rites de passage* (Paris, 1909); V. Turner, *The Ritual Process* (Chicago, 1969). See also P. Metcalf and R. Huntington, *Celebrations of Death. The Anthropology of Mortuary Ritual*[2] (Cambridge, 1991), 32–34; Eitrem (1915), 21. In other forms of funerary monument, this liminal stage might be otherwise expressed; for instance, the arch articulates a change of state by symbolizing a gateway between two realms. See A. von Domaszewski, "Die Triumphstrasse auf dem Marsfelde," *ArchRW* 12 (1909): 70–73; F. Noack, "Triumph und Triumphbogen," *Vorträge der Bibliothek Warburg* (1925–26) [1928]: 147–201; H. Petrikovitz, "Die Porta Triumphalis," *ÖJh* 28 (1933): 187–96; R. Schilling, "Janus le dieu introducteur, le dieu des passages," *MEFR* 72 (1960): 89–131; L. A. Holland, *Janus and the Bridge* (Rome, 1961).

38. On changing ritual, see V. Turner, "Symbols in African Ritual," A. Lehman and J. E. Myers, eds., *Magic, Witchcraft and Religion:*

An Anthropological Study of the Supernatural (Palo Alto, 1985).

39. See Verg. *Aen.* 5.545–88.

40. R. Brilliant, *Visual Narratives: Storytelling in Etruscan and Roman Art* (Ithaca, N.Y., 1984), 90–94.

41. "La difficoltà quasi insormontabile di lettura": S. Settis, A. La Regina, G. Agosti, and V. Farinella, *La Colonna Traiana* (Turin, 1988), 86–87.

42. K. Lehmann-Hartleben, *Die Traianssäule, ein römisches Kunstwerke zu Beginn der Spätantike* (Berlin-Leipzig, 1926).

43. R. Bianchi-Bandinelli, "La Colonna Traiana: Documento d'arte e documento politico (o della libertà dell'artista)," in *Dall'ellenismo al medio evo* (Rome, 1978), 139.

44. Lehmann-Hartleben (1926); W. Gauer, *Untersuchungen zur Trajanssäule. Erster Teil. Darstellungsprogramm und künstlerischer Entwurf, Monumenta artis romanae* 13 (Berlin, 1977), 45ff.; V. Farinella, "La Colonna Traiana: Un esempio di lettura verticale," *Prospettiva* 2.6 (1981): 2–9; Settis et al. (1988), 182–88 and 202–20; Brilliant (1984), 90–94.

45. The court measured 25 × 20.20 m., of which the Column took up 6.190 × 6.190 m.: see *LTUR,* 2:353 s.v. Forum Traiani (J. E. Packer); J. E. Packer and K. L. Sarring, "Il Foro di Traiano," *Archeo.* 7:11 (1992): 62–89, 92–93, esp. 73; Packer (1997), 113. The designer chose to begin the narrative at the bottom and spiral upward. If the illustrated rotulus was the inspiration for the narrative, the opposite arrangement would have been closer to the model; by beginning at the bottom, the sculptor better engages a viewer, again asking him to encircle the Column. Upward movement also better fits the Column's design: "The classical column is broadest at the bottom and thereby establishes a weight center, from which it tapers toward the top. This shape creates a strong connection with the ground and favors the upward thrust of rising toward a relatively free end." R. Arnheim, *The Dynamics of Architectural Form* (Berkeley, 1977), 50.

46. On this aspect of the Ara Pacis friezes, see F. Wickhoff, *Roman Art: Some of Its Principles and Their Application to Early Christian Painting,* trans. E. Strong (London, 1900), 31–35, 71–76, 101–5; O. Brendel, *Prolegom-*

ena to the Study of Roman Art (New Haven, Conn., 1979), 28–29.

47. Schol. Juv. 163–64; Gell. 13.25.2 ("Quaerebat Favorinus, cum in area fori [Traiani] ambularet et amicum suum consulem opperiretur causas pro tribunali cognoscentem"); *Cod. Theod.* 14.2.1; Novell. Valent. 19.4, 21.1.7, 21.2.6, 23.9, 27.8, 31.7M; S.H.A., *Comm.* 2.1 ("adhuc in praetexta puerili congiarium dedit atque ipse in Basilica Traiani praesedit"); Sid. Apoll. *Carm.* 2.544–45 ("nam modo nos iam festa vocant, et ad Ulpia poscunt / te fora, donabis quos libertate, Quirites"). See *LTUR,* 2:349 s.v. Forum Traiani (Packer).

48. B. Fehr, "Das Militär als Leitbild. Politische Funktion und gruppenspezifische Wahrnehmung des Traiansforums und der Traianssäule," *Hephaistos* 7–8 (1985–86): 39ff., contends that the libraries particularly catered to writers and professionals, that is, to those who needed books but could not necessarily afford to build their own extensive libraries.

49. Plut. *Vit. Alex.* 15; Robert (1939), 320. The visitor to Pelops's tomb at Olympia also encircled the tomb as a form of honor to the hero, as did the mounted ephebes on their visits to Neoptolemus's grave at Delphi, before sacrificing victims: Schol. Pind. *Ol.* 1.93.

50. *CIL* 6.960:

SENATUS . POPULUSQUE . ROMANUS
IMP . CAESARI . DIVI . NERVAE . F . NERVAE
TRAIANO . AUG . GERM . DACICO .
PONTIF
MAXIMO . TRIB . POT . XVII . IMP . VI .
COS . VI . P . P .
AD DECLARANDUM . QUANTAE . ALTI-
TUDINIS
MONS . ET . LOCUS . TA[NTIS OPE]
RIBUS . SIT . EGESTUS

[The Senate and People of Rome dedicated this to the emperor Caesar Nerva Trajan Augustus Germanicus Dacicus, son of the Divine Nerva, Pontifex Maximus, with tribunician power for the seventeenth time, imperator for the sixth time, consul for the sixth time, Father of his Country, to show how high was the montain, the site for great works after all, that was cleared away]. For this paraphrasing of Mau's interpretation, and for bibliography on the intensely problematic inscription, see F. Lepper and S. Frere, *Trajan's Column: A New Edition of the Cichorius Plates* (Gloucester, 1988), 52.

51. G. Boni, "Leggende," *Nuova Antologia,* s. 5.126 (1906): 3–39; idem, "Trajan's Column," *ProcBritAc* 3 (1907–8): 93–98.

52. A. Claridge, "Hadrian's Column of Trajan," *JRA* 6 (1993): 5–22. While I do not agree that the Column was initially designed without a spiral frieze, Claridge's argument stresses the novelty of the spiral staircase and forces us to reconsider the priorities in the Column's design. See also Lepper and Frere (1988), 20; M. Wilson Jones, "One Hundred Feet and a Spiral Stair: The Problem of Designing Trajan's Column," *JRA* 6 (1993): 23–38; S. Stucchi, "*Tantis viribus:* L'area della Colonna nella concezione generale del Foro di Traiano," *ArchCl* 41 (1989): 237–91.

53. See F. Panvini-Rosati, "La colonna sulle monete di Traiano," *AIIN* 5 (1958): 29–40; Settis et al. (1988), 59–60.

54. Lepper and Frere (1988), 13.

55. Amm. Marc. 16.10.14: "*elatosque vertices qui scansili suggestu consurgunt, priorum principum imitamenta portantes.*" The ambiguous text could refer to another monument type altogether.

56. *Var.* 7.6.1, trans. J. J. Pollitt. By medieval times, travel guides directed pilgrims toward the two *columnae cochlides* to witness the wonders of Rome. The author of the *Mirabilia* tells a visitor what to expect: "Trajan's winding pillar is 138 feet high, with 185 steps and 45 windows," details that one would experience on the interior of the shaft; only elsewhere does he add, "Here is a pillar of spectacular height and beauty, carved with the stories of [Trajan and Hadrian] like the pillar of Antoninus at his palace" (trans. Nichols [1986], 11, 39).

57. On towers incorporated into private estates, see A. M. Colini, "La torre di Mecenate," *RendLinc* 34 (1979): 239–50.

58. See Schmitt-Pantel (1982).

59. Amm. Marc. 16.10.15–16.

60. H. Schalles, "Forum und zentraler Tempel in 2. Jahrhundert n. Chr.," in *Die Römische Stadt im 2. Jahrhundert n. Chr. Colloquium in Xanten* (Bonn, 1992), 183–211.

61. G. Rodenwaldt, review of H. Lehner, *Das Römerlager Vetera bei Xanten. Ein Führer durch die Ausgrabungen des Bonner Provinzial-museums* (Bonn, 1926), *Gnomon* 2 (1926): 338–39. See also Fehr (1985–86), 44–45. Contra: J. B. Ward-Perkins, "Severan Art and Architecture at Lepcis Magna," *JRS* 38 (1948): 62.

62. Polyb. 6.27–34 and 42.

63. See J. E. Packer, *The Forum of Trajan in Rome: A Study of the Monuments* (Berkeley, 1997).

64. See Suet. *Dom.* 3.2; J. B. Campbell, *The Emperor and the Roman Army* (Oxford, 1984), 174. See also C. H. V. Sutherland, "The State of the Imperial Treasury at the Death of Domitian," *JRS* 25 (1935): 150–62; D. M. Robathan, "Domitian's Midas-Touch," *TAPA* 73 (1942): 130–44; Settis et al. (1988), 10–11.

65. Settis et al. (1988), 7.

66. See Settis (1988), 10–11; Campbell (1984), 164–74; emergencies such as military activity always created economic problems, because the empire lacked systematic budgeting. According to Campbell, in the first century A.C. yearly expenditure on the army consumed at least 40%, possibly 50%, of the state's available revenue. Cass. Dio (69.5.1) praises Hadrian for refraining from stirring up new wars and for terminating those which were in progress.

67. Cass. Dio 67.6; Settis et al. (1988), 6; Campbell (1984), 398–400; B. W. Jones, *The Emperor Domitian* (London, 1992), 126–59.

68. Campbell (1984), 398, writes: "An emperor would . . . have to bear in mind that military competence, real or imagined, could be a useful weapon of political propaganda against him." Trajan could look back upon the hostile senatorial tradition that ridiculed the military achievements of Tiberius, Claudius, and Domitian.

69. Just as Trajan surveyed the construction of such camps in the frieze, e.g., Scene XXXIX (Settis et al. [1988], p. 56).

70. Aul. Gell. 13.25.1. Settis et al. (1988), 39; Packer (1994); Packer and Sarring (1992), 92. E. Bernareggi, "Le opere di Traiano, imperatore spagnolo, nella documentazione numismatica," *Numisma* 25 (1975): 31–40, suggests that just such a propaganda campaign was being waged in Trajan's coinage: criticized for undertaking wars made necessary by Flavian spending and Nerva's lack of organization, Trajan followed his war coins with a series of coins displaying

architectural feats in Rome made possible by spoils.

71. Fehr (1985–86), 41.

72. Cass. Dio 68.17.1; Campbell (1984), 391. On the reasons for the Parthian War, see J. Guey, *Essai sur la guerre Parthique de Trajan (114–117)* (Bucharest, 1937); F. Lepper, *Trajan's Parthian War* (Oxford, 1948), and review by M. I. Henderson, *JRS* 39 (1949): 21.

73. See Cass. Dio 68.29.4–33.1 on toils and hardships endured in war, and 68.29.1 on Trajan's inability to retain land that he had already won. Campbell (1984), 395, 399. Pliny, in his Panegyric, praises Trajan for his moderation in not opening hostilities unnecessarily, but this speech was delivered in 100 and, Campbell suggests, "Pliny was presumably adapting what he says to suit Trajan's activities at the time."

74. Fehr (1985–86) suggests that the frieze was intended to allay civilian fear of the army by breaking down the barrier between military and civilian life. This long-standing fear manifested itself in the prohibition against military exercise within the *pomerium*. Literary sources reveal distrust of the army verging on antagonism on the part of the rest of the population. Emperors tried to minimize contact between army and civilians, perhaps for fear that city life would soften the soldiers. Thus the army had developed its own societal system apart from the rest of the population. He suggests that the Column's designers played down the violent acts of the soldiers to avoid aggravating this deep-seated fear in city-dwellers.

75. See Rodenwaldt (1926), 338–39; P. G. Hamberg, *Studies in Roman Imperial Art* (Copenhagen, 1945); L. Rossi, "Technique, Toil and Triumph on the Danube in Trajan's Propaganda Programme," *AntJ* 58 (1978): 81–87.

76. Especially in supplication scenes, e.g., LXXV–LXXVI; Settis et al. (1988), 127 and pls. 128–30.

77. The dead shown in battle scenes, in a variety of distorted poses, are Dacian, not Roman. There is only one scene on the whole frieze showing medical aid being given to Roman soldiers (XL), which may be more out of homage to army doctors than to reveal Roman vulnerability: Settis et al. (1988), 121 and pl. 58.

78. Settis et al. (1988), 129 and pl. 30.

79. E.g. Scene LXXV–LXXVI.

80. Dacians are shown in woods and mountains, while Romans are shown in cities, and while Dacian men fight Roman soldiers, Dacian women torture them (XLIV–XLVI); Settis et al. (1988), 134 and pls. 100–101, 67–68. On the torture scene, see R. Vulpe, "Prigionieri romani suppliziati da donne dacie sul rilievo della Colonna Traiana," *RivStorAnt* 3 (1973): 109–25.

81. Settis et al. (1988), pls. 179–83. See also F. S. Kleiner, "The Trophy on the Bridge and the Roman Triumph over Nature," *AntCl* 60 (1991): 182–92.

82. As precedents for this novel combination, Settis (1996), 232, suggests fortification towers containing staircases, or lighthouses; in both cases, the outside walls served to enclose a spiraling staircase rather than rooms for habitation or use.

83. Packer (1992), 73; idem (1994), 167, who estimates the height of the statue at at least 4 m.

84. J. E. Packer, "Trajan's Forum Again: The Column and the Temple of Trajan in the Master Plan Attributed to Apollodorus (?)," *JRA* 7, (1994), 177–78; idem (1997), 274–76.

85. The Basilica measured 600 × 200 Roman feet (176.28 × 58.76 m.) and 100 feet (29.38 m.) in height; the nave, defined by the interior columns, covered a rectangular area measuring 88.14 × 24.973 m. = 300 × 85 Roman feet. It had only two storeys (not three, as originally supposed). See *LTUR*, 2:353; Packer (1992), 73; idem (1997), 233, 437. In the event that the entrance to the forum fell on the northwest side (see R. Meneghini, "L'architettura del Foro di Ttraiano attraverso i ritrovimenti archeologici più recenti," *RM* 105 [1998], 127–48), a visitor would have been drawn to the towering column from a distance on the Via Lata. A massive propylon would have closed up the courtyard in a similar way to the traditional temple.

86. See A. Templer, *The Staircase: History and Theories* (Cambridge, Mass.-London, 1992), 52–84.

87. On the psychological sense of change induced by staircases, see MacDonald (1986), 71: "They are purveyors of changes not only of locale but of meaning – from the

street to the temple forecourt, for example, or from the street to the interior of the baths. . . ." (In the Column, the staircase reflects a change of state, from mortal to immortal.) See also Templer (1992), 7: "Stairs serve many roles in addition to their prosthetic function. These roles may modify or even dominate completely the mundane purposes of safe, comfortable and convenient ascent and descent. The stair has always been used to represent human spiritual aspirations and cosmography; to demonstrate secular power and authority, prestige and status; for aesthetic, architectural, and spatial manipulation; to make adjoining floors seem close, and the ascent a gentle transition; or to accentuate the separateness of spaces, with the staircase acting as bridge. Stairs convey meaning and have personalities. . . ."

88. K. Lynch, *The Image of the City* (Cambridge, Mass., 1960), 98.

89. The turning in itself could be disorienting: Luhrmann (1989), 227, describes the use of circular motion in contemporary rituals to induce disorientation.

90. Arnheim (1977), 158.

91. Ibid., 157. For measurements, see Wilson Jones (1993).

92. Stucchi (1989), 253.

93. I consider the vista from the Column of Marcus Aurelius in the following chapter.

CHAPTER SIX

1. Devon tombstone: D. J. Enright, ed., *The Oxford Book of Death* (Oxford, 1983), 322.

2. See D. Favro, *The Urban Image of Augustan Rome* (Cambridge, 1996), 193: "A building's eye-catching materials, large-scale or unusual form only become memorable when they can be observed. Siting is therefore crucial. To perceive a building as a landmark, observers need an appropriate distance and unencumbered sight lines, whether within the overall urban context or within a localized environment. In a crowded, densely built city such as Rome, arranging clear vistas of new structures was extremely difficult. Most buildings were seen from a skewed angle and thus appeared distorted. As a result, creation of an urban landmark required careful orchestration of how a project was perceived by observers."

3. Cic. *Fin.* 5.2, trans. C. Edwards.

4. C. Edwards, *Writing Rome: Textual Approaches to the City* (Cambridge, 1996), 42–43. See also F. Dupont, *Daily Life in Ancient Rome,* trans. C. Woodall (Oxford, 1992), 74: "Roman memory, lacking any anchorage in the inspired works of ancient poets, was rooted in the sacred ground of the city. To walk around Rome was to travel through its memory, past Romulus' cabin, Cacus' rock and Egeria's wood"; A. Vasaly, *Representations: Images of the World in Ciceronian Oratory* (Berkeley, 1993).

5. Edwards (1996), 29. See also Cic. *De or.* 2.351–54; *Ad Herenn.* 3.29–40; Quint. *Inst.* 11.2.17–22; F. Yates, *The Art of Memory* (Chicago, 1966); M. Carruthers, *The Book of Memory: A Study of Memory in Medieval Culture* (Cambridge-New York, 1990); B. Bergmann, "The Roman House as Memory Theater: The House of the Tragic Poet in Pompeii," *ArtB* 76 (1994): 225–56.

6. See Favro (1997), 4–11, 250: "An urban image forms in the minds of firsthand observers who read a cityscape as the cumulative product of all that has gone before and as a significant shaper of all that is to come"; see also M. Staeger's review, *BMCR* (1997).

7. See P. Zanker, *The Power of Images in the Age of Augustus,* trans. A. Shapiro (Ann Arbor, Mich., 1988), 51.

8. P. Zanker, *Forum Augustum. Das Bildprogramm* (Tübingen, 1968).

9. See Festus, p. 466ss. L.; Cic. *Off.* 3.16.66; F. Coarelli, *Il Foro Romano. Periodo arcaico* (Rome, 1983), 103; H. Cancik, "Rome as Sacred Landscape and the End of Republican Religion in Rome," *Visible Religion: Annual for Religious Iconography* 4 (1985): 250–65, esp. 252–53.

10. C. Nicolet, *Space, Geography, and Politics in the Early Roman Empire* (Ann Arbor, Mich., 1991), 57–84, 95–122. See also O. F. Robinson, *Ancient Rome: City Planning and Administration* (London-New York, 1992), 14–32; O. A. W. Dilke, *The Roman Land Surveyors* (New York, 1971). There may have been a publicly displayed map of the city as early as the reign of Augustus. See G. Gatti, *La pianta marmorea di Roma antica* (Rome, 1960), 218. Augustus's interest in chorography is readily manifested in his establishment of Rome's *regiones* (Suet. *Aug.*

30.1). For the map in the Porticus Vipsania, see Cass. Dio 55.8.3–4; D. Favro, "Reading the Augustan City," in P. J. Holliday, ed., *Narrative and Event in Ancient Art* (Cambridge, 1993), 230–57, esp. 245.

11. Favro (1993), 237–38; on transportation of materials, see J. C. Anderson, *Roman Architecture and Society* (Baltimore, 1997), 167. See, in general, F. Coarelli, *Il Campo Marzio dalle origini alla fine della repubblica* (Rome, 1997).

12. Favro (1993), 235; ead. (1996), 194, 206–7.

13. Ibid., 236, 245.

14. On Sulla: Livy *Epit.* 90; Appian, *BellCiv* 1.106; Plut. *Vit. Sull.* 38.4. On Hirtius: Livy *Epit.* 119; Vell. Pat. 2.62.4. Remains of Hirtius's tomb, a brick-faced concrete enclosure with a plain travertine coping, were found under the northwest corner of Palazzo della Cancelleria in 1938, along with cippi inscribed with his name. On Pansa: Livy *Epit.* 119; Vell. Pat. 2.62.4. A travertine tablet bearing Pansa's name was found in 1899 at the corner of Corso Vittorio Emanuele and Vicolo Savelli (*CIL* 6.37077). See Coarelli (1997), 591–602; L. Richardson, Jr., *A New Topographical Dictionary of Ancient Rome* (Baltimore, 1992), 356, 358; B. Nogara, *Monumenti romani scoperti . . . nell'Area del Palazzo della Cancelleria* (Rome, 1942); G. Waurick, "Untersuchungen zur Lage der römischen Kaisergräber in der Zeit von Augustus bis Constantin," *JRGZM* 20 (1973): 107–46, esp. 109. No record survives of a senatorial decree for Caesar's daughter Julia, but her burial in a tumulus on the Campus Martius may have been at the people's request: Livy *Epit.* 106; Plut. *Vit. Pomp.* 53.4, *Caes.* 23.4; Cass. Dio 39.64. On Julius Caesar's burial in this unlocated tumulus: Cass. Dio 44.51.1; Livy *Epit.* 106; Plut. *Vit. Pomp.* 53.4, *Caes.* 23.4; Cass. Dio 39.64. Although Agrippa had intended to be buried on the Campus Martius (Cass. Dio 54.28.5), his chosen site was probably not on public land but within his own private grounds, the Horti Agrippae, for which he did not need the Senate's permission.

15. Zanker (1968).

16. See K. Scott, "The Identification of Augustus with Romulus-Quirinus," *TAPA* 56 (1925): 82–105. He was not the first to do so: Julius Caesar adopted Romulus's dress and installed a statue of himself in Romu-

lus's Temple on the Quirinal (Cass. Dio 41.14.3; 43.45.3).

17. Cass. Dio 53.16. See A. Balland, "La casa Romuli au Palatin et au Capitole," *REL* 62 (1984): 57–80; J. C. Reeder, "Typology and Ideology in the Mausoleum of Augustus," *ClAnt* 11.2 (1992): 265–304, esp. 272 n. 43, for bibliography.

18. Cass. Dio 53.16.

19. Suet. *Aug.* 95.

20. E. Kornemann, "Zum Augustusjahr. 1. Octavians Romulusgrab. 2. Der Princeps als Hegemon im Ostem," *Klio* 31 (1938): 81–91. He sees the Mausoleum as a Romulan reference for what he sees as its old Italic tumulus form, reminiscent of Romulus's grave.

21. Livy 1.16.1. See also Florus 1.1.16; Solinus 1.20.

22. F. Coarelli, *Roma sepolta* (Milan, 1984), 142.

23. F. Coarelli, "L'apoteosi di Augusto e l'apoteosi di Romolo," *AnalRom,* suppl. 10 (1983): 41–46.

24. See, for instance, Coarelli (1983).

25. W. C. Loerke, "Georges Chédanne and the Pantheon: A Beaux Arts Contribution to the History of Roman Architecture," *Modulus. The University of Virginia School of Architecture Review* (1982). See also AIA abstract, P. B. F. J. Broucke, "The Caryatids from Hadrian's Villa at Tivoli and the Pantheon of Agrippa," *AJA* 103 (1999): 312.

26. SAH, Convention, St. Louis, 1996.

27. Cass. Dio 53.27.2–4, trans. W. L. MacDonald, *The Pantheon: Design, Meaning and Progeny* (Cambridge, Mass., 1976), 76.

28. As MacDonald (1976), 77, puts it: "By putting the Deified Julius inside, Augustus was given a connection with the gods, for whom he stood guard outside with Agrippa, his great minister and friend. Seen in this light, the original Pantheon takes on a strong dynastic and political coloring." See also K. de Fine Licht, *The Rotunda in Rome: A Study of Hadrian's Pantheon* (Copenhagen, 1968), 191–94.

29. F. Castagnoli, "Il Campo Marzio nell'antichità," *MemLinc* 8.1 (1947): 93–193, esp. 146; Loerke (1982), 51. See also M. T. Boatwright, *Hadrian and the City of Rome* (Princeton, N.J., 1987), 37: "If Agrippa's Pantheon had a monumental northern facade as the northernmost front of the Agrippan complex, it may have had a visual

axis with Augustus' Mausoleum, a somewhat earlier manifestation of Augustus'
ambitions."

30. Pliny *HN* 7.213; *RG* 19; Cass. Dio
54.19.1.

31. The route of the Sacra Via at the east end
of the Forum is uncertain. The Arch's
foundations rest on the Clivus Palatinus,
a fact that has led to the unlikely proposal
that it was moved when Hadrian's Temple of Venus and Roma was constructed:
see Richardson (1992), 30, 338–40. Some
scholars identify the Arch with a single-bay
arch depicted on the so-called Haterii relief in the Vatican Museums (inv. no. 9997,
Helbig [4] 1.778–80, no. 1076), described
in an accompanying inscription as *arcus in
sacra via summa*. See H. Kähler, "Triumphbogen," *RE* VII.A.1 (1939): 401; F. Castagnoli, "Gli edifici rappresentati in un rilievo
del sepolcro degli Haterii," *BullCom* 69
(1941): 62–65; W. Jensen, "The Sculptures
from the Tomb of the Haterii" (Ph.D. diss.,
University of Michigan, 1978), 117–20;
F. Coarelli, *Roma* (Rome, 1980), 93;
M. Pfanner, *Der Titusbogen, Beitrage zur Erschliessung Hellenistischer und Kaiserzeitlicher
Skulptur und Architektur* 2 (Mainz, 1983), 3;
M. Torelli, "Culto imperiale e spazi urbani
in età flavia dai rilievi Hartwig all'arco
di Tito," *Urbs: Espace urbain et histoire, 1er
siècle avant J.-C.–1er siècle après J.-C. CEFR*
98 (Rome, 1987): 563– 82, 573–78; S. De
Maria, *Gli archi onorari di Roma e dell'Italia
romana* (Rome, 1988), 72, 288, 294.

32. Torelli (1987), 563–82.

33. Ibid., 575. On the *Equus Domitani*, see
C. F. Giuliani and P. Verduchi, *Foro Romano: L'area centrale* (Florence, 1980), 45.
On the Forum Transitorium, see E.
D'Ambra, *Private Lives, Imperial Virtues:
The Frieze of the Forum Transitorium in
Rome* (Princeton, N.J., 1993). Torelli suggests that there was a main axis through
the Roman Forum from the Forum
Transitorium to the Temple of Castor and
the Athenaeum, the monumental entrance to the Palatine named after Minerva. The latter two buildings are,
however, considerably east of a central
axis running southwest from the Forum
Transitorium.

34. Torelli (1987), 575. See also D'Ambra
(1993), 33.

35. On Domitian's Palatine building projects,
see W. L. MacDonald, *The Architecture of
the Roman Empire, 1: An Introductory Study*[2]
(New Haven, Conn., 1982), 47–74.

36. See Coarelli (1983), 11ff. Its construction technique places it in the first century
B.C. or A.D., and a small fragment of marble decoration belonging to it is probably
Flavian: Torelli (1987), 573–74, and n. 50.
Suetonius (*Tit.* 1) reports that Titus was
born *in Palatio*. The *sodales Flaviales Titiales*,
mentioned in *CIL* 6.2004–9, were associated with this temple. See also Richardson
(1992), 224.

37. Torelli (1987), 576–78.

38. Torelli (1987), 578; De Maria (1988), 292;
G. Lugli, *Roma antica. Il centro monumentale*
(Rome, 1946), 524. Whether this arch was
Domitianic or Augustan, erected in honor
of Augustus's father, Octavius, is uncertain;
for an Augustan date, see, e.g., M. E. Blake,
*Ancient Roman Construction in Italy from the
Prehistoric Period to Augustus* (Washington,
D.C., 1947), 169; F. S. Kleiner, *The Arch of
Nero in Rome: A Study of the Roman Honor-
ary Arch before and under Nero* (Rome,
1985), 22–23.

39. Torelli (1987), 578–79.

40. Boatwright (1987), 111, n. 46.

41. See, for instance, J. E. Stambaugh, *The Ancient Roman City* (Baltimore, 1988), 72–73;
D'Ambra (1993), 45.

42. Estimates range from approximately one
hundred and twenty-five hectares to forty.
See C. C. Van Essen, "La topographie de la
Domus Aurea," *Meded* 17.12 (1954): 371–
98; I. Iacopi, *Domus Aurea* (Milan, 1999);
P. G. Warden, "The Domus Aurea Recon-
sidered," *JSAH* 40 (1981): 271–78; and
M. T. Griffin, *Nero, the End of a Dynasty*
(New Haven, Conn., 1985), 139.

43. Mart. *De Spect.* 2; Tac. *Ann.* 15.42–43; Suet.
Ner. 31. Larry F. Ball, "A Reappraisal of
Nero's Domus Aurea," *Rome Papers, JRA*,
suppl. 11 (Ann Arbor, Mich., 1994), 183–
254, concludes that the area of the Esquiline
Wing was barely inhabited before construc-
tion of the Domus Transitoria.; see also
Suet. *Ner.* 38, who states that granaries
were razed for construction on the Domus
Transitoria. Excavations in the area of the
Meta Sudans and Ludus Magnus indicate
that the fire did destroy an entire area of
Augustan/Tiberian/Claudian dwellings: see

LTUR, 2.51–55, s.v. Domus Aurea: Area dello Stagnum (G. Panella). For an assessment of the literary tradition, see M. P. O. Morford, "The Distortion of the Domus Aurea Tradition," *Eranos* 66 (1968): 158–79.

44. E. Champlin, "God and Man in the Golden House," *Horti Romani: Atti del convegno internazionale, Roma,* ed. M. Cima and E. La Rocca (Rome, 1998), 333–44; *LTUR,* 2:51–55, s.v. Domus Aurea: Area dello Stagnum (C. Panella).

45. Tac. *Ann.* 15.37, trans. M. Grant.

46. See also Tac. *Ann.* 14.15. Champlin (1998) notes many of the subversions: that at Tigellinus's party rafts on wine casks took the place of luxury yachts, rowed by male prostitutes, and elite women engaged in the activities of the nonelite; and the passage proceeds to describe Nero's marriage, disguised as a woman, to a male prostitute, and "everything was public which even in a natural union is veiled by night" (trans. M. Grant).

47. On which, see E. R. Varner, "Damnatio Memoriae and Roman Imperial Portraiture," (Ph. D. Diss., Yale University, 1993), 77–187.

48. Suet. *Otho* 7; Cass. Dio 65.4; Cass. Dio 65.4; Ball (1994), 227; Morford (1968), 165.

49. Pliny *HN* 36.4.37. On the fire of 80, see W. L. MacDonald, *The Architecture of the Roman Empire, I: An Introductory Study* (New Haven, Conn., 1982), 13, n. 36. The east block of the Esquiline Wing did not serve as barracks or storerooms in Flavian times as the west block did: see Ball (1994), 229; *LTUR,* 2:49–50, s.v. Domus Aurea (A. Cassatella); I. Iacopi, *Domus Aurea* (Milan, 1999), 13. MacDonald, 47, suggests that Titus lived on the Palatine. Late mentions of a Mica Aurea might refer to the Domus Titi: Warden (1981), 278.

50. Mart. *Spect.* 2, trans. Pollitt.

51. Pliny *HN* 34.84; Ball (1994), 205; *LTUR,* 2.56–63, s.v. Domus Aurea: Il Palazzo sull'Esquilino (L. Fabbrini).

52. A. Boethius, *The Golden House of Nero: Some Aspects of Roman Architecture* (Ann Arbor, Mich., 1960), 110–11. See Mart. *Spect.;* Cass. Dio 69.4.4.

53. Morford (1968), 163–64.

54. Griffin (1984), 104–18, 186. Otho took his name; Vitellius erected altars to him and

called for performances of his songs; members of the nonelite put up statues of him in the Forum, decorated his tomb with flowers, and posted edicts hoping for his return.

55. On Roman forms, see K. Welch, "The Roman Arena in Late-Republican Italy: A New Interpretation," *JRA* 7 (1994): 59–80.

56. *LTUR,* 2:264–66 s.v. Fornix Fabianus (L. Chioffi); De Maria (1988); 52–53, 264–66, 269–72; Kleiner (1985), 16–17, 25–27; idem, "The Study of Roman Triumphal and Honorary Arches 50 years after Kähler," *JRA* 2 (1989): 195–206, esp. 198–200; Richardson (1992), 23, 154.

57. J.-C. Richard, "Tombeaux des empereurs et temples des 'Divi': Notes sur la signification religieuse des sépultures impériales à Rome," *RHR* 170 (1966): 127–42.

58. In 56 B.C., for instance, Lucullus chose to be buried near his villa on his estate, and Pompey's ashes were sent from Egypt to his wife in Albanum for burial on his property. See Plut. *Vit. Pomp.* 80.5; G. McCracken, "The Villa and Tomb of Lucullus at Tusculum," *AJA* 46 (1942): 325–40; Waurick (1973), 124; J. Bodel, "Monumental Villas and Villa Monuments," *JRA* 10 (1997): 5–35. Later emperors built mausolea inside their residences: see Marasovic and Marasovic, *Diocletian Palace* (Zagreb, 1970); A. Frazer, "The Iconography of the Emperor Maxentius' Buildings in Via Appia," *ArtB* 48 (1966): 385–92.

59. Suet. *Aug.* 72; Richardson (1992), 130.

60. Suet. *Aug.* 5.1; *CIL* 6.2329, 2330b. Torelli (1987), 570; idem, *Typology and Structure of Roman Historical Reliefs* (Ann Arbor, Mich., 1982), 73; Richardson (1992), 45, 132, 137–38, 140; *LTUR,* I s.v. *Augustus, Divus, Sacrarium; Aedes* (Torelli), 143–45.

61. Torelli (1987), 570. Vespasian was born on the *vicus di Falacrinae* (Suet. *Vesp.* 2), Titus, in a *sordida aedes* near a *Septizonium* (Suet. *Tit.* 1). See also Richard (1966), 134.

62. Suet. *Vesp.* 23.

63. Suet. *Dom.* 13 and 4.

64. D'Ambra (1993), 40.

65. Suet. *Dom.* 5; B. W. Jones, *The Emperor Domitian* (London, 1992), 79–81.

66. MacDonald (1982); Anderson (1997).

67. Jones (1992), 79–98.

68. According to a variant tradition, the hill was named after the Sabine town Cures:

81–82; *LTUR,* 1.267–69. s.v. Ciconiae (C. Lega).

104. P. Gazzola, *Ponti romani: Contributo ad un indice systematico con studio critico bibliografico* (Florence, 1963), 41–42, no. 40.

105. Contra: S.H.A., *Hadr.* 19, which mentions only the temple.

106. *CIL* 6.973.

107. On the power of this heritage, see W. Weber in *CAH* XI.300.

108. See also MacDonald (1976), 100, on the Pantheon and tomb and cosmos.

109. Boatwright (1987), 58–62; Castagnoli (1947); V. Jolivet, "Les cendres d'Auguste: Note sur la topographie monumentale du Champ de Mars septentrionale," *Archeologia Laziale* 9 (1988): 90–96.

110. C. Hülsen, "Antichità di Monte Citorio," *RM* 4 (1889): 54, with Bianchini's drawings; La Rocca (1984), 107–8; Boatwright (1987), 493; *LTUR,* 1:75 (A. Danti). Richardson (1992), 149, identifies it as a consecration altar for Diva Fausina Maior.

111. L. Vogel, *The Column of Antoninus Pius* (Cambridge, Mass., 1973), 32.

112. C. Caprino, A. M. Colini, G. Gatti, M. Pallottino, and P. Romanelli, *La Colonna di Marco Aurelio* (Rome, 1955), 27ff.; M. Jordan-Ruwe, "Zur Rekonstruktion und Datierung der Marcussäule," *Boreas* 13 (1990): 53–69, esp. 62.

113. S. Maffei (1996), 304; G. Becatti, *Colonna di Marco Aurelio* (Milan, 1957); I. S. Ryberg, "Rites of the State Religion in Roman Art," *MAAR* 22 (1955); E. Angelicoussis, "The Panel Reliefs of Marcus Aurelius," *RM* 91 (1984): 140–205.

114. See S.H.A., *M. Ant.* 18; E. Petersen, A. von Domaszewski, and G. Calderini, *Die Marcussäule auf Piazza Colonna in Rom* (Monaco, 1896), 2; R. Valentini and G. Zucchetti, *Codice topografico della città di Roma* (Rome, 1940–53), 125, 176, 309. Caprino et al. (1955), 18, 32, hypothesize that the author of the *Mirabilia* saw the temple in the twelfth century and mistook it for an Antonine *palatium.* Recent excavations in the area have unearthed fragments of a soffit and marble tiles that may have belonged to this building: Maffei (1997), 303.

115. S. Maffei, *EAA,* Suppl. 2 (1996): 304–5: "Dal punto di vista storico-artistico, lo schiacciante confronto con la ricchezza compositiva del modello traianeo ha relegato per anni soto il marchio riduttivo di una scadente imitazione l'estrema essenzialità degli schemi iconografici della colonna, il cui acceso "espressionismo" è stato letto ed analizzato essenzialmente come punto chiave di trapasso dell'arte romana verso una completa dissoluzione del "classicismo," in nome di quel mutamento di stile "Stilwandel" che introduce alla nuova sensibilità tardoantica. Studi più recenti, a partire da un'interesse per i meccacnismi narrativi e i problemi di visibilità della Colonna Traiana (Brilliant) hanno riconosciuto nel radicale schematismo compositivo delle scene della *c. M.A.* una precisa volontà creativa, che pone il suo nuovo linguaggio formale al servizio di una sempre più ampia legibilità dei contenuti e di- una sempre più intensa efficacia communicativa, calibrata sapientemente sulle esigenze dell'osservatore."

116. D. E. E. Kleiner, *Roman Sculpture* (New Haven, Conn.,-London, 1992), 295.

117. Becatti (1957). See also P. G. Hamberg, *Studies in Roman Imperial Art* (Copenhagen, 1945), 157.

118. Caprino et al. (1955), 16; F. Fornari, "Scoperte di antichità a Piazza Colonna," *NSc* (1917): 9–26; Boatwright (1987), 63.

119. Boatwright (1987), 58–62.

120. See La Rocca (1984); M. T. Boatwright, "The '*Ara Ditis-Ustrinum* of Hadrian' in the Western Campus Martius and Other Problematic Roman Ustrina," *AJA* 89 (1985): 485–97; ead. (1987): 224–25; W. Weber, *CAH* XI.341. For a visual impression of the proximity of the two Antonine columns, see painting by G. P. Pannini, "Estrazione del lotto a Montecittorio," now in the collection of Norman Colville, London, illustrated in C. Pietrangeli, *Guide rionale di Roma. Rione III–Colonna* 2 (Rome, 1982), 93.

121. Mancini (1913), 3–15; Buzzetti (1984); Danti (1984); La Rocca (1984); Boatwright (1985), 493–94; Kampmann, "The Ustrinum in the Palazzo del Parlamento in Rome," *OpRom* 15 (1985): 67–78. For the acroteria, see A. Danti (1985), 423–33. Richardson (1992), 149, identifies the structure as a consecration altar to Diva Faustina Minor.

122. *LTUR,* 1:75 s.v. Arae Consecrationis (A. Danti).

123. Ibid.; Buzzetti (1984), 28.

124. Jolivet (1988).

125. Strab. 5.3.8; Jolivet (1988). See also E. Tortorici, "Alcune osservazioni sulla tavola 8 della *forma urbis* del Lanciani," *Topografia antica: Ricerchi e discussioni* (Rome, 1988), 7–15; J. R. Patterson, "Survey Article: The City of Rome, from Republic to Empire," *JRS* 82 (1992): 186–215, esp. 199. Most scholars place the ustrinum between Via Flaminia and the Mausoleum, because of the discovery there of Livilla's alabaster cinerary urn and imperial cippi with inscriptions such as *hic crematus est;* Helbig, 324–26; E. Q. Visconti, *Il Museo Pio Clementino* V (Rome, 1796), VII (Milan, 1822), 169–78; R. Lanciani, *Forma Urbis Romae* (1893–1901), pl. 8; C. Pietrangeli, *Scavi e scoperte di antichità soto il pontificato di Pio VI* (Rome, 1958), 67–70. Jolivet argues that if Augustus's ustrinum was monumentalized in the same way as later pyres, it could not have been used for further Julio-Claudian cremations, which would therefore have taken place in other locations near the Mausoleum.

126. Jolivet (1988), 94.

127. Jolivet (1988, 93–94, no. 23) notes that the association of acroteria with altar is still not definite, but relies on their findspot. For him, they are out of character with the cornice of the altar enclosure, which could be Hadrianic. He therefore prefers to identify Altar A with Hadrian and Altar B with Sabina. If this were the case, Marcus Aurelius's Column would have been designed to emphasize his tie to the founder of the Antonine dynasty. Boatwright (1987), 50, however, identifies the so-called Ara Ditis in the western Campus Martius as Hadrian's consecration altar.

128. S.H.A., *Comm.* 18–20; S.H.A., *M. Ant.* 17.11. While still alive he was divinized as Hercules and received sacrifices. A most likely date for this plan would be the earlier part of his reign, since in his last two years he appears to have attempted to disassociate himself from his father, to the extent of changing his name to L. Aelius Aurelius Commodus. See A. Birley, *Marcus Aurelius: A Biography* (New Haven, Conn., 1987), 90.

129. See A. Birley, *Septimius Severus: The African Emperor* (New Haven, Conn., 1989), on Pertinax's use of Marcus Aurelius as role model.

130. S.H.A., *Sev.* 24.1–2; either Septimius Severus's body was transported to Rome, or just his ashes in a golden urn. Dio Cassius (76.15.4) states that his ashes were transported in a porphyry urn, Herodian (3.15.7), in an urn of alabaster.

131. E. La Rocca, *Rilievi storici capitolini: Il restauro dei pannelli di Adriano e di Marco Aurelio nel Palazzo dei Conservatori* (Rome, 1986), pl. 23.

132. S.H.A., *M. Ant.* 26.2. *CAR II* (Rome, 1964), G nn. 152–68; Buzzetti (1984), 28; La Rocca (1984). See also S.H.A., *M.Ant.* 19: "Many tell that Commodus was actually conceived in adultery, since it is reasonably well known that Faustina chose both sailors and gladiators as lovers for herself at Caiea. When Marcus Aurelius was told about this so that he might divorce her – if not execute her – he reportedly said, "If we dismiss our wife, we must give back her dowry too." And what was her dowry but the empire, which he had received from his father-in-law when adopted by him at Hadrian's request." See Fantham et al., *Women in the Classical World* (Oxford, 1994), 355.

133. Marcus Aurelius had endeavored to cement his position from an even earlier date, making him Caesar in 166 (at age five), imperator in 176, consul, with *tribunicia potestas,* and Augustus in 177: S.H.A., *Comm.* 1.10–12.

134. So suggests H. Fuhrmann, "Ein Fragment des verlorene Reliefs am Sockel der Marcussäule," *RM* 52 (1937): 261–65, esp. 262, on the grounds that Commodus ended the war depicted in the frieze and commissioned the Column.

135. Fuhrmann (1937), 261–65, suggests that a relief fragment in the Museo Nazionale delle Terme showing a barbarian's head and upper torso against a backdrop of shields may belong to this relief (*Helbig*[4], 2, 227 no. 1527); Jordan-Ruwe (1990), 63.

136. Fuhrmann (1937), 262.

137. Cass. Dio 71.20; S.H.A., *M.Ant.* 28.1.

138. M. Hammond, "The Transmission of the Powers of the Roman Emperor from the Death of Nero in A.D. 68 to that of

Alexander Severus in A.D. 235," *MAAR* 24 (1956): 61–133.

139. When monuments of similar form are juxtaposed or planimetrically related, differences in dimension are surprisingly small and can be explained by reasons other than competitiveness – for instance, harmonious proportion or "magic" numbers.

CONCLUSION

1. F. E. Brown, *Roman Architecture* (New York, 1961), 9. Exceptions include W. L. Mac-Donald, *The Architecture of the Roman Empire, II: An Urban Appraisal* (New Haven-London, 1986); J. R. Clarke, *Roman Black-and-White Figural Mosaics* (New York, 1979); idem, *The Houses of Roman Italy, 100 B.C.–A.D. 250. Ritual, Space and Decoration* (Berkeley, 1991). See, most recently, J. Elsner, *Art and the Roman Viewer: The Transformation of Art from the Pagan World to Christianity* (Cambridge, 1995); D. Favro, *The Urban Image of Augustan Rome* (Cambridge, 1996); M. Koortbojian, "*In Commemorationem Mortuorum:* Text and Image Along the 'Streets of Tombs,' " in *Art and Text in Roman Culture,* ed. J. Elsner (Cambridge, 1996), 210–33.

2. See, e.g., J. E. Stambaugh, *The Ancient Roman City* (Baltimore, 1988); O. F. Robinson, *Ancient Rome: City Planning and Administration* (London-New York, 1992); E. J. Owens, *The City in the Greek and Roman World* (London, 1991); G. Wightman, "The Imperial Fora of Rome: Some Design Considerations," *JSAH* 56 (1997): 64–87. More specifically, M. Torelli, "Culto imperiale e spazi urbani in età flavia dai rilievi Hartwig all'arco di Tito," *Urbs: Espace urbain et histoire, ler siècle avant J.-C.–1er siècle après J.C. CEFR* 98 (Rome, 1987), 563–82; E. D'Ambra, *Private Lives, Imperial Virtues: The Frieze of the Forum Transitorium in Rome* (Princeton, N.J., 1993), 19–46. M. Trachtenberg, "Some Observations on Recent Architectural History," *ArtB* 70 (1988): 208–41, esp. 209, notes, "Near the 'center' of opinion [on what was lacking in recent architectural history], Richard Krautheimer and André Chastel were of similar minds that high among the things now crucial was to fill in the 'interstices' between great monuments, principally in the way of contextual and urbanistic research."

3. G. Waurick, "Untersuchungen zur Lage der römischen Kaisergräber in der Zeit von Augustus bis Constantin," *JRGZM* 20 (1973): 107–46.

BIBLIOGRAPHY

Abbondanza, L. "Osservazioni su alcuni rinvenimenti dell'area di Castel Sant'Angelo." In *Adriano e il suo Mausoleo,* ed. M. Mercalli, 55–61. Milan: Electa, 1998.

Abercrombie, S. *Architecture as Art.* New York: Harper and Row, 1984.

Agosti, G. "Ranuccio Bianchi-Bandinelli dall'invenzione del 'Maestro delle imprese di Traiano' alla scoperta dell'arte 'plebea.' " *AnnPisa,* s. 3, 16 (1986): 307–29.

Akerstrom, A. *Studien über die Etruskischen Gräber.* Uppsala: Almquist and Wicksell, 1934.

Alberti, G. *Codici Borgo San Sepolcro.* 1579.

Albertson, F. C. "An Augustan Temple Represented on a Historical Relief Dating to the Time of Claudius." *AJA* 91 (1987): 441–58.

Alexander, P. "Letters and Speeches of the Emperor Hadrian." *HSCP* 49 (1938): 141–77.

Alföldi, A. "Insignien und Tracht der römischen Kaiser." *RM* 50 (1935): 1–171.

—— *"Aiôn Plutonios — Saeculum Frugiferum."* In *Greece and the Eastern Mediterranean in Ancient History and Prehistory. Studies Presented to F. Schachermeyr,* ed. K. H. Kinz, 1-30. Berlin-New York: W. De Gruyter, 1977.

Allen, K. "The *Fasti* of Ovid and Imperial Propaganda." *AJP* 43 (1922): 250–66.

Altmann, W. *Die Römischen Grabaltäre der Kaiserzeit.* Berlin: Weidmann, 1905.

—— *Die Italischen Rundbauten.* Berlin: Weidmannsche Buchhandlung,1906.

Ambrogi, A. *Museo Nazionale Romano. Catalogo delle sculture* I.8. Rome: De Luca, 1985.

Amelotti, M. *Il testamento romano attraverso la prassi documentale.* Florence: Le Monnier, 1966.

Amelung, W. *Die Skulpturen des Vaticanischen Museums* 1. Berlin: Kommission bei Georg Reimer, 1903–56.

Anderson, J. C. "A Topographical Tradition in Fourth Century Chronicles: Domitian's Building Program." *Historia* 32 (1983): 93–105.

—— *The Historical Topography of the Imperial Fora.* Brussels: Latomus, 1984.

—— *Roman Architecture and Society.* Baltimore: Johns Hopkins University Press, 1997.

Andreae, B. "Studien zur römischen Grabkunst." *RM,* suppl. 9 (Heidelberg, 1963).

Angeletti, G. "Mausoleo di Adriano. Atrio: Restauro superfici lapidee." *Studi su Castel Sant'Angelo: Archivum arcis* 3 (1991): 155–57.

—— "Esito delle indagini attuate nel secondo tratto della rampa elicoidale." *Studi su Castel Sant'Angelo:Archivum arcis* 3 (1991): 158–60.

—— "Indagini termografiche nell'aula 'delle urne sepolcrali.' "*Studi su Castel Sant'Angelo: Archivum arcis* 3 (1991): 161–66.

—— "1987–1990: Scavi e restauri nel Mausoleo di Adriano." In *Adriano e il suo Mausoleo,* ed. M. Mercalli, 57–61. Milan: Electa, 1998.

Angelicoussis, E. "The Panel Reliefs of Marcus Aurelius." *RM* 91 (1984): 140–205.

Annequin, J. *Recherches sur l'action magique et ses représentations (Ier–IIe siècles après J.C.).* Paris: Les Belles Lettres, 1973.

Arce, J. *Funus imperatorum: Los funerales de los emperadores romanos.* Madrid: Alianza Editorial, 1988.

Arnaud, P. "L'image du globe dans le monde romain: Iconographie, symbolique." *MEFRA* 96.1 (1984): 53–116.

Arnheim, R. *The Dynamics of Architectural Form.* Berkeley, Los Angeles: University of California Press, 1977.

Arnold, D. *Building in Egypt. Pharaonic Stone Masonry.* Oxford: Oxford University Press, 1991.

Arthur, M. ' "Liberated' Women: The Classical Era." In *Becoming Visible: Women in European History,* ed. R. Bridenthal and C. Koonz, 96–104. Boston: Houghton Mifflin, 1987.

Artioli, R. *Castel Sant'Angelo.* Rome, 1923.

Attilia, L. "Il mausoleo di Augusto." In *Roma repubblicana dal 270 a.C. all'età augustea,* ed. F. Coarelli et al., 29–34. Rome: Quasar, 1987.

Aurigemma, S. *Villa Adriana.* Rome: Istituto Poligrafico Zecco dello Stato, Libreria dello Stato, 1984.

Aymard, A. "Relief funéraire romain représentant les jeux du cirque." *BAntFr* (1957): 71–72.

Bachelard, G. *The Poetics of Space.* Boston: Beacon Press, 1969.

Badian, E. "A Phantom Marriage Law." *Philologus* 129 (1985): 82–98.

Baehrens, A. *Poetae Latini Minores* 4. Leipzig: Teubner, 1881.

Bailey, D. M. "Alexandria, Carthage and Ostia (Not to Mention Naples)." In *Alessandria e il mondo ellenistico-romano. Studi in onore di A. Adriani II,* ed. N. Bonacase, and A. De Vita, 265–72. Rome: L'Erma di Bretschneider, 1983–84.

Ball, L. F. "A Reappraisal of Nero's Domus Aurea." *Rome Papers, JRA,* suppl. 11, 183–254. Ann Arbor, Mich., 1994.

Balland, A. "La casa Romuli au Palatin et au Capitole." *REL* 62 (1984): 57–80.

Bardon, H. *Les empereurs et les lettres latines d'Auguste à Hadrien.* Paris: Les Belles Lettres, 1968.

Barrett, A. R. *Caligula: The Corruption of Power.* London: B. T. Batsford, 1989.

Barringer, J. M. *Divine Escorts: Nereids in Archaic and Classical Greek Art.* Ann Arbor: University of Michigan Press, 1994.

Bartoli, A. *I monumenti antichi di Roma nei disegni degli Uffizi di Firenze.* Rome: C. A. Bontempelli, 1914–22.

———. "Il tempio di Antonino e Faustina." *MonAnt* 23 (1914): 949–74.

———. "L'architettura del mausoleo di Augusto." *BdA* 7 (1927): 30–46.

Barton, T. *Ancient Astrology.* London: Routledge, 1994.

———. "Augustus and Capricorn: Astrological Polyvalency and Imperial Rhetoric." *JRS* 85 (1995): 33–51.

Basso, M. *Guide to the Vatican Necropolis.* Vatican City: Tipografia Poliglotta Vaticana, 1986.

Bauman, A. *Women and Politics in Ancient Rome.* London-New York: Routledge, 1992.

Bayet, J. "L'immortalité astrale d'Auguste, ou Manilius commentateur de Virgile." *REL* 17 (1939): 141–71.

Beard, M. "The Sexual Status of the Vestal Virgins." *JRS* 70 (1980): 12–27.

———. "Rereading (Vestal) Virginity" In *Women in Antiquity: New Assessments,* ed. R. Hawley and B. Levick, 166–77. London: Routledge, 1995.

Beaujeu, J. *La religion romaine à l'apogée de l'empire, I: La politique religieuse des Antonins (96–192).* Paris: Les Belles Lettres, 1955.

Becatti, G. *Colonna di Marco Aurelio.* Milan: Editoriale Domus, 1957.

———. *La colonna coclide istoriata.* Rome: L'Erma di Bretschneider, 1960.

Bedon, R., "Les obélisques de Rome." *Archeologia* 216 (1986): 55–65.

———. "Les phares antiques." *Archeologia* 231 (1988): 54–66.

Belting-Ihm, C. "Ein römischer Circus-Sarkophag." *JRGZM* 8 (1961): 195–208.

Berczelly, L. "A Sepulchral Monument from the Via Portuense and the Origin of the Roman Biographical Cycle." *ActaAArtHist* 8 (1978): 49–74.

Bergmann, B. "The Roman House as Memory Theater: The House of the Tragic Poet in Pompeii." *ArtB* 76 (1994): 225–56.

Bergmann, M. *Der Koloss Neros, die Domus Aurea und der Mentalitätswandel im Rom der frühen Kaiserzeit, TrWPr* 13 (1933).

Bernareggi, E. "Le opere di Traiano, imperatore spagnolo, nella documentazione numismatica." *Numisma* 25 (1975): 31–40.

Bernhard, M. L. "Topographie d'Aléxandrie: Le tombeau d'Aléxandre et le mausoleum d'Auguste." *RA* 47 (1956): 129–56.

Bernhart, M. "*Consecratio*: Ein numismatischer Beitrag zur römischen Kaiserkonsekration." In *Festschrift F. Hommel* 2, 136–67. 1917.

Bertacchi, M. "Elementi per una revisione della topografia ostiense." *RendLinc,* s. 8, 15 (1960): 8-32.

Bertocchi, F. T. "Un nuovo mausoleo a Canosa." *Palladio* 11 (1961): 86–91.

Beurlier, E. *Essai sur le culte rendu aux empereurs romains.* Paris: E. Thorin, 1890.

Bianchi-Bandinelli, R. "Un problema di arte romana: Il 'Maestro delle imprese di Traiano.'" *Le Arti* 1 (1938–39): 325ff.

"Introduzione." *StMisc* 10 (1966): 9–20.

"La Colonna Traiana: Documento d'arte e documento politico (o della libertà dell'artista)." In *Dall'ellenismo al medio evo,* 123ff. Rome: Riuniti, 1978.

Bianchi-Bandinelli, R., and Torelli, M. *L'arte dell'antichità classica, 2: Etruria, Roma.* Turin, 1976.

Bianchini, F. *De Kalendario et Cyclo Caesaris ac de Paschali Canone S. Hippolyti Martyris. Dissertationes duae . . . Quibus Inseritur Descriptio, et Explanatio Basis, in Campo Martio Nuper Detectae Sub Columna Antonino Pio Olim Dicata.* Rome: Typis Aloysii & Francisci de Comitibus Impressorum Cameralium, 1703.

Bickermann, E. "Die römische Kaiserapotheose." *ArchRW* 27 (1929): 1–34.

"Consecratio." In *Le culte des souverains dans l'empire romain, Entr. Fond. Hardt* 19, ed. E. Bickermann and W. Den Boer, 3–25. Geneva: Fondation Hardt, 1973.

Billows, R. "The Religious Procession of the Ara Pacis Augustae: Augustus' *supplicatio* in 13 B.C." *JRA* 6 (1993): 80–92.

Birley, A. R. *Marcus Aurelius. A Biography.* New Haven, Conn.: Yale University Press, 1987.

Septimius Severus: The African Emperor. New Haven, Conn.: Yale University Press, 1989.

Hadrian: The Restless Emperor. London-New York: Routledge, 1997.

Birt, T. *Die Buchrolle in der Kunst.* Leipzig: B. G. Teubner, 1907.

Blake, M. E. *Ancient Roman Construction in Italy from the Prehistoric Period to Augustus.* Washington, D.C.: Carnegie Institution of Washington, 1947.

Roman Construction in Italy from Tiberius through the Flavians. Washington, D.C.: Carnegie Institution of Washington, 1959.

Bloch, H. *I bolli laterizi e la storia edilizia romana. Contributi all'archeologia e alla storia romana.* Rome: Ripartizione Antichità e Belle Arti, 1947.

Boatwright, M. T. "The '*Ara Ditis* – *Ustrinum* of Hadrian' in the Western Campus Martius and Other Problematic Roman Ustrina." *AJA* 89 (1985): 485–97.

Review of H. Stierlin, *Hadrien et l'architecture romaine* (Fribourg, 1984). *JSAH* 45 (1986): 408–10.

Hadrian and the City of Rome. Princeton, N.J.: Princeton University Press, 1987.

"The Imperial Women of the Early Second Century A.C." *AJP* 112 (1991): 513–40.

Bodel, J. "Monumental Villas and Villa Monuments." *JRA* 10 (1997): 5–35.

Boethius, A. "Nero's Golden House." *Eranos* 44 (1946): 442–59.

"*Et crescunt media pegmata celsa via* (Martial's *De Spectaculis* 2.2)." *Eranos* 50 (1952): 129–37.

The Golden House of Nero: Some Aspects of Roman Architecture. Ann Arbor: University of Michigan Press, 1960.

Bonanno, A. *Portraits and Other Heads on Roman Historical Relief up to the Age of Septimius Severus.* Oxford: British Archaeological Reports, 1976.

Boni, G. "Leggende." *Nuova Antologia,* s. 5, 126 (1906): 3–39.

"Esplorazione del Forum Ulpium." *NSc* 4 (1907): 361–427.

"Trajan's Column." *ProcBritAc* 3 (1907–8): 93–98.

Bonner, C. "Desired Haven." *HThR* 34 (1941): 49–67.

Borbein, A. "Die Ara Pacis Augustae. Geschichtliche Wirklichkeit und Programm." *JdI* 90 (1975): 242–66.

Borgatti, M. *Castel Sant'Angelo in Roma.* Rome: La Libreria dello Stato, 1931.

Borrelli, L. *Le tombe di Pompei a schola semicircolare.* Naples, 1937.

Boschung, D. "Tumulus Iuliorum – Mausoleum Augusti." *Hefte des Berner Archaeol. Seminars* 6 (1980): 38–41.

Antike Grabaltäre aus den Nekropolen Roms, Acta Bernensia 10. Berne, 1987.

Bouche-Leclerq, A. *Manuel des institutions romaines.* Paris: Hachette et Cie., 1886.

Boyance, P. "Le sens cosmique chez Virgile." *REL* 32 (1954): 220–49.

Brandt, O. "Recent Research on the Tomb of Eurysaces." *OpRom* 19 (1993): 13–17.

Brelich, A. "Trionfo e morte." *SMSR* 14 (1938): 189–93.

Gli eroi greci. Un problema storico-religioso. Rome: Edizione dell'Ateneo, 1958.

Brendel, O. J. *Prolegomena to the Study of Roman Art.* New Haven, Conn.: Yale University Press, 1979.

The Visible Idea: Interpretations of Classical Art. Washington, D.C.: Decatur House Press, 1980.

Brilliant, R. *Gesture and Rank in Roman Art: The Use of Gesture to Denote Status in Roman Sculpture.* New Haven, Conn.: Academy, 1963.

Visual Narratives: Storytelling in Etruscan and Roman Art. Ithaca, N.Y.: Cornell University Press, 1984.

Brommer, F. "Aion." *Marburger Winckelmann-Programm* (1967), 1–5.

Brown, F. E. *Roman Architecture* New York: G. Brazillier, 1961.

Brown, R. "The Palace of the Sun in Ovid's *Metamorphoses.*" In *Homo Viator,* ed. M. Whitby, P. Hardie, and M. Whitby, 211–20. Bristol: Bristol Classical Press, 1987.

Brües, E. *Raffaele Stern. Ein Beitrag zur Architekturgeschichte in Rom zwischen 1790 und 1830.* Diss., University of Bonn, 1958.

Buchner, E. *Die Sonnenuhr des Augustus: Nachdruck aus RM 1976 und 1980 und Nachtrag über die Ausgrabung 1980/1981.* Mainz: P. Von Zabern, 1982.

"*Horologium Augusti.* Neue Ausgrabungen in Rom." *Gymnasium* 90 (1983): 494–508.

"Ein Kanal für Obelisken. Neues vom Mausoleum des Augustus in Rom." *AntW* 27 (1996): 161–68.

Burkert, W. *Greek Religion.* Cambridge, Mass.: Harvard University Press, 1985.

Bush, A. C., and McHugh, J. J. "Succession to the Throne of Rome through 192 A.D." *JIES* 2 (1974): 259–77.

Buzzetti, C. "Nota sulla topografia dell'Ager Vaticanus." *QITA* 5 (1968): 105–11.

"Ustrini imperiali a Montecitorio." *BullCom* 89.1 (1984): 27–28.

Callmer, C. "Antike Bibliotheken." *OpArch* 3 (1944): 144–93.

Calza, G. *La necropoli del Porto di Roma nell'Isola Sacra.* Rome: La Libreria dello Stato, 1940.

Calza, R. *Scavi di Ostia, 5: I Ritratti,* 1. Rome: La Libreria dello Stato, 1964.

Camozzi, G. "La consecratio nelle monete da Cesare ad Adriano." *RIN* 14 (1901): 27–53.

Campbell, J. B. *The Emperor and the Roman Army.* Oxford: Oxford University Press, 1984.

Camps, G. "Nouvelles observations sur l'architecture et l'âge du Medracen, mausolée royal de numide." *CRAI* (1973): 470–516.

Cancik, H. "Rome as Sacred Landscape and the End of Republican Religion in Rome."

Visible Religion: Annual for Religious Iconography 4 (1985): 250–65.

Caprino, C.; Colini, A. M.; Gatti, G.; Pallottino, M; and Romanelli, P. *La Colonna di Marco Aurelio.* Rome: Bretschneider, 1955.

Carandini, A. *Vibia Sabina.* Florence: L. S. Olschki, 1969.

Carettoni, G. "Due nuovi ambienti dipinti sul Palatino." *BdA* 46 (1961): 189–99.

Carruthers, M. *The Book of Memory: A Study of Memory in Medieval Culture.* Cambridge-New York: Cambridge University Press, 1990.

Casson, L. *The Ancient Mariners: Seafarers and Sea Fighters of the Mediterranean in Ancient Times.* Princeton, N.J.: Princeton University Press, 1991.

Travel in the Ancient World. Baltimore: Johns Hopkins University Press, 1994.

Castagnoli, F. "Gli edifici rappresentati in un rilievo del sepolcro degli Haterii." *BullCom* 69 (1941): 62–65.

"Il Campo Marzio nell'antichità." *MemLinc* 8.1 (1947): 93–193.

"Installazioni portuali a Roma." In *The Seaborne Commerce of Ancient Rome: Studies in Archaeology and History,* ed. J. H. D'Arms and E. C. Kopff, 35–39. Rome: American Academy in Rome, 1980.

"Influenze alessandrine nell'urbanistica della Roma augustea." In *Alessandria e il mondo ellenistico-romano. Studi in onore di A. Adriani* 3, 520–26. Rome: L'Erma di Bretschneider, 1984.

Castriota, D. *The Ara Pacis Augustae and the Imagery of Abundance in Later Greek and Early Roman Imperial Art.* Princeton, N.J.: Princeton University Press, 1995.

Cecchelli, C. "Le chiese della Colonna Traiana e la leggenda di Traiano." In *Studi e documenti sulla Roma sacra I (Miscellanea della R. Deputazione Romana di Storia Patria),* ed. C. Cecchelli, 95–125. Rome: R. Deputazione alla Biblioteca Vallicelliana, 1938.

Cerfaux, L., and Tondriau, J. *Le culte des souverains dans la civilisation Gréco-Romaine.* Tournai: Desclée & Cie., 1957.

Champlin, E. "Hadrian's Heir." *ZPE* 1 (1976): 79–89.

"God and Man in the Golden House." In *Horti Romani. Atti del convegno internazionale, Roma,* ed. M. Cima and E. La Rocca, 333–44. Rome: L'Erma di Bretschneider, 1998.

Charlesworth, M. P. "Providentia and Aeternitas." *HThR* 29 (1936): 107–32.

Christofle, M. *Le tombeau de la Chrétienne.* Paris: Arts et Metiers Graphiques, 1951.

Ciancio Rossetto, P. *Il sepolcro del fornaio Marco Virgilio Eurisace a Porta Maggiore.* Rome: Istituto di Studi Romani, 1973.

Clapham, A. W. "Roman Mausolea of the Cartwheel Type." *ArchJ* 79 (1922): 93–100.

Claridge, A. "Hadrian's Column of Trajan." *JRA* 6 (1993): 5–22.

Clarke, J. R. *Roman Black-and-White Figural Mosaics.* New York: New York University Press, 1979.

——. *The Houses of Roman Italy, 100 B.C.–A.D. 250. Ritual, Space and Decoration.* Berkeley-Los Angeles: University of California Press, 1991.

Clarke, S., and Engelbach, R. *Ancient Egyptian Construction and Architecture.* New York: Dover Publications, 1990.

Clayton, P., and Price, M. J. *The Seven Wonders of the Ancient World.* London: Routledge, 1989.

Coarelli, F. "Il sepolcro degli Scipioni." *DialArch* 6 (1972): 36–106.

——. *Roma.* Rome: Laterza, 1980.

——. "L'apoteosi di Augusto e l'apoteosi di Romolo." *AnalRom,* suppl. 10 (1983): 41–46.

——. *Il Foro Romano. Periodo arcaico.* Rome: Quasar, 1983.

——. *Roma sepolta.* Milan: A. Curcio, 1984.

——. "Porticus adonaea, aedes heliogabali, aedes iovis ultoris. La tomba di Antinoo?" *MEFRA* 98.1 (1986): 230–53.

——. *Il sepolcro degli Scipioni a Roma.* Rome: Fratelli Palombi Editori, 1988.

——. *Il Campo Marzio dalle origini alla fine della repubblica.* Rome: Quasar, 1997.

Coarelli, F., and Thebert, Y. "Architecture funéraire et pouvoir: Réflexions sur l'hellénisme numide." *MEFRA* 100.2 (1988): 761–818.

Colini, A. M. "La torre di Mecenate." *RendLinc* 34 (1979): 239–50.

Colini, A. M., and Giglioli, C. Q. "Relazione della prima campagna di scavo nel Mausoleo di Augusto." *BullCom* 54 (1926) [1927]: 191–234.

Colonna, G. "Un aspetto oscuro del Lazio antico. Le tombe del VI–V secolo a.C." *PP* 32 (1977): 160–61.

Colvin, H. *Architecture and the Afterlife.* New Haven-London: Yale University Press, 1991.

Condurachi, E. "Riflessi della propaganda politica e della strategia militare sui rilievi della Colonna di Traiano." In *L'esame storico-artistico della Colonna Traiana. Colloquio italo-romano, Roma 25 Ottobre 1978,* ed. E. Condurachi, 7–19. Rome: Accademia nazionale dei Lincei, 1982.

Conlin, D. A. "The Reconstruction of Antonia Minor on the Ara Pacis." *JRA* 5 (1992): 209–15.

——. *The Artists of the Ara Pacis. The Process of Hellenization in Roman Relief Sculpture.* Chapel Hill: University of North Carolina Press, 1997.

Corbaud, E. *Le bas-relief romain à représentations historiques.* Paris: A. Fontemoing, 1899.

Corbett, J. H. "The Succession Policy of Augustus." *Latomus* 33 (1974): 87–97.

Corbier, M. "Divorce and Adoption as Roman Familial Strategies." In *Marriage, Divorce, and Children in Ancient Rome,* ed. B. Rawson, 47–78. Oxford: Oxford University Press, 1991.

——. "Male Power and Legitimacy through Women: The *Domus Augusta* under the Julio-Claudians." In *Women in Antiquity: New Assessments,* ed. R. Hawley and B. Levick, 178–93. London: Routledge, 1995.

Cordingley, R. A., and Richmond, I. A. "The Mausoleum of Augustus." *BSR* 10 (1927): 23–25.

Couchoud, P. L., and Audin, A. "Le carré magique." *Latomus* 17 (1958): 518–27.

Coupelle, P., and Demargne, P. *Fouilles de Xanthos, III: Le monument des Néréides (l'architecture).* Paris: Klincksieck, 1958.

Crawford, O. C. "Laudatio funebris." *CJ* 37 (1941–42): 17–29.

Csillag, P. *The Augustan Laws on Family Relations.* Budapest: Akadémia Kiadó, 1976.

Cumont, F. "L'éternité des empereurs romains." *RHLR* 1 (1896): 435–52.

——. "L'aigle funéraire d'Hierapolis et l'apothéose des empereurs." *Etudes syriennes* (1917).

——. *Recherches sur le symbolisme funéraire des romains.* Paris: P. Geuthner, 1942.

——. "Les lampes et les cierges allumés sur les tombeaux." *Miscellanea G. Mercati* 5, 41–47. Vatican City: Biblioteca Apostolica Vaticana, 1946.

——. *Lux Perpetua.* Paris: P. Geuthner, 1949.

——. *After Life in Roman Paganism.* New York: Dover Publications, 1959.

Curtius, L. *Das antike Rom.* Vienna: A. Schroll, 1944.

D'Ambra, E. "Pudicitia in the Frieze of the Forum Transitorium." *RM* 98 (1991): 243–48.

——— *Private Lives, Imperial Virtues. The Frieze of the Forum Transitorium in Rome.* Princeton, N.J.: Princeton University Press, 1993.

D'Onofrio, C. *Gli obelischi di Roma.* Rome: Bulzoni, 1967.

——— *Castel Sant'Angelo: Images and History.* Rome: Romana Società Editrice, 1984.

Daniel-Lacombe, H. *Le droit funéraire à Rome.* Paris: H. Picard, 1886.

Danti, A. "Nuove acquisizioni per la topografia antica del Campo Marzio settentrionale (ustrino di Marco Aurelio)." *L'Urbe* 47, n.s. 3–4 (1984): 143–46.

Darwell-Smith, R. *Emperors and Architecture: A Study of Flavian Rome.* Brussels: Latomus, 1996.

De Asin, M., and Otero, M. L. "The Pharos of Alexandria." *ProcBritAc* 19 (1933): 277–92.

De Fine Licht, K. *The Rotunda in Rome. A Study of Hadrian's Pantheon.* Copenhagen: Gyldendal, 1968.

De Franciscis, A., and Pane, R. *Mausolei romani in Campania.* Naples: Edizioni Scientifiche Italiane, 1957.

De Grummond, N. "Pax Augusta and the Horae on the Ara Pacis." *AJA* 94 (1990): 663–77.

De Launay, R. "Les fallacieux détours du labyrinthe." *RA* 2 (1915): 114–25, 348–63, 3 (1916): 116–26, 387–98, 4 (1916): 119–28, 286–94, 413–21.

De Maria, S. *Gli archi onorari di Roma e dell'Italia romana.* Rome: L'Erma di Bretschneider, 1988.

De Rossi, J. B. *Inscriptiones Christianae Urbis Romae.* Rome: Ex Officina Libraria Pontificia, 1888.

De' Spagnolis, M. "Contributi per una nuova lettura del Mausoleo di Adriano." *BdA* 61 (1976): 62–68.

De Verrall, M. "Two Instances of Symbolism in the Sixth *Aeneid*." *CR* 24 (1910): 43–46.

De Vos, A., and De Vos, M. *Pompei, Ercolaneo, Stabia. Guida archeologiche laterza.* Rome: G. Laterza, 1982.

De Vos, M. *L'Egittomania in pitture e mosaici romano-campani della prima età imperiale.* Leiden: E. J. Brill, 1980.

De Wit, J. "Vergilius Vaticanus und die nordafrikanische Mosaiken." *Mnemosyne* 3.1 (1934): 29–31.

Deedes, C. N. "The Labyrinth." In *The Labyrinth,* ed. S. H. Hooke, 1–44. London: Society for Promoting Christian Knowledge, 1935.

Deer, J. *The Dynastic Porphyry Tombs of the Norman Period in Sicily, DOS* 5. Cambridge, Mass.: Harvard University Press, 1959.

Delplace, D. *Le griffon, de l'archaïsme à l'epoque impériale. Etude iconographique et essai d'interprétation symbolique.* Brussels-Rome: Institut Historique Belge de Rome, 1980.

Demus-Quatember, M. *Etruskischer Grabarchitektur.* Baden-Baden: B. Grimm, 1958.

Deubner, L. "Die Apotheose des Antoninus Pius." *RM* 27 (1912): 1–20.

Dilke, O. A. W. *The Roman Land Surveyors.* New York: Barnes and Noble, 1971.

Dixon, S. "A Family Business: Women's Role in Patronage and Politics at Rome, 80–44 B.C." *ClMed* 34 (1983): 91–112.

Dobias, J. "Le monnayage de l'empereur Marc-Aurèle et les bas-reliefs historiques contemporains." *RN* 4.35 (1932): 127–61.

Donini, A. *Ponti su monete e medaglie.* Rome: P. & P. Santamarie, 1959.

Doob, P. R. *The Idea of the Labyrinth from Classical Antiquity through the Middle Ages.* Ithaca, N.Y.: Cornell University Press, 1990.

Doublet, G. "Communications: Lettre à M. Héron de Villefosse sur la mosaique d'Hadrumète qui représentait Thesée, le Minotaure et le labyrinthe." *CRAI* (1892): 318–29.

Dragendorff, H., and Krueger, E. *Das Grabmal von Igel.* Trier: Kommissionsverlag von Jacob Lintz, 1924.

Dressel, H. "Der Matidiatempel auf einem Medallion des Hadrianus." In *Corolla Numismatica in Honour of Barclay Head,* ed. G. F. Hill, 16–28. Oxford: H. Frowde, 1906.

Dupont, F. "The Emperor-God's Other Body." In *Fragments for a History of the Human Body,* ed. M. Feher, R. Naddaff, and N. Tazi, 397–419. New York: Urzone, 1989.

——— *Daily Life in Ancient Rome.* Trans. C. Woodall. Oxford: Blackwell, 1992.

Duret, L. "Néron-Phaethon ou la témérité sublime." *REL* 66 (1988): 139–55.

Edwards, C. *Writing Rome: Textual Approaches to the City.* Cambridge: Cambridge University Press, 1996.

Edwards, I. E. S. *The Pyramids of Egypt*. Harmondsworth: Penguin Books, 1949.

Eisner, M. "Zur Typologie der Mausoleen des Augustus und des Hadrian." *RM* (1979): 319–24.

——— *Zur Typologie der Grabbauten in Suburbium Roms*. Mainz: P. Von Zabern, 1986.

Eitrem, S. *Opferritus und Voropfer der Griechischen und Römer*. Kristiania [Oslo]: In Kommission bei J. Dybwad, 1915.

Elsner, J. *Art and the Roman Viewer: The Transformation of Art from the Pagan World to Christianity*. Cambridge: Cambridge University Press, 1995.

——— "Inventing Imperium: Texts and the Propaganda of Monuments in Augustan Rome." In *Art and Text in Roman Culture*, ed. J. Elsner, 32–53. Cambridge: Cambridge University Press, 1996.

Empereur, J.-Y. *Alexandria Rediscovered*. London: British Museum Press, 1998.

Enright, D. J., ed. *The Oxford Book of Death*. Oxford: Oxford University Press, 1983.

Erkell, H. "Statius' *Silvae* 1.1 und das Templum Gentis Flaviae." *Eranos* 56 (1958): 173–82.

Ermann, A. "Römische Obelisken." *Abhandlungen der Königlich preussischen Akademie der Wissenschaften* 4 (1917): 3–47.

Fantham, E.; Foley, H. P.; Kampen, N. B.; Pomeroy, S. B.; and Shapiro, A. L., eds. *Women in the Classical World*. Oxford: Oxford University Press, 1994.

Farinella, V. "La Colonna Traiana: Un esempio di lettura verticale." *Prospettiva* 2.6 (1981): 2–9.

Farnell, L. R. *The Cults of the Greek States*. Oxford: Oxford University Press, 1896–1909.

Farquharson, A. S. L. "On the Names of Aelius Caesar, Adopted Son of Hadrian." *CQ* 2 (1908): 1–8.

Farrar, L. *Ancient Roman Gardens*. Stroud: Sutton Publishing, 1998.

Favro, D. "Reading the Augustan City." In *Narrative and Event in Ancient Art*, ed. P. J. Holliday, 230–57. Cambridge: Cambridge University Press, 1993.

——— *The Urban Image of Augustan Rome*. Cambridge: Cambridge University Press, 1996.

Fea, C. *Miscellanea filologica, critica e antiquaria* 1. Rome, 1790.

Fears, J. R. "The Solar Monarchy of Nero and the Imperial Panegyric of Q. Curtius Rufus." *Historia* 25 (1976): 494–96.

——— *Princeps a Diis Electus: The Divine Election of the Emperor as a Political Concept in Rome*. Rome: American Academy in Rome, 1977.

——— "Jupiter and Roman Imperial Ideology." *ANRW* 2.17.1 (1981): 3–141.

Fedak, J. *Monumental Tombs of the Hellenistic Age. A Study of Selected Tombs from the Pre-Classical to the Early Imperial Era*. Toronto: University of Toronto Press, 1990.

Feeley-Harnik, G. "Issues in Divine Kingship." *Annual Review of Anthropology* 14 (1985): 273–313.

Fehr, B. "Das Militär als Leitbild. Politische Funktion und gruppenspezifische Wahrnehmung des Traiansforums und der Traianssäule." *Hephaistos* 7–8 (1985–6): 39–60.

Fellmann, R. *Das Grabmal des Lucius Munatius Plancus bei Gaeta*. Basel: Verlag des Instituts für Ur- und Frühgeschichte der Schweitz, 1957.

Ferguson, J. *The Religions of the Roman Empire*. Ithaca, N.Y.: Cornell University Press, 1970.

——— *Utopias of the Classical World*. London: Thames and Hudson, 1975.

Ferrill, A. *Caligula, Emperor of Rome*. London: Thames and Hudson, 1991.

Festugière, A. J. "Le symbole du phénix et le mysticisme hermétique." *MonPiot* 38 (1941): 147–51.

Fiaccadori, G. "The Tomb of Alexander the Great." *PP* 263 (1992): 128–31.

Fiorilli, E. "A proposito del Mausoleo di Augusto." *BdA* 7 (1927): 214–19.

Fishwick, D. "Ovid and Divus Augustus." *CP* 86 (1991): 36–41.

Fittschen, K., and Zanker, P. *Katalog der römischen Porträts in den Capitolinischen Museen und den anderen kommunalen Sammlungen der Stadt Rom III, Kaiserinnen und Prinzessinbildnisse, Frauenporträts*. Mainz: P. Von Zabern, 1983.

Fitzgerald, W. "Aeneas, Daedalus and the Labyrinth." *Arethusa* 17 (1984): 51–65.

Flambard, J.-M. "Deux toponymes du Champs de Mars: *ad Ciconias, ad Nixas*." *CEFR* 98 (1987): 191–210.

Fleming, A. "Vision and Design: Approaches to Ceremonial Monument Typology." *Man* 7 (1972): 57–73.

Florescu, F. B. *Das Siegesdenkmal von Adamklissi: Tropaeum Traiani*. Bucharest: Verlag der Akademie der Rumänischen Volksrepublik, 1965.

Flory, M. B. "*Sic Exempla Parantur:* Livia's Shrine to Concordia and the Porticus Liviae." *Historia* 33 (1984): 309–30.

Flower, H. I. *Ancestor Masks and Aristocratic Power in Roman Culture.* Oxford: Clarendon Press, 1996.

Fontana, C. *Discorso sopra l'antico Monte Citatorio situato nel Campo Marzio. . . . Rome:* Stamperia di Giuseppe Nicolò de Martiis, 1708.

Formigé, J. *Le trophée des Alpes (La Turbie).* Paris: Centre Nationale de Recherche Scientifique, 1949.

Fornari, F. "Scoperte di antichità a Piazza Colonna." *NSc* (1917), 9–26.

Foucher, L. *Découvertes archéologiques à Thysdrus en 1961.* Tunis: Imp. Du Secrétariat d'Etat aux Affaires Culturelles et à l'Information, 1961.

"Annus et Aion." In *Le temps chez les Romains,* 197–203. Paris: A. & J. Picard, 1976.

Franchi, L. "Rilievo con pompa funebre e rilievo con gladiatori al museo dell'Aquila." In *Sculture municipali dell'area sabellica tra l'età di Cesare e quella di Nerone, StMisc* 10, ed. R. Bianchi-Bandinelli, 23–32. Rome: De Luca, 1963–64.

Frank, R. I. "Augustus' Legislation Concerning Marriage and Children." *CSCA* 8 (1975): 41–52.

Fraser, P. M. *Ptolemaic Alexandria.* Oxford: Clarendon Press, 1972.

Frazer, A. "The Cologne Circus Bowl: Basileos Helios and the Cosmic Hippodrome." In *Essays in Memory of Karl Lehmann,* ed. L. F. Sandler, 105–13. New York: Institute of Fine Arts, New York University, 1964.

"The Iconography of the Emperor Maxentius' Buildings in Via Appia." *ArtB* 48 (1966): 385–92.

"The Roman Imperial Funeral Pyre." *JSAH* 27.3 (1968): 209.

"The Pyre of Faustina Senior." In *Studies in Classical Art and Archaeology. A Tribute to P. H. von Blanckenhagen,* ed. G. Kopcke and M. B. Moore, 271–74. New York: J. J. Augustin, 1979.

Freshfield, E. H. "Notes on a Vellum Album Containing some Original Sketches of Public Buildings and Monuments, Drawn by a German Artist Who Visited Constantinople in 1574." *Archaeologia* 72 (1921–22): 87–104.

Frischer, B. "*Monumenta et Arae Honoris Virtutisque Causa:* Evidence of Memorials for Roman Civic Heroes." *BullCom* (1983): 51–86.

Fuchs, G. "Varros Vogelhaus bei Casinum." *RM* 69 (1962): 222.

Fuhrmann, H. "Ein Fragment des verlorene Reliefs am Sockel der Marcussäule." *RM* 52 (1937): 261–65.

Fullerton, M. D. "The *Domus Augusti* in Imperial Iconography of 13–12 B.C." *AJA* 89 (1985): 473–83.

Gagé, J. *'Basileia.' Les Cesars, les rois d'Orient et les mages.* Paris: Les Belles Lettres, 1968.

Galinsky, G. K. "Venus in a Relief on the Ara Pacis Augustae." *AJA* 70 (1966): 223–43.

"Augustus' Legislation on Morals and Marriage." *Philologus* 125 (1981): 124–44.

"Venus, Polysemy, and the Ara Pacis Augustae." *AJA* 96 (1992): 457–75.

Augustan Culture. Princeton, N.J.: Princeton University Press, 1996.

Gardner, J. F. *Women in Roman Law and Society.* Bloomington-Indianapolis: Indiana University Press, 1986.

Gardthausen, V. *Augustus und seine Zeit* 1. Leipzig: B. G. Teubner, 1891.

Der Altar des Kaiserfriedens, Ara Pacis Augustae. Leipzig: Viet & Comp., 1908.

Garnsey, P., and Saller, R. *The Roman Empire: Economy, Society and Culture.* Berkeley-Los Angeles: University of California Press, 1987.

Gatti, G. "Il Mausoleo di Augusto. Studio di ricostruzione." *Capitolium* 10 (1934): 457–64.

"Nuove osservazioni sul Mausoleo di Augusto." *L'Urbe* 3.8 (1938): 1ff.

La pianta marmorea di Roma antica. Rome: Comune di Roma, 1960.

Gauer, W. *Untersuchungen zur Trajanssäule. Erster Teil. Darstellungsprogramm und künstlerischer Entwurf, Monumenta artis romanae* 13. Berlin: G. Mann, 1977.

Gazda, E. K., and Haeckl, A. E. *Images of Empire: Flavian Fragments in Rome and Ann Arbor Rejoined.* Ann Arbor: University of Michigan, Kelsey Museum of Archaeology, 1996.

Gazzola, P. *Ponti romani. Contributo ad un indice systematico con studio critico bibliografico.* Florence: L. S. Olschki, 1963.

Gerade, P. "Le règlement successorial d'Hadrien." *REA* 52 (1950): 258–77.

Geyer, U. *Der Adlerflug im römischen Konsekrationszeremoniell.* Diss., University of Bonn, 1967.

Gibbs, S. L. *Greek and Roman Sundials.* New Haven, Conn.: Yale University Press, 1976.

Giglioli, G. Q. "Il sepolcreto imperiale." *Capitolium* 6 (1930): 532–67.

Giuliani, C. F. "Domus Flavia: Una nuova lettura." *RM* 84 (1977): 91–106.

"La rivoluzione adriana, revisione archeologica I." *L'architettura, cronache e storia* 279.1 (1979): 45–51.

Giuliani, C. F., and Verduchi, P. *Foro Romano. L'area centrale.* Florence: L. S. Olschki, 1980.

Götte, H. R. "*Disiecta membra* eines traianischen Frieses." *AA* 98 (1983): 239–46.

Götze, B. *Ein römisches Rundgrab in Falerii, Baugeschichte des römischen Adels- und Kaisergrabes.* Stuttgart: W. Kohlhammer, 1939.

Grabar, O. "From Dome of Heaven to Pleasure Dome." *JSAH* 49 (1990): 15–21.

Grafton Milne, J. "Greek and Roman Tourists in Egypt." *JEA* 3 (1916): 76–80.

Greenhalgh, M. *The Survival of Roman Antiquities in the Middle Ages.* London: Duckworth, 1989.

Gregorovius, F. *Die Gräbmaler der römischen Päpste.* Leipzig: F. A. Brockhaus, 1857.

Grenfell, B. P., and Hunt, A. S., eds. *Fayum Towns and Their Papyri.* London: Egypt Exploration Fund, 1900.

Grenier, J.-C. "La tombe d'Antinoos à Rome." *MEFRA* 98 (1986): 217–53.

Grether, G. "Livia and the Roman Imperial Cult." *AJP* 67 (1947): 222–52.

Griffin, M. T. *Nero, the End of a Dynasty.* New Haven, Conn.: Yale University Press, 1985.

Grimal, P. *Les jardins romains.* Paris: E. De Boccard, 1943.

Review of H. Stierlin, *Hadrien et l'architecture romaine* (Fribourg, 1984). *REL* (1984): 541–42.

Grinsell, L. *Egyptian Pyramids.* Gloucester: J. Bellows, 1947.

Grisar, H. "Il sepolcro dell'imperatore Ottone II nel paradiso dell'antica Basilica Vaticana." *Civiltà cattolica* 55 (1904): 463–73.

Groh, V. "La Colonna di Traiano." *RendLinc,* s. 6.1 (1925): 40–57.

Gros, P. *Aurea templa: Recherches sur l'architecture religieuse de Rome à l'epoque d'Auguste.* Rome: Ecole Française de Rome, 1976.

Gsell, S. *Essai sur le règne de l'empereur Domitien.* Paris: Thorin et Fils, 1894.

Histoire ancienne de l'Afrique du Nord. Paris: Hachette, 1913–20.

Guarducci, M. "Documenti del primo secolo nella necropoli Vaticana." *RendPontAcc* 29 (1956-57) [1958]: 111–37.

The Tomb of St. Peter. New York: Hawthorne Books, 1960.

"La religione di Adriano." In *Les empereurs d'Espagne,* 209–21. Paris: Editions du Centre National de la Recherche Scientifique, 1965.

Guey, J. *Essai sur la guerre Parthique de Trajan (114–17).* Bucharest: Moniteur Officiel et Imprimeries de l'Etat, Imprimerie Nationale, 1937.

"La date de la 'pluie miraculeuse' (172 après J.C.) et la colonne Aurelienne I." *MEFR* 60 (1948): 105–28.

"Encore la 'pluie miraculeuse,' mage et dieu." *RPhil* 22 (1948): 16–62.

"La date de la 'pluie miraculeuse' (172 après J.C.) et la colonne Aurelienne II." *MEFR* 61 (1949): 93–118.

Gullini, G. "Apollodoro e Adriano. Ellenismo e classicismo nell'architettura romana." *BdA* 53 (1968) [1971]: 63–80.

Gury, F. "Aion juvénile et l'anneau zodiacal: L'apparition du motif." *MEFRA* 96:1 (1984): 7–28.

Güven, S. "Displaying the *Res Gestae* of Augustus: A Monument of Imperial Image for All." *JSAH* 57 (1998): 30–45.

Guye, S., and Michel, H. *Mesures du temps et de l'espace, horloges, montres et instruments anciens.* Fribourg: Office du Livre, 1970.

Haarlov, B. *The Half-Open Door. A Common Symbolic Motif within Roman Sepulchral Sculpture.* Odense: Odense University Press, 1977.

Habachi, L., and Buchner, E. *Die unsterblichen Obelisken.* Mainz: P. Von Zabern, 1982.

Hadzi, M. L. Review of L. Vogel, *The Column of Antoninus Pius* (Cambridge, Mass., 1973). *ArtB* 57 (1975): 123–25.

Haftmann, W. *Das italienische Saülenmonument.* Leipzig: Teubner, 1939.

Halfmann, H. *Itinera Principum.* Stuttgart: F. Steiner Verlag Wiesbaden, 1986.

Hallett, J. P. *Fathers and Daughters in Roman Society. Women and the Elite Family.* Princeton, N.J.: Princeton University Press, 1984.

"The Role of Women in Roman Elegy: Counter-Cultural Feminism." In *Women in the Ancient World: The Arethusa Papers,* ed. J. Peradotto and J. P. Sullivan, 241–44. Albany: State University of New York Press, 1984.

Halsberghe, G. H. *The Cult of Sol Invictus.* Leiden: E. J. Brill, 1972.

Hamberg, P. G. *Studies in Roman Imperial Art.* Copenhagen: E. Munskgaard, 1945.

Hammond, M. "The Transmission of the Powers of the Roman Emperor from the Death of Nero in A.D. 68 to that of Alexander Severus in A.D. 235." *MAAR* 24 (1956): 61–133.

Hanell, K. "Das Opfer des Augustus an der Ara Pacis." *OpRom* 2 (1960): 31–123.

Hanfmann, G. M. A. *The Seasons Sarcophagus in Dumbarton Oaks.* Cambridge, Mass.: Harvard University Press, 1951.

Hannah, R. "*Praevolante Nescio Qua Ingenti Humana Specie . . .* A Reassessment of the Winged Genius on the Base of the Antonine Column." *BSR* 57 (1989): 90–105.

Hardie, P. *Virgil's Aeneid: Cosmos and Imperium.* Oxford: Clarendon Press, 1986.

Hartwig, P. "Ein römisches Monument der Kaiserzeit mit einer Darstellung des Tempels des Quirinus." *RM* 19 (1904): 26–33.

Haspels, C. H. E. *The Highlands of Phrygia: Sites and Monuments.* Princeton, N.J.: Princeton University Press, 1971.

Hautecoeur, L. *Mystique et Architecture. Symbolisme du Cercle et de la Coupole.* Paris: A. et J. Picard, 1954.

Heidenreich, R. "Tod und Triumph in der römischen Kunst." *Gymnasium* 58 (1951): 326–40.

Helbig, W. *Führer durch die öffentlichen Sammlungen klassischer Alterthümer in Rom.* Tübingen: E. Wasmuth, 1963–72.

Helm, R. "Eusebius Werke: Chronik des Hieronymus." *GCS* 7 (1956): 191.

Henderson, M. I. Review of F. A. Lepper, *Trajan's Parthian War* (Oxford, 1948). *JRS* 39 (1949): 21.

Hersey, G. *Pythagorean Palaces: Magic and Architecture in the Italian Renaissance.* Ithaca, N.Y.: Cornell University Press, 1976.

Herter, "Die Rundform in Platons Atlantis und ihre Nachwirkung in der Villa Hadriani." *Rheinisches Museum für Philologie* 96 (1953): 1–20.

Hertz, R. "Contribution à une étude sur la représentation collective de la mort." *Année sociologique* 10 (1907): 48–137.

Hirschfeld, O. "Die kaiserlichen Grabstätten in Rom." *Kleine Schriften* (Berlin, 1913): 1149–68.

Holland, L. A. *Janus and the Bridge.* Rome: American Academy in Rome, 1961.

Holliday, P. J. " 'Ad Triumphum Excolendum': The Political Significance of Roman Historical Painting." *Oxford Art Journal* 3.2 (1980): 3–8.

"Roman Triumphal Painting: Its Function, Development and Reception." *ArtB* 79 (1997): 130–47.

Holloway, R. R. "The Tomb of Augustus and the Princes of Troy." *AJA* 70 (1966): 171–73.

Hölscher, T. "Actium und Salamis." *JdI* 99 (1984): 205–14.

Monumenti statali e pubblici. Rome: L'Erma di Bretschneider, 1994.

Hommel, P. *Studien zu den römischen Figurengiebeln der Kaiserzeit.* Berlin: G. Mann, 1954.

Hopkins, K. *Conquerors and Slaves.* Cambridge: Cambridge University Press, 1978.

Death and Renewal. Cambridge: Cambridge University Press, 1983.

Hübner, E. "Zum Denkmal des Trimalchio." *Hermes* 13 (1878): 414–22.

Hülsen, C. "Antichità di Monte Citorio." *RM* 4 (1889): 54.

"Trajanische und hadrianische Bauten im Marsfelde in Rom." *ÖJh* 15 (1912): 124–42.

Humann, K., and Puchstein, O. *Reisen in Kleinasien und Nordsyrien.* Berlin: Dietrich Reimer, 1890.

Humphrey, J. *Roman Circuses: Arenas for Chariot Racing.* Berkeley-Los Angeles: University of California Press, 1986.

Hyde, J. K. "Medieval Descriptions of Cities." *Bull. J. Rylands Lib.* 48 (1965–6): 308–40.

Iacopi, I. *Domus Aurea.* Milan: Electa, 1999.

Iversen, E. *Obelisks in Exile 1: The Obelisks of Rome.* Copenhagen: Gad, 1968.

Jacoby, F. *Fragmente der griechischen Historiker.* Berlin: E. J. Brill, 1926.

Jeffrey, L.-H. *The Local Scripts of Archaic Greece.* Oxford: Clarendon Press, 1961.

Jensen, W. "The Sculptures from the Tomb of the Haterii." Ph. D. diss., University of Michigan, 1978.

Jeppesen, K., Hojland, F., and Aaris-Sorensen, K. *The Mausolleion at Halikarnassos.* 1, *The Sacrificial Deposit.* Copenhagen: Jutland Archaeological Society, Commission, Glydendalske Boghandel Nordisk Forlag, 1981.

Jeppesen, K., and Luttrell, A. *The Mausolleion at Halikarnassos.* 2, *The Written Sources and the Archaeological Background.* Aarhus: Jysk Arkaeologisk Selskab, 1986.

Johansen, K. F. *The Attic Grave-Reliefs of the Classical Period. An Essay in Interpretation.* Copenhagen: E. Munksgaard, 1951.

Johnson, M. J. "Late Antique Imperial Mausolea." Ph. D. diss., Princeton University, 1988.

Jolivet, V. "Les cendres d'Auguste. Note sur la topographie monumentale du Champ de Mars septentrionale." *Archeologia Laziale* 9 (1988): 90–96.

Joly, E. "Nuove lucerne con vedute di porto nell'Antiquarium di Sabratha." *LibAnt* 5 (1968): 35–54.

Jones, B. W. *The Emperor Domitian.* London: Routledge, 1992.

Jordan, H., and Hülsen, C. *Topographie der Stadt Rom im Altertum.* Berlin: Weidmannsche Buchhandlung, 1871–1907.

Jordan-Ruwe, M. "Zur Rekonstruktion und Datierung der Marcussäule." *Boreas* 13 (1990): 53–69.

Joyce, H. "Hadrian's Villa and the 'Dome of Heaven.' " *RM* 97 (1990): 347–81.

Kagis McEwen, I. "Hadrian's Rhetoric I. The Pantheon." *Res* 24 (1993): 55–66.

Kähler, H. *Der Fries vom Reiterdenkmal des Aemilius Paullus in Delphi.* Berlin: G. Mann, 1965.

Kampen, N. B. *Image and Status: Roman Working Women in Ostia.* Berlin: G. Mann, 1981.

"The Muted Other." *ArtJ* (Spring 1988), 15–19.

"Between Public and Private: Women as Historical Subjects in Roman Art." In *Women's History and Ancient History,* ed. S. B. Pomeroy, 218–48. Chapel Hill-London: University of North Carolina Press, 1991.

"The Muted Other: Gender and Morality in Augustan Rome and Eighteenth-Century Europe." In *The Expanding Discourse: Feminism and Art History,* ed. N. Broude and M. D. Garrard, 160–69. New York: Icon Editions, 1992.

"Gender Theory in Roman Art." In *I, Claudia: Women in Ancient Rome,* ed. D. E. E. Kleiner and S. B. Matheson, 14–25. New

Haven, Conn.: Yale University Press, 1996.

Kampmann, H. "The Ustrinum in the Palazzo del Parlamento in Rome." *OpRom* 15 (1985): 67–78.

Kantorowicz, E. H. *The King's Two Bodies: A Study in Medieval Political Theology.* Princeton, N.J.: Princeton University Press, 1957.

Keinast, D. "Zur Baupolitik Hadrians in Rom." *Chiron* 10 (1980): 391–412.

Kern, H. *Labyrinthe. Erscheinungsformen und Deutung 5000 Jahre Gegenwart eines Urbilds.* Munich: Prestel-Verlag, 1982.

Kitzinger, E. "Observations on the Samson Floor at Mopsuestia." *DOP* 27 (1973): 133–44.

Kleiner, D. E. E. *Roman Group Portraiture: The Funerary Reliefs of the Late Republic and Early Empire.* New York: Garland Publishers, 1977.

"The Great Friezes of the Ara Pacis Augustae. Greek Sources, Roman Derivatives and Augustan Social Policy." *MEFRA* 90 (1978): 753–85.

"Women and Family Life on Roman Imperial Altars." *Latomus* 46 (1987): 545–54.

Roman Sculpture. New Haven-London: Yale University Press, 1992.

"Imperial Women as Patrons of the Arts in the Early Empire." In *I Claudia: Women in Ancient Rome,* ed. D. E. E. Kleiner and S. B. Matheson, 28–53. New Haven, Conn.: Yale University Press, 1996.

Kleiner, D. E. E., and Kleiner, F. S. "The Apotheosis of Antoninus and Faustina." *RendPontAcc* 51–52 (1978–80): 389–400.

Kleiner, D. E. E., and Matheson, S. B. *I Claudia: Women in Ancient Rome.* Exh. cat., Yale University Art Gallery, New Haven, Conn.: Yale University Press, 1996.

Kleiner, F. S. *The Arch of Nero in Rome: A Study of the Roman Honorary Arch before and under Nero.* Rome: G. Bretschneider, 1985.

"The Study of Roman Triumphal and Honorary Arches 50 Years after Kähler." *JRA* 2 (1989): 195–206.

"The Arches of Vespasian in Rome." *RM* 97 (1990): 127–36.

"The Trophy on the Bridge and the Roman Triumph over Nature." *AntCl* 60 (1991): 182–92.

Kleiner, G. *Diadochen-Gräber.* Wiesbaden: F. Steiner, 1963.

Knight, W. F. J. "Virgil and the Maze." *CR* 93 (1929): 212–13.

———. "A Prehistoric Ritual Pattern in the Sixth *Aeneid.*" *TAPA* (1935): 256–73.

Koch, G., and Sichtermann, H. *Römische Sarkophage.* Munich: Beck, 1982.

Kockel, V. *Die Grabbauten vor dem Herkulaner Tor in Pompeii.* Mainz: P. Von Zabern, 1983.

Köppel, G. M. "Fragments from a Domitianic Monument in Ann Arbor and Rome." *Bulletin. Museum of Art and Archaeology. The University of Michigan* 3 (1980): 15–29.

———. "Die historischen Reliefs der romischen Kaiserzeit I. Stadtrömische Denkmäler unbekannter Bauzugehörigkeit aus augusteischer und julisch-claudischer Zeit." *BJb* 183 (1983): 61–144.

———. "Die historischen Reliefs der römischen Kaiserzeit IV: Stadtrömischen Denkmäler unbekannter Bauzugehörigkeit aus hadrianischer bis konstantinischer Zeit." *BJb* 186 (1986): 1–90.

Koortbojian, M. "*In Commemorationem Mortuorum*: Text and Image along the 'Streets of Tombs.'" In *Art and Text in Roman Culture,* ed. J. Elsner, 210–33. Cambridge: Cambridge University Press, 1996.

Kornemann, E. *Mausoleum und Tatenbericht des Augustus.* Leipzig: B. G. Teubner, 1921.

———. "Zum Augustusjahr. 1. Octavians Romulusgrab. 2. Der Princeps als Hegemon im Ostem." *Klio* 31 (1938): 81–91.

Kovacsovics, W. K. *Römische Grabdenkmäler.* Waldsassen-Bayern: Stifland-Verlag, 1983.

Kraft, K. "Der Sinn des Mausoleums des Augustus." *Historia* 16 (1967): 189–206.

Kranz, P. *Jahreszeiten-Sarkophag: Entwicklung und Ikonographie des Motivs der Vier Jahreszeiten auf Kaiserzeitlichen Sarkophagen und Sarkophagdeckeln.* Berlin: G. Mann, 1984.

Kranz, W., ed., *Die Fragmente der Vorsokratiker . . . von Hermann Diels.* Berlin: Weidmannsche Buchhandlung, 1951.

Kraus, T. *Das römische Weltreich.* Berlin: Proyläen Verlag, 1967.

Krautheimer, R. *Rome, Profile of a City, 312–1308.* Princeton, N.J.: Princeton University Press, 1980.

Kraay, C. M., and Hirmer, M. *Greek Coins.* New York: H. N. Abrams, 1966.

Krencker, D., and Schede, M. *Der Tempel in Ankara (Denkmäler Antiker Architektur, III).* Berlin-Leipzig: W. de Gruyter, 1936.

Küthmann, C. "Zur Gemma Augustea." *AA* 65–66 (1950–51): 89–103.

Kuttner, A. L. "Some New Grounds for Narrative. Marcus Antonius's Base (*The Ara Domitii Ahenobarbi*) and Republican Biographies." In *Narrative and Event in Ancient Art,* ed. P. Holliday, 198–229. Cambridge: Cambridge University Press, 1993.

———. *Dynasty and Empire in the Age of Augustus: The Case of the Boscoreale Cups.* Berkeley-Los Angeles: University of California Press, 1995.

L'Orange, H. P. *Studies in the Iconography of Cosmic Kingship in the Ancient World.* Oslo: H. Aschehoug, 1953.

La Rocca, E. *La riva a mezzaluna: Culti, agoni, monumenti funerari presso il Tevere nel Campo Marzio occidentale.* Rome: L'Erma di Bretschneider, 1984.

———. *Rilievi storici capitolini: Il restauro dei pannelli di Adriano e di Marco Aurelio nel Palazzo dei Conservatori.* Rome: De Luca, 1986.

Lambert, R. *Beloved and God: The Story of Hadrian and Antinous.* New York: Carol Publishing Group, 1992.

Lancaster, L. "Building Trajan's Column." *AJA* 103 (1999): 419–39.

Lanciani, R. *Forma Urbis Romae.* Mediolani: Apud Ulricum Hoepli, 1893–1901.

———. *The Destruction of Ancient Rome.* New York: MacMillan, 1899.

Lavagne, H. "Le tombeau, mémoire du mort." In *La mort, les morts et l'au-delà dans le monde romain.* Caen, 1987.

Le Gall, J. *Le Tibre, fleuve de Rome dans l'antiquité.* Paris: Presses Universitaires de France, 1953.

———. "Les romains et l'orientation solaire." *MEFRA* 87 (1975): 287–320.

Lefkowitz, M. R. "Wives and Husbands." *GaR* 30 (1983): 31–47.

Lehmann, K. "The Dome of Heaven." *ArtB* 27 (March 1945): 1–17.

Lehmann-Hartleben, K. *Die antiken Hafenanlagen des Mittelmeers.* Leipzig: Dieterichsche Verlagsbuchhandlung, 1923.

———. *Die Traianssäule, ein römisches Kunstwerke zu Beginn der Spätantike.* Berlin-Leipzig: W. De Gruyter & Co., 1926.

———. "L'Arco di Tito." *BullCom* 62 (1934): 89–122.

Lepper, F. *Trajan's Parthian War.* Oxford: Oxford University Press, 1948.

Lepper, F., and Frere, S. *Trajan's Column: A New Edition of the Cichorius Plates.* Gloucester: Alan Sutton, 1988.

Levi, D. "Aion." *Hesperia* 13 (1944): 269–314.

Linderski, J. "The Augural Law." *ANRW* II.16.3 (1968): 2, 146.

Ling, R. *Roman Painting.* Cambridge: Cambridge University Press, 1991.

Lissi Caronna, E. "Roma. Rinvenimenti in Piazza Capranica 78." *NSc* (1972): 398–403.

Llewellyn, N. *The Art of Death.* London: Reaktion Books, 1991.

Loerke, W. C. "Georges Chédanne and the Pantheon: A Beaux Arts Contribution to the History of Roman Architecture." *Modulus. The University of Virginia School of Architecture Review* (1982), 40–55.

"A Rereading of the Interior Elevation of Hadrian's Rotunda." *JSAH* 49 (1990): 22–43.

Lugano, P. P. *Santa Maria Nova.* Rome: Casa Editrice "Roma," 1923.

Lugli, G. *Roma antica. Il centro monumentale.* Rome: G. Bardi 1946.

"La tomba di Traiano." In *Omagiu lui Constantin Daicoviciu,* 333–38. Bucharest, 1960.

Luhrmann, T. M. *Persuasions of the Witch's Craft: Ritual Magic and Witchcraft in Present-Day England.* Oxford: Basil Blackwell, 1989.

Lynch, K. *The Image of the City.* Cambridge, Mass.: MIT Press, 1960.

MacCormack, S. G. *Art and Ceremony in Late Antiquity.* Berkeley-Los Angeles: University of California Press, 1981.

MacDonald, W. L. *The Pantheon, Design, Meaning and Progeny.* Cambridge, Mass.: Harvard University Press, 1976.

The Architecture of the Roman Empire, I: An Introductory Study. New Haven-London: Yale University Press, 1982.

"Roman Architects." In *The Architect: Chapters in the History of the Profession,* ed. S. Kostof, 44–51. Oxford: Oxford University Press, 1986.

"Apollodorus." In the *Macmillan Encyclopedia of Architects,* 1:91–94. New York: Free Press, 1982.

The Architecture of the Roman Empire, II: An Urban Appraisal. New Haven-London: Yale University Press, 1986.

"Sorting Out Roman Architecture." *AJA* 102 (1998): 614–17.

MacDonald, W. L., and Pinto, J. *Hadrian's Villa and Its Legacy.* New Haven-London: Yale University Press, 1995.

MacMullen, R. "Women in Public in the Roman Empire." *Historia* 29 (1980): 208–18.

Paganism in the Roman Empire. New Haven-London: Yale University Press, 1981.

"Women's Power in the Principate." *Klio* 68 (1986): 434–43.

Maffei, S. "La 'felicitas imperatoris' e il dominio sugli elementi." *Studi classici e orientali* 40 (1990): 329–67.

Magi, F. "Il circo Vaticano in base alle più recenti scoperte, il suo obelisco e i suoi 'carceres.'" *RendPontAcc* 45 (1972/73): 37–73.

"L'iscrizione perduta dell'Arco di Tito: Una ipotesi." *RM* 82 (1975): 99–116.

Malaise, M. *Les conditions de pénétration et de diffusion des cultes egyptiens en Italie.* Leiden: E. J. Brill, 1972.

Manca di Mores, G. "Terrecotte architettoniche e problemi topografici: Contributi all'identificazione del Tempio di Quirino sul colle Quirinale." *AnnPerugia* 20.6 (1982–83): 332–33.

Manodori, A. "Memorie sparse del Mausoleo di Adriano." In *Adriano e il suo Mausoleo,* ed. M. Mercalli, 149–59. Milan: Electa, 1998.

Mansuelli, G. A. "Il monumento commemorativo romano." *BCSSA* 12 (1958): 3–23.

Marasovic, J., and Marasovic, T. *Diocletian's Palace.* Zagreb: Zova, 1970.

Marchetti, D. "Scoperte nella Regione IX." *NSc* (1890), 153.

"Di un antico molo per lo sbarco dei marmi riconosciuto sulla riva sinistra del Tevere." *BullCom* (1891): 45ff.

"Scoperte nella Regione IX." *NSc* (1892): 110ff.

Marrou, H.-I. *Mousikos aner. Etudes sur les scènes de la vie intellectuelle figurant sur les monuments funéraires romains.* Grenoble: Didier et Richard, 1938.

Martin, J.-P. "Hadrien et le phénix: Propagande numismatique." In *Mélanges d'histoire ancienne offerts à William Seston.* Paris, 1974.

Martin, R. *Recherches sur l'agora grecque.* Paris: E. De Boccard, 1951.

"Le monument des Néréides et l'architecture funéraire." *RA* (1971), 327–37.

Martines, G. "La struttura della Colonna Traiana. Un esercitazione di meccanica alessandrina." *Prospettiva* 32 (1983): 60–71.

Matheson, S. B. "The Divine Claudia: Women as Goddesses in Roman Art." In *I Claudia:*

Women in Ancient Rome, ed. D. E. E. Kleiner and S. B. Matheson, 182–93. New Haven, Conn.: Yale University Press, 1996.

Matthews, W. H. *Mazes and Labyrinths. A General Account of Their History and Developments.* London: Longmans, Green and Co., 1922.

Mattingley, H. "The Consecration of Faustina the Elder and Her Daughter." *HThR* 41 (1948): 147–51.

McCracken, G. "The Villa and Tomb of Lucullus at Tusculum." *AJA* 46 (1942): 325–40.

McFayden, D. "The Date of the Arch of Titus." *CJ* 11 (1915–16): 131–41.

McGowan, E. P. "Tomb Marker and Turning Post: Funerary Columns in the Archaic Period." *AJA* 99 (1995): 615–32.

McNamara, J. A. "*Matres Patriae/Matres Ecclesiae:* Women of the Roman Empire." In *Becoming Visible: Women in European History,* ed. R. Bridenthal, C. Koonz, and S. Stuard, 107–29. Boston: Houghton Mifflin, 1987.

Meneghini, R. "L'architettura del Foro di Traiano attraverso i ritrovimenti archeologici più recenti." *RM* 105 (1998): 127–48.

Mercalli, M. "The Angel of the Castle, Its Iconography, Its Significance." In *The Angel and Rome,* ed. B. Contadi and M. Mercalli, 67–93. Rome: Fratelli Palombi, 1987.

Merlin, A., and Poinssot, A. "Factions du cirque et saisons sur des mosaïques de Tunisie." *Mélanges Ch. Picard* 2, 732–45. Paris: Presses Universitaires de France, 1949.

Metcalf, P., and Huntington, R. *Celebrations of Death: The Anthropology of Mortuary Ritual.* Cambridge: Cambridge University Press, 1991.

Mikocki, T. "Les impératrices et les princesses en déesses dans l'art romain." *Eos* 78 (1990): 209–18.

Sub specie deae: Les impératrices et princesses romaines assimilées à des déesses. Etude iconologique. Rome: G. Bretschneider, 1995.

Miller, S. G. "Macedonian Tombs: Their Architecture and Architectural Decoration." *Studies in the History of Art,* 10: *Macedonia and Greece in Late Classical and Early Hellenistic Times,* ed. E. N. Borza and B. Barr-Sharrar. Washington, D.C., 1982.

Mocchegiani Carpano, C. "Indagini archeologiche nel Tevere." *QArchEtr* 5 (1981): 144.

Mommsen, T. "Trimalchios Heimath und Grabschrift." *Hermes* 13 (1878): 106–21.

Moretti, G. *Ara Pacis Augustae.* Rome: Istituto Poligrafico dello Stato, Libreria dello Stato, 1948.

Moretti, M. *New Monuments of Etruscan Painting.* University Park: Pennsylvania State University Press, 1970.

Morford, M. P. O. "The Distortion of the Domus Aurea Tradition." *Eranos* 66 (1968): 158–79.

Morris, J. "The Dating of the Column of Marcus Aurelius." *JWarb* 15 (1952): 33–47.

Murray, W. M., and Petsas, P. M. *Octavian's Campsite Memorial for the Actian War.* Philadelphia, Penn.: American Philosophical Society, 1989.

Musso, L. "Ascensione ad astra e iconografia funeraria sulla composizione di due sarcofagi romani del III secolo." *Scienze dell'antiquità. Storia, archeologia, antropologia* 1 (1987): 319–38.

Catalogo della Galleria Colonna in Roma. Sculture, ed. F. Carinci, H. Keutner, L. Musso, and M. G. Picozzi, 182–83. Rome: Bramante Editrice, 1990.

Nardoni, D. *La Colonna Ulpia Traiana.* Rome: Edizione Italiane di Letteratura e Scienze, 1986.

Nash, E. "Obelisk und Circus." *RM* 64 (1957): 232–59.

Nichols, F. M. *The Marvels of Rome.* New York: Italica Press, 1986.

Nicolet, C. *Space, Geography, and Politics in the Early Roman Empire.* Ann Arbor: University of Michigan Press, 1991.

Noack, F. "Triumph und Triumphbogen." *Vorträge der Bibliothek Warburg* 1925–26 [1928]: 147–201.

Nock, A. D. "Sarcophagi and Symbolism." *AJA* 50 (1946): 140–70.

Nogara, B. *Monumenti romani scoperti . . . nell'Area del Palazzo della Cancelleria.* Rome: Reale Istituto di Studi Romani, 1942.

North, J. A. "These He Cannot Take." *JRS* 73 (1983): 169–74.

Nueser, K. *Anemoi. Studien zur Darstellung der Winde und Windgottheiten in der Antike.* Rome: G. Bretschneider, 1982.

Nylander, C. *Ionians in Pasargadae. Studies in Old Persian Architecture.* Uppsala: Almquist and Wiksell, 1970.

Ostrowski, J. A. "Personifications of Rivers as an Element of Roman Political Propaganda." *EtTrav* 15 (1990): 309–19.

Owens, E. J. *The City in the Greek and Roman World.* London: Routledge, 1991.

Packer, J. E. "Trajan's Forum Again: The Column and the Temple of Trajan in the Master Plan Attributed to Apollodorus (?)" *JRA* 7 (1994): 163–82.

— *The Forum of Trajan in Rome: A Study of the Monuments.* Berkeley-Los Angeles: University of California Press, 1997.

— "Report from Rome: The Imperial Fora, a Retrospective." *AJA* 101 (1997): 307–30.

Packer, J. E., and Sarring, K. L. "Il Foro di Traiano." *Archeo* 7.11 (1992): 62–89, 92–93.

Palmer, R. E. A. "Jupiter Blaze, Gods of the Hills and Roman Topography of *CIL* VI 377." *AJA* 80 (1976): 43–56.

— "Studies in the Northern Campus Martius." *TAPS* 80.2 (1990): 52–55.

Panofsky, E. *Tomb Sculpture.* London: Thames and Hudson, 1964.

Panvini Rosati, F. "La colonna sulle monete di Traiano." *AIIN* 5 (1958): 29–40.

Paris, R. "Propaganda e iconografia: Una lettura del frontone del Tempio di Quirino sul frammento del "rilievo Hartwig" nel Museo Nazionale Romano." *BdA* 73 (1988): 27–38.

— ed. *Dono Hartwig: Originali ricongiunti e copie tra Ann Arbor e Roma. Ipotesi per il Templum Gentis Flaviae.* Rome: Giunti, 1994.

Patterson, J. R. "Survey Article: The City of Rome: From Republic to Empire." *JRS* 82 (1992): 186–215.

Pensa, M. "Rappresentazioni di monumenti sulle monete di Adriano." *RIN* 80 (1978): 27–78.

Pepe, L. "Sul monumento sepolchrale di Trimalchione." *Giornale italiano di filologia* 10 (1957): 293–300.

Perrin, Y. "Nicolas Ponce et la Domus Aurea de Néron. Une documentation inédite." *MEFRA* 94 (1982): 843–91.

— "D'Aléxandre à Néron. Le motif de la tente d'apparat. La salle 29 de la Domus Aurea." In *Neronia 4. Alejandro Magno, Modelo de los emperadores romanos,* ed. J. M. Croisille, 211–29. Brussels: Latomus, Revue des Etudes Latines, 1990.

Petersen, E. "Sitzungsprotocolle." *RM* 10 (1895): 95–96.

— *Ara Pacis Augustae.* Vienna: A. Hölder, 1902.

— "Funde." *RM* 19 (1904): 154–61.

Petersen, E.; von Domaszewski, A.; and Calderini, G. *Die Marcussäule auf Piazza Colonna in Rom.* Munich: F. Bruckmann, 1896.

Petrie, W. F. M. *Royal Tombs of the Earliest Dynasties* 1. London: Egypt Exploration Fund, 1900–1901.

Petrikowitz, H. "Die Porta Triumphalis." *ÖJh* 28 (1933): 187–96.

Pfanner, M. "Codex Coburgensis Nr. 88: Die Entdeckung der porta triumphalis." *RM* 87 (1980): 327ff.

— *Der Titusbogen, Beitrage zur Erschliessung Hellenistischer und Kaiserzeitlicher Skulptur und Architektur 2.* Mainz: P. Von Zabern, 1983.

Pflaum, H.-G. "Le règlement successorial d'Hadrien." *HAC* (1963): 95–122.

— "Les impératrices de l'époque des Antonins dans l'*Historia Augusti*." *HAC* 4 (1979/81):

Piazzesi, G. "Gli edifici: Ipotesi ricostruttive." *ArchCl* 41 (1989): 125–96.

Picard, G.-C. "Sur quelques représentations nouvelles du phare d'Aléxandrie, et sur l'origine aléxandrine des paysages portuaires." *BCH* 76 (1952): 61–95.

— "Le Trophée de Trajan à Adam Klissi." *RA* (1962), 91–94.

Picard, C. *Les trophées romains. Contribution à l'histoire de la religion et de l'art triomphale de Rome.* Paris: E. De Boccard, 1957.

Picard, C., and Picard, G. "Recherches sur l'architecture numide." *Karthago* 19 (1977–78): 15–33.

Pierce, J. R. "The Mausoleum of Hadrian and the Pons Aelius." *JRS* 15 (1925): 75–103.

Pietilä-Castrén, L. *Magnificentia Publica. The Victory Monuments of the Roman Generals in the Era of the Punic Wars.* Helsinki: Societas Scientiarum Fennica, 1987.

Pietrangeli, C. *Guide rionale di Roma. Rione III – Colonna* 2. Rome: Fratelli Palombi Editori, 1982.

Piganiol, A. *Recherches sur les jeux romains.* Strasbourg: Libraire Istra, 1923.

Platner, S. B., and Ashby, T. *A Topographical Dictionary of Ancient Rome.* London: Oxford University Press, H. Milford, 1929.

Plowden, E. *Commentaries or Reports.* London: S. Brooke, 1816.

Pollini, J. "Studies in Augustan 'Historical' Reliefs." Ph.D. diss., University of California, Berkeley, 1978.

Pollitt, J. J. *The Art of Rome, c. 753 B.C.–A.D. 337: Sources and Documents.* Cambridge: Cambridge University Press, 1983.

Art in the Hellenistic Age. Cambridge: Cambridge University Press, 1986.

Pollock, G. "Modernity and the Spaces of Femininity." In *Vision and Difference. Femininity, Feminism and the Histories of Art,* ed. G. Pollock, 50–90. London: Routledge, 1988.

Pomeroy, S. B. *Goddesses, Whores, Wives, and Slaves. Women in Classical Antiquity.* New York: Schocken Books, 1975.

"The Relationship of the Married Woman to Her Blood Relatives in Rome." *Ancient Society* 7 (1976): 215–27.

Prayon, F. "Architecture." In *Etruscan Life and Afterlife,* ed. L. Bonfante, 174–201. Detroit: Wayne State University Press, 1986.

Price, S. R. F. "From Noble Funerals to Divine Cult: The Consecration of Roman Emperors." In *Rituals and Royalty: Power and Ceremonial in Traditional Societies,* ed. D. Cannadine and S. Price, 56–105. Cambridge: Cambridge University Press, 1987.

Prieur, J. *La mort dans l'antiquité romaine.* Rennes: Ouest France, 1986.

Puech, H.-C. "Le gnose et le temps." In *En quête de la gnose* 1:215–70. Paris: Gallimard, 1978.

Purcell, N. "Livia and the Womanhood of Rome." *PCPS,* n.s. 32 (1986): 78–105.

"Tomb and Suburb." In *Römische Gräberstrasse,* ed. H. Von Hesberg and P. Zanker. Munich: Verlag der Bayerischen Akademie der Wissenschaften in Kommission bei der C. H. Beckschen Verlagsbuchhandlung, 1987.

Quet, M.- H. "Pharus." *MEFRA* 96 (1984): 789–845.

Quilici, L. *Via Appia da Porta Capena ai colli Albani.* Rome: Fratelli Palombi Editori, 1989.

Raditsa, L. "Augustus' Legislation Concerning Marriage, Procreation, Love Affairs and Adultery." *ANRW* II.13 (1980): 278–339.

Rakob, F. "Architecture royale numide." In *Architecture et société de l'archaisme grec à la fin de la république romaine, Rome 1980,* 326ff. Rome: Ecole Française de Rome, 1983.

"Adriano – Imperatore e architetto." In *Adriano e il suo Mausoleo,* ed. M. Mercalli, 7–19. Milan: Electa, 1998.

Reddé, M. "La représentation des phares à l'époque romaine." *MEFRA* 91.2 (1979): 845–72.

Reeder, J. C. "Typology and Ideology in the Mausoleum of Augustus." *ClAnt* 11.2 (1992): 265–304.

Richard, F. "Les dieux des phares." *Sefunim* 6 (1981): 37–45.

Richard, J.-C. "Les aspects militaires des funérailles impériales." *MélRome* 78 (1966): 313–25.

"Tombeaux des empereurs et temples des 'Divi': Notes sur la signification religieuse des sépultures impériales à Rome." *RHR* 170 (1966): 127–42.

" 'Mausoleum': d'Halicarnasse à Rome, puis à Aléxandrie." *Latomus* 29 (1970): 370–88.

Richardson, L., Jr. *A New Topographical Dictionary of Ancient Rome.* Baltimore: Johns Hopkins University Press, 1992.

Richlin, A. "Approaches to the Sources on Adultery at Rome." In *Reflections of Women in Antiquity,* ed. H. P. Foley, 379–404. New York: Gordon and Breach Science Publishers, 1981.

Richmond, I. A. *Roman Archaeology and Art.* London: Faber, 1969.

Ridgway, B. S. *Hellenistic Sculpture I. The Styles of ca. 331–200 B.C.* Madison: University of Wisconsin Press, 1990.

Ridley, R. T. "*Augusti Manes Volitant per Auras*: The Archaeology of Rome under the Fascists." *Xenia* 11 (1986): 19–46.

Rivoira, T. "Di Adriano architetto e dei monumenti Adrianei." *RendLinc* 18 (1909): 172–77.

Robathan, D. M. "Domitian's Midas-Touch." *TAPA* 73 (1942): 130–44.

Robert, F. *Thymélé, recherches sur la signification et la destination des monuments circulaires dans l'architecure religieuse de la Grèce.* Paris: E. De Broccard, 1939.

Robinson, O. F. *Ancient Rome: City Planning and Administration.* London-New York: Routledge, 1992.

Rodenwaldt, G. Review of H. Lehner, *Das Römerlager Vetera bei Xanten. Ein Führer durch die Ausgrabungen des Bonner Provinzialmuseums* (Bonn, 1926). *Gnomon* 2 (1926): 338–39.

"Über den Stilwandel in der antoninischen Kunst." *Abhandlungen der Preussischen Akademie der Wissenschaft zu Berlin, Phil.-Hist. Klasse* 3 (1935).

"Römische Reliefs: Vorstufen zur Spätantike." *JdI* 55 (1940).

Rodocanachi, E. *Les monuments de Rome après la chute de l'empire.* Paris: Hachette et Cie., 1914.

Rodríguez-Almeida, E. "Il Campo Marzio settentrionale: Solarium e pomerium." *RendPontAcc* 51–52 (1978–80): 195–212.

"Alcune note topografiche sul Quirinale di epoca domizianea." *BullCom* 91.1 (1986): 49–60.

Roes, A. "L'aigle du culte solaire syrien." *RA,* ser. 6, 36 (1950): 129–46.

"L'aigle psychopompe de l'époque impériale." In *Mél. Ch. Picard* 2:881–91. Paris, 1949.

Roos, A. G. "Het Regenwonder op de zuil can Marcus Aurelius." *Meded* 6.1 (1943): 30ff.

Roscher, W. *Ausführliches Lexikon der griechischen und römischen Mythologie.* Leipzig: B. G. Teubner, 1893.

Rose, C. B. *Dynastic Commemoration and Imperial Portraiture in the Julio-Claudian Period.* Cambridge: Cambridge University Press, 1997.

Rossi, L. "Technique, Toil and Triumph on the Danube in Trajan's Propaganda Programme." *AntJ* 58 (1978): 81–87.

Roullet, A. *The Egyptian and Egyptianising Monuments of Imperial Rome.* Leiden: E. J. Brill, 1972.

Rousselle, A. "Personal Status and Sexual Practice in the Roman Empire." In *Fragments in the History of the Human Body* 3:300–333. New York: Zone, 1989.

Roux, G. *L'architecture de l'Argolide aux IVe et IIIe siècles avant J.-C.* Paris: E. De Boccard, 1961.

"Un chef-d'oeuvre d'architecture gréco-lycienne: Le 'monument des Néréides.' " *REG* 88 (1975): 182–89.

Rushford, G. "Funeral Lights in Roman Sepulchral Monuments." *JRS* 5 (1915): 149–64.

Rushforth, G. M. "Magister Gregorius de Mirabilibus Urbis Romae: A New Description of Rome in the 12th Century." *JRS* 9 (1919): 14–58.

Rutledge, H. C. "Virgil's Daedalus." *CJ* 62 (1967): 309–11.

"The Opening of *Aeneid* 6." *CJ* 67 (1972): 110–15.

Ryberg, I. S. "Rites of the State Religion in Roman Art." *MAAR* 22 (1955).

Rykwert, J. *The Idea of a Town.* Princeton, N.J.: Princeton University Press, 1976.

The Dancing Column: On Order in Architecture. Cambridge, Mass.: MIT Press, 1996.

Santangelo, M. "Il Quirinale nell'età classica." *MemPontAcc* 5 (1941): 77–214.

Sauter, H. "Der römische Kaiserkult bei Martial und Statius." *Tübinger Beiträge zur Altertumsissenschaft* 21 (1934): 150–52.

Schalles, H. "Forum und zentraler Tempel im 2. Jahrhundert n. Chr." In *Die Römische Stadt im 2. Jahrhundert n. Chr. Colloquium in Xanten,* 183–211. Bonn, 1992.

Scheid, J. "*Contraria facere*: Renversements et deplacements dans les rites funéraires." *Archeologia e storia antica* 6 (1984): 117–39.

Schilling, R. "Janus le dieu introducteur, le dieu des passages." *MEFR* 72 (1960): 89–131.

"Roman Festivals and Their Significance." *Acta Classica* 7 (1964): 44–56.

Schmitt-Pantel, P. "Evergétisme et mémoire du mort." In *Le mort, les morts dans les sociétés anciennes,* ed. G. Gnoli and J. P. Vernant, 177–88. Cambridge: Cambridge University Press, 1982.

Schulten, P. N. *Die Typologie der römische Konsekrationsprägungen.* Frankfurt: Numismatischer Verlag Schulten, 1974.

Schütz, M. "Zur Sonnenuhr des Augustus auf dem Marsfeld." *Gymnasium* 97 (1990): 432–57.

Scott, K. *The Imperial Cult under the Flavians.* Stuttgart-Berlin: W. Kohlhammer, 1936.

"The Identification of Augustus with Romulus-Quirinus." *TAPA* 56 (1925): 82–105.

Scullard, H. H. *The Elephant in the Greek and Roman World.* London: Thames and Hudson, 1974.

Serafin, P. "La moneta al tempo di Adriano." In *Adriano e il suo Mausoleo,* ed. M. Mercalli, 187–225. Milan: Electa, 1998.

Settis, S.; La Regina, A.; Agosti, G.; and Farinella, V. *La Colonna Traiana.* Turin: G. Einaudi, 1988.

Sherman, C. R. "Taking a Second Look: Observations on the Iconography of a French Queen, Jeanne de Bourbon (1338–1378)." In *Feminism and Art History: Questioning the Litany,* ed. N. Broude and M. D. Garrard, 100–117. New York: Harper and Row, 1982.

Shipley, F. W. *Res Gestae Divi Augusti.* London: W. Heinemann, 1924.

"Chronology of the Building Operations in Rome from the Death of Caesar to the Death of Augustus." *MAAR* 9 (1931): 7–60.

Simon, E. "Zur Bedeutung des Greifen in der Kunst des Kaiserzeit." *Latomus* 21 (1962): 749–80.

———. *Die Götter der Griechen.* Munich: Hirmer Verlag, 1980.

———. *Augustus, Kunst und Leben in Rom um die Zeitenwende.* Munich: Hirmer Verlag, 1986.

———. *Die Götter der Romer.* Munich: Hirmer Verlag 1990.

Soubiran, J. "L'astronomie à Rome." In *L'astronomie dans l'antiquité classique,* 167–83. Paris: Belles Lettres, 1979.

Spaeth, B. S. "The Goddess Ceres in the Ara Pacis Augustae and the Carthage Relief." *AJA* 98 (1994): 65–100.

———. *The Roman Goddess Ceres.* Austin: University of Texas Press, 1996.

Spannagel, M. "Wiedergefundene Antiken: Zu vier Dal-Pozo-Zeichnungen in Windsor Castle." *AA* (1979), 348–77.

Squadrilli, T. "Il Mausoleo di Adriano." *Capitolium* 50.7–8 (1975): 20–31.

Staeger, M. Review of D. Favro, *The Urban Image of Augustan Rome* (Cambridge, 1996). *BMCR* (1997).

Stambaugh, J. E. *The Ancient Roman City.* Baltimore: Johns Hopkins University Press, 1988.

Steinmetz, H. "Windgötter." *JdI* 25 (1910): 1–55.

Stevens Curl, J. *A Celebration of Death: An Introduction to Some of the Buildings, Monuments and Settings of Funerary Architecture in the Western European Tradition.* London: Constable, 1980.

Stierlin, H. *Hadrien et l'architecture romaine.* Fribourg: Office du Livre, 1984.

Strong, D. E. "Late Hadrianic Architectural Ornament in Rome." *BSR* 21 (1953): 118–51.

Strong, E. *La scultura romana da Augusto a Costantino.* Florence: Fratelli Alnari, 1923–26.

———. "Terra Mater or Italia?" *JRS* 27 (1937): 114–26.

Stuart-Jones, H. "Notes on Roman Historical Sculptures." *BSR* 3 (1906): 213–71.

Stucchi, S. "L'Arco detto 'di Portogallo' sulla Via Flaminia." *BullCom* 73 (1949–50): 101–22.

———. "Fari, campanili e mausolei." *AquilNost* 30 (1959): 15–32.

———. "*Tantis viribus*: L'area della Colonna nella concezione generale del Foro di Traiano." *ArchCl* 41 (1989): 237–91.

Stuhlfauth, G. "Der Leuchturm von Ostia." *RM* 53 (1938): 139–63.

Stuveras, R. *Le putto dans l'art romain.* Brussels: Latomus, 1969.

Sutherland, C. H. V. "The State of the Imperial Treasury at the Death of Domitian." *JRS* 25 (1935): 150–62.

Syme, R. "Hadrian the Intellectual." In *Les empereurs d'Espagne,* 243–53. Paris, 1965.

———. "Astrology in the *Historia Augusta.*" *HAC* 1972–4 (1976): 291–309.

———. "Journeys of Hadrian." *ZPE* 73 (1988): 162–68.

Tarn, W. W. "The Battle of Actium." *JRS* 21 (1931): 173–99.

Templer, J. *The Staircase: History and Theories.* Cambridge, Mass.-London: MIT Press, 1992.

Thiersch, H. *Pharos, Antike und Islam.* Leipzig: B. G. Teubner, 1909.

———. "Die Alexandrinische Königsnekropole." *JdI* 25 (1910): 55–97.

Thompson, D. L. Review of L. Vogel, *The Column of Antoninus Pius* (Cambridge, Mass., 1973). *AJA* 78 (1974): 208.

Thornton, M. K., and Thornton, R. L. *Julio-Claudian Building Programs: A Quantitative Study in Political Management.* Wauconda, Ill.: Bolchazy-Carducci Publishers, 1989.

Tomei, M. A. "La regione Vaticana nell'antichità." In *Adriano e il suo Mausoleo,* ed. M. Mercalli, 23–38. Milan: Electa, 1998.

———. "Nuovi elementi di recenti acquisiti." In *Adriano e il suo Mausoleo,* ed. M. Mercalli, 55–61. Milan: Electa, 1998.

———. "Il Mausoleo di Adriano: La decorazione scultorea." In *Adriano e il suo Mausoleo,* ed. M. Mercalli, 101–47. Milan: Electa, 1998.

Torelli, M. *Typology and Structure of Roman Historical Reliefs.* Ann Arbor: University of Michigan Press, 1982.

———. "Culto imperiale e spazi urbani in età flavia dai rilievi Hartwig all'arco di Tito." In *Urbs: Espace Urbain et Histoire, 1er Siècle avant J.-C.–1er Siècle après J.-C. CEFR* 98, 563–82. Rome: Ecole Française de Rome, 1987.

Tortorici, E. "Alcune osservazioni sulla tavola 8 della *forma urbis* del Lanciani." In *Topografia antica: Ricerchi e discussioni,* 7–15. Rome, 1988.

Toynbee, J. M. C. *Roman Medallions.* New York: The American Numismatic Society, 1944.

———. Review of F. Magi, *I rilievi flavi del Palazzo della Cancelleria* (Rome, 1945). *JRS* 37 (1947): 187–91.

"Ruler Apotheosis in Ancient Rome." *NC* 7 (1947): 126–49.

Death and Burial in the Roman World. London: Thames and Hudson, 1971.

Trachtenberg, M. "Some Observations on Recent Architectural History." *ArtB* 70 (1988): 208–41.

Traversari, G. *L'Arco dei Sergii.* Padua: CEDAM 1971.

Treggiari, S. "*Digna condicio*: Betrothals in the Roman Upper Class." *EchCl* 28 (1984): 419–51.

Roman Marriage. Oxford: Clarendon Press, 1991.

Tupet, A. M. "La mentalité superstitieuse à l'époque des Julio-Claudiens." *REL* 62 (1984): 206–35.

Turcan, M. " 'Aedes Solis' au Grand Cirque." *REL* 36 (1958): 255–62.

Turcan, R. *Les sarcophages romains à représentations dionysiaques: Essai de chronologie et d'histoire religieuse.* Paris: E. De Boccard, 1966.

"Littérature astrologique et astrologie littéraire dans l'antiquité classique." *Latomus* 27 (1968): 329–405.

"Le piédestal de la Colonne Antonine à propos d'un livre récent." *RA* 2 (1975): 305–18.

Turcan-Deleani, M. "Les monuments représentes sur la Colonne Trajane, schématisme et réalisme." *MEFR* 70 (1958): 149–76.

Turner, V. *The Ritual Process.* Chicago: Aldine Publishing Co., 1969.

"Symbols in African Ritual." In *Magic, Witchcraft and Religion: An Anthropological Study of the Supernatural,* ed. A. Lehman and J. E. Myers. Palo Alto, Calif.: Mayfield Pub. Co., 1985.

Üblacker, M. *Das Teatro Marittimo in der Villa Hadriana.* Mainz: P. Von Zabern, 1985.

Ungaro, L., and Milella, M. *I luoghi del consenso imperiale. Il Foro di Augusto, il Foro di Traiano.* Rome: Progetti Museali, 1995.

Valadier, G. *Narrazione artistica dell'operato finora nel ristauro dell'Arco di Tito letta nell'Accademia Romana di Archeologia.* Rome: Stamperia de Romania, 1822.

Valentini, R., and Zucchetti, G. *Codice topografico della città di Roma.* Rome: Tipografia del Senato, 1940–53.

Van Buren, A. W. "The Ara Pacis Augustae." *JRS* 3 (1913): 134–41.

Van Buren, A. W., and Kennedy, R. M. "Varro's Aviary at Casinum." *JRS* 9 (1919): 59–66.

Van den Broek, R. *The Myth of the Phoenix According to Classical and Early Christian Traditions.* Leiden: E. J. Brill, 1972.

Van Essen, C. C. "La topographie de la Domus Aurea." *Mededelingen der Koninklijke nederlandse akademie van wetenschappen, afd. Letterkunde* 17.12 (1954): 371–98.

Van Gennep, A. *Les rites de passage.* Paris: E. Nourry, 1909.

Varner, E. R. "Damnatio Memoriae and Roman Imperial Portraiture." Ph.D. diss., Yale University, 1993.

"Domitia Longina and the Politics of Portraiture." *AJA* 99 (1995): 187–206.

Vasaly, A. *Representations: Images of the World in Ciceronian Oratory.* Berkeley-Los Angeles: University of California Press, 1993.

Vermeule, C. C. *The Goddess Roma in the Art of the Roman Empire.* Cambridge, Mass.: Spink and Son, 1959.

Greek Sculpture and Roman Taste. Ann Arbor: University of Michigan Press, 1977.

Versnel, H. S. *Triumphus. An Inquiry into the Origin, Development and Nature of the Roman Triumph.* Leiden: E. J. Brill, 1970.

Veyne, P. "Les idéaux collectifs dans l'art funéraire." *REL* 37 (1959): 43–45.

A History of Private Life I. From Pagan Rome to Byzantium. Ed. P. Veyne, trans. A. Goldhammer, 169–71. Cambridge, Mass.-London: Harvard University Press, 1987.

Vignoli, I. *De Columna Imperatoris Antonini Pii Dissertatio.* Rome: Franciscum Gonzagan, 1705.

Visconti, C. L. "Delle scoperte avvenute per la demolizione delle Torri della Porta Flaminia." *BullCom* (1877): 184–252.

Visconti, E. Q. *Il Museo Pio Clementino* V, VII. Milan: N. Bettoni, 1796, 1822.

Vogel, L. "Circus Race Scenes in the Early Roman Empire." *ArtB* 51 (1969): 155–60.

The Column of Antoninus Pius. Cambridge, Mass.: Harvard University Press, 1973.

Voisin, J.-L. "*Exoriente sole* (Suetone, Nér. 6). D'Aléxandrie à la Domus Aurea." In *CEFR* 98, 509–43 (1987).

Vollgraff, W. "Le péan delphique à Dionysos." *BCH* 48 (1924): 97–208.

von Domaszewski, A. "Die Triumphstrasse auf dem Marsfelde." *ArchRW* 12 (1909): 70–73.

von Hesberg, H. "Das Mausoleum des Augustus." In *Kaiser Augustus und die verlorene*

Republik, 244–51. Mainz: P. Von Zabern, 1988.

Römische Grabbauten. Darmstadt: Wissenschaftliche Buchgesellschaft, 1992.

von Hesberg, H., and Panciera, S. *Das Mausoleum des Augustus. Der Bau und seine Inschriften.* Munich: Verlag der Bayerischen Akademie der Wissenschaften, 1994.

von Massow, W. *Die Grabmäler von Neumagen.* Berlin-Leipzig: Walter de Gruyter & Co., 1932.

von Sydow, W. "Ein Rundmonument in Pietrabbondante." *RM* 84 (1977): 294–96.

Vulpe, R. "Prigionieri romani suppliziati da donne dacie sul rilievo della Colonna Traiana." *RivStorAnt* 3 (1973): 109–25.

Wace, A. J. B. "Studies in Roman Historical Reliefs." *BSR* 4 (1907): 258–63.

Walker, S. *Memorials to the Roman Dead.* London: British Museum Publications, 1985.

Wallace-Hadrill, A. "The Emperor and His Virtues." *Historia* 30 (1981): 298–323.

"The Social Structure of the Roman House." *BSR* 56 (1988): 43–97.

"Engendering the Roman House." In *I Claudia: Women in Ancient Rome,* ed. D. E. E. Kleiner and S. B. Matheson, 104–15. New Haven, Conn.: Yale University Press, 1996.

Walton, F. R. "Religious Thought in the Age of Hadrian." *Numen* 4 (1957): 165–70.

Ward-Perkins, J. B. "Severan Art and Architecture at Lepcis Magna." *JRS* 38 (1948): 62.

"Nero's Golden House." *Antiquity* 30 (1956): 209–19.

"Columna divi Antonini." In *Mélanges d'histoire ancienne et d'archéologie offerts à Paul Collart,* 345–52. Lausanne: Bibliothèque Historique Vaudoise, 1976.

Roman Imperial Architecture. Harmondsworth: Penguin Books, 1981.

Warden, P. G. "The Domus Aurea Reconsidered." *JSAH* 40 (1981): 271–78.

Waters, K. A. "Traianus Domitiani Continuator." *AJP* 90 (1969): 385–405.

Waurick, G. "Untersuchungen zur Lage der römischen Kaisergräber in der Zeit von Augustus bis Constantin." *JRGZM* 20 (1973): 107–46.

Wegner, M. "Bemerkungen zu den Ehrendenkmälern des Marcus Aurelius." *AA* 53 (1938): 157–95.

Die Herrscherbildnisse in Antoninischer Zeit. Berlin: G. Mann, 1939.

Hadrian, Plotina, Marciana, Matidia, Sabina. Berlin: G. Mann, 1956.

"Schmuckbasen des antiken Rom." *Orbis Antiquus* 22 (1966):

Weinstock, S. *Divus Julius.* Oxford: Clarendon Press, 1971.

Weitzmann, K. *Illustrations in Roll and Codex.* Princeton, N.J.: Princeton University Press, 1970.

Welch, K. "The Roman Arena in Late-Republican Italy: A New Interpretation." *JRA* 7 (1994): 59–80.

Welter, G. "Zwei vorrömische Grabbauten in Nordafrika." *RM* 42 (1927): 84ff.

Whitehead, J. "Biography and Formula in Roman Sarcophagi." Ph. D. diss., Yale University, 1984.

"The 'Cena Trimalchionis' and Biographical Narration in Roman Middle Class Art." In *Narrative and Event in Ancient Art,* ed. P. J. Holliday, 299–325. Cambridge: Cambridge University Press, 1993.

Wickhoff, F. *Roman Art: Some of Its Principles and Their Application to Early Christian Painting.* Trans. E. Strong. London: W. Heinemann, 1900.

Wightman, G. "The Imperial Fora of Rome: Some Design Considerations." *JSAH* 56 (1997): 64–87.

Wilson Jones, M. "One Hundred Feet and a Spiral Stair: The Problem of Designing Trajan's Column." *JRA* 6 (1993): 23–38.

Windfeld-Hansen, H. "Les couloirs annulaires dans l'architecture funéraire antique." *Acta Instituti Romani Norvegiae* 2 (1962): 35–63.

Winkes, R. "Pliny's Chapter on Roman Funerary Customs in Light of *Clipeatae Imagines.*" *AJA* 83 (1979): 481–84.

Wolff, H. "Welchen Zeitraum stellt der Bilderfries der Marcus-Säule dar?" *Ostbairische Grenzmarken. Passauer Jahrbuch für Geschichte, Kunst und Volkskunde* 32 (1990): 9–29.

Wood, S. "Agrippina the Elder in Julio-Claudian Art and Propaganda." *AJA* 92 (1988): 409–26.

Wrede, H. *Consecratio in Formam Deorum: Vergöttlichte Privatpersonen in der römischen Kaiserzeit.* Mainz: P. Von Zabern, 1981.

Wuilleumier, P. "Cirque et astrologie." *MEFR* 44 (1927): 184–209.

Yarden, L. *The Spoils of Jerusalem on the Arch of Titus: A Reinvestigation.* Stockholm: Svenska Instituet Rom, 1991.

Yates, F. *The Art of Memory.* Chicago-London: University of Chicago Press, 1966.

Yavetz, Z. "The *Res Gestae* and Augustus' Public Image." In *Caesar Augustus: Seven Aspects,* ed. F. Millar and E. Segal, 1–36. Oxford: Clarendon Press, 1984.

Zahn, E. *Die Igeler Säule bei Trier, Rheinische Kunststätten* 6–7. Cologne-Deutz: Rheinischer Verein für Denkmalpflegeund Landschaftsschutz, 1968.

Zanker, P. *Forum Augustum. Das Bildprogramm.* Tübingen: E. Wasmuth, 1968.

———. "Das Trajansforum in Rom" *AA* (1970): 499–544.

———. *The Power of Images in the Age of Augustus.* Trans. A. Shapiro. Ann Arbor: University of Michigan Press, 1988.

Zimmer, G. *Römische Berufdarstellungen.* Berlin: G. Mann, 1982.

Zwikker, W. *Studien zur Markussäule I.* Amsterdam: N.v. Noord-Hollansche Uitgevers Mij., 1941.

INDEX